STUDIES OF
CONTEMPORARY THAILAND

STUDIES OF CONTEMPORARY THAILAND

ROBERT HO & E. C. CHAPMAN (eds)

RESEARCH SCHOOL OF PACIFIC STUDIES

Department of Human Geography
Publication HG/8 (1973)

AUSTRALIAN NATIONAL UNIVERSITY · CANBERRA

Inquiries should be made to the publisher,

Department of Human Geography,
Australian National University,
Canberra

National Library of Australia Catalogue Card no. and
ISBN 0 7081 0294 8

Library of Congress Catalogue Card no. 72-97053

Registered in Australia for transmission by post as a book

Distributed by Australian National University Press
P.O. Box 4,
Canberra, A.C.T., 2600

Printed by authority of the Registrar,
The Australian National University
1973

1816404

ACKNOWLEDGEMENTS

When the seminar on Thailand was first proposed, Robert Ho and I anticipated
that it would be a very modest affair, involving four or five papers and
perhaps about 15 participants.   As the number of papers in this monograph indicates, however, the response of potential contributors was very
much greater than expected and a large proportion of the 51 particpants
made substantial contributions to the success of the meeting, as chairmen
or discussants at particular sessions, or in open discussions around the
seminar table.

In the months leading up to the seminar our initial proposals and
subsequent preparations were strongly supported at the Australian National
University by Professor Sir John Crawford, then Vice-Chancellor, and by
Professor O.H.K. Spate, then Director of the Research School of Pacific
Studies.   Preparations were also made very much easier through the help
of His Excellency Mr T.K. Critchley, Australian Ambassador to Thailand,
Dr Rongpet Sucharitkul (then Counsellor and Chargé d'Affaires at the
Royal Thai Embassy in Canberra) and by officers of the Australian Depart-
ment of Foreign Affairs and the Department of Trade.   At the seminar
itself, we were fortunate to have the assistance of several distinguished
scholars closely associated with Thailand or neighbouring countries of
Southeast Asia in recent years, who acted as chairmen or discussants.
Sir John Crawford chaired the first session, concerned with recent
changes in the Thai economy, and also led the discussion; at subsequent
sessions we were helped in a similar way by Professor H.W. Arndt,
Professor B.L.C. Johnson, Dr G.J.R. Linge, Associate Professor J.W.
McGarity, Mr Douglas Miles, Mr L.F. Myers, Dr Ronald Ng, Dr Prachoom
Chomchai, Professor O.H.K. Spate, Professor Wang Gungwu, and Dr Gehan
Wijeyewardene.   All contributed immeasurably to the proceedings.

Preparation of the papers for publication was beginning, early in
1972, when Robert Ho died.   After several months delay while I was in
Thailand, preparation of this monograph was resumed with the encouraging
cooperation of my co-authors.   Without exception, they willingly up-dated
their original papers where this seemed desirable and a number also took
the opportunity to make substantial revisions.   At this stage also, most
valuable assistance was received from several scholars in both Australia
and Thailand; I would like to record my gratitude particularly to

Professor T.H. Silcock (who had been unable to attend the seminar owing to World Bank commitments), Dr Chaiyong Chuchart, Mr Richard Davis and Dr Varin Wonghanchao.   The appearance of the monograph reflects the skills of cartographers who drew the maps and diagrams (Ian Heywood in the Department of Human Geography; Peter Daniell and Pam Millwood in the Department of Geography, School of General Studies), photographer Ken Lockwood (Department of Human Geography), Pauline Falconer who typed the entire work, and Bill Hobart, Paula Power and the staff of Central Duplicating who gave technical assistance and printed the monograph. Thanks are also due to Marianne Henderson and Edith Parr for typing, and Gladys Bartholomeuz for duplicating the original papers for the seminar.

Finally, the publication of this monograph owes most to three people whose encouragement and support began long before the seminar; Lisa Ho, Nancy Clark and Gerard Ward, who took up appointment as Head of the Department of Human Geography at the end of 1971.   Nancy Clark and Gerard Ward have acted as subsidiary editors, generous with their time and the most tolerant of colleagues.   I am deeply grateful to them both.

E.C. Chapman
Canberra, 1 June 1973

TABLE OF CONTENTS

ACKNOWLEDGEMENTS

CONTENTS

  List of Tables
  List of Figures
  Conventions

PREFACE - Sir John Crawford

ROBERT HO - O.H.K. Spate

CHAPTER

TABLE OF CONTENTS - Continued

LIST OF TABLES

LIST OF TABLES - Continued

LIST OF TABLES - Continued

LIST OF TABLES - Continued

LIST OF FIGURES

LIST OF FIGURES - Continued

14.3A   Regression lines for the relationship between volume   322
        shipments and distance to Bangkok for movements from the
        provinces to the capital

14.3B   Regression lines for the relationship between volume   322
        shipments and distance from Bangkok for movements from the
        capital to the provinces

14.4   Standardised residuals from regression for freight flows   323
        to Bangkok from the provinces by inland waterway, coastal
        shipping, railway, and truck for specified dates

14.5   Standardised residuals from regression for freight flows   327
        from Bangkok to the provinces by inland waterway, coastal
        shipping, railway, and truck for specified dates

14.6A   Transport surface showing provinces with surplus freight   333
        as hillocks and those with net inflows over outflows as
        hollows

14.6B   Reversed transport surface showing provinces with deficits   334
        as hillocks and those with a surplus as hollows

14.7   Constituent provinces and representative nodes for the   336
        twelve transport zones in Thailand

14.8   A schematic representation of the main lineaments of   337
        Thailand's national transport system

14.9   Flow chart of the simulator   339

15.1   Litchfield plan: land use 1990   346

15.2   First revised metropolitan plan: land use 1990   351

15.3   Motor vehicle registrations, Bangkok-Thon Buri 1957-1969   356

15.4   Greater Bangkok plan 2000   358

15.5   Plan of the new national administrative centre   362

CONVENTIONS

The practice in this monograph has been to use metric measurements,
converting Thai data to the metric equivalents.   In Thailand it is now
common practice to use the metric system for distance measurements and
most weight measurements, but to retain the traditional Thai measurement
of area (rai).   In the few instances where rai has been used in this
book, its metric equivalent has been stated as well.

1 rai = 1600 sq. metres = 0.16 hectares

The Thai unit of currency, the baht, has retained parity with the
United States dollar in the 1960s and early 1970s, to 1973.

US $1.00 = Baht 20.80

The use of Thai words in the text has generally been avoided, except
for baht, changwat (province), amphoe (district) and tambon (sub-district).
The transliteration of Thai place-names in this monograph follows the
official rules and practice of the Royal Institute of Thailand, as adopted
by the Thai Cabinet in 1967.   Dates are shown in the text, tables and
figures according to the Christian calendar, but in a few instances
Buddhist Era (B.E.) dates are also included; appropriately, Thailand
retains the Buddhist system of year-numbering which is 543 years ahead of
the Christian system.   1973 = B.E. 2516.   The Thai fiscal year begins
on 1 October and is conventionally stated in the literature according to
the Buddhist calendar year which follows: for example, Fiscal Year
1972-73 began on 1 October 1972 and is known as FY2516.

PREFACE

Following the events of the Second World War Australia has developed a
keen awareness of her geographical position in relation to the countries
of Asia.   As one Australian writer observed:

> We are near Asia but not part of it...Our interest in
> Asia is important because we live nearby...our role
> in Asia is partly that of a transmission belt...partly
> that of a modifier...and is partly, too, the role of a
> good neighbour, trying to get on well with Asians and
> not using them as pawns in our own interests.[1]

This awareness of the importance of Asia to Australia has become
particularly apparent in the work of our universities which, through both
teaching and research, are helping to foster in Australians a greater
understanding of the history, cultures, economies and political systems
of their Asian neighbours.   The founding fathers of the Australian
National University saw the need for special emphasis on deepening this
understanding and, under the Act establishing it on 1 August 1946, the
university was empowered to set up a Research School of Pacific Studies.
It was originally proposed that this School be called the Research School
of Pacific and Asiatic Affairs.   Certainly the study of Asian countries
has featured largely in the School's research projects over the years and
the longer title describes more aptly the range of its activities.

The ANU has been fortunate in having T.H. Silcock, Gehan Wijeyewardene
and the late Robert Ho on its research staff in Pacific Studies to help
stimulate an interest in Thai affairs.   The ANU Press has issued several
publications dealing with Southeast Asia in general and some dealing
specifically with Thailand.   Three of the latter have been by Silcock
and include his imaginative sketches from Thai life under the title Proud
and Serene.   In more serious vein, the economy of Thailand and its
position vis à vis Australia's international horizons have come under
scrutiny in ANU publications during the past few years.

A further step towards developing Australia's understanding of Asian
countries was taken with the provision at the ANU of a degree course in

---

1 J.D.B. Miller, 'Australia and the Future in Asia', Röntgen Oration,
Canberra, 1 October 1968.

Asian studies in 1962. The work of the Faculty of Asian Studies allows for a wide range of subjects relating to Asian civilisations, including the philosophico-religious system of Buddhism which has particular relevance to our comprehension of the Thai outlook. The presence here of Thai students, both at undergraduate and post-graduate level, is contributing to a greater appreciation by each country of the other's customs and ways.

In the Geography Department of the Faculty of Arts considerable interest has been devoted to Thailand, particularly under the leadership of E.C. Chapman whose field work programme in Thailand marks an important collaboration with the University of New England.

The publication of this current collection of seminar papers owes most to the initiative and organisation of Robert Ho and E.C. Chapman. The seminar was the last major contribution by Ho before his death and the publication of the papers is by way of memorial to him and his work. The scope of the papers - from general and particular aspects of economic development to issues of border security and foreign aid - illustrates the extent of Australian research interest in Thailand. It bodes well for a sustained interest in Thai affairs and, hopefully, will help Australians in their efforts to 'get on well with' one of their neighbours.

Australian National University   J.G. Crawford
Canberra.

ROBERT HO, 1921-1972

The death from a heart attack of Robert Ho in January 1972 came as a shock to his many friends within and without the Australian National University. He had had what we only then realised was a premonitory attack a couple of years earlier, and his inherent ebbullience had naturally been somewhat dulled; but, with Ted Chapman, he had played the major role in organising the remarkably successful Thailand symposium of which the papers are presented here, and there was nothing to prepare us for the sudden end; rather the reverse, for he seemed to have recovered, and at 50 there should have been many useful years yet before him. This volume must stand as an inadequate tribute from his colleagues to his memory, and to his widow Lisa, whose courage in the midst of her deep grief won the admiration of us all.

I first met Bobby Ho when I was lecturing, mainly on Asian themes, in the LSE-King's College Joint School of Geography just after the war: not many undergraduates remain in memory as distinct personalities after so many years, but he stood out by a certain quicksilvery manner, bright and humorous. That there was much more than brightness and humour was abundantly shown by his remarkably successful term as Professor of Geography in the University of Malaya, Kuala Lumpur. The reputation of a Department diffuses itself in intangible and undefinable ways, but is nevertheless unmistakable to those whose antennae are attuned to the signals. It was common knowledge that the Department at KL, without fuss or réclame, had established itself, under Ho's guidance, as one of the very best in South and Southeast Asia. And that meant hard work and devotion.

When, in 1965, the opportunity came to attract Ho as a Senior Fellow to what was then the Department of Geography in the Research School of Pacific Studies, I was motivated not only by this sterling record and his wide range of interests in Southeast Asian geography, though these of course were paramount to our purposes, but also by my memory of his personal quality. Bobby very soon fitted into the life of the School, and it was all the sadder that ill health so soon robbed him of the opportunity of developing his full potential. His professional output was not great, but it must be remembered that the war intervened when he had barely started on his career as a student, so that he was nearly 30 when he took his M.A.; and ill health shadowed his last years. Nevertheless these years saw the publication of a number of papers based on his intensive fieldwork in Malaysia. It is particularly unfortunate that he was not able to publish the results of his more recent work on the plural society of Malaysia. His papers on Southeast Asian subjects show an enviable range, from geomorphology by pedology to the economics of agricultural development in Malaysia; and all of them are stout substantial stuff, carefully researched and presented.

The abiding remembrance of Bobby Ho is of his geniality and his acuteness of mind: he was never assertive but always, except when under the burden of ill health, gay and alert. It is a tragedy that his heart should have given way just when his powers and his projects seemed on the point of maturity.

O. H. K. Spate
October 1972

CHAPTER 1

STUDIES OF CONTEMPORARY THAILAND: AN INTRODUCTION

E.C. Chapman*

1. THE SEMINAR

The chapters which follow in this monograph were initially prepared as papers for a seminar on 'Contemporary Thailand', held at the Australian National University in September 1971; the papers were later revised by their authors during the second half of 1972.   The seminar and this volume were first suggested by Robert Ho, in an effort to bring together some of the recent work by Australian-based academics concerned with the progress of economic development in Thailand.   As the seminar took shape, and became more ambitious in scope than we had first planned, invitations to participate were accepted by scholars and officials from Thailand, New Zealand, England and the United States.   In all the preliminary arrangements and in the actual organisation of the seminar, Robert Ho played the major role.   It is appropriate therefore that his name appears, as we intended, as the senior editor of a volume of papers which he inspired in the last year of his life.

The seminar coincided almost exactly in time with the end of Thailand's second National Economic and Social Development Plan (1967-71). Overall, the five years beginning in October 1966 had been a period of remarkable economic growth, but by the end of the 1960s there was clear evidence of marked sectoral and spatial inequalities in its distribution. The annual growth rate of Gross National Product averaged 8.1 per cent in 1961-66 and in 1967-69.   Rapid expansion had occurred in the metro-politan industries and services, such as manufacturing, construction, banking and insurance, where growth had little impact on the four-fifths of the population who depend on agriculture for their liveli-hood.   In agriculture, by contrast, the annual rate of growth was so low in the Second Plan period (3.8 per cent, 1967-69) that it barely kept pace with population increase.   Improvements in agricultural

---

* Mr Chapman is Reader in Geography, School of General Studies, in the Australian National University.

production and rural incomes inevitably became main goals for the Third
Plan period, beginning in October 1971.

As its major focus therefore, the seminar was concerned with the
economic and social development of Thailand during the second half of
the 1960s.   The key study, which opened the first session, was the
review of recent economic progress prepared by Mrs Richter and Dr Edwards
(Chapter 2).   It was followed by Dr Prachoom's appraisal of Thai manufacturing (Chapter 3) and a group of papers concerned with agricultural
development (Chapters 4-8).   The second half of the meeting, reflected
in Chapters 9-16, was less directly concerned with economic and social
changes: five studies dealt with different aspects of the politically
'sensitive' northern hills and southern provinces, bordering Malaysia;
two case studies were related to the urgent need for effective government
planning (Chapters 14 and 15); and finally, two papers dealt with foreign
aid to Thailand, as seen from the Australian and Thai viewpoints.   In
the following paragraphs an attempt has been made to highlight a few of
the main points which emerged in the seminar papers and in discussions
which they generated.

2.   THE ECONOMY REVIEWED

While the rate of economic growth remained high and relatively uniform in
the 1960s, a number of major economic changes were taking place in Thailand.
Traditionally, the Thai economy has depended upon its export trade, centred
upon rice, rubber, tin and teak, but in the 1960s their combined share of
total merchandise exports fell from 70 per cent to 50 per cent, and
between 1965 and 1969 the annual trade deficit suddenly increased at an
alarming rate: the value of merchandise imports rose by two-thirds, while
merchandise exports remained almost unchanged (Ingram, 1971:314, 317).
The resulting crisis would have been much worse, except for an equally
spectacular growth in the surplus from services, mainly derived from the
tourist trade and heavy American military expenditure in Thailand during
the Vietnam war.   While the war dragged on Thailand's economy benefited,
but in the 1970s the country faces the likelihood of a sharp reduction in
foreign military expenditure, uncertain trading prospects for crops which
are replacing rice as exports, and the rapid growth of population at a
rate variously estimated at between 3.0 and 3.4 per cent per annum.

Appropriately, Richter and Edwards begin their review of recent
economic developments (Chapter 2) with an examination of population data
and population projections based on the rather dubious results of the
1970 census.   It was conducted hurriedly and processed slowly, under the
stress of budget restrictions imposed by the Budget Scrutiny Committee
during Thailand's brief experience of parliamentary democracy between
1969 and 1971.   The population in 1970 may have been 36,000,000, as an
official estimate suggests (Fuhs and Vingerhoets, 1972:6), or 37,500,000
(as Richter and Edwards argue), but whatever the total and the actual
rate of growth may be, the inescapable fact is that Thailand is now facing
a massive increase in its teenage population and in their requirements
for schools and jobs.   In 1970 it is estimated that 46 per cent of the
population was under 15 years of age and 10,300,000 were of school age
(5-14).   By 1980, Richter and Edwards estimate that the school-age
population will have increased by 49 per cent; and even a conservative
estimate of the 'labour force explosion', which is now occurring, anti-
cipates the need for 33 per cent more jobs between 1970 and 1980 (Fuhs
and Vingerhoets, 1972:7).   Most of this increased demand will occur in
rural areas, where the recent progress of agriculture has been so poor
overall that a substantial addition of low income and under-employed
workers seems inevitable.

The future population problems are magnified by the presumed
continuation of high fertility.   In 1970 it is estimated that the birth
rate was still 40 per thousand, and in that year the Thai government
finally responded to pressure and adopted voluntary family planning as
official policy.   Following that decision, it has been assumed that any
significant reduction of fertility will depend upon the effectiveness of
government support for family planning (Richter and Edwards; Fuhs and
Vingerhoets, 1972:7).   There is scattered evidence, however, that in
some parts of Thailand modern birth control measures came into common
use up to five years before the government's decision in 1970.   Missionary hospitals and clinics appear to have played an important role in
introducing modern methods, at least in the northern region, but perhaps
the most remarkable and significant aspect is the speed of adoption in
rural areas.   A study of two villages in Saraphi District of Chiang Mai
Province, made in 1969, showed that 45 per cent of married women aged

20-44 were using modern birth control techniques (Cunningham, Yoddumnurn and Ratanasupa, 1970:169); and in 1972, in a more remote rural situation, Davis found that in a village of 43 households in central Nan Province where modern birth control measures were first adopted about 1967, all except four or five married women aged 20-44 were using some form of birth control (Richard Davis, personal information).   If such rapid adoption of family planning has been widespread in Thailand, the government's efforts may well achieve a reduction in the annual population growth rate to 2.5 per cent by 1976, as set out in the Third Plan.

Turning from population problems to the performance of Thai agriculture in the 1960s, Richter and Edwards in Chapter 2 and Norman in Chapter 5 examine recent and prospective trends in the area, production and yield for rice and 'upland' (unirrigated) crops.   It is clear from these studies and from recent data published by the Ministry of Agriculture (Table 1.1) that within the period of the Second Plan expansion of the total cultivated area continued at an average annual rate of 2.5 per cent, compared with population increase at 3.0 to 3.4 per cent.

Table 1.1: Major crops: percentage changes in area, production and yield
during the Second Plan period to 1970

| | Planted area 1970 (000 ha) | Changes from 1965-66 to 1969-70 (per cent) | | |
		Area	Production	Yield
All crops	10,813	+10		
Rice	7,376	+ 6	+26	+24
Upland food crops	1,498	+39		
maize	829	+23	+70	+44
mungbeans	239	+171	+17	-29
cassava	224	+79	+93	+ 8
sugar-cane	206	+48	+51	+ 4
Oil seeds	556	+12		
castor beans	46	+5	+ 8	+ 3
peanuts	104	-19	-29	- 5
sesame	30	+ 1	+ 2	+ 5
soybeans	59	+66	+73	+ 1
coconuts[a]	316	+24	-35	?
Fibre crops	503	-13		
cotton	31	-22	-53	-23
kapok and bombax	51	- 7	0	+ 4
kenaf	421	-13	-37	-26
Rubber[b]	855	+46	+31	-11
Tobacco (Virginia)	25	+36	+23	- 8

a   The total area includes non-fruiting trees and for this reason yield data are
    not shown.
b   Tappable area only.

Note: Percentages have been calculated from the averages for 1965-66 and 1969-70
       (calendar years).

Source: Ministry of Agriculture, 1972: Tables 4, 11, 14, 15-28, 32 and 33.

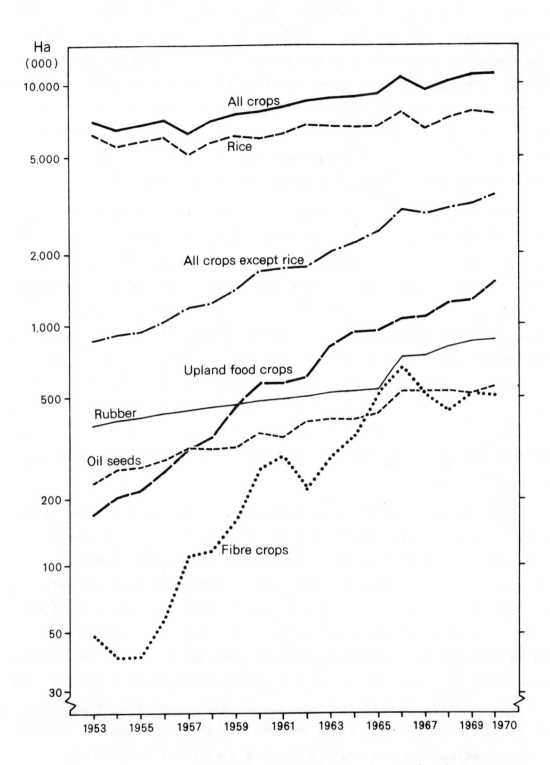

Fig. 1.1   Trends in area planted for rice and other crops
           1953-70.   Data on the planted area for rice,
           rubber and individual crops grouped as 'upland
           food crops', 'oil seeds' and 'fibre crops' are
           shown in Table 1.1.

Source: Ministry of Agriculture, 1972: Tables 4, 11, 14,
           15-28, 32 and 33.

In the late 1960s also, marked differences became evident in the area and yield trends for maize and other major export crops. As Fig. 1.1 indicates, the forward thrust of maize and other major upland food crops continued strongly while the expansion of oil seed and fibre crops stopped. The position of maize, however, was unique by 1970. Excluding rice and maize, all 15 main field and tree crops registered only small percentage increases in yield, or yield decreases, during the Second Plan period. Maize continued its spectacular increase in area, while the rice area increased at a very slow rate (Table 1.1).

The importance of these trends is enhanced by the vital contribution which the 'new' crops are making to Thailand's export trade, at a time when the traditional exports are declining in importance. In 1969, shipments of maize and cassava (both mainly to Japan), tobacco, oil seeds, kenaf and beans altogether contributed 27 per cent of Thailand's merchandise exports, far ahead of rice (20 per cent) and rubber (18 per cent) (Ingram, 1971:312, 314). With the continuing uncertainty of international markets for rice and the maintenance of the rice premium which reduces domestic prices and at the same time acts as a disincentive for Thailand's rice farmers, the new export crops seem destined to be of permanent significance in the kingdom's foreign trade during the 1970s.

With yields for many crops decreasing, or increasing only slightly during the Second Plan period, what are the prospects for a substantial increase in agricultural productivity during the 1970s? Norman's comments in Chapter 5 provide rather mixed encouragement. He notes that Thailand, compared with other tropical countries, already obtains relatively high yields for several 'problem' crops such as peanuts, cassava and soybeans. On the other hand, he indicates that mungbeans, sesame and castor beans are among the group where yields may be improved relatively easily, in much the same way as maize yields were improved during the 1960s by an intensive varietal selection programme, carried out with American assistance. A further possibility which Norman emphasises is the improvement of yields through the concentration of crops in areas where growing conditions are more favourable; for example, his proposal that peanuts might replace rice on many existing rice-fields of the Northeast where water supply is often inadequate for a good padi

crop.   In the initial concentration or dispersion of the new crops historical factors played a major role (Silcock, 1970:82-106) and often the
dispersion into equally favourable, or more favourable areas was rather
slow.   Cassava, for example, was concentrated in the area southeast
from Bangkok and only in the 1970s is it being established rapidly in
parts of the upper central plain, near Kamphaeng Phet.

Compared with the agricultural sector, Thailand's manufacturing
made spectacular progress after 1960, but again the prospects in the
1970s are somewhat clouded.   Dr Prachoom, in Chapter 3, examines the
success of the existing industrial development strategy, focussed on
import substitution, at the end of the Second Plan Period.   He concludes
that Thailand faces, in many instances, 'the prospective dilemma of
having to protect inefficient infant industries indefinitely, or [of]
letting them collapse at the end of the promotional period'.   For the
future he argues for a change to labour-intensive rather than capital-
intensive industries, making more use of the products of Thailand's
farms and aiming at providing employment for workers in rural areas.
This proposal, and Thailand's experience of poorly diffused economic
growth, can be matched in most developing countries.   The problem for
the future is in implementation; it will require strong government action
to establish profitable, labour-intensive industries in provincial areas -
in time to have much impact in absorbing under-employed rural labour.

The combination of major development characteristics in Thailand
during the 1960s (chequered agricultural progress, capital-city concentration of manufacturing, rapid increase of the rural population) has
resulted in marked income disparities between the four major regions.
Differences between the incomes of town-dwellers and villagers living
in the same region are so great that regional averages are extremely
gross generalisations, but in the absence of more precise information
the estimates of per capita income used in preparation of the Third Plan
remain striking enough: in 1970, estimated per capita income was US $304
for the Central region (including Bangkok-Thon Buri), $177 for the South,
$122 for the North and $87.50 for the Northeast (Fuhs and Vingerhoets,
1972:21).   Effective regional planning and strong government action to
implement regional development will be needed in the 1970s, if these
disparities in income are to be reduced.

3.   AGRICULTURAL CHANGES

The set of five papers concerned with agricultural development (Chapters
4-8) begins with an historical overview by Wijeyewardene, assessing the
relevance of Wittfogel's theory of 'hydraulic (irrigation-based) societies' to Thailand.   He argues that Thailand has acquired an agro-
managerial bureaucracy in recent decades, through its concern for
irrigation works whether or not they substantially aided productivity.
In general support of Wijeyewardene's arguments, much of Judd's paper
(Chapter 6) is concerned with the ways in which productivity objectives
of the Greater Chao Phraya Basin irrigation project have not so far been
achieved, since the dams and distribution canals were completed in 1964.
Further support is to be found in Jacobs' recent appraisal of the 'patri-
monial' administrative system practised in Thailand (Jacobs, 1971).   In
his terms, World Bank loans and foreign aid for irrigation or other
development activities provide the means ('prebends') by which the traditional administrative system and bureaucracy are maintained, with productivity objectives tending to fall into second place.

The chapters by Norman, Judd, Ng and Chapman bring the discussion
of agricultural development down to regional earth.   Important themes
recur in these papers.   Norman's discussion of the extent to which
Thailand's agricultural potential remains unrealised posits the need for
more planning and for wide-ranging government support for agricultural
development; Judd gently emphasises the stark lack of comprehensive
planning in the development of the Chao Phraya Project in the central
plain during the 1960s; Ronald Ng shows by multivariate analysis of data
from 15 villages in the Northeast that farm variations in rice yields are
to be explained more by cultural factors, such as the extent of farmers'
specialisation on rice production, than by physical constraints such as
the sandy soils and poor irrigation facilities to which the rural poverty
of this region is usually attributed.   Finally, Chapter 8 further
emphasises the critical importance of the 'farmer variable' in rural
development, and at the same time underscores a theme common to all four
papers; that the achievement of increased productivity of land and farm
labour in Thailand will hinge upon the performance of Thai government
agencies, notably in extension work.

4. PROBLEMS IN THE ETHNIC BORDERLANDS

In recent years economic and social pressures have compelled the Thai
government to become actively involved in many national problems where
solutions are not easily achieved, including the complex problems of its
northern and southern borderlands. In both areas counter-insurgency
operations have taken a heavy toll in money and lives, since 1967. In
both areas also, international relationships are involved: in the south
the Malay-speaking Muslim population predominates in three provinces
bordering Malaysia; and in the north the United Nations and United States
have exerted considerable pressure on the Thai government since 1964, with
the object of better narcotics control.

In the north most attention has been given to the opium problem in
the 'high hills'. Opium poppies are grown above about 1000 metres in a
broad belt around the border of Thailand from the provinces of Tak and
Mae Hong Son to Nan, Loei and Phetchabun (Fig. 1.2). The crop has long
been a main element of the shifting cultivation (swidden) economies of
several tribal groups, numbering about 100,000 people and comprising
approximately one-third of the total hill-tribe population in northern
Thailand. Geddes (Chapter 9) examines the extent of the opium problem
and the proposed measures for its eradication, particularly among the
Meo who are numerically the largest and also the most migratory of the
opium-producing groups. Miles (Chapter 11) discusses the child-adoption
practices by which the Yao (the second most numerous group of opium-
growers) increase their labour force in a situation where labour rather
than land is the chief constraint on the swidden economy. Hinton
(Chapter 10) takes up the more widespread problem of land shortage in
the northern hills (with special reference to the Karen, the largest
tribal group) in a typical situation where population growth from natural
increase and trans-border migration has ruptured the previous balance of
man and land in the swidden system.

It is clear from the studies of Geddes, Miles and Hinton in this
volume, as well as from other studies already published or soon to appear,[1]

---

[1] An additional paper presented at the seminar by Mr F.G.B. Keen on 'The
fermented tea industry of Northern Thailand' was concerned with Thai settlement in the lower hills zone; by agreement between the author and editors it
has been included for publication in Peter Kunstadter and E.C. Chapman (eds),
Farmers in the forest: economic development and marginal agriculture in
Northern Thailand, University Press of Hawaii (forthcoming).

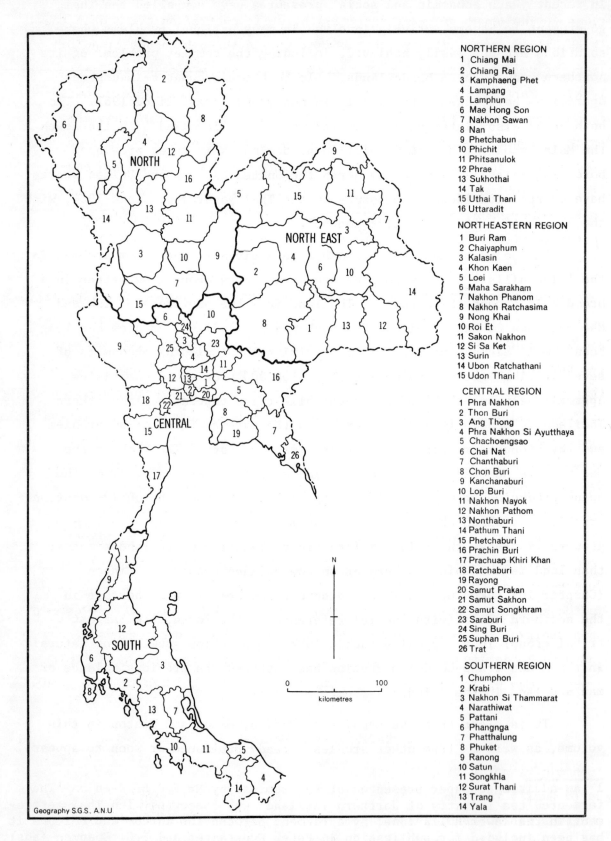

NORTHERN REGION
1 Chiang Mai
2 Chiang Rai
3 Kamphaeng Phet
4 Lampang
5 Lamphun
6 Mae Hong Son
7 Nakhon Sawan
8 Nan
9 Phetchabun
10 Phichit
11 Phitsanulok
12 Phrae
13 Sukhothai
14 Tak
15 Uthai Thani
16 Uttaradit

NORTHEASTERN REGION
1 Buri Ram
2 Chaiyaphum
3 Kalasin
4 Khon Kaen
5 Loei
6 Maha Sarakham
7 Nakhon Phanom
8 Nakhon Ratchasima
9 Nong Khai
10 Roi Et
11 Sakon Nakhon
12 Si Sa Ket
13 Surin
14 Ubon Ratchathani
15 Udon Thani

CENTRAL REGION
1 Phra Nakhon
2 Thon Buri
3 Ang Thong
4 Phra Nakhon Si Ayutthaya
5 Chachoengsao
6 Chai Nat
7 Chanthaburi
8 Chon Buri
9 Kanchanaburi
10 Lop Buri
11 Nakhon Nayok
12 Nakhon Pathom
13 Nonthaburi
14 Pathum Thani
15 Phetchaburi
16 Prachin Buri
17 Prachuap Khiri Khan
18 Ratchaburi
19 Rayong
20 Samut Prakan
21 Samut Sakhon
22 Samut Songkhram
23 Saraburi
24 Sing Buri
25 Suphan Buri
26 Trat

SOUTHERN REGION
1 Chumphon
2 Krabi
3 Nakhon Si Thammarat
4 Narathiwat
5 Pattani
6 Phangnga
7 Phatthalung
8 Phuket
9 Ranong
10 Satun
11 Songkhla
12 Surat Thani
13 Trang
14 Yala

Geography S.G.S. A.N.U

Fig. 1.2   Thailand: provinces and statistical regions.

that the complex inter-relationships between tribal groups and between the Thai and lowland populations do not lend themselves to limited solutions.   The opium problem, for example, while centred on the Meo in the 'high hills' zone, affects other tribal groups through competition for land, as well as through labour recruitment, opium addiction and trade links.   Furthermore, if profitable replacements for the land-intensive opium crop can be found they are likely to require more land than the existing economy, thereby putting additional stress on available land resources.   For United Nations agencies concerned with narcotics control the problem is primarily one of eliminating opium.   For Thailand, on the other hand, opium-production may be only a transient problem contained within the complex of development problems affecting its tribal people.

The 'minorities problem' in the southernmost provinces is critically different.   It is a long-standing problem and the opposing Thai-Buddhist and Thai-Muslim groups are strongly polarised, with few bridges between the two cultures.   Donald and Elise Tugby point out, in Chapter 12, that 'consensus formation between Thai-Muslims and the bureaucracy cannot come about because there are so few channels of upward communication'. Other important factors in preventing integration are the strength of Islam as a culturally unifying force and, as Suhrke indicates in Chapter 13, the rural and inward-looking character of Thai-Muslim society.   At the present time the prospects for rapid improvement in relationships are not bright.   However, in Fig. 13.2 Suhrke illustrates the recent encouraging response of Thai-Muslims in Pattani to greater educational opportunities, following Thai government action to improve its schools in the southern provinces.   If further action follows, to provide career opportunities for many educated Thai-Muslims within the bureaucracy, the southern borderlands may gradually acquire a significant group of 'culture brokers' who will reduce the communications barrier between the two groups.

5.   THE PLANNING PROCESS

Economic planning is a new art in Thailand, introduced in 1959 on the World Bank's recommendation to overcome the 'haphazard planning' of previous years (IBRD, 1959:Chapter VIII).   Social planning was not given formal recognition until the Second Plan in 1966.   Despite the existence

of elaborate planning machinery in the form of the NEDB (now the National
Economic and Social Development Board) for more than a decade, rigorous
planning is still an alien concept to a large part of the Thai bureaucracy.   This is not really surprising.   If objective planning were to
be applied within the administrative system itself it would certainly
cost many government officers their jobs, where Departments are over-
staffed and the marginal productivity of labour is low (Ingram, 1971:303);
and at higher levels in the administration, measures to reduce the serious
duplication of responsibilities in competing Departments and Ministries
remain pre-requisite for the effective implementation of regional development programmes.   Few changes have taken place.   At the present time
one effect of duplication is that sometimes two agencies collect similar
data, leading to the existence of alternative data sets of varying
reliability (Silcock, 1970:14-36); more commonly, the data collected by
one agency are often unknown to a related Department or Division, or if
known they remain unused.   Obviously there is much waste of time in un-
coordinated data collecting, and this contributes to inadequate analysis
of available information for use in planning.

With these strictures in mind, the studies by Rimmer (Chapter 14)
and Sternstein (Chapter 15) provided the seminar with useful illustrations: the first as an example of the type of analytical pre-development
study, based on existing data, which transport planning needs in Thailand;
the second as an example of the alarming confusion which seems to be
occurring very widely in Thailand in the preparation and implementation
of plans, away from the draughting tables in the NESDB.

Rimmer is concerned to show the pattern of domestic freight movements in Thailand by railway, coastal shipping, inland waterway and road
trucking, as a preliminary step to objective assessment of the role of
road transport around 1970.   Initial construction of the highway system
had then largely been completed and further massive expenditure was proposed, for extensions during the Third Plan period.   He uses methods
which have become well-established in transport geography, with additional refinements in cartographic technique to map the 'transport surface' (Figs 14.6A and 14.6B) and in the testing of a simulation model of
inter-provincial freight flows.   Perhaps the most important conclusion,
however, is not mentioned at the end of his study: it is the evidence

from his study as a whole of how much can be done with existing transport
data, despite the occasional pleas of 'inadequate information' for poorly
justified decisions on the construction of new highways by foreign aid
agencies.

Turning from Rimmer's illustration of how pre-development planning
in Thailand might proceed, Sternstein's account of the planning tangle in
Bangkok (Chapter 15) comes as a shock if one had expected that development at the centre would be well ordered, despite what happens at the
periphery.   Sternstein spent just over five years as municipal adviser
to Bangkok and Thon Buri until early 1971, and his review of Bangkok's
plans helps to explain how the capital was allowed to deteriorate during
the 1960s into its present condition, like 'any mean modern city of recent
generations'.   He summarises the proximate cause, as 'two offices promoting
two separate plans for the same city, cannot create intelligent growth'.
Unfortunately, the inter-agency rivalry which has bedevilled city planning
in Bangkok is still characteristic of the kingdom at large, and while this
situation is allowed to persist the implementation of development proposals
will inevitably be handicapped.   For planning to become really effective
some major changes are probably needed in the administrative system, but
recent changes in the Ministry of Agriculture (in 1973 a new Planning
Division has been set up, headed by an economist drawn from NESDB and
responsible to the Under-Secretary) provide grounds for hope, at least
for the future of agricultural planning.

6.   FOREIGN AID

The last two studies (Chapters 16 and 17) were prepared for the seminar
by Khun Piew Phusavat, currently head of the agency which coordinates
foreign aid to Thailand, and by the Australian Department of Foreign
Affairs.   Australia's programme of assistance to Thailand has been small,
but it is part of an immensely significant factor in Thailand's economic
development over the past two decades.   Between 1950 and 1968 foreign
grants and loans comprised about one-third of total Thai government
capital expenditure (Ingram, 1971:305), approaching US $400 per capita
of the Thai population.   In addition, foreign military aid (including

Australia's assistance under the SEATO programme) and American payments
for materials and services during the Vietnam war provided a further
strong boost to the Thai economy during the late 1960s.

Apart from the sheer magnitude of foreign assistance in money
terms, the World Bank and foreign countries associated with Thailand in
bilateral arrangements have exerted a powerful influence on the kind of
economic development undertaken with foreign help, and its geographic
distribution.   Agriculture, for example, attracted only a small part
of bilateral aid during the First and Second Plans.   In 1970 agriculture received only 11.7 per cent of all technical assistance (Table
16.2), despite the fact that four-fifths of the population live in farm
households.   Further, many aid projects were undertaken without cost-
benefit studies or other thorough feasibility investigations, contributing to the mis-allocation of both Thai funds and foreign assistance.
The Tak-Mae Sot Highway, built with Australian aid, is one example: as
Chapter 17 indicates, this road 'was undertaken after comparatively little
investigation' for a total cost of $A16,000,000 of which Thailand contri-
buted two-thirds and Australia one-third.   The small volume of traffic
to be seen today on this bitumen-sealed, two lane highway is testimony
to Australia's rashness.   Unfortunately, it is not a solitary example;
but fortunately, in the case of Australian aid, the assistance is provided to Thailand as a grant and not as a repayable loan.

By the end of the 1960s foreign aid to Thailand was rapidly
decreasing in annual total, reflecting reductions in the activities of
the United States Agency for International Development (AID) soon after
the first Nixon Administration took office in 1968.   As Khun Piew shows
in the valuable attachment to his paper, total grant aid to Thailand fell
by almost half and American aid by 58 per cent between 1967 and 1971
(Table 16.1); the American share decreased from 78 per cent to 60 per
cent of total technical aid to Thailand in four years.   This big reduction in USAID operations probably had much less effect on economic
development than the figures suggest, however, since almost half the
American civil assistance to Thailand has been devoted to 'thwarting
subversion and insurgency', mainly through assistance to the para-
military police forces (under the heading 'Public Safety', in Table 16.1)
and to community development.

The remarkable expansion of technical assistance in the mid-1960s undoubtedly put a heavy strain on the Thai agencies responsible for administering and coordinating foreign aid within the framework of the Second Plan.   Khun Piew shows, in Chapter 16, that total grant assistance increased from US $27,592,000 to $70,262,000 between 1965 and 1967 (Table 16.1).   In 1970 the total had fallen to US $48,187,000:   40 per cent of this amount was provided by the United Nations Special Fund and 12 countries (not including the United States) and supported 65 major projects (Tables 16.5, 16.7, 16.9).   Viewed in these terms, some reduction in foreign aid in the 1970s may well have advantages, in allowing the closer coordination of aid projects for agricultural and regional development, and better evaluation of progress by the Thai agencies and foreign donors.

7.   CONCLUSION

The papers presented in this monograph and its orientation, towards an evaluation of Thailand's socio-economic situation at the beginning of the Third Plan period in October 1971,   reflect the interests of the Australia-based academics and officials who came together for the Australian National University seminar in September of that year.   For those of us involved, the seminar served to widen our field of view and to heighten our awareness of the problems which Thailand is now facing. It is hoped that the publication of the revised seminar papers will benefit a wider audience concerned with 'contemporary Thailand', in much the same way.

REFERENCES

Cunningham, C.E., Yoddumnurn, B. and Ratanasupa, W., 1970.   'Aspects of
        maternity and birth control in two Saraphi villages', in
        Cunningham, C.E., Doege, T.C. and Na Bangxang, H. 1970
        Studies of health problems and health behavior in Saraphi
        District, North Thailand, Faculty of Medicine, Chiang Mai
        University, Chiang Mai, Thailand.

Fuhs, F.W. and Vingerhoets, J., 1972.   Rural manpower, rural institutions
        and rural employment in Thailand, Manpower Planning Division,
        National Economic Development Board, Bangkok.

International Bank for Reconstruction and Development, 1959.   A public
        development program for Thailand, Baltimore.

Ingram, J.C., 1971.   Economic change in Thailand, 1850-1970, Stanford
        University Press, Stanford.

Jacobs, N., 1971.   Modernization without development, Praeger.

Ministry of Agriculture, 1972.   Agricultural statistics of Thailand, 1970
        Bangkok.

Silcock, T.H., 1970.   The economic development of Thai agriculture,
        Australian National University Press, Canberra.

CHAPTER 2

RECENT ECONOMIC DEVELOPMENTS IN THAILAND

H.V. Richter and C.T. Edwards*

1. INTRODUCTION

Over recent years Thailand has made remarkable economic progress.
Economists are now concerned that much of this success may have been
fortuitous, arising out of circumstances unlikely to recur.   In this
paper we seek to provide an analysis of recent economic trends to give
some indications of the causes of progress and of the problems to be
overcome if progress is to continue.   Five principal spheres are considered: population and work force; land use, agricultural production
and surpluses for export; the diversification of the economy and growth
of manufacturing industry; foreign trade and the balance of payments;
and finally, expenditure trends, both private and public.

Before discussing details of economic activity it should be noted
that statistical data in Thailand are a matter of some controversy.
Different government agencies produce alternative sets of estimates on
the size and composition of the population and on the workforce, the
volume and value of crop production (especially rice), manufacturing
and other activities.   There are frequently wide and unexplained dis-
crepancies between the various estimates.   The figures themselves are
often subject to doubt, and the methods of valuation, especially of
aggregates, are sometimes dubious, so that bias is introduced.   Nevertheless methods and principles of measurement on which the estimates of
the different agencies are based are thought to have remained reasonably
uniform throughout recent years, so that data from the same source may
be adequate to show trends over time.

* Mrs Richter is Research Fellow in the Department of Economics, Research
School of Pacific Studies, Australian National University.   Dr Edwards is
Senior Lecturer in the Department of Economics, School of General Studies,
Australian National University.

2.   POPULATION

Preliminary figures from the 1970 census place Thailand's population in
mid-1970 at 34,200,000.   The rate of natural increase is three per cent
a year.   By contrast, projections based on the 1960 census place the
population closer to 37,500,000 growing at between 3.1 and 3.4 per cent
a year.

On the basis of the 1960 census figure of 26,300,000, the 1970 census
figure would give an average annual rate of population growth for the
period 1960-70 of 2.7 per cent.   However, demographic research has indicated that the 1960 census figure under-estimated the size of the population.   Based on an adjusted 1960 census figure of 27,200,000, the population growth rate for the period 1960-70 would fall to 2.3 per cent a year.
The 1960 census showed a population growth rate in that year of 3.2 per
cent.   For 1970, the growth rate was placed at three per cent, although
most indicators suggest a higher rate.   If the 1970 census figure is
approximately correct, the resulting average annual growth rates for the
period 1960-70 suggest that either there was a significant dip in the
birth rate during this period or a rise followed by a fall in the death
rate.   There is no evidence to corroborate either of these propositions.
It would, therefore, seem possible that the preliminary 1970 census figure
under-estimates the size of the population.

Demographic studies indicate that, before 1960, the birth rate had
remained constant at 45 per thousand for the previous 40 to 50 years.
Allowing for a decline in the birth rate to 40 per thousand in 1970
together with a decline in the death rate from 13 per thousand in 1960
to 10 per thousand in 1970, the projections give a minimum figure for
the 1970 population of 37,000,000 (36,000,000 if the unadjusted 1960
census figure is used as the base).   Available evidence suggests that
the decline in the birth rate has not been as great as that assumed in
the above projection but that the decline in the death rate has been
greater, giving a slightly higher population growth rate for the period
1960-70 than that used in the projection.   Thus it would seem that, by
mid-1970, Thailand's population was between 36,000,000 and 37,500,000,
with a presumption that the actual figure is towards the upper end of
this range.

Thailand's population has grown rapidly throughout this century
(Table 2.1).   Migration raised the growth rate before the Second World
War, especially in the first two decades of this century, but natural
increase accounted for the major part of total growth.   The main post-
war development has been a dramatic rise in the rate of natural increase
due almost entirely to a fall in mortality; the death rate, around 30
per thousand after the war, had fallen below 20 per thousand by 1955
and reached 13 per thousand in 1960.   Since the imposition of strict
immigration quotas between 1947 and 1950, the net effect of migration
on population growth has been negligible.   Overall, Thailand now has
the dubious distinction of being among the select group of countries -
all less developed - which have the highest natural population growth
rates in the world.   The increase in population growth rate has already
had a major impact.   Over the 20 years 1951-1970, Thailand's population
rose by over 17,000,000.   During the century 1850-1950, it had risen by
only 14,000,000.

Table 2.1:   Adjusted census counts and population
             growth rates, 1919-60

Census date	Population '000	Average annual rate of growth since last estimate
1919	9,966	–
1929	12,433	2.2
1937	14,549	2.0
1947	17,890	2.1
1960	27,170	3.2

Note: Based on the 1960 adjusted census count, the
        preliminary 1970 census count of 34,150,000
        would give a rate of population growth for the
        period 1960-70 of 2.3 per cent per annum.
        Based on the actual 1960 census count, the
        rate of growth for the same period would rise
        to 2.7 per cent per annum.

Source: Caldwell, 1967:35.

Table 2.2: Population projections by age group and dependency ratios, 1970-90

Age Group	Millions				Per cent				Average Annual Rate of Growth			
	1970	1980	1985	1990	1970	1980	1985	1990	1970-80	1980-85	1985-90	1970-90
1. 0-14	17.2	23.6	27.0	29.6	45.6	45.1	43.9	42.0	3.25	2.70	1.91	2.78
(0-4)	6.8	9.2	10.1	10.7	18.1	17.5	16.5	15.1	3.03	2.02	0.99	2.25
(5-14)	10.3	14.4	16.8	19.0	27.5	27.6	27.4	26.9	3.39	3.10	2.46	3.06
2. 15-64	19.3	27.2	32.3	38.5	51.3	51.8	52.8	54.6	3.50	3.53	3.55	3.52
(15-19)	3.9	5.5	6.5	7.8	10.4	10.5	10.7	11.0	3.50	3.49	3.47	3.49
(20-64)	15.4	21.7	25.8	30.8	40.9	41.3	42.1	43.6	3.49	3.54	3.58	3.53
3. 65 +	1.1	1.6	2.0	2.4	3.0	3.1	3.2	3.4	3.98	3.76	3.77	3.87
4. Total (1 + 2 + 3)	37.5	52.4	61.3	70.5	100.0	100.0	100.0	100.0	3.40	3.17	2.86	3.21
5. Dependents (1 + 3)	18.3	25.3	28.9	32.0	51.3	51.8	52.8	54.6	3.30	2.77	2.04	2.84
6. Potential Labour Force Ratios (per 100 aged 15-64)	16.3	23.0	27.4	32.6	43.4	43.8	44.6	46.2	3.51	3.54	3.55	3.53
7. Child Dependency Ratio (1 + 2 + 2)	189.0	186.9	183.4	176.9								
8. Total Dependency Ratio (4 + 2)	194.8	192.9	189.5	183.1								

Note: The assumptions used in this projection were
(a) fertility: slight fertility decline beginning in 1970 such that the birth rate would fall by one-third to 1990.
(b) mortality: moderate mortality decline corresponding to a yearly increase of one half year in the expectation of life at birth.

Source: Chalothorn, 1970.

In 1967, 86 per cent of the population lived in rural areas
(especially in the Central Plain and Northeast).   The urban population
has grown more rapidly than total population since the war, but urbanisation is low and is largely confined to one metropolis (Bangkok-Thon Buri).[1]
The urban-rural division of the population reflects the underlying
occupational pattern.   In 1966, 80 per cent of employed persons were
engaged in agriculture (including forestry and fishing), four per cent
in industry, two per cent in construction and 14 per cent in service
activities.

Immigration, border changes and, more recently, refugee movements,
have slightly diversified the ethnic composition of the population.
The Chinese (mostly in Bangkok and other urban areas) and the Malays
(confined to the extreme south of Thailand) are the most important
minority groups.

Rapid natural population growth has significant implications for
the future size of the total population, its age structure and the rate
of growth of the labour force.   Table 2.2 presents one possible population projection.   It is assumed that Thailand's current population is
37,500,000 and is growing by 3.4 per cent a year.   The projection allows
for a decline in fertility by one-third between 1970 and 1990 and further
marginal decreases in mortality.   A faster decline in fertility is
possible if the central government gives strong support to a national
family planning policy.   Such support has not yet been coordinated
partly because recent military developments in neighbouring countries
have strengthened the plausibility of the case against birth control,
partly because population pressure on land and food supplies has not
been an acute political issue and partly because more prosperity in the
past decade eroded the case for long-term planning.   The economic
situation is now changing - but because family planning is a long range
policy with little immediate impact, it is not clear yet whether it
will receive a more central place in government policy, particularly

---

1 Caldwell (1967:45-6) pointed out that in 1960, the size relationship
between the populations of Bangkok-Thon Buri, Chieng Mai and Khorat -
the three largest urban centres in Thailand - was 100:4:2.

in view of growing insurgency problems in Thailand.[2]   Nevertheless, some
decline in fertility seems likely as a result of a piecemeal extension of
the existing family planning programme, observed increases in the age of
marriage and the desire for family planning, and a continued relative
increase in the extent of urbanisation.

Table 2.2 indicates that Thailand's population may increase by
almost 90 per cent between 1970 and 1990 to reach 70,000,000. In itself
this rapid growth is not a new phenomenon but the absolute size of the
projected increase is much larger than that of the last two decades and
is likely to place far greater strain on the economy.   While a more
rapid decline in the death rate than that projected would not significantly affect the 1990 estimate, a greater decline in fertility would,
but the effect would be small if this decline were delayed a decade.

Because of sustained high fertility, the child dependency ratio is
high in Thailand by comparison with countries with lower fertility.   In
1970, 46 per cent of the population was under 15 years of age.   A high
dependency ratio restrains the capacity of the economy to save (by sus-
taining a high average consumption-income relationship) and diverts a
significant part of the saving that does occur into demographic investment in a future generation, such as schools.   The projected decline in
fertility after 1970 lowers the rate of growth of the child population
and reduces the child dependency ratio but the reduction in this ratio
is slight in the first decade and the decrease to 1990, while important,
is not substantial.   In 1990, 42 per cent of the population is still
projected to be under 15 years of age.   If the projection proves to be
reasonably accurate, Thailand will continue to have an economically
inefficient age structure for the remainder of this century.

While the rate of growth of the child population declines significantly, that of the school-age population (5-14 years) falls much less
and that of the pre-tertiary and tertiary population (15-9 years) is

_____

2 Family planning on a voluntary basis was approved early in 1970 as
part of government policy.   A five year population plan aimed at reducing the population growth rate to 2.5 per cent a year by the end of
1976 by providing more extensive family planning services has been
included in the Third Five Year National Economic and Social Development
Plan (1972-76).

virtually unaffected.   Between 1970 and 1990, the population 5-14 years
is projected to increase 84 per cent and that of 15-9 years 100 per cent.
The coming decades will see an unflagging demand for primary education
facilities and an accelerating demand for the relatively more expensive
secondary and tertiary facilities.   This finding contrasts sharply with
the position in Singapore where, as a result of a substantial fall in
fertility, the demand for additional primary education facilities has
virtually ceased.

The rate of growth of the population of working age (defined as all
persons aged 15-64), which was comparatively steady for several decades
at just below two per cent a year, has increased significantly since 1965
and, regardless of what now happens to fertility, will shortly reach 3.5
per cent a year and stabilise around this level for the remainder of the
century.   Because of the projected fall in the rate of growth of the
child dependent population, the share of the population of working age
will rise from 51 per cent in 1970 towards 55 per cent in 1990, doubling
in aggregate figures.

Estimates of the potential labour force based on 1970 participation
rates indicate a similar overall growth pattern.   For 1966-67, a labour
force survey placed unemployment at two per cent of the potential labour
force.   Almost all of this unemployment occurred in urban areas (and
especially in Bangkok-Thon Buri).   This figure is low because most of
Thailand's population lives in rural areas and no account was taken of
under-employment.   Nevertheless, it would seem fair to conclude that
sustained high economic growth in the post-war period absorbed almost
all of the increase in the potential labour force to 1965.   Since then,
the rate of growth of the potential labour force has jumped and there are
now indications that the rate of economic growth may not be as rapid in
the future as in the past.   While the major part of the increase in the
potential labour force will be absorbed into the rural community, a more
rapid relative growth of the urban population in the future will bring
about a marked rise in the number and probably in the percentage of the
potential labour force that is unemployed.

Table 2.3: Gross Domestic Product by industrial origin
US$million, in constant 1962 prices[a]

	1960	%	1969[b]	%	Annual Growth[c] %
Agriculture, forestry and fishing	1032	38.2	1646	30.5	5.3
Mining and quarrying	29	1.1	92	1.7	13.7
Manufacturing	352	13.0	887	16.4	10.8
Construction	131	4.9	365	6.8	12.1
Electricity, water supply	12	0.4	69	1.3	21.5
Transport and communication	203	7.5	367	6.8	6.8
Wholesale and retail trade	426	15.8	905	16.7	8.7
Banking, insurance and real estate	52	1.9	198	3.7	16.0
Ownership of dwellings	77	2.9	105	1.9	3.5
Public administration and defence	125	4.6	229	4.2	7.0
Other services	261	9.7	539	10.0	8.4
Gross Domestic Product	2700	100.0	5403	100.0	8.0
Net factor income from abroad	-4		2		
Gross National Product	2696		5405		
Per capita GNP $[d]	102		156		4.8

a   Converted from baht at 20.8 = US$1.00
b   Preliminary
c   Change between 1960 and 1969
d   Based on National Statistical Office's estimates of population,
       26,392,000 in 1960, 34,738,000 in 1969.

Source: Bank of Thailand, Monthly Report (citing National Accounts
              Division, NEDB).

3.   GROWTH AND CHANGING STRUCTURE OF THE ECONOMY

Over the past two decades all major branches of the economy grew at a
fairly rapid pace.   This pace may prove difficult to maintain.   During
the same period some structural transformation took place.   The extent
of the structural change which has occurred should not, however, be
exaggerated.   In 1969 agriculture, including fishing and forestry,
still occupied nearly four-fifths of the work force, contributed almost
a third to Gross Domestic Product and earned at least three-quarters of
the value of commodity exports.   Rice remained overwhelmingly the most
important crop, occupying almost twice the area of land under all other
crops.   Moreover, according to calculations made for 1962/3 by Silcock
(1967:237), over half of all rice produced did not enter the market, but
was consumed on farms.   Nevertheless, a significant change has been
going on, as much within sectors as between sectors, and the element of
subsistence production within the economy is declining.

Table 2.3 shows the recent growth and changing composition of
national income.   It will be seen that Gross Domestic Product doubled in
terms of constant 1962 prices between 1960 and 1969, showing an annual
average growth rate of eight per cent over the period.   Agriculture
expanded satisfactorily, value added growing by an annual average of 5.3
per cent during the nine years, though with marked yearly variations.
Agricultural growth was outpaced by other sectors, notably manufacturing,
construction, banking and real estate and services, so that its share of
Gross Domestic Product, which had been over 40 per cent in 1958 (Panitpakdi,
1967:106) declined to 38 per cent in 1960 and to 30 per cent in 1969.
These estimates are given in constant prices, but, since little inflation
took place over the period, an adjustment to current prices would not
significantly affect the patters shown.[3]

According to the estimates presented in Table 2.3, per capita Gross
National Product in terms of constant 1962 prices rose from the equivalent

---

[3] The index of wholesale prices in Bangkok-Thon Buri, based on 1958 =
100, rose to 115 by 1969.   At current prices the share of agriculture,
fishing and forestry in GDP is estimated at 39.9 per cent in 1960 and
at 31.8 per cent in 1969.

of US$102 in 1960 to US$156 in 1969.   The disparity between urban and
rural incomes is thought to have widened somewhat, since a larger share
of the increase flowed to urban factors.   It will be remembered, however, that it is often argued that the rural sector, especially the rice
sector, is undervalued in the national accounts.   This is partly because
rice, including the large share consumed on farms, was valued before 1971
at the artifically low prices maintained by the government through its
rice premium (export tax) policy.   Fishing by farmers for their own consumption, an important element in their domestic economy, is entirely
omitted from the estimates (Panitpakdi, 1967:112).   Similarly it is not
clear whether the non-farming activities undertaken by farm families in
trading, house construction, home industries and the like are given anything like their true weight in the national accounts.

4.   EXPANSION AND DIVERSIFICATION OF AGRICULTURAL PRODUCTION

Many different factors affected the growth and diversification of farm
production, both on the supply and demand side, and there was a marked
difference in response between regions.   The pattern of expansion is
quite different if one looks at the rice sector or at the so-called upland crops, such as maize, cassava, kenaf, and beans.   Since 1950 rice
production has increased more slowly than population while consumption
per head appears to have risen.   Export surpluses have declined.   From
figures available it would appear that roughly half of the growth in
rice output can be attributed to the extension of area cultivated and
about half to better yields per hectare since the mid-1950s.

Upland crop development, in contrast, has been directed largely
to export markets.   Starting from a very small base, output has almost
quintupled since the beginning of the 1950s, probably some four-fifths
of the increase being attributable to an extension of acreage.   Whereas
in 1950 only 12 per cent of the total area sown was devoted to non-rice
crops, by 1967 their share had grown to nearly 35 per cent.

(i)   Land use

Since data on land use in Thailand are scattered, a summary of
available statistics is presented below.   It is government policy that
half the area of the country should remain under forest, to protect the

watersheds and valuable timbers.   This limit is now being approached.
There are, however, large areas of waste and of sparsely settled land,
especially in the outer provinces (Table 2.4).

Table 2.4:   Land use
'000 hectares

	1960	1963	1965	1965 %
Arable area	10,077	10,604	11,415	22
of which irrigated	(1,636)	(1,764)	(2,275)	(20[a])
Forest and grazing	30,004	27,135	27,354	53
Unclassified	11,319	12,998	12,631	25
Total Kingdom	51,400	51,400	51,400	100

a Per cent of arable area.

Source: Statistisches Bundesamt, 1970:14.

Data from the 1963 Census of Agriculture show the concentration of
holdings in two regions, the Central region and the Northeast, and the
fairly large average size of farms there (Table 2.5).

Table 2.5:   Farm holdings by region, 1963

	Number of holdings '000	Area in holdings '000 ha.	Average size of holdings ha.	Area irrigated[a] '000 ha. State projects	Private projects	Per cent irrigated by projects
Central	723	3101	4.3	1328	44	44
North	777	2009	2.6	81	75	8
Northeast	1221	4227	3.5	105	3	3
South	493	1812	3.7	–	49	3
Total	3214	11,149	3.5	1514	171	15

a 1964.   Excludes tanks and manually operated systems.   These are important
   outside the Central region.

Source: National Statistical Office, 1965:   Tables 78 – from Census of
          Agriculture;   Tables 93 and 94 – from Royal Irrigation Department.

More up-to-date data show the recent expansion of irrigation
facilities, which has almost wholly benefited the Central region.   1967
data (Table 2.6) cover both State and private systems, including those
manually operated by farmers.   The definition of 'irrigation' is not
the same in the two systems.   By 1967, 2,630,000 hectares were classified as irrigated, four-fifths of which was in the Central Plain.
There was at this date another 1,630,000 hectares of additional projects
at the construction or planning stage, of which State reservoirs were
scheduled to provide 1,000,000 hectares of double cropping facilities
by the end of 1971.   These new projects would benefit other regions
equally with the Central region.

Table 2.6: Irrigated land, 1967

'000 hectares

Regions	Central	Northern	N'Eastern	Southern	Total
Irrigated	2129	220	226	56	2631
Planned[a]	774	484	266	106	1630
(of which Double Crop[b])	(436)	(550)	(70)	-	(1055)
Irrigable	2903	704	492	162	4261

a   Includes projects under construction. Data are for rainy season.
b   Data are for dry season, reservoirs only. For a number of these
      reservoirs the area irrigable is larger in the dry season than
      in the rainy season.

Source: Ministry of Agriculture, 1970: Tables 110 and 113.

(ii) Agrarian conditions

Since land shortage has not, at least until recently, been a pressing
problem, save in localities near Bangkok and some other towns, Thai farming
has traditionally been characterised by owner-occupiers working holdings of
relatively uniform size.   Only one-fifth of the cultivated area was held
in farms over 10 hectares in the early 1960s while very small holdings were
usually vegetable or fruit plots in the neighbourhood of towns and villages
(Table 2.7).

There has recently been concern that agrarian conditions are deterio-
rating, and that fragmentation of holdings into smaller, less economic,
units is occurring, together with increasing tenancy.   There was a 50 per
cent increase in the number of farms throughout the country between 1953

Table 2.7:   Farm holdings by size, 1963

Size[a]	Number of holdings '000	%	Amount of land '000 ha.	%
Under 1 ha.	595.2	18.5	284.8	2.6
1-4 ha.	1597.5	49.7	3427.9	30.7
4-10 ha.	847.3	26.4	4958.6	44.5
Over 10 ha.	174.4	5.4	2478.0	22.2
Total	3214.4	100.0	11,149.3	100.0

a Original data in rai, size groups under 6 rai, 6-25 rai,
   25-60 and over 60.

Source: Statistisches Bundesamt, 1970:14.

and 1963 and a decline in the average size of farm from 4.4 to 3.5 hectares though it is uncertain whether the statistics for the two years are comparable.   At the same time the area sown to the principal crops per head of total population in Thailand seems to have declined very little over the past two decades (Table 2.8) so that farmers' utilisation of their land may have risen.

Similarly there is concern that peasants are losing their land to landowners.   This is especially said of the rice lands north of Bangkok, extending up to the Ayutthaya district.   No countrywide study of agrarian conditions has been made.   A survey carried out by the National Statistical Office in 1968 (NEDB, 1969, appendix) of 498,000 farms in the Central region, estimated that 59 per cent of households there wholly owned their land, 16 per cent partly owned and partly rented it, and 25 per cent wholly rented. It was not stated what share of the area was in each category.   The findings in this fairly commercialised region would not, however, be typical of conditions in the rest of the country.

(iii) Growth and change in production

The area planted to all crops rose 56 per cent between 1950-52 and 1965-67 to a total of 10,000,000 hectares.   Non-rice crop areas quadrupled between the two periods, to occupy 3,300,000 hectares, one-third of the sown area (Table 2.8).   Much of the land in Thailand, especially in

Table 2.8: Area planted of principal crops, 1950-1967

('000 hectares)

	Rice[a]	Rubber	Maize	Kenaf	Tobacco[b]	Oil seeds[c]	Cassava[d]	Garden crops	Fruits	All non-rice	All crops total	Area per head
1950	5540	337	36	5	31	180	13	n.a.	n.a.	752	6292	0.325
1951	5959	352	41	14	42	194	13	n.a.	n.a.	829	6789	0.335
1952	5368	368	45	11	44	197	14	n.a.	n.a.	851	6219	0.298
1953	6172	384	48	10	54	201	14	n.a.	n.a.	890	7062	0.329
1954	6997	400	53	6	55	229	14	n.a.	n.a.	947	6504	0.294
1955	5790	416	56	8	56	235	14	n.a.	n.a.	979	6748	0.296
1956	6024	430	82	17	57	251	39	n.a.	n.a.	1070	7093	0.302
1957	5075	444	97	12	62	282	38	38	71	1334	6409	0.265
1958	5758	456	127	20	61	280	44	43	68	1390	7148	0.287
1959	6065	469	200	44	62	283	63	48	77	1567	7633	0.297
1960	5921	481	286	140	59	335	72	61	109	1894	7815	0.296
1961	6179	493	307	190	42	319	99	90	152	2068	8247	0.303
1962	6659	502	328	114	42	363	123	118	147	2021	8680	0.310
1963	6601	524	418	153	41	372	140	123	175	2377	8978	0.311
1964	6540	529	552	218	51	368	105	117	173	2538	9077	0.305
1965	6479	532	577	384	72	409	102	117	242	2855	9334	0.305
1966	7375	731	653	530	86	477	130	186	274	3519	10,895	0.345
1967	6410	737	744	348	63	462	141	188	275	3475	9885	0.302

a The figures are for the crop years 1950-1 to 1967-8.
b Tobacco figures are obtained by adding local and Virginian varieties.
c Includes castor beans, groundnuts, sesame and coconuts.
d Until 1956 figures are for Chon Buri province.

Source: Ministry of Agriculture, 1970: Table 4.

the delta, is suitable only for rice growing, owing to flooding and to
heavy and impermeable subsoils.   But where switching to other crops is
technically possible, commercial conditions have clearly favoured non-
rice crops for many years.   Profits from rice growing were slender,
owing to the operation of the rice premium, which was designed not only
to provide the government with its principal direct source of revenue
from the agricultural sector, but also to keep down prices for domestic
purchasers of rice.   Farmers made the rational choice of first securing
their family needs of rice.   Those either more enterprising or with
larger farms then put an increasing share of their surplus land under
export crops, such as maize, kenaf and cassava or switched to high value
cash crops for local sale, often persuaded by Bangkok traders and their
agents.

The earliest and most rapid response both in expansion and diversification of land use took place in the Central region, where a greater
than average share of output is marketed.   Somewhat later a similar
change took place in the Northeast, with other regions changing more
slowly (Silcock, 1970:174).   This expansion and diversification was made
possible by three principal factors on the supply side: public investment
in irrigation and flood control schemes;   extensions to the road network
which opened up new localities to the market;   and private investment,
mainly in tractors.

(iv) Agricultural inputs

By 1970 there were reported to be 19,000 tractor units in Thailand,
older ones mainly of the 40 h.p. class, with newer units often of 70 h.p.
or more (Department of Trade and Industry, 1970:241).   According to one
estimate (Chancellor, 1971:14-5) 'data...indicate that the area tilled
(single pass basis)...represents 55 per cent of the area in annual crops[4]
...tractors made possible the tillage of large areas of hard upland soils.'
Owners were mainly farmer-contractors working machines round the clock
during the five months tillage season with relays of drivers, so that each
machine worked on the average 1360 hours a year (Chancellor, 1971:5).

---

4 This seems most unlikely unless it refers to crops other than wet rice.
The survey was carried out between mid-August and early December.

The principal benefit, in Chancellor's view, was not in direct extra
profits or higher yields either to contractors or their clients, but in
the profitable use to which farmers put the time saved by mechanised
tillage.

Comparatively little fertiliser is used in Thailand, particularly
in open fields, because its use is uneconomic at present price relationships, and because of potential losses due to flooding.   Nitrogen is the
main plant nutrient needed for both upland crops and the new rice varieties
in the principal areas.   Freight and handling charges on imported supplies
are high[5], while the local factory, established at Mae Moh in 1966 on
lignite deposits in the North, is a high cost producer far from markets.
Wholesale prices of nitrogen to farmers in the Central Plain were reported
in 1969 to be seven baht per kg (US$336 per tonne) compared to farm prices
of 2.2 to 4.4 baht/kg N in most other countries (Department of External
Affairs, 1970:40).   In 1970, with prices of good quality padi in the
range of US$45-48 per tonne, the ratio of fertiliser to padi prices was
seven to one.   This is a striking contrast to the position in Indonesia
where a two to one ratio is aimed at through subsidised sales of urea at
around US$80 a tonne.

(v)   The rice sector

According to estimates of the Rice Department of the Ministry of
Agriculture, production of padi increased from an average of 6,900,000
tonnes in 1950/1-1952/3 to an average of 11,200,000 tonnes in the three
seasons running to 1969/70.   This would be an increase of 62 per cent
over the period or a growth rate of about 2.5 per cent annually over the
past 20 years.   The sown area expanded by 26 per cent between the two
periods, and average yield by 29 per cent.   If these estimates are to
be believed it appears that the long term decline in yields in the first
half of this century noted by Ingram (1955:49), which had been caused by
the extension of rice cultivation to marginal lands, has been reversed
(Table 2.12).

---

5 There are no tariffs on imported fertiliser, but urea and ammonium
sulphate are subject to import control to ensure a market for output of
the Mae Moh plant.

Rice yields are still low by standards of some other tropical countries. They are roughly two-thirds of those of Western Malaysia for
example. The improvement which has recently taken place is probably due
mainly to an extension of water control and the application of more labour.
The new high yielding seeds developed at the International Rice Research
Institute in the Philippines are not yet being used in bulk, the Thais
preferring quality to quantity. IR8 is in any case too short in stature
for the flood plains of the Delta. Experiments are, however, being conducted in government stations with hybrid IRRI – native varieties, which
are reported to be doing well (Department of External Affairs, 1970), so
that disease resistant, better flavoured and higher yielding crosses may
soon be available for distribution on a trial basis, mainly for the
irrigated areas.

(vi) Upland crops

The great increase in upland crop production which has occurred over
the past two decades is largely attributable to acreage expansion. Table
2.8 gives estimates of planted areas of the principal crops. These show
that in the three seasons 1950-52 the average area sown to rice was
5,622,000 hectares, or 87 per cent of the total. Rubber occupied 352,000
hectares (5.5 per cent) and all other crops 458,000 hectares,[6] (7.1 per
cent). By 1965-67 rice occupied 6,755,000 hectares (67 per cent) and
rubber 666,000 hectares (6.6 per cent). Other crops occupied 2,616,000
hectares, 26 per cent of the sown area.

During the 1950s yields of almost all crops rose as farmers adopted
new seeds, planted on better land and became accustomed to new techniques.
By the mid-1960s, however, yields of many crops had declined, although
most still retained a fair part of the gain of the 1950s. In the case of
the important oilseeds group, however, yields were actually lower than at
the beginning of the 1950s (Table 2.9).

Some of the decline in yields during the 1960s may be attributable
to seasonal factors. Crop estimates for 1968 and 1969 (Bank of Thailand,
April 1971) show substantial increases in the harvests of many crops.

6 This is an underestimate, as it does not include garden crop and fruit
areas, included in data from 1957 onwards.

Table 2.9: Area, output and yield of field crops other than rice

	Area '000 ha	Output '000 tonnes	Yield kg/ha
1950-2 average			
Maize, mungbeans and cassava	90	108	1200
Sugar cane	66	1202	18,212
Oilseeds[a]	210	760	3619
Fibres[b]	53	39	736
Tobacco	39	35	897
Total	458	2144	
1959-61 average			
Maize, etc	387	1062	2744
Sugar cane	143	4185	29,265
Oilseeds	335	1204	3594
Fibres	264	579	2193
Tobacco	54	63	1167
Total	1183	7093	
Change compared to 1950-2	+ 158%	+ 213%	
1965-7 average			
Maize, etc	912	1954	2143
Sugar cane	138	4278	31,000
Oilseeds	492	1382	2809
Fibres	574	933	1625
Tobacco	72	81	1125
Total	2188	8628	
Compared to 1959-61	+ 85%	+ 22%	
Compared to 1950-2	+ 378%	+ 302%	

a Castor beans, peanuts, sesame, soybeans and coconuts.
b Cotton, kapok and bombax, jute, kenaf and ramie.

Source: Ministry of Agriculture, 1970: Tables 15, 24, 35.

But it is also possible that the yield declines of the mid-1960s are part of a long term trend caused by the spread of cultivation to lands of lesser quality or to a loss of soil fertility through intensive use without suffi- cient replenishment by fertilisers. It has been argued that upland crop production may have reached a plateau under present techniques (Welsch, 1971:89-104). It has also been argued that the diversification of agri- culture, which was so striking a feature in the 1950s, has recently run out

of steam and that no new products have been introduced during the past
decade (NEDB, 1969:6).

1816404

(vii) <u>Rubber</u>

The doubling of rubber output from 114,500 tonnes in 1950 to about
275,000 tonnes in 1970 is due to an expansion of area, which more than
offset a decline in yields.   Area and yield statistics are available only
to 1967 (Ministry of Agriculture, 1970:Table 55).   These estimate that
tappable area rose 144 per cent from 261,000 hectares in 1950 to 637,000
in 1967.   Planted area was 337,000 and 737,000 hectares respectively.
Production was 219,300 tonnes in 1967.   Yields per tapped hectare
declined by 22 per cent over the period from 439 kg/ha to 344 kg/ha.
Thai yields are not much over half those of West Malaysia and are roughly
comparable with those of Indonesian smallholders.   Only about six per
cent of the Thai area has so far been replanted to the latest high yielding
strains.   Government policy is to subsidise the replanting of between 16,000
and 23,000 hectares a year, or two to three per cent of the planted area,
a somewhat slow rate of progress.

5.   EXPANSION OF MANUFACTURING INDUSTRY[7]

During the past decade the manufacturing sector has gone through a phase
of dynamic growth, following a long period of stagnation.   In terms of
constant 1962 prices its contribution to Gross Domestic Product grew at
an annual average of 11 per cent between 1960 and 1969 and the sector's
share at current prices rose from 12.5 per cent to 14.6 per cent.   Up to
1967 the construction industry grew even more rapidly.   And although its
growth slackened somewhat in the following two years, its contribution to
GDP   was   6.6 per cent in 1969.   These are quite significant shares of
national income compared to many other developing countries and represent
substantial recent investment.   Manufacturing has of course grown from a

---

7 This section draws heavily on the work of C. Isarangkun, both from his
unpublished Ph.D thesis, 'Manufacturing Industries in Thailand,' Australian
National University, 1969 and the work he did for the first author as a
research assistant.   His assistance is gratefully acknowledged.

Table 2.10: Basic statistics of major manufacturing industries, 1963

	Total census		Firms employing 10 or more workers			
	No. of establishments	No. employed	No. of establishments	No. employed	Gross receipts a $'000	Value added a $'000
Food manufacturing industries	23,773	93,542	1,395	42,187	156,788	39,565
Rice-mills	18,413	48,625	643	12,977	68,961	10,682
Sugar-mills	534	19,064	375	18,528	24,967	11,115
Beverage industries	110	7,616	61	7,384	49,015	37,758
Alcoholic drinks	49	4,719	40	4,672	29,219	24,144
Breweries	2	805	2	805	n.a.	n.a.
Non-alcoholic beverages	58	2,083	19	1,907	10,823	5,633
Tobacco	287	12,360	142	11,784	75,363	54,316
Cigarette and cigar-factories	63	5,551	7	5,287	70,798	52,486
Redrying tobacco leaf factories	146	6,442	128	6,859	3,481	1,265
Textiles	68,722	160,351	302	25,168	42,339	12,741
Cotton textiles factories	30,753	55,057	112	10,039	9,921	2,804
Spin, weave, dye and finish of silk	25,038	57,739	36	1,274	1,350	501
Gunny-bag mills	7	8,642	6	8,639	9,442	5,037
Wood and cork manufacturers	23,863	63,085	490	19,932	39,577	14,575
Saw-mills and plywood factories	585	19,037	421	18,279	37,075	13,574
Basketry etc.	21,434	38,013	9	129	42	17
Non-metallic mineral products manufacture	7,766	28,634	219	11,488	38,980	21,125
Manufacture of glass and glass products	20	2,503	14	2,480	7,323	4,174
Manufacture of cement and cement products	84	2,829	5	2,696	25,244	13,939
Bricks	1,867	6,299	443	709	244	160
Pottery	4,211	8,893	37	1,083	265	188
Total for all industries	164,002	481,213	3,584	154,956	542,172	232,711

a Original data in baht, converted here at US$1.00 = 20.8 baht.
Source: National Statistical Office, 1967-8.

very small base, and much remains on a cottage scale.   Basic statistics
from the 1964 census covering the year 1963 are given in Table 2.10, compiled by Isarangkun.   They show a total of 481,000 workers in 164,000
enterprises, of whom a third worked in textiles, nearly a quarter in food,
drink and tobacco and 13 per cent in saw mills and basketry.   There have
been three main sources of growth of the manufacturing sector over the
past decade.

(i)   Raw material processing

There has been an expansion of plants processing local raw materials,
partly for the home market and partly for export.   These new or enlarged
plants are located both in the provinces and in the Bangkok-Thon Buri
area.   In some cases expansion appears to have run well ahead of supplies,
so that over-capacity exists in many sectors, notably rice milling, sugar,
gunny sacks and wood manufacture (Isarangkun, 1969:256).   In other cases
capacity seems to be running ahead of demand, as for example in motor
tyres, where production potential will probably be around 1,000,000 units
by 1972.

The tin smelter, established in 1965 at Phuket to process local ores
to ingot form, exports almost the whole of its output.   It is jointly
owned by United States and Dutch interests and has been operating over
the past three years close to its rated capacity of 26,000 tonnes a year.

(ii)   Construction materials

The second source of expansion has been in the mushroom growth of
factories and workshops, often quite small, turning out products for the
construction industry (such as bricks, tiles, galvanised iron and frames)
whose production is afforded natural protection by high freight costs.
The one branch in this category whose output is on a sizeable factory
scale is cement, demand for which has been stimulated by dam construction,
road and bridge works and building programmes.   Output, which was only
400,000 tonnes in 1957, reached 2,600,000 in 1970.   Here again, however,
over-capacity may prove a problem, as each of the three firms operating
is enlarging, so that if all plans are carried out, capacity will reach
4,500,000 tonnes in 1972.   During the mid-1960s some 160,000 tonnes of
cement were exported annually, so that it may be that part of the surplus
will again find export markets.

These two sectors, the processing of raw materials and the production
of construction materials, accounted for almost two-thirds of the increase
in value added in manufacturing between 1964 and 1967 (NEDB, 1967).

(iii) Import substitution industries

Finally there has been a sizeable development of new industries,
almost all in the import substitution field and protected by tariffs or
quotas.   Most of these factories are located in the Bangkok-Thon Buri
area, and produce mainly consumer goods, often from imported raw materials
and parts.   This category includes textiles, clothing, the assembly of
cars, radios and television sets, paper, paints, plastics, soap and pharma-
ceuticals.   The change of government policy in the early 1950s away from
the previous stress on state enterprise in industry and low protection for
private enterprises has stimulated this development.   A Promotion of
Industrial Investment Act of 1954, as amended in 1960, 1962 and 1965 now
offers a familiar range of tariff and tax concessions to promoted industries, together with assurances on the remittance of capital and profits
(Isarangkun, 1969:232-3).   There are distinct lags, however, in the
government provision of a long promised industrial estate, and in other
services, such as electricity, water and telephone.

By the end of 1969 the registered capital of promoted companies had
reached 6,217,000,000 baht (US$299,000,000), one-third in wholly Thai-
owned enterprises and two-thirds in joint Thai-foreign firms.   Of total
registered capital, 67 per cent was Thai, 10.6 per cent Japanese, 5.4 per
cent United States, 4.8 per cent Taiwanese, 5.3 per cent European and 2.3
per cent other Asian countries (Stikker and Hirono, 1971:411).   Development of promoted industries has been made possible by the granting of
fairly high protective tariffs, ranging from 10 per cent nominal rate for
food products, 20 to 67 per cent for cotton, wool and synthetic fabrics
and 10 to 60 per cent for paper, chemicals, footwear and clothing.

The whole strategy of industrialisation by import substitution is
being increasingly criticised in Thailand.   It is inward oriented, and
moreover the captive market it aims at is the urban enclave rather than
the mass rural market, so that the scale of production is necessarily
small.   A proliferation of competing firms encouraged by promotion

measures has further split the market, reduced capacity utilisation and added to costs.   It has proved relatively capital intensive in a country which will soon face mounting employment problems.   Only some 96,000 employees work in promoted industries, and the whole manufacturing sector absorbs only four to five per cent of the work force, including part time employees.   Moreover, with its heavy dependence on imported capital equipment and raw materials, its net benefit to the balance of payments is doubtful.

6.   FOREIGN TRADE AND THE BALANCE OF PAYMENTS

(i)   Export performance

Thailand has been praised for its dynamic export record since the end of the Second World War.   It has been portrayed by Hla Myint and others as one of the developing countries which has benefited from the adoption of outward looking trade policies, and whose enconmic growth could be described as export-led (Myint, 1967:1).   Exports have not only grown substantially in value but have diversified in composition and direction with the development of new products and new markets.   Between 1960 and 1966 the average rate of growth of export values was 8.5 per cent a year, and the ratio of exports to Gross Domestic Product was 15.4 per cent.

Since 1966 the continuous expansion in export earnings has come to a virtual halt, so that their ratio to Gross Domestic Product declined to 11.3 per cent in 1969.   But the striking diversification in the commodity pattern of exports has continued.   An analysis of the trade returns reveals how important the postwar shift in composition has been.[8]   In 1952

---

8 Michaely (1962:6-12) demonstrated in a study of 44 countries in the mid-1950s that Thailand had an especially highly concentrated export pattern. Thailand's coefficient was calculated by Michaely at 68.3 in 1954.   A recalculation on the same formula with more recent data shows a change to 44.8 by 1963, 40.7 in 1967 and 35.9 in 1968.   The coefficient

$$C_x = 100 \frac{}{i} \quad \frac{x_i}{} {}^2 \quad \text{where } x_i \text{ is the value of a country's}$$

exports of commodity i and x is the value of its total exports.

rice brought in nearly two-thirds of export value, but in 1970 only 17
per cent.   Diversification up to 1966 took place against a background of
rising or steady rice sales.   In this period increased sales of rubber,
tin, maize, kenaf and tapioca contributed most to growth.   Since that
date exports of these latter commodities failed to expand sufficiently
to offset falls in rice earnings.   The value of exports of the seven
principal commodities taken as a group (including rice and teak) was
thus eight per cent lower in 1970 than four years earlier (Table 2.11).

Loss from this group of seven major exports has however been made
good by a rise in 'other exports', which in 1970 contributed 30 per cent
to total value, compared to under nine per cent in 1952.   It would be
interesting to know the composition of this 'other export' group, which
is growing quite rapidly.   Published Thai trade statistics account for
less than one-third of it, giving details of a number of minor items,
mainly rural and fishery commodities.   It is difficult to judge what
share of the gain is fortuitous.   It may, for example, include substantial American procurement orders for Vietnam.   If it is more solidly
based, this would be a most healthy development, probably leading to a
resumption of long term growth in total export earnings.

Table 2.11:   Changes in composition of exports 1966 and 1970

| | U.S. $'000,000[a] | | | Per cent of total value | |
	1966	1970[b]	Change	1966	1970
Rice	192.4	121.3	-71.1	28.4	17.1
Kenaf[c]	77.6	33.0	-44.6	11.4	4.6
Teak	11.7	7.4	- 4.2	1.7	1.0
Sub-total	281.6	161.7	-119.9		
Rubber	89.5	107.5	+18.1	13.2	15.1
Maize	73.1	88.7	+15.7	10.8	12.5
Tin	63.3	77.7	+14.4	9.3	10.9
Tapioca	31.0	58.7	+27.7	4.6	8.3
Sub-total	256.8	332.7	+76.0		
Other products	139.4	216.4	+77.0	20.6	30.4
Total	677.8	710.9	+33.0	100.0	100.0

a   Converted at baht 20.8 = US$1.00.   Errors in additions due to
    rounding.   Includes re-exports of about $15,000,000 in 1966
    and $25,000,000 in 1970.
b   Preliminary.
c   Includes jute.

Source: Bank of Thailand, Monthly Report.

(ii) <u>Rice</u>

Thailand must earn more foreign exchange if it is to maintain the
present pace of development without running down foreign exchange reserves
too sharply or increasing overseas obligations and income payable abroad.
It seems doubtful whether it can look to greatly improved rice sales to
contribute to growth, although government planners are hoping that exports
will again rise to 1,500,000 tonnes a year.   In 1970 the record was
gloomy.   Exports (Table 2.12) remained just over the 1,000,000 tonne
level, but the unit price fell sharply to US$116 per tonne, compared
with US$138 in 1969 and US$170 in 1968.   By early 1971 unit prices had
declined to around US$90.   In April and May 1971 the export premium,
which constituted about one-third of f.o.b. prices of privately traded
rice in 1968-69 was abolished on most grades, as much to maintain prices
to farmers as to stimulate exports.[9]

It is impossible to forecast world market prospects for a commodity
in which world trade supplies only about five per cent of consumption.
The marginal nature of trade can create large swings in demand according
to harvests in importing countries.   Moreover the market must cope with
supplies from the United States and Japan, sold on preferential terms,
and with the emergence of new sellers, who are a step ahead of Thailand
in the 'green revolution'.   However the position might well alter rapidly.
Both the United States and Japan are constantly reminded by Thailand of
the disruptive impact of their food aid programmes on traditional Thai
markets such as Indonesia and the Philippines, and Japan at least appears
to be listening.   Moreover Asian countries now concentrating on import
replacement policies for rice may modify policies as the green revolution
moves through different phases, giving comparative cost considerations
preference over security.   The main markets have recently been Malaysia,
Singapore, India and Hong Kong.

The supply side is also doubtful, for Thailand seems to be following
the same pattern as its neighbour and competitor, Burma.   Increasing home
consumption is cutting deeply into former export surpluses.   Table 2.12
shows the dramatic change which has taken place since the 1930s, when
roughly half the crop was exported.   According to calculations based on

---

9 The export duty of around four per cent ad valorem remains in force.

Table 2.12: Rice: exports, production, yield, consumption, 1934-38 average, 1955-70

	Exports			Production[a]			Exports[b] as % of production (milled basis)	Domestic retention[c]	
	Volume tonnes milled rice ('000)	Volume Index (1958 = 100)	Price Index (1958 = 100)	padi metric tonnes ('000)	harvested area hectares ('000)	yields kg per ha		total tonnes milled rice ('000)	kg per capita
1934- (av.)	1388	123	24	4357	3370	1293	49	1488	106
1955	1248	110	94	5709	4524	1262	33	2520	111
1956	1226	108	92	7334	5376	1364	25	3614	154
1957	1570	139	96	8297	5762	1440	29	3906	162
1958	1133	100	100	5570	4287	1299	31	2543	102
1959	1092	96	90	7053	5169	1364	24	3563	139
1960	1203	106	82	6770	5263	1286	27	3265	124
1961	1576	139	87	7835	5643	1388	30	3594	133
1962	1271	112	97	8177	5656	1446	24	4126	147
1963	1418	125	92	9279	6191	1499	23	4706	163
1964	1896	167	88	10,029	6354	1578	29	4723	159
1965	1905	167	87	9558	5971	1601	30	4403	144
1966	1508	133	101	9218	5925	1556	25	4576	144
1967	1482	121	120	11,846	6878	1722	19	6336	193
1968	1068	94	135	9595	5601	1713	17	5265	156
1969	1023	90	110	10,772	6259	1721	14	6087	175
1970	1060	94	91	13,346	7246	1842	12	7748	216

a Figures refer to the crop year ending in the year stated, Rice Department estimates.
b Small scale exports of rice flour and vermicelli have not been taken into account. Padi has been
   converted to milled rice at the rate of 66 per cent.
c Production of rice, milled basis, minus exports, includes seed, stock and waste.

Sources: Bank of Thailand, 1958-; I.M.F., 1948-; National Statistical Office, 1956-.

these statistics, exports averaged less than 17 per cent of production
between 1967 and 1969, and in 1970, a poor marketing year when unsold
stocks accumulated, the share was only 12 per cent.   How farm padi prices
and supplies will adjust to the recent abolition of export premiums on
most grades remains to be seen.   An immediate rise in volume shipped may
be expected as there are heavy stocks to clear.   But if domestic consumption continues its present trend and production fails to grow, the export
surplus would disappear within this decade.

(iii) Other exports

In contrast to rice, almost all other exports find their main markets
in developed countries.   They are thus very dependent on industrial conditions there and face competition not only from other developing countries
but also from synthetic substitutes and from domestic suppliers.   The
latter are often subsidised or protected by tariffs and quotas.   Japan
is Thailand's largest market, but although its share of exports has increased recently, it does not play the dominating role that it does in
Thailand's import market.   It takes just over one-fifth of total exports,
being the principal purchaser of rubber, maize and kenaf.   The United
States holds second place with 14 per cent of the total, and buys half to
two-thirds of tin bloc shipments and an important share of rubber and
tapioca.   Otherwise markets are fairly well diversified, with no country
taking more than 10 per cent of total value.

Market conditions for tin, maize and tapioca have not changed substantially since the mid-1960s (Corden and Richter, 1966:133-7).   Prices,
while fluctuating, have remained fairly strong for the princiapl products,
save kenaf.   Prospects for the main exports, however, are not buoyant.
In some cases supply limitations have proved a problem.   Some new off-
shore reserves of tin have been located but the search for other ores has
so far had limited success.   Kenaf production cannot be expanded greatly
owing to the very heavy demands this commodity makes on soil and water.
The best teak stands have been worked out and the home market absorbs a
much larger share of production than formerly.   Earlier in this chapter
the question was posed whether output of upland crops and rubber could be
expanded greatly without changes in agricultural techniques involving increased use of commercial inputs.   It is largely on the answer to this
question, and the farmers' response to change where needed, that the
expansion of exports depends.

(iv)   Earnings from services

United States military expenditure in the area has been a very
important source of foreign exchange earnings over the past few years –
so important that it is sometimes argued that the efforts of entrepreneurs have been diverted from export promotion towards supplying American
needs.   Foreign exchange earnings from United States military spending
are estimated at US$200-300,000,000 annually over the past five years.
This sum is equivalent to around one-third of the value of commodity
exports, which brought in US$687,000,000 a year between 1966 and 1970.
The major part of military services consisted of direct United States
government expenditures on the construction and maintenance of air bases,
ports, roads and other facilities.   At the peak, some 100,000 Thais were
employed at the bases.   Spending by the 48,000 United States troops
stationed in the country was also important before the recent withdrawal
commenced.   Income from these sources averaged US$196,000,000 annually
between 1966 and 1970 (Table 2.14).   To this must be added the spending
of United States troops on 'R. and R.' leave in Thailand;   United States
procurement purchases;   and remittances from Thai troops and contract
workers employed in Vietnam.   These three sources have provided an
estimated annual average of just under US$80,000,000 between 1966 and
1969 (Benoit, 1971:635).

United States spending on military services will obviously drop as
the Vietnam withdrawal proceeds, and indeed they have already begun to
decline.   But how fast and how far they will fall it is impossible to
judge.   The tourist industry is the only other significant invisible
export earner.   Its recent performance has proven rather disappointing
and there is under-utilisation of hotel and tourist facilities in Bangkok.
Promotion of tourism and commodity exports would have to be vigorous to
make good the loss of income from United States war expenditures.

(v)   Imports

The strong growth and changing pattern of imports over the past decade
reflects both Thailand's recent prosperity and its industrialisation and
development expenditures.   Part of the recent rise, too, must be attributed to the direct and indirect impact of United States military spending
in the area.   United States expenditure-induced imports have been

estimated by the NEDB at around US$100,000,000 in 1967 and 1968, or about
eight per cent of imports of goods and services.

The bulk of the growth, however, is due to the development effort.
Imports rose by an annual average of nearly 11 per cent between 1960 and
1970 and their composition altered.   Capital goods, intermediate products
and raw materials, which formed 43 per cent of total value 10 years ago,
reached 60 per cent in 1970 (Table 2.13).   Thus it is hard to prune
imports without affecting development.   Additional duties were imposed
on many consumer goods and passenger vehicles in July 1970, slowing down
imports of these categories.   The overall value of imports rose less
than four per cent in 1970, compared to a rise of nearly eight per cent
between 1968 and 1969.

Over two-thirds of imports come from four suppliers, the average
share of total value for 1966-69 being Japan 35.6 per cent, United States
16.8 per cent (military goods are excluded), West Germany 8.5 per cent
and the United Kingdom 8.4 per cent.   These countries provide most
foreign aid in grants, loans, investment and credits for industry.

Table 2.13:   Growth and composition of imports[a]
US $'000,000

	Consumer goods	Capital goods	Intermediate products and raw materials	Other[b]	Total
1960	161.8	113.8	83.9	103.1	462.6
% of total	35.0	24.6	18.1	22.2	100.0
1970	264.3	445.3	324.8	260.9	1295.3
% of total	20.4	34.5	25.1	20.1	100.0
Growth p.a.%	5.0	14.6	14.5	9.7	10.8

a   Includes non-monetary gold;   excludes military goods.
b   Over 80 per cent consists of vehicles and parts, fuel and lubricants.
Source: Bank of Thailand, 1971: Table III 6.

(vi)   The balance of payments

The last surplus on foreign trade was in 1956.   During the next nine
years the annual trade deficit averaged US$80,000,000 and since then it has
risen sharply.   Up to 1966 the trade deficit was more than balanced by
earnings from services and foreign grants (Table 2.14).   Even after that

Table 2.14: Balance of payments
US $'000,000[a]

	1962	1966	1967	1968	1969	1970[P]
Trade balance, net[b]	-94.4	-215.4	-391.8	-512.0	-543.2	-578.8
Services, net	24.4	197.5	284.3	297.5	281.4	257.5
(of which military[c])	(9.8)	(124.2)	(197.6)	(236.4)	(222.6)	(197.1)
Transfer payments net	43.8	47.2	57.6	74.4	57.1	49.8
(of which U.S. grants)	(26.7)	(21.1)	(38.4)	(56.4)	(41.6)	(29.5)
Balance of goods, services and transfers	-26.1	+29.3	-49.9	-140.1	-204.7	-271.6
Capital inflow, net	71.9	65.6	104.4	114.7	121.2	107.8
Errors & omissions	16.5	63.1	6.7	46.9	35.4	35.4
Overall balance	+62.3	+158.0	+61.2	+21.5	-48.0	-128.4
Level of official reserves[d]	523	924	1008	1021	985	906
Reserves as % of imports[e]	95.7	104.6	95.1	87.8	79.4	70.2

a Converted from baht at 20.8 = US$1.00.
b Exports f.o.b., imports c.i.f. including non-monetary gold, excluding military goods.
c U.S. government expenditure on construction and maintenance of airbases, ports, roads etc. plus
   estimated local spending of U.S. troops stationed in Thailand.
d End year. Includes gold and I.M.F. gold tranche.
e As per cent of customs values, excluding non-monetary gold.
P Provisional.

Source: Bank of Thailand, 1971: Tables III 11 and III 13.

date, rising capital inflows more than offset the current account deficit
so that foreign exchange reserves continued to mount until the end of 1968.
During the past two years, however, the balance of payments as a whole has
been in deficit.   This is in spite of the fact that net earnings from
services averaged US$264,000,000 a year between 1966 and 1970 and that
foreign grants averaged US$50,000,000.   US$37,000,000 annually came from
the United States and the remainder from West Germany, Colombo Plan countries and Japan.

Official reserves have fallen by over US$100,000,000 over the past
two years but they still remain high, at over US$900,000,000.   This is
well over their level of five years ago, and is sufficient to pay for
eight month's imports.

7.   INCOME AND EXPENDITURE

Thailand's GNP grew rapidly during the decade 1960-9 and this led to several
significant changes in the composition of expenditure on GNP.   These changes
are summarised in Table 2.15.

(i)   Aggregate trends

Consumption expenditure, which dominates total expenditure, has grown
less rapidly than GNP.   Thus, while consumption per head has risen four
per cent per annum on average, the share of consumption in GNP has declined
from 84.3 per cent in 1960 to 79.1 per cent in 1969.   Public consumption
has, however, grown more rapidly than private consumption and its share of
expenditure on GNP has risen slightly (from 9.8 per cent in 1960 to 10.7
per cent in 1969).

Savings is the difference between GNP and consumption.   Since consumption grew less rapidly than GNP, savings grew considerably more rapidly,
and its share of GNP jumped from 15.7 per cent in 1960 to 20.9 per cent in
1969.   This is a remarkable achievement for a country with such a low per
capita income, and with such a high rate of population growth.   While the
gains from recent growth have been widely distributed, the sharp rise in
the savings ratio would seem to suggest that the distribution of income has
become more uneven.

If the rise in the savings ratio has been remarkable, the increase in the investment ratio has been even more so.   The share of gross investment (fixed investment plus any change in stocks) rose from 15.7 per cent in 1960 to 27.3 per cent in 1969, and that of fixed investment from 14.2 per cent to 25.5 per cent.   Private fixed investment rose markedly each year after 1961, although the increase in 1965 was small and the rate of growth has eased since 1967.   Public fixed investment has also grown dramatically but, for budgetary reasons, the rate of growth was severely curtailed in 1969.

Domestic savings financed the major part of investment up to 1966. In 1967, a poor harvest slowed the growth of GNP.   Consumption demand increased slightly more rapidly than in previous years, and as a result savings fell.   Investment, however, continued to rise strongly, largely in response to the increase in United States military expenditure in Thailand and to the growth of investment in promoted industries.   Consequently, a large gap emerged between savings and investment; this gap, which was steady at around 14 per cent between 1962 and 1966, rose to 29 per cent in 1967, and to 39 per cent in 1968.   As a result of severe restraints on the growth of government capital expenditure, and a rise in savings, the gap then narrowed to 22 per cent in 1969.   After 1966, imports rose not only because GNP rose, but also to close the gap between domestic savings and investment.   Because of the openness of Thailand's economy, inflationary pressure was modest, the brunt of the internal disequilibrium being borne by an adverse movement in the current account of the balance of payments.   United States military expenditure and grant assistance provided the foreign exchange to cover the current account deficit, but, as these flows levelled off in 1969, a foreign exchange constraint on growth became apparent for the first time in the decade.

Exports, fixed investment and government consumption represent the main sources of autonomous demand in Thailand.   In 1961 the share of exports in GNP was broadly equivalent to that of fixed investments.   However, by contrast with fixed investment, the direct contribution of exports to the growth of GNP has been patchy.   Exports pushed up the growth rate in 1961 and during the period 1964-66, but it was essentially fixed investment which sustained Thailand's high rate of growth during the decade.

Nevertheless, the overall balance of payments situation has made an
important indirect contribution to growth.   On current account, imports
exceed exports, and the gap has widened markedly since 1966.   But, until
1969, net autonomous capital flows from abroad more than offset this gap,
and the nation's external reserves rose each year.   The rise in reserves
increased the liquidity of the commercial banks and thus enhanced their
ability to make advances, a factor which supported the strong growth of
fixed investment demand.   In addition, investment in Thailand has a
high import content, but the growth of exports and of capital inflow freed
investment from any foreign exchange constraint.   The annual increase in
external reserves reached a maximum of US$158,000,000 in 1966.   There-
after the annual increase dropped significantly and external reserves
actually fell in 1969 and 1970.   Consequently, bank liquidity has become
tighter and the growth of fixed investment demand has slowed since 1967,
and would have slowed still more but for the growing dependence by the
government sector on expansionary finance in recent years.

The weakening of world demand for rice combined with slackening
expansion of upland crop production and high internal population growth
threaten to restrain the future growth of Thailand's export earnings.
In consequence, the future course of investment demand will be the main
determinant of economic growth in Thailand.   But the slow growth of
export earnings combined with a decline in United States military expenditure is likely to preclude rapid growth of domestic savings.   In these
circumstances, the future course of investment will be significantly influenced by the response of the government sector.   The growth of investment demand can be sustained at a reasonably high level by expanding
deficit financing within the government sector provided external reserves
are regarded as expendable.   Otherwise an endeavour must be made to bring
about a closer relationship between government spending and the transfer
of resources from the private to the public sector.   This will most
probably restrain the rate of growth of private fixed investment and of
output, but it will also bring about a closer relationship between GNE
and GNP than now prevails and, in so doing, will ease the pressure on
the import side of the balance of payments.

Table 2.15: Expenditure on Gross National Product and savings

Item	Value US$'000,000,000		Share of GNP (per cent)		Annual rate of growth (per cent)								
	1960	1969	1960	1969	1961	1962	1963	1965	1966	1967	1968	1969	1960-69
1. Consumption	2.27	4.34	84.3	79.1	5.1	6.7	7.1	7.5	8.2	8.4	9.0	8.7	7.5
Private	2.01	3.76	74.5	68.4	5.3	6.3	6.8	7.1	8.2	8.0	8.4	8.3	7.2
Public	0.26	0.59	9.8	10.7	4.0	9.4	9.4	10.5	7.9	11.2	1.31	11.7	9.2
2 Investment	0.38	1.40	14.2	25.5	6.4	19.0	19.1	8.6	22.3	20.7	11.7	10.5	15.5
Private	0.28	0.97	10.2	17.7	3.9	14.2	17.3	4.9	24.4	21.2	11.0	14.4	15.1
Public	0.11	0.43	3.9	7.8	13.1	30.0	22.7	16.9	17.9	19.9	13.0	2.7	16.6
3. Change in stocks	0.04	0.10	1.5	1.8	-55.8	331.4	57.9	45.6	175.9	-115.1	288.4	106.3	10.8
4. Statistical discrepancy	0.03	0.009	1.2	0.2									
5. Gross national expenditure	2.73	5.85	101.3	106.6	3.43	11.0	9.8	7.9	12.6	7.8	12.6	9.8	8.9
6. Trade balance	-0.03	-0.37	-1.1	-6.8	208.2	-306.1	-75.7	-6.6	-32.6	-152.0	-91.4	6.2	-32.6
Exports [a]	0.43	0.96	15.9	17.5	19.4	-1.0	4.7	8.6	21.7	9.2	-1.1	1.6	9.3
Imports [a]	0.46	1.33	17.0	24.2	4.8	19.1	12.8	8.5	22.5	21.5	15.3	-0.7	12.6
7. Gross domestic product	2.70	5.48	100.2	99.8	6.8	6.9	8.8	8.1	12.4	5.1	7.4	11.4	8.2
8. Net factor income from abroad	-0.01	0.01	-0.2	0.2									
9. Gross national product	2.69	5.49	100.0	100.0	5.8	7.5	8.6	8.1	12.3	5.2	9.1	11.2	8.2
10. Gross national savings	0.42	1.15	15.7	20.9	9.2	11.7	15.9	10.8	30.4	-6.3	9.6	21.3	11.8

a Exports and imports of goods and services.

Source: Data provided by National Accounts Division, NEDB.

(ii)   Government expenditure

The government sector has grown significantly over the past decade, its share of GNP rising from 13.7 per cent in 1960 to 18.5 per cent in 1969 (Table 2.15).   This sector consists of the central government, local governments (including municipalities) and numerous state enterprises.   Detailed accounts for the whole of the public sector are not available.   However, since the central government accounts for more than 90 per cent of total government sector operations, it is reasonable to confine the discussion to an analysis of central government transactions.

The central government has consistently managed to record a surplus of current revenue over current expenditure (Table 2.16).   Between FY (Fiscal Year)[10] 1961 and FY 1967, this surplus (government saving) covered some 50 per cent of capital expenditure and transfer payments.   Despite the rapid growth of capital expenditure, budget deficits were small (although the size of the deficit rose sharply in FY 1967 as a result of rapid growth of both current and capital expenditure) and were more than covered by domestic borrowing from the commercial banks, the Government Savings Bank and by external loans and grants.   As a result of overestimating expenditure and underestimating revenue, budget deficits were inflated well above the realised levels and loan raisings, based on the inflated estimated deficits, largely served to increase the government's cash balances with the Central Bank.

FY 1968 saw a change in the pattern of government finances.   Current expenditure grew more rapidly than revenue so that government savings decreased and, at the same time, capital expenditure rose by 33 per cent. As a result, the size of the budget deficit increased.   While external loans and grants rose slightly, domestic borrowing from the commercial banks and the Government Savings Bank declined; a slower growth of deposits lowered the ability of the banks to purchase bonds and the attractiveness of government bonds was reduced because interest was made subject to company tax from the beginning of 1968.   In these circumstances, the government was forced to reduce its cash balances and to borrow from the Central Bank - both expansionary sources of finance.

---

10 The fiscal year runs from 1 October to 30 September, e.g. FY 1961 begins on 1 October 1960.

Table 2.16: Government expenditure and finances, selected years

	Value US$'000,000 FY1961	FY1970[a]	Annual rate of growth (per cent)						
			FY1961-65	FY1966-70	FY1966	FY1967	FY1968	FY1969	FY1970
1. Current revenue, of which	345.2	913.4	13.5	10.5	11.3	15.1	11.1	11.7	4.5
Tax revenue, of which	320.9	839.3	11.9	11.2	9.3	16.3	11.7	11.9	5.0
Income tax	32.8	102.4	13.1	14.4	11.7	20.9	14.8	14.3	7.9
Personal	22.2	60.1	8.1	16.1	9.0	19.7	17.9	15.3	11.4
Corporate	10.6	42.3	21.7	12.2	15.1	22.3	10.9	13.0	3.4
Export duties	60.7	55.9	6.6	-5.6	-10.1	-14.2	9.2	22.1	-30.5
Rice premium	39.9	36.1	10.8	-8.5	-14.4	-13.1	20.0	10.8	-39.3
Rice tax	9.1	7.8	0.8	-6.8	10.3	-9.8	-22.2	5.9	1.3
Rubber tax	10.2	10.1	-0.1	10.3	-13.4	-29.6	-63.0	521.6	-8.7
Import duties	109.7	278.3	7.9	16.0	5.7	32.1	13.7	10.3	9.1
Business tax	44.6	178.0	21.3	10.6	23.3	19.7	7.3	9.1	6.8
Excise tax	50.7	193.3	15.3	17.1	17.3	12.3	15.2	17.7	11.4
2. Current expenditure, of which	294.2	828.7	8.9	15.0	15.0	23.2	14.0	12.3	10.5
General administration	42.8	100.5	1.6	11.9	40.6	17.8	29.2	8.8	-5.4
Defence and police	97.1	285.0	7.2	21.2	2.8	17.1	20.4	19.6	28.0
Agriculture	12.5	44.7	16.9	12.5	18.6	15.7	16.7	11.5	6.5
Transport	10.6	35.3	16.8	16.1	0.0	22.2	25.9	12.5	4.9
Education	67.8	134.6	5.1	10.9	7.7	10.9	19.4	11.5	2.4
Health	11.5	29.1	16.4	3.9	18.4	17.3	0.2	6.4	-6.9
Interest payments	16.8	80.6	13.9	26.5	10.8	29.5	16.8	13.0	49.9
3. Government saving (1 - 2)	50.9	84.7	26.1	-11.2	-0.1	-13.2	-3.5	8.2	-31.5
4. Capital expenditure, of which	63.9	299.2	26.7	14.1	7.4	23.5	32.6	2.3	0.9
Agriculture	17.3	79.7	15.5	20.6	22.5	39.8	30.1	-10.7	30.1
Transport	224.5	111.8	18.9	19.0	13.8	53.9	28.8	10.9	-9.0
Education	8.2	55.4	22.3	25.9	20.8	11.3	75.3	15.6	11.1
Health	0.9	7.4	45.7	10.9	13.3	0.0	3.9	24.5	16.7
5. Transfer payments	28.8	91.2	16.4	16.3	-8.4	19.3	9.3	0.7	39.3
6. Budget deficit [3 - (4 + 5)]	41.8	305.8	17.4	36.7	10.3	75.0	55.6	0.0	28.1
7. Deficit financed by									
External grants	25.0	52.9							
External loans (net)	1.9	10.3							
Domestic borrowing	48.6	194.2							
Commercial banks	14.4	20.7							
Government savings bank	10.1	20.7							
Bank of Thailand	16.3	145.7							
Public	7.7	7.2							
Cash balances	38.5	4.6							
Other	8.6	43.8							

a Provisional revised estimates

Data provided by Bank of Thailand.

In FY 1969 and FY 1970, current expenditure rose 11 per cent on average despite expenditure restraint. Government saving was whittled down. The increase in capital expenditure in both years was negligible. Nevertheless, the size of the budget deficit increased. With a decline in external loan and grant finance and in domestic borrowing from the commercial banks and the Government Savings Bank, the government was forced to rely more heavily on expansionary Central Bank finance. By increasing the money supply, this pattern of finance placed pressure on the balance of payments. In July 1970, the government raised import tax rates in an endeavour to restrain the growth of imports. It was also hoped that revenue would increase, but it was appreciated that, if imports were restrained, the growth of import duty revenue would also be restrained. In fact, there has been little growth of import duty revenue or of total revenue, a decrease in rice premium revenue negating modest expansion elsewhere. Current expenditure has, however, continued to rise and, partly as a result of a carry forward of unspent allocations from FY 1970, capital expenditure has also increased. In consequence, FY 1971 has seen still heavier dependence on Central Bank borrowing and the pressure on the balance of payments can be expected to intensify in the future.

Current expenditure amounted to 76.0 per cent of central government expenditure in FY 1961, capital expenditure 16.5 per cent and transfers 7.5 per cent. Between FY 1961 and FY 1965, current expenditure grew less rapidly than either capital expenditure or transfers and its share of total expenditure fell. However, since then, current expenditure has grown by 15 per cent per annum on average and its share of total expenditure has increased from 65.7 per cent in FY 1965 to 68.0 per cent in FY 1970.

Expenditure on defence and police accounted for almost 35 per cent of current expenditure in FY 1970. The next important expenditure heads are education (16 per cent), general administration (12 per cent), debt service (10 per cent) and economic services (10 per cent). Defence and police force expenditure, which grew more slowly than total current expenditure between FY 1961 and FY 1965, has increased substantially each year since FY 1966 in response to growing insurgency problems. Interest payments have also risen strongly as a result of a steady increase in

government indebtedness.   Education expenditure, which grew very slowly
between FY 1961 and FY 1966, increased more markedly thereafter but, with
the tightening of the government financial position, its growth rate was
cut sharply in FY 1970.   General administration, economic services and
health expenditure have been similarly affected.

Preliminary estimates for the Third Plan (1972-76) place the growth
of government expenditure at 8.8 per cent per annum, current expenditure
rising by 9.2 per cent per annum and capital expenditure by 8.0 per
cent per annum on average.   Given no significant decrease in the rate
of growth of defence and police force expenditure, it will prove increasingly difficult to hold the rate of growth of current expenditure
to the 10 per cent level achieved in FY 1970, let alone 9.2 per cent per
annum.   With the student-age population growing rapidly, the demand for
education services at all levels, primary, secondary and tertiary, will
grow apace.   Education services are already deficient;   demand for
secondary and tertiary education far exceeds available positions.   Continued restraint will simply lead to a further deterioration of existing
standards.   Further economies in the provision of services are possible,
but the price of failing adequately to maintain the infrastructure,
especially roads, irrigation schemes and urban facilities, would be high
and considerable productivity potential would be forgone.   Moreover, the
projected continued growth of capital expenditure will necessitate further
growth of associated current expenditures.   With the outstanding debt
rising, interest payments will rise.   Further, some adjustment of public
service salaries, which are very low in comparison with those of the
private sector, may be necessary in the future.

The growth of capital expenditure, which averaged 24 per cent a year
between FY 1961 and FY 1968, was severely curtailed in both FY 1969 and FY
1970.   Under the First Development Plan (1961-66), primary emphasis was
placed on the development of water resources (in particular, the Greater
Chao Phraya flood control and irrigation project and the Yanhee multi-
purpose project) and on the transportation system, especially of highways.
Normal planning problems developed;   in some instances, feasibility studies
were inadequate, in others, project preparation was deficient and, in
general, shortages of skilled manpower (especially engineers) and physical

and administrative bottlenecks became apparent as the plan progressed.
The Second Plan (1967-71) again placed primary emphasis on agricultural
development and on extending the transportation and communication system.
In addition, greater attention was given to alleviating regional income
disparities, particularly in the Northeast where per capita income is
lowest, and to strengthening regional security.   While broad targets
were set, the plan was worked out on an annual basis to ensure a flexible
response to current economic trends and thus to avoid excessive pressure
on domestic and external resources.

     Expenditure on agriculture (mostly water resource development which
includes hydro-electric power generation) and transportation accounted
for some 65 per cent of total capital expenditure during the decade
1961-70.   Capital expenditure on education, starting from a very low
base in FY 1961, has grown rapidly and has increased its share of capital
expenditure from 12.8 per cent in FY 1961 to 19.0 per cent in FY 1970.
Capital expenditure on community services such as health, sewerage and
water supply has broadly grown in step with the growth of total capital
expenditure, but its share of the total is small.

     The severe restraint on the growth of capital expenditure in FY 1969
and FY 1970 was inopportune.   The need for further capital expenditure
in agriculture, transportation, education, urban (particularly Bangkok-
Thon Buri) and village development is considerable;   rapid population
growth is constantly adding to the task ahead.   Concern for stable monetary conditions and for ample foreign exchange reserves together with
increased spending on national security has severely affected the development budget.

     The Third Plan continues to place primary emphasis on the further
development of the agricultural sector and on the transport and communication system, but the share of expenditure on education and community
facilities is to increase;   total expenditure under the Plan is budgeted
at US$5,000,000,000, almost double that budgeted for the Second Plan.
If the Plan is to be successfully implemented, a serious attempt must be
made to channel more domestic resources to the government sector.

(iii) Government finance

Tax revenue, which accounts for 90 per cent of total central
government revenue, increased slightly faster than GNP in the past decade
and thus marginally raised its share of GNP to around 12.7 per cent in
1969.   The growth rate, however, fell to five per cent in FY 1970 and
the increase in FY 1971 has been negligible.

Indirect taxes dominate the tax structure.   Income tax revenue,
which has grown more rapidly than total tax revenue since FY 1961,
accounted for only 12.2 per cent of total tax revenue in FY 1970.   The
main indirect taxes are those on international trade (import duties and
export taxes) and businesses (part of which is derived from levies on
imported goods) and excise taxes.

Import duty revenue accounted for 33.2 per cent of total tax revenue
in FY 1970.   Levies on consumer goods account for about half of this
revenue;   intermediate goods (particularly chemicals, fuels, lubricants
and basic metals) and capital goods (metal products, machinery and
transport equipment) share the balance almost equally.   Import duty
revenue grew less rapidly than total tax revenue in the first half of
the decade, but more rapidly thereafter, as a response to the fast growth
of imports after 1965 and duty rate increases.   Much potential revenue
was forgone as duty exemptions were granted for consumer goods imported
by United States personnel serving in Thailand and a large proportion of
these goods were later sold within Thailand on a duty-free basis.

In contrast to import duties, the returns from export taxes have
fluctuated and their share of tax revenue has fallen from 18.9 per cent
in FY 1961 to 6.7 per cent in FY 1970.   The rice export premium dominates
export duty revenue.   Until 1967, the premium was a specific tax and,
because the premium rate was unchanged, revenue varied directly with
export volume.   There was little change in export volume until the
favourable 1963/4 and 1964/5 crop years.   In response, revenue jumped
in FY 1964 and FY 1965, but smaller exports thereafter cut revenue substantially;   the revenue yield for FY 1967 was little above that achieved
in FY 1961.   Because world demand was strong and rice was being diverted
from the domestic to the world market, the government converted the
premium from a specific to an ad valorem basis in January 1967 and

subsequently, to ensure adequate supplies to the domestic market, raised the premium rate on several occasions. As a result of the premium increases and a favourable harvest in 1968/9, revenue rose in FY 1968 and again in FY 1969. The fall in the world price of rice after 1968 coincided with a serious deterioration in the state of Thailand's balance of payments. In an endeavour to support export earnings, the rice premium was progressively reduced. In consequence, rice export premium revenue fell 40 per cent in FY 1970. In April and May 1971, the premium was abolished on grades of rice other than cargo rice. This will virtually eliminate export taxes as an important source of government revenue.

Business taxes are levied on locally manufactured products, imported goods and a range of domestic services (public utilities, hotels, restaurants, bank and insurance activities). The tax is levied on gross receipts, and rates vary from two per cent (3-7 per cent if imported) for most intermediate goods and basic items of consumption (food and clothing), to between 12 and 30 per cent for finished goods. Following a change in the tax base in 1961, business tax revenue rose substantially in FY 1962 and it has since maintained its share of total tax revenue at 21 per cent. Almost half of the revenue raised in FY 1970 was obtained from importers. Problems of tax avoidance and evasion are serious and centre on classification of goods for tax purposes, determination of gross receipts and collection of revenue from small business and service activities. Moreover, since the tax is levied when goods are sold, its incidence on the price of goods is haphazard, being a function of the degree of integration of production processes.

Excise taxes, which accounted for 23 per cent of total tax revenue in FY 1970, are levied on a narrow range of products, some of which are monopolised by the government (tobacco, playing cards). Petroleum, tobacco and alcoholic beverages account for more than 90 per cent of total excise tax revenue.

By comparison with the Philippines, which has a higher per capita income than Thailand but raised only 10 per cent of GNP in tax revenue, Thailand's tax effort appears satisfactory. Ceylon and Malaysia both have a higher tax/GNP ratio (16 and 17 per cent respectively). In these countries, income and export taxes are relatively more important than in

Thailand.   In a large measure, the difference is explained by the importance of the estate plantation sector in these countries;   as a share of
GNP, personal income tax revenue is not markedly higher in Malaysia than
in Thailand, but company tax revenue is substantially higher.

There is, however, considerable scope for raising additional tax
revenue in Thailand.   Company tax rates are very low (15 per cent on
the first US$25,000 of profit, 20 per cent on the next US$25,000 and 25
per cent on any excess).   In Malaysia, the company tax rate is 40 per
cent.   Personal tax rates are well graduated, but personal allowances
are high and in consequence a major part of the potential taxpaying public
is exempted.   The present net from personal income tax is very small.
In addition, despite improvement over the past decade, administrative
problems plague both forms of income taxation;   tax avoidance and tax
evasion are widespread.

Apart from developing income taxation, property taxation is also in
need of reform.   Urban development has and will continue to produce rising
rental values.   The government should share in such gains.   Property tax
is a municipal tax.   Owner-occupied premises are presently exempt from
tax.   There is much tax evasion, and the legislation encourages tax
avoidance by imposing a different tax rate on rented buildings and furni-
shings.   Similarly, rural land taxation is light and betterment charges
for such government services as irrigation and roads are poorly developed.
In addition, there would seem to be scope for introducing an inheritance
tax and perhaps an annual wealth tax.

Such tax adjustments would be politically difficult but the potential
for an increase in existing sources of revenue seems to be limited.   The
import duty structure has developed on an ad hoc basis and rationalisation
is needed to reduce levies on intermediate and capital good imports and
raise those on consumer good imports.   However, given the present balance
of payments problem and the projected slow growth of export earnings,
future growth of imports and thus of import duty revenue will be restrained.
Despite upward rate adjustments in July 1970, import duty revenue for the
year 1970 was slightly below that raised in 1969.   Business tax is, in
part, also a tax on imports.   As such, its growth will also be restrained,
but growth of domestic demand will raise the revenue yield.   Excise duties

on petroleum, tobacco and alcoholic beverages are already quite high.
Further increases are possible and, with the growth of population, demand
will rise and thus broadly sustain the growth rate of revenue from excise
duty.   At current tax rates and allowance levels, income tax revenue will
increase, but the decline in the rate of growth of GNP after 1969 has
slowed the growth of this revenue source.   Combined with the decline in
export tax revenue, total revenue barely increased in FY 1971.   It would
seem that politically difficult decisions will have to be made if revenue
is to grow in step with the planned increase in government expenditure in
the future (nine per cent per annum on average).   Even if this is achieved,
the budget deficit (which was equal to 34 per cent of revenue in FY 1970)
will grow by nine per cent per annum.

While the task of raising tax revenue will prove difficult, that of
raising finance by selling government bonds outside of the banking system
is even more intractable.   In Malaysia, Singapore and Ceylon, a substantial flow of government finance is obtained by tapping the annual flow of
contributions to nationally established Employees' Provident Funds and,
to a lesser extent, insurance companies and other non-bank institutions.
These institutions have not been developed on a comparable scale in
Thailand.   Consequently, the market for government securities is virtually
confined to the banking system.

Government bonds can be used by the commercial banks as collateral
to borrow from the Bank of Thailand up to 80 per cent of their face value
at seven per cent.   Selling bonds to the commercial banks is therefore
potentially similar to selling bonds to the Bank of Thailand; both are
highly expansionary sources of finance.

The commercial banks and the Government Savings Bank absorbed 90
per cent of the increase in government domestic debt between December 1961
and December 1968.   Prior to 1968, the government's need for this source
of finance was not pressing.   Bonds were issued on favourable terms with
interest of eight per cent per annum tax free to permit the banks to fulfil
and maintain minimum reserve and local assets requirements and to avoid
foregoing borrowing power under various loan acts.   Since loan raisings
were adequate, the government reduced the attractiveness of bonds in
January 1968 by making interest subject to company taxation.   Unfortunately,

this move coincided with two other developments.   First, the government's need for loan finance jumped after the middle of 1968.   Second,
a smaller increase in foreign assets in 1968 and a decline thereafter
reduced the liquidity and thus the ability of the banks to buy bonds.
The domestic debt rose 16 per cent between December 1968 and December
1970 (from US$722,000,000 to US$1,137,000,000) and the Bank of Tahiland
was forced to absorb 72 per cent of this increase.

External loan and grant finance is the only other major source of
government finance.   Grant finance, derived mainly from the United States,
rose between FY 1967 and 1969 but has since declined.   Recent developments in the United States indicate that foreign aid will be reduced in
the future;   Thailand can expect to share in this reduction.   External
loans have not been a major source of finance and, in recent years,
repayments have risen thus reducing the net value of this source of
finance.   Thailand will continue to obtain external loan finance, but
the flow is unlikely to increase because detailed feasibility studies
which would satisfy the requirements of international lending bodies are
rarely prepared satisfactorily.

The government sector is facing a crisis.   In the short term, the
rise in expenditure will have to be financed by increased borrowing from
the Bank of Thailand.   This will negate the adverse effect on bank
liquidity of the fall in international reserves and thus maintain the
growth of demand, including demand for imports.   Assuming no substantial rise in the rate of growth of export earnings, a further reduction
in international reserves would seem likely.   Given the high level of
these reserves, some decrease can be justified.   But if this decrease is
to be a short term policy measure, an effort must be made first to raise
the level of taxation (by introducing new taxes, by rate and allowance
adjustments for existing taxes and by improving tax administration);   and
secondly to develop institutions, such as a National Employees' Provident
Fund, which can be an important avenue for transferring resources from
the private to the public sector.   Failing action here, government expenditure will be subject to the vagaries of the balance of payments, a
situation not conducive to effective development planning.

(iv) Money supply

Throughout the decade, the money supply increased roughly in step with the growth of GNP (Table 2.17).   Up until 1967, the accumulation of foreign assets was the main expansionary force; this increased the liquidity of the commercial banks and thus enhanced their ability to make loans.   But two factors offset these expansionary forces.   First, there was a marked rise in time and savings deposits and secondly, net public sector operations were either contractionary or non-expansionary in this period.   The government sector increased its cash balances with the Bank of Thailand until the end of 1965.

Since 1967, the situation has been reversed.   The government is exercising a strong expansionary influence on the growth of the money supply because of increased reliance on the Bank of Thailand to finance its deficit.   However, this effect has been offset in part by the continued strong rise of time and savings bank deposits and by a decrease in the level of external reserves after 1968.   The rate of growth of the money supply slowed in 1969 and the increase in 1970 was also small, falling below the rate of growth of GNP.

CONCLUSION

The major problems in Thailand's economy at the present moment centre on the balance of payments and government finances.   Slow growth of export earnings and a decline in United States expenditure will restrain growth. In part, the government sector can offset these depressing effects, but if this is to happen, Thailand must reconcile itself to a steady fall in its external reserves, and the decrease will not be significantly reduced even if the government sector succeeds in diverting more resources from the private sector to itself by way, for example, of increased taxation. If this is not acceptable, the growth of government expenditure will have to be restrained.   If this occurs, liquidity problems will tend to restrain the growth of private investment.   Combined with the projected slow growth of export earnings, this would imply a much lower growth potential for the Thai economy in the 1970s than that achieved during the 1960s.

Table 2.17: Analysis of changes in money supply, 1961–70

(Baht '000,000,000)

Year ended	1961	1962	1963	1964	1965	1966	1967	1968	1969	1970[a]
1. Domestic credit	0.34	1.24	1.29	1.06	1.88	2.45	3.16	4.86	5.82	8.59
Claims on government (net)	-0.49	0.04	0.17	-0.58	-0.18	0.36	0.82	2.15	2.67	3.97
Claims on private sector	0.83	1.20	1.12	1.64	2.06	2.09	2.34	2.71	3.15	4.62
2. Quasi money [b]	-0.63	-1.69	-1.25	-3.13	-1.07	-3.35	-2.90	-2.98	-3.58	-3.58
3. Other items [b]	-0.30	-0.79	-0.57	-0.20	-1.05	-0.47	-0.27	-1.11	-0.70	-1.65
4. Total domestic factors (1 + 2 + 3)	-0.59	-1.24	-0.53	-2.27	-0.24	-1.37	-0.01	0.77	1.54	3.36
5. Foreign assets	1.59	1.24	1.34	1.44	1.99	3.32	1.07	0.46	-0.92	-2.40
6. Money supply										
(i) Annual change	1.00	0.00	0.81	0.83	1.75	1.95	1.06	1.23	0.62	0.96
(ii) Total supply	11.08	11.08	11.89	11.06	12.81	14.76	15.83	17.07	17.69	18.64
(iii) Rate of growth (per cent)	9.9	0.0	7.3	-7.0	15.8	15.2	7.2	7.8	3.6	5.4
7. Rate of growth of GNP (per cent)	5.8	7.5	8.6	6.6	8.1	12.3	5.2	9.1	11.2	7.5

a   End November 1970

b   Minus means increase

Source: IMF, various issues.

In the longer term, the main problems to be tackled are the expansion of agricultural production (depending on the availability of land and on the adoption of yield raising techniques), the provision of education and employment for the rapidly rising population, and further diversification of the structure of the economy.

REFERENCES

Asian Development Bank, 1971.   Southeast Asia's economy in the 1970s,
          Longman, London.

Bank of Thailand, 1958-.   Monthly report, Bangkok.

Benoit, E., 1971.   'Im acts of the end of Vietnam hostilities, IV,
          Thailand', in Asian Development Bank, 1971: 628-46.

Caldwell, J.C., 1967.   'The demographic structure', in Silcock, ed. 1967:
          27-64.

Chalothorn, T., 1970.   Population projection for Thailand 1960-1990,
          National Statistical Office, Bangkok.

Chancellor, W.C., 1971.   'Tractor contract operations in Thailand and
          Malaysia', Rice policy conference: current papers on rice
          technology. The International Rice Research Institute,
          Manila, Paper 7.

Corden, W.M. and Richter, H.V., 1967.   'Trade and the balance of payments',
          in Silcock, 1967: 128-50.

Department of External Affairs, 1970.   Second report to the Ministry of
          Agriculture, Part A, Thai-Australian Chao Phya Research
          Project, Canberra.

Department of Trade and Industry, May 1970.   'Equipment needed for Thai's
          agricultural "revolution" ', Overseas Trading, Canberra,
          pp. 240-1.

International Monetary Fund (I.M.F.), 1948-.   International Financial
          Statistics, Washington, D.C.

Ingram, J.C., 1955.   Economic change in Thailand since 1850, Stanford
          University Press, Stanford.

Isarangkun, C., 1969.   'Manufacturing industries in Thailand', unpub-
          lished Ph.D. thesis, Australian National University, Canberra.

Michaely, M., 1962.   Concentration in international trade, North Holland,
          Amsterdam.

Ministry of Agriculture, 1955.   Thailand economic farm survey, 1953,
          Bangkok.

Ministry of Agriculture, 1970.   Agricultural statistics of Thailand, 1967,
          Bangkok.

Myint, H., 1967.   'The inward and outward looking countries of Southeast
          Asia', Malayan Economic Review, 12, pp. 1-13.

National Economic Development Board (NEDB), 1967   National income of
        Thailand, Bangkok.

National Economic Development Board (NEDB), 1969.   Agricultural develop-
        ment strategy for Thailand, Bangkok.

National Statistical Office, 1956-.   Statistical yearbook, Bangkok.

National Statistical Office, 1967-8.   Report of the 1964 industrial
        census, Bangkok.

Nuttonson, M.Y., 1963.   The physical environment and agriculture of
        Thailand, American Institute of Crop Ecology, Washington,
        D.C.

Panitpakdi, P., 1967.   'National accounts estimates of Thailand', in
        Silcock, 1967:105-27.

Silcock, T.H. (ed.) 1967.   Thailand, social and economic studies in
        development, Australian National University, Canberra.

Silcock, T.H., 1967.   'The rice premium and agricultural diversification',
        in Silcock, ed. 1967:231-57.

Silcock, T.H., 1970.   The economic development of Thai agriculture,
        Australian National University Press, Canberra.

Statistisches Bundesamt, 1970: Länderkurzberichte Thailand, Wiesbaden.

Stikker, D. and Hirono, R., 1971.   'The impact of foreign private
        investment', in Asian Development Bank, 1971:370-420.

Welsch, D.E., 1971.   'Agricultural problems in Thailand and some
        policy alternatives', Bangkok Bank, Monthly Review, 12, No.3,
        pp. 89-104.

CHAPTER 3

THAILAND'S INDUSTRIAL DEVELOPMENT: RATIONALE, STRATEGY AND PROSPECTS

Prachoom Chomchai*

1. INTRODUCTION: INDUSTRIAL CHANGES SINCE THE SECOND WORLD WAR

An important stimulus to war-time and post-war production in Thailand was
the high rate of inflation experienced especially during the war, quite
apart from the huge unsatisfied demand for both domestic and foreign goods
built up during the war.   War-time inflation could easily be explained
with the help of the simple quantity theory of money: baht notes were
issued against yen credits not only to finance an export surplus vis-à-vis
Japan but also to finance local Japanese expenditure, and budget deficits
were similarly financed by borrowing directly from the central bank.

Table 3.1:   Thailand gross geographical product by industrial origin
(percentages)

	1938/9	1950
Agriculture, forestry and fishing	45.6	57.3
Mining and quarrying	3.2	1.6
Construction		0.6
Manufacturing	9.9	12.6
Electricity and water	0.6	0.2
Commerce	26.9	15.1
Transportation and communication	2.8	1.1
Government (general)	5.0	4.0
Personal service and other	6.0	7.5
Total	100.0	100.0

Source: Gould (1953) in Ingram, 1971:146).

Different sectors experienced varying rates of inflation in the 10
years before 1950 and changes in relative prices certainly encouraged the
advance of some sectors, relative to others (Table 3.1).   Many other factors
also affected the situation; for example, the mining industry and transportation both suffered from war-time destruction and deterioration of equipment

---

* Dr Prachoom Chomchai is Professor and Dean, Faculty of Economics,
Chulalongkorn University, Bangkok.

while manufacturing, in contrast, was stimulated by the long interruption
of foreign trade.   It should be pointed out, however, that the relative
strength of 'manufacturing' indicated in Table 3.1 is due partly to the
inclusion of value-added by the processing of agricultural products
(Ingram, 1971:145-6).

In the past two decades the major branches of the Thai economy have
grown substantially, but so very unevenly that considerable structural
transformation has taken place.   The sectors which advanced most rapidly
in the 1960s were manufacturing, construction, banking, insurance and real
estate, and especially electricity and water supply (Table 3.2).   Compared
with the fast growth in these industries, agriculture has made relatively
slow progress except for the sub-sector of fisheries where the rate of
expansion has been remarkable.   Table 3.2 also illustrates the sharp
variations in rates of growth which occurred during the early period of
the Second Plan (1967-69), compared with the First Plan (1961-66).   Again,
fisheries and forestry were exceptions to the poor growth of the agricultural economy;   it is also evident that growth in the tertiary sector, in
general, tended to accelerate during the Second Plan period, presumably
because of relatively high income elasticities of demand.

Table 3.2:   Growth rates of Gross National Product by industrial origin at
             1962 prices, 1961-1969

	Average (1961-1966)	Average (1967-1969)	Average (1961-1969)
Agriculture	6.4	3.8	5.5
Crops	(6.6)	(1.6)	(4.9)
Livestock	(3.0)	(3.0)	(3.0)
Fisheries	(17.9)	(22.7)	(19.5)
Forestry	(3.5)	(8.8)	(5.3)
Mining and quarrying	15.3	10.5	13.7
Manufacturing	11.2	10.2	10.9
Construction	12.9	10.8	12.2
Electricity and water	22.9	20.8	22.2
Transport and communication	6.1	8.3	6.9
Wholesale and retail trade	8.2	10.0	8.8
Banking, insurance and real estate	15.8	16.3	16.0
Ownership of dwellings	3.0	4.2	3.4
Public administration and defence	5.4	10.4	7.1
Services	7.9	9.5	8.4
Gross domestic product	8.1	8.0	8.1
Gross national product	8.1	8.1	8.1

Source: Office of the National Economic Development Board, 1971.

When relative shares are examined in Tables 3.2 and 3.3, the most striking developments during the 1960s were clearly the decline in agriculture and the increasing role of secondary industries. The relative decline of agriculture is more significant because Thailand's exports are mostly agricultural products, and about 80 per cent of the labour force is still employed in agriculture. In absolute terms, of course, the money value of agriculture's contribution to gross national product has steadily increased, though it has grown less fast than the other sectors.

Within agriculture, as Table 3.2 shows, the overall growth rate of the crop and livestock sub-sectors in the period 1961-69 was particularly disappointing. Despite increased diversification, however, rice has remained the predominant crop from various viewpoints. In terms of the cultivated area, padi still accounted for almost 70 per cent of the total in 1965-67, although its proportion had declined from almost 90 per cent in 1950-52 (Ministry of Agriculture, 1970). Rice has also remained predominant from the point of view of export earnings. The combined share of the four main export commodities (rice, rubber, tin and teak) fell drastically between 1950 and 1969 and, while that of rice also fell sharply, by 1969 it was still in the front rank of export earners. Of course, considerable diversification has taken place in Thailand's merchandise exports, newcomers being maize, cassava, kenaf, oilseeds, beans, shrimp and other primary products. Their importance can be gauged from the fact that in 1969 their combined share in total merchandise exports amounted to approximately 30 per cent which exceeded that of rice. When this is added to the share of the four principal commodities, the total share of the main primary products in Thailand's merchandise exports was approximately 80 per cent in 1969.

Table 3.3: Percentage distribution of Gross Domestic Product at 1962 prices, 1960-1969

		1960	1969
I	Primary		
	(a) Agriculture	38.1	30.5
	(b) Mining	1.1	1.7
II	Secondary		
	(a) Manufacturing	13.1	16.4
	(b) Construction	4.9	6.8
III	Tertiary		
	(a) Commerce	20.6	22.3
	(b) Transport and communications	7.5	6.8
	(c) Electricity and water supply	0.4	1.9
	(d) Services	14.3	14.2
		100.0	100.0

Source: As for Table 3.2.

There is, of course, considerable danger in the development of new agricultural exports such as kenaf, maize and cassava owing to the instability of their markets.   Ingram has warned (1971:313-4) that 'as the residual supplier of nations that produce these items themselves, Thailand must be prepared for wide fluctuations in specific products.   It needs to develop a flexible agriculture, capable of shifting quickly from one crop to another as market conditions warrant'.   While this is sound advice, it will not be easily implemented within the space of a few years.   On the other hand, Thailand also needs to develop its non-agricultural exports and services, although as Ingram notes (1971:314), 'only tourism offers much promise as a source of foreign exchange earnings'.

Finally in this brief review of recent performances in the various sectors of the Thai economy, it is appropriate to comment upon the implications of differential growth for per capita incomes.   A critical consideration is the extent to which agricultural production is undervalued. Usher (1968) and Silcock (1970, Ch.2) have argued that undervaluation seriously affects the measurement of agriculture's contribution to Thailand's gross national product.   Pursuing the same argument, Ingram has used 1968 data to calculate income per head in agriculture and the non-agricultural industries.   Ingram's calculations, shown in Table 3.4, lead him to conclude that, without adjustments for possible undervaluation, 'income per capita in non-agricultural activities is 8.7 times as large as income per capita in agriculture.   While differentials in favor of the nonagricultural sector have commonly been observed in other countries, they usually range from 4:3 to 2:1.   A differential of 8.7:1 can scarcely be believed' (Ingram, 1971:236).

Table 3.4:   Income per head in agriculture and other sectors in Thailand in 196

	Population	GNP originating (000,000 baht)	GNP per capita (baht)
Agriculture	27,000,000	37,000	1,370
Non-agricultural activities	6,700,000	80,300	11,980
Total	33,700,000	117,300	3,480

Note: The proportion of the employed population in agriculture here is 80 per cent.

Source: Ingram, 1971:236.

Faced with this apparently absurd result, Ingram cites Usher's cautious calculations of per capita incomes using 1963 data (incorporating many adjustments) which indicated a ratio of about 3:1 in favour of the non-agricultural sector.

In his calculations Ingram possibly overestimates the proportion of economically active population engaged in agriculture and at the same time underestimates the contribution that agriculture makes to Gross National Product.   On the other hand, an even more recent calculation by the Bangkok Bank, shown in Table 3.5, using more specific data for the size of the economically active population in 1961 and 1971, has produced results which are somewhat more favourable to agriculture: the ratios are 6.9:1 for 1961 and 7.2:1 for 1971.

Table 3.5:   Income distribution in Thailand, 1961-1971

	1961	1971
Economically active population in agriculture (millions)	10.34	12.75
Contribution to GDP of agriculture (million baht)	23,111.00	37,300.00
Per capita income in agriculture (baht)	2,230.00	2,920.00
Economically active population in non-agricultural activities (million)	2.34	4.25
Contribution to GDP of non-agricultural activities (million baht)	35,895.00	89,100.00
Per capita income in non-agricultural activities (baht)	15,350.00	21,000.00

Source: Calculations based on Bangkok Bank Limited, 1972:33-34.

The persistent undervaluation of agricultural output which limits the value of these calculations arises partly because rice, including the large share consumed on farms, is valued at the artificially low prices maintained by the government through its rice premium policy (Richter and Edwards, in chapter 2 of this volume).   Moreover, fishing by farmers for their own consumption, an important element in their domestic subsistence economy, is entirely omitted from the estimates (Panitpakdi, 1967:112).   Similarly, it is not clear whether non-farming activities undertaken by farm families in trading, house construction, home industries and other such activities are given anything like their true weight in the national accounts (Usher, 1966:433-4; Trescott, 1970:61).

Relative under-valuation of agriculture may also result from the over-valuation of other sectors, notably public administration, defence and manufacturing, though the position may not be as bad as Ingram suggests. He argues that the full cost of government payrolls is included as value-added and hence as part of the national product, despite the fact that 'the marginal productivity of labour (in government service) is close to zero -- if indeed it is not negative' and, consequently, that 'a substantial part of the government payroll could more properly be treated as a transfer payment' (Ingram, 1971:303-5).   This may well be true, but the author's impression is that Ingram goes too far in view of the fact that the civil service has constituted the back-bone of all development efforts.   Indeed, the under-employment of some civil servants may well be amply compensated for by the exertion of the more active and dedicated members of the service. Further, an important factor in the overvaluation of manufacturing has been the maintenance of high prices for manufactures behind the tariff wall.

2.   RATIONALE OF PLANNED INDUSTRIALISATION

After a decade or so of planned industrial development, it has been vaguely assumed in Thailand that there will be further industrialisation in the years to come.   It has not been made clear why this should necessarily be the case.   For instance, an official statement puts it in the following terms:-

'Accelerated industrial development is an objective of the Second Plan which has been adopted in order to realize a structural change in the economy with the manufacturing sector growing, creating employment opportunities and utilising greater supplies of indigenous raw materials' (Office of NEDB, 1967:115).   The Third Plan (1972-1976) adds the promotion of export and labour-intensive industries and more integration with the agricultural sector (NEDB, 1972:54-5).   While the official objectives are clear from official statements, one needs some economic justification for the choice of manufacturing industry.   It has not been made explicit

whether the strategy of industrial development followed in the past will
still be adopted.

One of the soundest and most important reasons for embarking on a
programme of industrialisation is that it may be a way of increasing the
national income of the country (Bryce, 1960:8).   To what extent the manufacturing sector is able to achieve this particular aim depends on its relative
importance in the economy as well as on its rate of expansion.

The relative importance of manufacturing as well as its rate of
growth can be gauged from Tables 3.1, 3.2 and 3.3, though data in the
first table are not in real terms.   Manufacturing increased its relative
share in GDP from about 10 per cent in 1938 to about 16 per cent in 1969,
which indicates relatively fast rates of growth.

Both the Gross Domestic Product and Gross National Product, in real
terms (1962 prices), grew between 1961 and 1969 at the annual rate of 8.1
per cent.   Manufacturing grew faster than the overall rate, that is, at
10.9 per cent per annum, while the dominating agricultural sector, with an
annual growth rate of 5.5 per cent, lagged behind.   This experience is by
no means limited to Thailand, as a recent ECAFE study reported (ECAFE,
1970a:6).

> 'In general (of countries in the ECAFE region), while the
> industrial sector has been expanding rapidly, its relative
> size is still too small to counter a setback in other sectors.
> It can easily be seen that the effect of a rapidly-growing
> industrial sector on total output may be entirely offset by
> a relatively greater negative change in another sector,
> typically agriculture.   This has been brought home to countries
> which were occasionally confronted with an agricultural decline
> or falling world prices for their primary export commodities.
> The notion of a rapidly-growing industrial sector leading the
> economy in development is thus a goal, whose achievement is
> only possible when the industrial sector has become predominant.

> It is painfully true that, as things stand, overall economic growth
> in the developing countries of the ECAFE region has been determined
> largely by a slowly-moving agricultural sector.   In most of these
> countries agricultural output grew between 1952 and 1966 at less
> than 4 per cent annually, and, since the agricultural sector
> accounts for between 30 and 50 per cent of the gross national
> product in these countries, its low growth rate, in the absence
> of fast rates of growth in other non-industrial sectors, was
> bound to result in a poor rate of growth of the national product.
> Action designed to accelerate growth is therefore required on the
> agricultural as well as the industrial fronts'.

THAILAND

Table 3.6

Table 3.7

Source

ECAFE

Svetanant

Thailand

Agriculture

Manufacturing

Mining

Construction

Electricity

Transport

Commerce

Services

1953-60

1960-67

On the basis

While all this

Another sound

Israngkun

Bryce

On the basis of figures in Table 3.6, another ECAFE study estimates that between 1960 and 1967 the increase in manufacturing output in Thailand made a larger contribution than agriculture to the increase in national income. It concludes that, for very rapid economic growth to be possible, rapid industrialisation is essential.

Table 3.6: Percentage contribution of manufacturing and agricultural output to the increase in Gross Domestic Product, 1953-60 and 1960-67

| | Manufacturing | | Agriculture | |
	1953-60	1960-67	1953-60	1960-67
Thailand	7	19	35	15

Source: ECAFE, 1970b:20.

While all this is true, one has to agree with Israngkun (1969:262) that, because of the relatively small size of manufacturing industry in Thailand at the present time, 'it will take several decades before the sector can assert its role as a leading sector in the Thai economy'. Thus the government's objective of 'realising a structural change in the economy' is inevitably a long-term one.

Another sound reason for industrialisation is the employment of the unemployed or partially employed (Bryce, 1960:9). Table 3.7 gives the employment situation in Thailand in the mid-1960s.

Table 3.7: Percentage distribution of employment in Thailand 1960 and 1966

	1960	1966
Agriculture	83.0	79.8
Mining	0.2	0.3
Manufacturing	3.6	4.7
Construction	0.6	0.8
Electricity	0.1	0.2
Transport	1.3	1.6
Commerce	6.0	7.1
Services	5.2	5.5
	100.0	100.0

Source: Svetanant, 1969:53.

INDUSTRIAL DEVELOPMENT   75

Despite its increased importance, manufacturing still employs a
relatively small proportion of the total labour force, the dominant role
being played again by agriculture.   As Israngkun suggests (1969:262),
it will take several decades before the sector can assert its role as an
'employer of the bulk of the increasing labour force'.   Thus the official
objective of 'creating employment opportunities' through manufacturing is
also inevitably a long-term one.

Table 3.8 below gives an idea of the rate of labour absorption in
various sectors of the economy.   While manufacturing had a very high rate
of labour absorption between 1954 and 1960, its ability to absorb labour
had been much reduced by 1960-66.   It is apparent that during the era of
planned industrial development, manufacturing has rapidly changed its
fundamental nature: it has become more capital-intensive. Disequilibrium
in the factor markets seems to have had a pervasive impact on the structure
of the manufacturing sector.   For instance, market wages are higher than
shadow wages based on the estimated marginal productivity of labour, as
has been cogently argued by Marzouk (1972:302-3).   Again, the costs of
capital (largely imported) may be artificially held down by the apparent
overvaluation of the baht (Marzouk, 1972:303).   Moreover, pricing policies
pursued by such capital-intensive activities as power generation tend
artificially to keep down the cost of using capital.   In sum, it may well
be that factor prices in Thailand do not reflect the true scarcity of
capital and the relative abundance of labour.   A situation similar to what

Table 3.8:   Index of labour absorption (L/Q) 1954-1960 and 1960-1966

	1954-1960	1960-1966
Mining	8.911	0.808
Manufacturing	4.308	0.784
Commerce	2.615	0.772
Electricity	2.342	1.006
Services	2.334	0.685
Construction	1.828	0.921
Communication	1.266	0.804
Agriculture	0.597	0.441

Note: Q denotes the rate of growth of GDP per annum.
       L denotes the rate of growth of employment per annum.

Source: Svetanant, 1969:41, 44.

Kindleberger calls 'structural disequilibrium at the factor level' (1968:
489-90) appears to be developing.   If such a situation is allowed to
develop strongly, future expansion of manufacturing activity cannot be
relied upon to absorb a massive increase in the labour force (likely to
result from rapid population growth and the advent of the green revolution)
unless a transformation of the industrial structure does take place.

Capital intensity in itself may not be a bad thing from the viewpoint
of employment creation; for through its forward and backward linkages and
lateral effects, industrial expansion with increasing capital intensity
can indirectly have a decisive impact on the employment situation.   Unfortunately, as Thailand is an open economy, backward linkages and lateral
effects, instead of creating local employment opportunities, are likely
to have encouraged the import of the required intermediate products from
abroad.   The pattern of import substitution to be examined lends much
support to this argument.

In such an open economy as Thailand's, it is doubtful whether the
Third Plan's objective of integrating manufacturing with agriculture can
easily be realised.   Industrial investment may not, as has been pointed
out, have had substantial backward linkages in the domestic economy.
Conversely, agricultural development in the past has had few linkages with
industry.   Fertilisers, tractors and agricultural implements in general
have not been produced at home despite the existing demand, because imports
are so readily available.   Whether linkages are allowed to have significant
local impact depends largely, of course, on government investment policies
and the response of the private sector to economic incentives.

Employment creation apart, as Thailand is gradually entering the
phase of export substitution, it appears that the objectives of encouraging
export and labour-intensive industries are consistent, in that it may be
believed that Thailand has a comparative advantage in products with a high
labour content.   It needs to be emphasised that the number of workers
employed may not accurately reflect the amount of labour input.   For
instance, if labour is underutilised because of the seasonal nature of
work, the number employed at harvest time tives a misleading impression
of the quantity of labour intake (Myrdal, 1968:1013-4).

Table 3.9 shows some of the principal manufactured exports from Thailand to the developed countries in descending order of labour intensity of production.   While the crude index calculated by Kerdpibul is affected by the fact that labour is not homogeneous throughout the economy, it does suggest that Thailand tends to export goods of a high labour content to the developed countries.

Table 3.9:   Thailand's manufactures exported to developed countries, 1965

Products	Index of labour intensity	Export value (000,000 baht)
Woven products	2.5384	1,077.79
Rubber products	1.2917	2.48
Wood products	1.0710	262.41
Non-metallic products	0.6646	22.39
Paper products	0.3077	0.94
Metal products	0.3466	6.96
Clothing	0.2018	19.57
Chemicals	0.1672	25.12
Articles for household decorations	0.1578	0.54
Leather products	0.1074	26.60
Electrical appliances	0.0857	7.86

Source: Kerdpibul, 1970:18-19.

If Thailand has a comparative advantage in the production of goods of a high labour content, it must be emphasised nevertheless that such advantage can exist only in real terms.   In money terms, her absolute advantage in such products may be significantly reduced or even eliminated if it is true, as has been suggested, that market wage rates are higher than shadow ones based on the marginal physical productivity of labour and if it is also true that the baht rate of exchange is overvalued.

It is to be noted that manufactures incorporating the labour-intensive products listed in Table 3.9 generally make extensive use of raw materials which are locally available in Thailand.   With this combination, the process of export substitution is likely to satisfy the official criteria of employment creation and of greater dependence on local materials.   In this case, removal of disequilibrium in factor markets and adjustment of the baht exchange rate will form an integral part of Thailand's future development policy.

3. STRATEGY OF PLANNED INDUSTRIALISATION

While it may not be possible to attribute to the government a consistent
and well-integrated strategy of industrialisation, there are already some
elements from which a strategy could be developed.

First, the role of direct government participation has been crucial.
The immediate post-war need for industrialisation encouraged the government
to establish a number of industrial enterprises ranging from sugar to paper,
gunny bag, plywood, glass containers and cigarettes (Marzouk, 1972:195).
The public sector's participation in industrialisation was not so much a
reflection of political ideology as a response to the widely-held belief
that the industrial sector, being new and uncharted, would not be responsive to private incentives in the same way as agriculture. The policy
of direct government participation continued into the early 1950s, when
the emphasis shifted to government encouragement of private enterprise and
provision of infrastructural facilities. The legacy of the past is still
evident, however: public enterprises continue to play a major role in
several industries.

Secondly, the rice 'premium' (and rice export duty) imposed in 1955,
virtually abolished in 1971 and substantially revived in mid-1972, has
functioned almost accidentally as a key instrument of industrial development. The premium helps to redistribute incomes in favour of the urban
dwellers, since domestic rice prices are kept down (Kridakara, 1970).
The government view seems to be that depression of the domestic prices of
rice is desirable because it holds down the cost of living in urban areas
and reduces the pressure for higher wages and salaries; at the same time
it encourages exports and enables infant industries to compete with imports
(Myint, 1972:31). This essentially boils down to using the premium as an
anti-inflation device and as an instrument for long-term industrialisation
and modernisation. In the long run, Ingram thinks the premium can also
become one instrument of development strategy: 'it is necessary to force
savings in the traditional agricultural sector and transfer them to the
non-agricultural (modern) sector'. On the assumptions that the supply
of rice is inelastic and that surplus labour exists in the agricultural
sector, a dual-economy model deriving from Lewis's (Lewis, 1954) can
indeed be applied and the conclusion reached 'that the premium would
promote economic development' (Ingram, 1971:258).

Of course, the growth of industry requires investment, and this can
be financed basically in one of three ways: from within the industrial
sector itself, from a surplus in other sectors of the economy, or from
abroad.   Not much is known about financing from within the industrial
sector; on the other hand, it is clear that through a series of investment
promotion acts some success has been achieved in attracting foreign capital
to Thailand's manufacturing.   The rice premium though perhaps not by
design, has become a crucial element in financing industrial investment
from the agricultural sector.   It has functioned essentially by holding
down the price of rice and thereby turning the terms of trade against the
rice farmers.   What is surprising is that all this has taken place while
little or no improvement in farm productivity has occurred.   Ingram (1964:
118) has shown that 'rice farmers obtained increasingly favourable terms
of trade from the 1860s to the end of the century', and, while they may
have suffered an unfavourable change from the turn of the century up to
1910, little or no change took place between 1910 and 1930.   The imposition
of the premium in 1955 must, therefore, have had some harsh and abrupt consequences for rice farmers who had enjoyed relatively favourable terms of
trade.   The unfavourable change in the terms of trade due to imposition of
the rice premium automatically transferred resources out of rice farming;
some of these resources could have gone into cultivation of other crops in
the process of agricultural diversification, as well as into other non-
industrial sectors.   It is difficult to say how much has gone into
manufacturing alone.

What is known is that the net transfer of funds is taking place all
the time, from rural areas to the capital city.   Rozental (1970) has shown
that the provincial branches of commercial banks collect rural savings and
channel them into the Bangkok-Thon Buri area.   He recommended retention
of such funds in the provinces.   More recently, the National Economic
Development Board has called on all commercial banks to prevent the drain
of funds from the provinces to the metropolis; it stated that only a
quarter of funds deposited in the provinces are being retained for use
there (Bangkok Post, 17 September 1972).

Thirdly, the strategy of industrial development in Thailand has
generally been inward-looking, since it emphasises import substitution

with high protection barriers.   This is a serious departure from pre-war
practice, when tariffs were imposed only for revenue purposes (Myint, 1972:
28).   In general, consumer and intermediate goods provided locally are now
protected by high tariffs ranging from 40 to 60 per cent ad valorem.
Capital equipment, raw materials and components not locally produced are
subject to lower tariffs of 5 to 15 per cent ad valorem.   Moreover, such
tariffs are supplemented by specific rates on some products (Sophonpanich,
1970:105).

It is not sufficient, however, to know the ad valorem and the specific rates of tariffs.   What is more relevant is, of course, the effective
rate of protection.   Table 3.10 shows that protection is higher as a
result of the privileges granted under the Promotion of Industrial Investment Act (1962) and that the effective rates of protection favour consumer
goods.   Among consumer goods, the non-durable category is especially favoured.

Table 3.10:   Effective rates of protection in Thailand

	z_1	z_2	Ratio (z_2/z_1)
Fats and oils	73	185	2.52
Cereal products	16	88	5.55
Textile fabrics	70	104	1.48
Dairy products	112	250	2.23
Automobiles	118	122	1.03
Motorcycles and bicycles	66	95	1.43
Petroleum products	104	164	1.58
Thread and yarn	62	98	1.59
Glass and glass products	58	72	1.25
Paper and paper products	51	65	1.26
Rolling mill products	49	89	1.81
Rubber goods	57	86	1.50
Electrical machinery	45	58	1.28
Non-electrical machinery	38	53	1.40
Agricultural machinery	7	21	2.78

Note: The effective rate of protection has been calculated according to
Corden, (1966:222), as follows:-

$$z = \frac{w-v}{v}$$

z = rate of protection of value added
w = actual value in domestic prices
v = hypothetical free trade value added

z_1 is the effective rate of protection calculated from the Customs Tariff
Code of 1960, a standardised input-output table (based on Belgium and
Netherlands data) and international trade weights.

z_2 is similarly calculated, but privileges granted under the Promotion of
Industrial Investment Act (1962) are also included.

Source: Suwankiri, (1970:76).

In economic theory, such high protection penalises the export sector owing to the overvaluation of the local currency.   In other words, over-valuation of the baht defended by high protection is one of the factors retarding the growth of the export sector, constituted largely by agriculture.   Fortunately, because of relatively low supply elasticities of exported agricultural products, the handicap is less than in the case of manufactured exports.   In the long run, of course, growth of exported manufactures will be hampered by such high protection, and this is a relevant consideration for the Third Plan which aims at promoting manufactured exports.

Table 3.11 shows that the import content of private consumption has fallen, as a result of import substitution, between 1960 and 1969.   The fall was sharper in the case of finished consumption goods, since more consumption goods were made domestically from imported materials.

Table 3.11: Import substitution of consumption goods, 1960-1969

	Import content of consumption expenditure[a]	Ratio of finished consumption goods to private consumption expenditure
1960	11.2	8.5
1969	10.8	6.6

a   Import of finished consumption goods and materials chiefly for consumption goods as a percentage of private consumption expenditure.

Source: Calculated from data provided by the Department of Customs and office of National Economic Development Board.

Table 3.12 gives an idea of the extent of import substitution in capital goods.   These figures reflect not only the domestic production of capital goods, but also the type of capital formation: for example, the construction of indigenous types of buildings requires little or no imports.

Table 3.12: Import content of gross domestic fixed capital formation, 1960-1969

	Ratio of import of capital goods to gross domestic fixed capital formation	Ratio of import of capital goods and materials chiefly for capital goods to gross domestic fixed capital formation
1960	31.3	40.8
1969	29.0	36.4

Source: As for Table 3.11.

The reduction in the import content of capital formation in Thailand between
1960 and 1969 can be attributed, in large measure, to the rapid expansion in
construction work for which the domestic supply of cement has greatly
increased.

With more elaborate tools for measuring import substitution, Ingram
concludes, that, in general, 'the primary effect of investment promotion in
Thailand has not been a substitution of domestic production for imports, but
a substitution of one kind of imports for another - in particular, a substitution of imported new materials, components, and capital goods for imports
of the products now turned out by promoted firms' (1971:297).   In his view
'Thailand's investment programme from 1959 to 1970 has primarily stimulated
firms to capture the small, tariff-sheltered domestic market' (1971:298).

In sum, we may note a number of unwelcome consequences of Thailand's
policies towards industrial investment during the past 10 years or so,
which will require careful consideration in the future strategy of industrialisation.   First, as Ingram mentions (1971:298) 'promoted firms tend
to design their plants to produce only for the sheltered domestic market,
which means they build small-scale plants'.   Since many new firms aim at
the urban enclave rather than the mass rural market, the scale of production
is necessarily small.   Furthermore, the proliferation of competing firms
encouraged by promotion measures has further split the market, reduced
capacity utilisation and added to costs (Richter and Edwards, in chapter 2
of this volume).   Secondly, the over-entry of firms into industries
encouraged by high tariffs has frequently resulted in alternative and competing versions of the same product, so that the size of the market for many
does not justify backward integration and has thereby increased dependence
upon imported intermediate manufactures.   Thirdly, and as a consequence of
the previous problem, firms constrained by the small size of their Thailand
market will obviously not aim at exporting, but at the same time the high
prices which they must charge for their output will in turn weaken the
competitive position of potential exporters who purchase these products
for further manufacture.   Fourthly, as Richter and Edwards note, industrialisation has proved relatively capital-intensive in a country which will
soon face mounting employment problems (1973, in chapter 2 of this volume).
Finally, as a consequence of the pattern of substituting one import for

another, combined with Thailand's heavy dependence on imported capital
and raw material for manufacturing industry, the net benefit of industrialisation to the balance of payments has been in doubt (Richter and
Edwards, in chapter 2 of this volume).

4.   PROSPECTS FOR PLANNED INDUSTRIALISATION

Despite the many handicaps discussed above, manufacturing industry grew
rapidly in Thailand in the 1960s and the prospects for further industrialisation are promising.   For one thing, there is a plentiful supply of cheap
labour.   It is clear from Table 3.13 that Thailand enjoys a low level of
wages when compared with countries at similar stages of development, such
as Malaysia or the Philippines.   This is partly due, as noted earlier,
to the role of the rice premium in keeping down domestic rice prices.
Quite apart from the low level of wages, it is also true that wages have
risen very little in recent years.   Indeed, real wages in manufacturing
may actually have fallen between 1964 and 1969 (ILO, Yearbook of Labour
Statistics 1970:563), a fact which may incidentally have helped to finance
industrial investment from the manufacturing sector itself.   Another
favourable factor is the local availability of industrial raw material
derived from forests, mines and increasingly diversified cropping.

Table 3.13:   Wages in several Asian countries
(in US$)

Country	Average daily earnings (male and female)	Minimum daily wages (unskilled male workers)
Republic of China (1967)	1.17	0.61-0.76
Indonesia (1970)	–	–
Japan (1968)	6.51	1.08
Republic of Korea (1968)	1.36	0.37-0.40
West Malaysia (1968)	–	1.08
Philippines (1968)	2.07	–
Singapore (1968)	2.51	1.30
Thailand (1968)	1.32	0.50

Source: ILO, Yearbook of Labour Statistics, 1970:

No less favourable than the ready availability of cheap labour and
materials is Thailand's ability to achieve a rapid rate of economic growth
without a substantial increase in the price level.   This has been due to
the successful balancing between the growth of money and the growth of output against a background of the relative constancy of money velocity
(Trescott, 1971:27).   Factors contributing to stability have been the
structure of the monetary system itself, the absence of major internal
disturbances and the government's restraint on expenditure (Trescott,
1971:276-7).

In order that Thailand's latent comparative advantage may be realised,
a radical change in the nation's industrial strategy must take place.   In
particular, the strategy of inward-looking industrialisation, suited to the
phase of import substitution, must be entirely overhauled to orient the
economy to export substitution.   This transformation will be difficult to
achieve.   Even the presumed comparative advantage in the production of
labour-intensive products may be more apparent than real: once promotional
privileges have been eliminated these products may no longer be competitive
in the world market.   Indeed, it could well be that very few industries
promoted so far in Thailand can genuinely qualify as 'infant industries'.
Very few of the promoted industries would have passed the 'Mill test' of
being able to acquire sufficient skill and experience to overcome a historical handicap and the 'Bastable test' of being able to achieve a
sufficient saving in costs to compensate for the high costs of the learning
period (Kemp, 1960:65-7).   If the Mill and Bastable tests are too severe,
it is also doubtful whether many of the promoted industries could pass the
more general 'Meade test' of being able to generate external economies
during growth so that the community gains to an extent which justifies the
price paid in terms of protection (Meade, 1955:chapter 16).

The prospective dilemma of having to protect inefficient infant
industries indefinitely, or letting them collapse at the end of the promotional period, would become a smaller problem if certain distortions were
removed.   If it is true that factor prices in Thailand do not reflect the
relative scarcities of various factors, efforts must be made to bring them
into line with their marginal physical productivities.   The proposal by

the government to fix minimum wages will be of no help unless they are fixed with an eye to such equilibrium levels.   Moreover, if it is true that the baht exchange rate is over-valued, steps should be taken to bring it to an equilibrium level, however difficult this may be.   In effect, this means restoration of the price mechanism, to the extent which may be feasible, taking into account such distortions as are caused by State monopolies and the rice premium.

REFERENCES

Bangkok Bank Limited, 1972. Rai-ngan Prachampea 2514 (Report for the Year 1971), Bangkok.

Bryce, M.D., 1960. Industrial development - a guide for accelerating economic growth. McGraw Hill, New York.

Corden, W.M., 1966. 'The structure of a tariff system and the effective protection rate', Journal of Political Economy, 74, No.3, pp. 221-37.

Cowan, C.D. (ed.), 1964. The economic development of South-East Asia, Praeger, New York.

ECAFE, 1970a. Laying the foundations for accelerated and integrated industrial growth in the second development decade, paper prepared for the Second Session Asian Conference on Industrialisation (Tokyo), Bangkok (mimeo).

ECAFE, 1970b. Industrialisation policies: achievements and problems, paper prepared for the Second Session Asian Conference on Industrialisation (Tokyo), Bangkok (mimeo).

Gould, J.S., 1953. Thailand's national income and its meaning, National Economic Council, Bangkok (mimeo). Quoted in Ingram, 1971:146.

ILO, 1970. Yearbook of labour statistics, Geneva.

Ingram, J.C., 1964. 'Thailand's rice trade and the allocation of resources', in Cowan (ed.), 1964:102-26.

Ingram, J.C., 1971. Economic Change in Thailand 1850-1970, Stanford University Press.

Israngkun, C., 1969. Manufacturing industries in Thailand, unpublished Ph.D thesis, Australian National University, Canberra.

Kerdpibul, U., 1970. 'Karnsuksa tung kwamsamat kong pratetthai nai karnkayai karnsong sinka usahakam pai chamnai nai tangpratet' (A study of Thailand's ability to expand her manufactured exports), Journal of Economics and Public Administration, 2, No.3, pp. 14-28.

Kemp, M.C., 1960. 'The Mill-Bastable infant-industry dogma', Journal of Political Economy, 68, pp. 65-67.

Kindleberger, C.I., 1968. International Economics, Irwin, Homewood Illinois.

Kridakara, H.S.H. Prince Sithiporn, 1970. Some aspects of rice farming in Siam, Bangkok.

Kurihara, K.K., 1968.   'Theoretical objections to agriculture-based economic development', Indian Journal of Economics, pp. 169-70.

Lewis, W.A., 1954.   'Economic development with unlimited supplies of labour', Manchester School, 20, pp. 105-38.

Marzouk, G.A., 1972.   Economic development and policies: case study of Thailand, Rotterdam University Press, Rotterdam.

Meade, J.E., 1955.   Trade and welfare, Oxford University Press, London.

Ministry of Agriculture, 1970.   Agricultural statistics of Thailand 1967, Bangkok.

Myint, H., 1972.   Southeast Asia's economy - development policies in the 1970s, Penguin Books, Harmondsworth.

Myrdal, G., 1968.   Asian drama: an inquiry into the poverty of nations, Pantheon, New York.

Office of the National Economic Development Board, 1967.   The second national economic and social development plan 1967-71, Bangkok.

Office of the National Economic Development Board, 1971.   National income of Thailand 1968-69 edition, Bangkok.

Office of the National Economic Development Board, 1972.   Paen patana setakit Lae sangkom haeng chat chabab teesam P.S. 2515-2519 (Third national economic and social development plan B.E. 2515-2519), Bangkok.

Panitpakdi, P., 1967.   'National accounts estimates of Thailand', in Silcock (ed.), 1967:105-27.

Rozental, A.A., 1970.   Finance and development in Thailand, Praeger, New York.

Silcock, T.H. (ed.), 1967.   Thailand: social and economic studies in development, Australian National University, Canberra.

Silcock, T.H., 1970.   The economic development of Thai agriculture, Australian National University Press, Canberra.

Sophonpanich, C., 1970.   'Protection and industrialisation in developing countries', Warasarn Setasert (Journal of Economics), 5, No.2, pp. 97-109.

Suwankiri, T., 1970.   'The structure of protection and import substitution in Thailand', Warasarn Setasert (Journal of Economics), 5, No.1, pp. 53-109.

Svetanant, P., 1969.   Employment problems in Thailand, unpublished M.A. thesis, University of the Philippines.

Trescott, P.B., 1970.   'Measurement of Thailan's economic growth, 1946–
        1965', <u>Warasarn Setasert</u> (Journal of Economics), 4, No.1,
        pp. 16–106.

Trescott, P.B., 1971.   <u>Thailand's monetary experience – the economics
        of stability</u>, Praeger, London.

Usher, D., 1966.   'Income as a measure of productivity: alternative
        comparisons of agricultural and non-agricultural productivity
        in Thailand', <u>Economica</u>, 33, No.132, pp. 430–41

Usher, D., 1968.   <u>The price mechanism and the meaning of national income
        statistics</u>, New York.

CHAPTER 4

HYDRAULIC SOCIETY IN CONTEMPORARY THAILAND?

Gehan Wijeyewardene*

1. INTRODUCTION

This paper is concerned with certain aspects of the theory of hydraulic societies (Wittfogel, 1957) as they apply to contemporary Thailand.[1] In essence the theory is materialist and determinist. The physical properties of water, the fact of its uneven distribution over the earth's surface, and its absolute necessity for agricultural production means that post-Neolithic man has in many parts of the world faced some hard choices. In certain favoured areas, pre-eminently Western Europe, successful agriculture depended only on rainfall for its supply of water. In such areas there developed the institutions typical of European feuda- lism, where the power of the centralised state was balanced by the coun- tervailing power of a nobility holding strong rights in private property. But in arid and semi-arid areas, agriculture could often be carried on only by the laborious and continuing control of water. The organisational requirements of irrigation works and their maintenance result in the development of an agro-managerial bureaucracy and a despotic state in which neither free labour nor strong private property evolves. In this, its simplest form, the argument suggests that rainfall agriculture is associated with strong private property, a low level of centralised authority and European-style feudalism, while irrigation-based agricul- ture is associated with weak private property, a highly centralised state and Oriental despotism. The gross typology is substantially modified by distinguishing between 'compact' and 'loose' hydraulic societies. To anticipate the final section of this paper, I might mention that despotism is held to be associated with societies which have erected major flood control and protective works.

* Dr Wijeyewardene is Senior Fellow in the Department of Anthropology and Sociology, Institute of Advanced Studies, Australian National University.

1 By 'contemporary' I refer mainly to the period 1965-6 when my field data were collected. Published sources for subsequent years are rather scarce.

If irrigation-based agriculture and hydraulic enterprise is
associated with despotism, two questions present themselves.   First,
do all despotisms, particularly those with inexorable Oriental features,
arise out of hydraulic society?   Second, does irrigation always lead to
despotism?   Wittfogel seems to answer, in a rather complex way, 'yes'
to the first question, and 'no' to the second.   For Russia he argues
that the incipient feudalism of the Kievan Republic was overthrown by
a hydraulic and despotic ideology carried westward by the Tartars, and
that communism is merely a new form of the old ideology in action.
Nazi Germany was also an Oriental aberration.   In both cases, despotism
was an ideological intrusion which was established despite the absence
of a hydraulic base.   At the same time, he considers that communism in
China is the resurgence of Oriental despotism in its most acute form.
Despotism, then, is always a product of hydraulic forms -- though
ideological borrowing may give rise to non-hydraulic derivatives.   But
all this does not mean that the Tennessee Valley Authority and the Snowy
Mountains Hydro-Electric Authority are forerunners of a new despotism.
Where strong private property has established strong liberal and democratic forms of society, irrigation agriculture, hydro-electric power
and water control are no more than technological adjuncts to the growth
of still more free and prosperous societies.

All this leaves out those countries which have neither a developed
industrial base nor bourgeois democratic institutions;   neither strong
private property nor a liberal pluralistic polity.   What does Wittfogel
himself have to say about such countries?   Unfortunately, he views their
situation merely in terms of their contamination by communist ideology
which he considers synonymous with Oriental despotism:

> 'Does this mean that one after the other the ideologically
> penetrated countries will cease resisting the political
> erosion to which Communist strategy is exposing them?
> Such a turn is entirely possible.   And although its con-
> sequences would entail far more than an 'Asiatic restora-
> tion,' in one respect it deserves this title: it would
> be a spectacular manifestation of a retrogressive societal
> development' (Wittfogel, 1957:446).

As a result, Wittfogel's hypothesis has become entangled with the politics
of the cold war.   My concern, however, is with a more basic issue: namely,

the effects that water controls exert on the evolution of a non-industrial
society.   To do so, I examine some of the effects of the Thai irrigation
programme, first at the level of the whole society, and then at the level
of a village and its individual farmers in North Thailand.   The main aim
is to investigate the applicability of the hydraulic thesis to developing
nations in the latter half of the 20th century.

2.   EARLY IRRIGATION WORKS

Historically the hydraulic status of the Thai kingdoms is by no means
beyond doubt.   Wittfogel has but a passing reference (1957:32) with the
emphasis on the transportation of the rice surplus to the capital.   The
only citation is Virginia Thompson and the citation is misleading.
Thompson notes frequent references in the 17th and 18th centuries to the
superior quality of Siamese rice;   ruins of irrigation works in eastern
Siam;   and traces in Sawankhalok and Sukhothai provinces of the irrigation works on which the capitals depended for their food supply.   Irrigation works were constructed during the Ayutthayan period by the government
and by individuals - but not until the reign of Chulalongkorn, when rice
became the major export, was the paramount importance of waterways, both
for communication and irrigation, actively recognised (Thompson, 1967:
514).   She then proceeds to note the existence of small irrigation works
in the north and contrasts this with the central plain where 'canals
exist as waterways, but not until modern times have there been any irrigation works' (1967:515).

The irrigation works of eastern Thailand are in many ways a special
case;   this region is mainly a semiarid plateau and was nearer the centres
of control of the indubitably hydraulic civilisations of Cambodia (Coedes,
1966:88-109).   For the Mae Nam Ping - Chao Phraya valley the evidence seems
to suggest a very much lower level of 'agro-managerial despotism' than
that reached in neighbouring Cambodia.   Briefly the evidence indicates
the existence of small scale irrigation systems in the North, largely
maintained by local communities, and some irrigation and water control
works around royal capitals in the central plain.   Undoubtedly there
were transportation canals but even these supplemented the rivers as the
major communication link between north and south.   For a balanced view

I cite in its entirety Quaritch Wales' summary of the historical,
archaeological and epigraphic evidence.

> 'The Siamese are a riverine people and had little use for
> roads, which indeed would have been difficult of construc-
> tion in a low alluvial country subject to heavy rains. A
> system of canals was therefore a necessity for trade and
> as a means of communication in both peace and war, some
> of the canals being deliberately cut with the sole object
> of moving troops and supplies. To develop the rice-
> growing lands, canals for irrigation became necessary,
> but this was on the whole a later undertaking than the
> cutting of canals for inland navigation. This canal system,
> particularly in the deltaic region, required the construc-
> tion of numerous bridges.
>
>   The inscription of Rama Gamhen mentions the existence of
> a 'sritbhansa' at Sukodhaya, which Professor Coedes tran-
> slates as a 'digue', presumably some kind of irrigation
> work. References to similar undertakings and navigation
> canals in the Northern Annals indicate that the Thai were
> familiar with such works long before this time. The later
> inscriptions of Sukhodaya also mention roads as well as
> canals. In A.D. 1498 the deepening and clearing of two
> ancient canals is recorded in the Annals of Ayudhya, while
> the inscription of the Siva statue at Kambenbejra and dated
> A.D. 1510 records among other royal works the restoration
> of an irrigation canal. About A.D. 1534 a very important
> work for the future history of Siam was begun. This was
> the cutting of Glon Pankok Hyai and its branch which linked
> between them the ends of a big curve of the Menam. The
> citadel of Bangkok was built to guard the lower mouth of
> this canal, and it formed the nucleus of the modern capital
> of Siam. Through the erosive action of the stream, the
> canal widened until it was able to receive the main mass
> of the river which forsook its ancient winding course and
> has since flowed through the canal on the banks of which
> the present city of Bangkok was built. In all several
> thousand kilometres of canal were dug since that period,
> and tens of thousands of acres of unproductive land were
> made fit for cultivation by irrigation' (Wales, 1965:229-30).

While Virginia Thompson's statement that 'not until modern times
have there been any irrigation works' (1967:515) is an exaggeration, Wales
suggestion of extensive irrigation must be balanced against her judgment
and his own statement of the facts.   I would argue that though irrigation has always been a factor in the Thai socio-political system since
Sukhothai, it is a factor that should not be over-rated. The major
interest in waterworks was for communication purposes - and this not only
for 'transporting the rice surplus to the capital'.   In fact the history

of hydraulic society and despotism in Thailand appears to lend support
to Wittfogel's more general thesis - as the growth of despotism seems
not directly connected to ecological and productive factors.   Coedes
has made the point that the famous stele of Rama Kamhaeng gives a
picture of early Thai kingship entirely different from the practices
of Khmer royalty as evidenced in Cambodian epigraphy.   Sukhothai was
a successor kingdom to the dwindling Khmer empire so that the principles
of hydraulic despotism could not have been unknown to its founders.
Perhaps Coedes is right that the antipathy of Theravada Buddhist Thai
to Shaivite Khmer led the former to make 'an express effort to go
against everything that had been done by their former masters' (1966:
144).   The limited evidence does indicate that Sukhothai was not a
despotism.   The Thai historian Kachorn Sukhabanij (cited by Broman,
1968) has suggested the very plausible hypothesis that Sukhothai was
the end product of a number of 'beach-head states' established in the
river valleys of Northern Thailand and Laos as Thai-type culture and
perhaps some of the ancestors of the modern Thai moved southwards.
Broman (1968) has further suggested that the socio-political organisation of these beach-head states may not have been very different from
that of the tribal T'ai who still inhabit similar ecological niches today.
Their ecology is not unfamiliar to anthropologists as the Shan variant
has been discussed at length in relation to Kachin political structure
(e.g. Leach, 1954).   Basically these are stratified societies based on
wet-rice agriculture.   It would seem that in such environments some
water control would always be necessary, but in the absence of extensive
terracing, a limit on population, territorial extent and political
differentiation would be placed by the geographical nature of the river
valleys.   However it is not unexpected that powerful Thai kingdoms arose
in the extensive Chiang Mai valley and in Sukhothai - the northern reaches
of the central plain.   The polity the Thai brought with them was primi-
tively hydraulic and not, in the technical sence, despotic.[2]   Despotism

---

2 A somewhat similar point has been made by Leach, for Ceylon (Leach,
1959).   Leach's article makes two main points.   First, there is no
evidence that the monarchs of ancient Ceylon (Sinhala, more accurately
Sinhale) had access to vast teams of forced labour to construct irrigation works.   The irrigation works in Ceylon's dry zone are of two types,
small village tanks which were for the most part built and maintained by
their users and large scale works which have been built up over centuries.

was fully introduced with the reforms of Borom Trailokanath, though the
kingdom of Ayutthaya appears from the start to have been based on Khmer
models (Coedes, 1966:146).   Borom Trailokanath was undoubtedly influenced
in his administrative reforms by his Khmer advisors (Wales, 1965:70), but
it is more than likely that the objective factors demanding an agro-
managerial hydraulic society were the basis of Ayutthayan despotism.[3]

This brief historical excursion has been necessary to support the
point of view that though traditionally Thai society may be said to be
hydraulic, it was much more unevenly and much less extensively so until
the 19th century.   It was then that the need for extensive irrigation
and water control became apparent for a number of reasons including
increasing population, the development of rice exports and the devas-
tating floods which struck the central plain in 1831.   The bulk, if
not all the major hydraulic projects were the result of western advice
and influence and coincided with the dismantling of the despotic state.

3. MODERN IRRIGATION

The modern history of irrigation may be said to have begun in 1892 with
the Siam Canals, Land and Irrigation Company and the Rangsit system whereby
the developing company was to acquire rights to the land adjacent to its
canals.   The operation appears to have broken down through legal tangles
and lack of engineering foresight.   The next significant period was from

---

2 (cont'd) Leach argues therefore that though Sinhale was a hydraulic
society, it had no Oriental despot.   The second point is that the small
caste communities in reciprocal relationship with each other and subject
to a local baron were ecologically adapted to the environment and the
hydraulic technology.   Though Leach is very likely right on both counts,
this does not I think have much to do with the basic Wittfogel theory.
There is no particular reason why we should pay more attention to Wittfogel's hatred of 20th century despotism than to anybody else's.   His
historical insights however must be taken seriously and separated from
his political commitments.   Leach's main attack is on the latter.   On
the description and interpretation of the hydraulic society of Sinhale,
I doubt there would be great disagreement between them.

3 I have elsewhere argued that these historical events are partially
responsible for some aspects of Thai rural social structure (Wijeyewardene 1967:80; 1969:11-2).

1899 to 1909, during which Homan van der Heide established the basis for
the irrigation system of the southern part of the central plain.   His
programme was discontinued because of its heavy expense.   In 1913 Sir
Thomas Ward studied irrigation possibilities in Thailand and submitted
a report which appears to have been the basis for the remarkable expansion of irrigation; first, up to the outbreak of the Second World War,
and then again since 1949.   Contrary to Ward's advice, work began with
the Rangsit scheme in 1916 and was completed in 1922.   Irrigation was
not an immediate success.   The Rangsit system deprived Ayutthaya of
some of its water and there was no significant increase in rice exports
as a result of the scheme.   By the time of the 1932 revolution a good
part of Ward's programme had been implemented at a cost of about 34,000,000
baht.   The programme appeared to be running down however, and Thompson
notes that in 1932 appropriations did little more than meet maintenance
costs.   The process of running down continued till after the Second World
War (Thompson, 1967:514-20).

Revitalisation followed the FAO mission in 1947.   Table 4.1 gives
the area irrigated by works completed between 1907 and 1967.   In addition
to 1,445,500 hectares irrigated by operational works in 1967, a further
area of 117,760 hectares was irrigated from works which were then incom-
plete.   In the 60 years between 1907 and 1967 the area under irrigation
increased 66 times.   This may be compared with the expansion of agriculture and of population (Table 4.2).

Table 4.1:   Area irrigated by completed State
             irrigation works, excluding tanks,
             1907-1967 (thousand ha)

Year	Area	Year	Area
1907	21.9	1957	803.7
1924	130.7	1958	828.2
1931	344.3	1959	835.6
1936	355.5	1960	850.0
1941	362.6	1961	856.4
1949	375.0	1962	890.5
1950	612.9	1963	1352.4
1954	715.3	1964	1414.2
1955	758.9	1965	1426.0
1956	787.7	1967	1445.5

Source: National Statistical Office, 1967/9:
          195-6.

Table 4.2:   Expansion of agriculture and population, 1907-1965

Year	Total area planted (million ha)	Total rice area planted (million ha)	Population (million)
1907	n.a.	1.8[a]	n.a.
1911	n.a.	n.a.	8.3[b]
1919	n.a.	2.6[a]	9.2[b]
1929	n.a.	3.2[a]	11.5[b]
1937	n.a.	3.4	14.5[b]
1941	n.a.	4.0	n.a.
1947	n.a.	4.8	17.4[b]
1949	n.a.	5.3	19.1[c]
1950	6.3	5.5	19.6[c]
1954	6.5	5.6	22.1[c]
1955	6.8	5.8	22.8[c]
1956	7.1	6.0	23.4[c]
1957	6.4	5.1	24.1[c]
1958	7.2	5.8	24.9[c]
1959	7.6	6.1	25.6[c]
1960	7.8	5.9	26.3[b]
1961	8.2	6.2	27.2[c]
1962	8.7	6.7	28.0[c]
1963	9.0	6.6	28.8[c]
1964	9.1	6.5	29.7[c]
1965	9.3	6.5[d]	30.6[d]

Sources: Total area planted from Silcock, 1970:54.
Total rice area planted from Ministry of Agriculture, 1966:46-7.

a   Average over 10 years
b   Census (Caldwell, 1967:29)
c   Estimate (Ministry of Agriculture, 1966:178)
d   Silcock, 1970:54

These figures help us to approach, very tentatively, an assessment of the impact of irrigation on agricultural production.   My overall impression is that expenditure on irrigation has outstripped gains in productivity but the evidence for this is slight.   The proportion of the area under rice to total planted area has been falling in recent years, from 90 per cent in 1950 to slightly under 70 per cent in 1965.   We may assume from this that in the first decade of this century the total area under cultivation was about 1,900,000 hectares.   Between then and 1965 state irrigated land increased by about 6000 per cent, while the total area cultivated increased

by 400 per cent, the area under rice by 300 per cent and the population by
about 300 per cent.   In 1965 the area cultivated under state-aided irrigation (i.e. including People's irrigation and tanks) was just under 1,760,000
hectares - about 20 per cent of the total cultivated area.   The 1967
figure was 1,808,000 hectares (National Statistical Office, 1967-9:194).
In the National Economic Development Plan for 1961-66 irrigation was
allotted just over 2,135,000 baht out of budget appropriations and another
730,000,000 baht from foreign loans.   Total expenditure, from all sources,
was 32,657,900 baht (National Economic Development Board, 1964).

There are two separate issues involved here and they are not easy to
keep apart.   In the first place the success of the irrigation programme
may be judged by the degree to which agricultural development and productivity are commensurate with expenditure on the programme.   Whether the
programme is successful or not the growth of irrigation systems may or
may not lead to increasing bureaucratic (agro-managerial) control of the
economy and the polity.   The Wittfogel hypothesis is that the association
is positive.   The second issue only arises if the expenditure and effort
involved in the irrigation programme are disproportionate.   We are then
faced with explaining the continuance of the programme.   At this point
it is the second issue with which I am concerned.   The figures presented
in the preceding paragraph indicate that the rapid increase in land under
irrigation did not appreciably affect the expansion of land under cultivation.   Productivity is much more difficult to assess and I present the
following evidence with the comment that the total impact does not seem
to have been a dramatic one.

For many reasons the Thai government has restricted the uncontrolled
extension of agriculture by an overall policy of maintaining half of the
total land area under forest (Silcock, 1967:298;   1970:202).   Nevertheless expansion of rice land has kept pace with population growth.   This
is not unexpected in a country which does not show signs of great over-
population despite massive population increase.   However, increasing
irrigation facilities did not prevent substantial declines in average
yields of rice during the 1940s and early 1950s.   Though the figures
have picked up in recent years, yields are still 15 per cent below those
for the early decades of this century (Ministry of Agriculture, 1966:46-7).

The quite distinct movement away from rice cultivation to other crops is partly responsible.   In 1950 crops other than rice accounted for 11.9 per cent of total planted area; in 1965 the percentage had increased to 30.7 per cent (Silcock, 1970:54).   In 1951 the value of crops other than rice accounted for 38.9 per cent of the total, and 54.7 per cent in 1964. Between 1951 and 1964 the value of all crops increased by 75 per cent whereas the planted area increased by only 35.8 per cent.   Inflation does not account for all of the rise.   The price of rice was 16 per cent higher in 1964 than in 1951, but general fluctuations throughout the period suggest that this figure should be treated with caution and there is no doubt that an increase in productivity has taken place (Ministry of Agriculture, 1966).   The evidence then is mixed and the question needs much closer investigation.   There are however prima facie grounds to look for reasons other than the more obvious for the burgeoning of the irrigation programme.

My implication is that we have the growth of an agro-managerial bureaucracy.   True the numbers involved in the actual management of agriculture and waterworks may be small proportionately, but this is partly a consequence of technological differences of the 20th century. During the historical periods over which hydraulic societies developed, the maintenance of waterworks served not only agriculture but also transport and communication.   It is significant that roughly one-third of the allocations in the First National Economic Development Plan are for transport and communications.   Whatever Thailand may have been throughout her history, there is no doubt that today she is a hydraulic society; one, however, without an Oriental despot.   It is to the mechanisms and consequences of agro-managerial rule that we must now turn, that is, to the bureaucracy.

4.   THE BUREAUCRACY

The Thai bureaucracy is one of the best studied aspects of Thai society. Here I have space to refer to only a few main points.   Siffin (1966) and Riggs (1966:329 et al.,) have examined the stratified nature of the bureaucracy, drawn attention to the actual rulers of the country and the pyramidal nature of the bureaucracy through which it governs.   Skinner

(1958), among others, has documented the mechanisms by which the Thai elite
control the operations of Chinese industrial and commercial leaders.   Evers
and Silcock (1967) have suggested that the mobility which may have characterised Thai society in the past has gradually been eroded.   Historically
Wales (1965) gives the impression that Borom Trailokanath installed a
highly centralised bureaucracy in the 15th century.   Riggs, however, has
more recently suggested a rather different history for the Thai bureaucracy.
He has argued that Borom laid down the theory of administration which has
been accepted ever since but was nowhere near implemented until the reign
of Rama IV (Mongkut).   In theoretical terms, the kingship was balanced
between the Saivite ideology of the god-king and the Buddhist cakravartin
implementing and governed by the Dharmasastra.   Mongkut tipped the balance
in favour of the latter and laid the ideological basis for modern bureaucratic control.   The reforms of Rama V (Chulalongkorn) marked 'the shift
from a traditional, largely ceremonial regime to one in which decision-
making and the effective exercise of governmental powers dramatically
grew in importance' (Riggs, 1966:108).   The revolution of 1932 merely
legitimised the transference of this power from the monarchy to the bureaucracy.   It would be quite futile to argue that the major pre-occupation
of this bureaucracy is the construction and maintenance of hydraulic works.
Yet to the extent that the economy is basically agrarian, that the backbone
of this agrarian economy has come to depend on state financed irrigation,
that despite the persistent comments by foreign experts (e.g. FAO, 1948;
Silcock, 1970) both government and farmer consider the provision of
irrigation water a duty of the state, and that so much enterprise in
Thailand is either directly or indirectly state controlled, the Thai
bureaucracy is an agro-managerial bureaucracy.

I wish now to present evidence suggesting that the bureaucracy is to
be seen not as representative of all sections of the population or even of
a particular class, but rather that the bureaucracy is a class itself.
There are difficulties in deciding how many government servants (khaaraa-
tchakaan) there are in the country, though Siffin's estimate seems reasonable (Siffin, 1966:151, 273).   He gives the figure for civil employment
in 1962 as 240,000.   Riggs gives, for 1958, the figure of 350,000 'civil
and military officials of the Thai government' (Riggs, 1966:328).   Of

these 150,000 were in the armed forces under the Ministry of Defence.
Presumably Rigg's figures exclude employees of such enterprises as the
Tobacco Monopoly, Thai Airways and the Bank of Thailand.   Riggs estimates that in 1958 officials constituted 1.4 per cent of the population
of roughly 25,000,000.   A very rough check of the 1960 population census
figures for the 'economically active' allows an estimate of those engaged
in 'middle class occupations'.   Unfortunately the estimate excludes
industrial entrepreneurs, mining magnates and wealthy farmers.   However,
it is unlikely that this would put the middle and upper-middle class
figure significantly above the half-million mark, say, two per cent of the
population in 1960.   Hence it seems reasonable to estimate that about
three-quarters of the economically active middle and upper-middle class
population are officials of the Thai government.   This excludes 200,000
labourers and other non-status employees in government agencies and public
enterprises (Siffin, 1966:151).

In its official ideology, no doubt sincerely held, the bureaucracy
is concerned with national development and security.   National development means a strong and prosperous economy in which benefits will accrue
to all sections of the population.   The irrigation programme is the most
spectacular manifestation of this ideology.   But the government has also
attempted to direct agricultural expansion - balancing expansion against
conservation, discouraging the growth of tenancy and the fragmentation of
holdings.   These questions have recently been discussed by Silcock (1970).

Part of this policy deals with land tenure.   Thai land law is complicated, but we may simplify.   An individual may take out a title to
unused land (in areas approved by the government);   this title, known as
bai caung, gives the holder the right to clear and use the land within a
specified period.   This certificate is not transferable, except by inheritance.   When the land has been cleared and shows evidence of use, the
certificate is marked daj tham prajood laew ('use has been made of it')
and an estimate of boundaries and area is made;   this title is now
transferable.   Full land certificates are only issued when the area has
been fully surveyed, giving an ultimate form of title known as canoot.
In 1966 the total area for which such certificates had been issued was
2,160,000 hectares.   Since 1943 the average increase has been about
10,560 hectares per year, and in the 1960s about 16,000 per year (National

Statistical Office, 1966-9:199).   In the 1960s the increase in area
planted has averaged just under 320,000 hectares per year.

Clearly, by the standards Wittfogel has used, Thailand today has
strong private property.   Yet private property does not form a counter-
vailing power to the centralised government.   It appears that in practice, if not in ideology and in policy, there is a movement of landed
property into the hands of the bureaucracy and of the class which they
appear to dominate.[4]   Among peasants I have spoken to personally, there
is a clear belief that when land becomes available, those with access
to the District Land Offices have much better chances of acquiring it
than any farmer - except when a colonisation scheme is involved.   This
claim is borne out to some extent by the impression that most district
government officials appear to own scattered pieces of land, many of
which are not put to intensive use.   This is only an impression and
should be treated as such.   We may assume, however, that the system
favours (because it does not forbid) government officials acquiring
choice land.

5. NORTHERN THAILAND

The final section of this paper deals with a small People's irrigation
system in Northern Thailand and some of the effects on it of national
irrigation development.   It may appear that disproportionate space is
given to a description of the problems of this small group of farmers,
but it is necessary to identify some of the basic mechanisms through which
irrigation development is changing the social structure of 20th century
Thailand.   These involve questions of some theoretical and methodological

---

4 Douglas Miles drew attention, during the symposium, to the fact that
traditionally agro-managerial bureaucracies held little or no private
property in land.   This is an important point and if the theory of
hydraulic societies is to be applied seriously to the developing countries
this difference must be taken into account and explained.   I am also
grateful to Paul Alexander for pointing out that the bureaucratic dominance of developing societies is much more far-reaching than implied in
the control of hydraulic technology.   My argument in the paper however,
applies mainly to Thailand and merely suggests an approach to other areas.
It may also be useful to add here that in the district in which I lived
such enterprises as petrol sheds, eating houses, transport, the hire of
tractors, all tend to be largely controlled by government officials,
their spouses or retired officials.

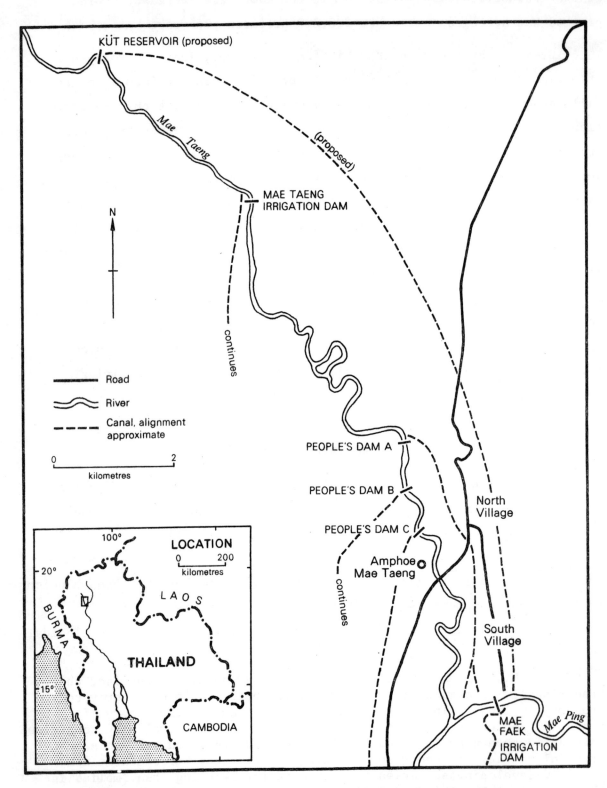

Fig. 4.1 Irrigation facilities around Amphoe Mae Taeng.

importance.   It is not sufficient to say that economic power at all
levels is shifting into the hands of the bureaucracy.   At some stage
one must show how it shifts and why it shifts.   It is with this in mind
that I now turn to South Village.

South Village lies in the Mae Taeng district of Chiang Mai province
about 40 kilometres north of the city just off the main road (Fig. 4.1).
Its present location is a consequence of the completion of the Mae Taek
irrigation dam in 1936.   There is now an all-weather road between the
Chiang Mai-Fang road and the irrigation works.   South Village straddles
this road.   In August 1966 the village had a population of 389 persons
in 86 households.

The economic basis of the village is not the Mae Faek irrigation
system (which waters fields on the other side of the river in San Sai
district), but the rice fields watered by the South Village People's
irrigation system.   This system serves an area of approximately 96 hectares, of which 64 are in the territory of South Village, and the balance
in the territory of North Village.   The latter lies on the main road, is
a small market and commercial centre and is the location for a Tobacco
Monopoly barn.   It is therefore no longer a mainly agricultural village.
The South Village wet-rice land neither wholly belongs to, nor is wholly
cultivated by, residents of the village.   Most cultivators are resident
in South Village; the rest come from North Village and three villages on
the right bank of the Mae Taeng.   The irrigation system consists of a
main canal roughly 3.5 km in length and a temporary dam across the Mae
Taeng (People's irrigation dam A in Fig. 4.1).   The dam forces the water
into the canal and theoretically that is all that has to be done.   In
fact maintenance makes many demands and work on the irrigation system is
by far the most onerous task of the cultivation year, so that state irrigation is a very substantial boon to the farmer even if productivity does
not increase.   Up to 1965 each cultivator spent about 30 days of each rice
cultivation season working on the irrigation system.

The South Village system is about 80 years old.   The area under
irrigation has been slowly extended and some minor extensions were still
going on in 1966.   It is reasonable to say, however, that the limits of
the system have been reached.   There were two larger systems in the area

up to 1965 (People's dams B and C in Fig. 4.1) which watered fields on
the right bank of the Mae Taeng and some way beyond the Mae Taeng-Mae
Ping junction.   These two systems have now (since 1965) been superseded
by the new Mae Taeng State irrigation system.

People's irrigation systems are loosely supervised by the Irrigation
Department.   This supervision becomes much tighter as incorporation into
the national system comes closer.   The day to day running of the South
Village system is in the hands of the farm operators.   Every man who gets
water from the system has an obligation to maintain the irrigation works.
The authority of the district administration may be used to enforce this
obligation.   The cultivators elect a headman to take charge of the system.
Once elected he remains in office until he resigns, is removed, or dies.
The South Village system also has a clerk and an assistant headman.   The
usual practice appears to be that an assistant is chosen from each village
served by the system.

Up to 1965 the South Village system appears to have worked extremely
successfully.   This is not to imply that the farmers were generally prosperous - average landholdings were small and tenancy was high.   Yet water
was more than adequate for the needs of all and average yields were high.
In spite of this there was a general feeling of despondency in 1966 and
many of the most successful owner cultivators were talking of selling and
moving elsewhere.   Within the space of little more than a year a system
which had worked with only minor disputes between landlord and tenant
appears to have acquired a deep malaise.   The whole affair is an extremely
minor one, but it does cast some light on the issues raised earlier.

Water is not uniformly available for all South Village fields.   The
lowest portions are part of the flood plain of the Mae Taeng and every few
years there is the risk of losing the whole crop in a flood.   In good
years however, the highest returns come from these portions.   In addition,
off-season vegetable crops do well.   The middle terrace is the safest
sector and is suitable for off-season crops such as tobacco.   The high
terrace gets sufficient water in good years, but there is always the risk
that insufficient water will spoil the main rice crop.   It is not used
for off-season crops to any significant extent.   Some of the newest fields
are on the high terrace.

In 1965 two main disputes occurred, as a result not only of the development of State irrigation in the area, but also of increasing winter cultivation and an exceptionally swollen river.   In that year, the Mae Taeng state irrigation scheme was serving 4,320 hectares (National Statistical Office, 1965:190), compared with a total of not more than 960 hectares watered by People's systems A, B and C in previous years. The building of the Mae Taeng dam just up-river from dam A reduced water levels at the latter;   and as dams B and C were no longer operating, levels below dam A also fell.   The 1965 season was characterised by numerous complaints about lack of water and excessive work on the system. The Irrigation Department also appears to have been worried about the scarcity of water, as it built a control gate in the canal a little way south of the dam.   Ironically, when heavy rains came later, a portion of the bank below dam A was washed away and the canal was breached;   this may have been due to the removal of dams B and C.   Whatever the cause, the result was that water in the irrigation system was maintained at service levels only after the Irrigation Department opened the control gate.   Even so, water had to be rationed by the headman, apparently at the request of the Department.   There were allegations that equity was not maintained.   The position was not helped by the flooding of the river over the lower fields and the almost immediate plague of caterpillars which followed.   Dissatisfaction culminated in a no-confidence move against the headman in April 1966.

In November 1965 there were more immediate issues.   There was fear that the winter crops would not have enough water.   As noted above, winter crops can only be grown on certain parts of the wet-rice land. It is the practice that a tenant may cultivate during the winter a part or all of his tenement without paying any extra rent.   Others pay rent. Many villagers who have no access to wet-rice land also cultivate during the winter and this is a substantial, if not crucial part of their liveli- hood.   Winter cultivation does not usually carry with it an obligation to work on the irrigation system.   The dispute centred on the repairs necessary for the system.   The cultivators/share-croppers argued that repairs would constitute a permanent improvement to the system and that they had no security of tenure, and that therefore repairs were the obligation of the owners.   Many cultivators also argued that they did

no winter cultivation anyway.   The owners said it was not their business
to work on the canal.   A compromise was suggested that the cultivators
and owners should share the obligation -- all the actual labour being done
by the cultivators but the owners paying for half of it.   The owners did
not agree;   one of their main reasons being an interesting status argument
that having given land to a tenant it was then inappropriate to pay him.
No compromise was reached.   At the end of December a further breach
occurred downstream from the Irrigation Department control gate.   The
entire canal was now below the level of the river and that winter the
irrigation system operated without a dam.

In April 1966, as the new season approached, the discontent of the
previous year came to a head with widespread allegations against the irrigation headman and his assistant.   However, a meeting held to discuss the
issue voted unanimously to express its confidence in these officials.   It
is useful to look briefly at the objective facts which gave rise to the
dissatisfaction.   On a near-complete crop return survey for 1964 and 1965
the returns in padi were, for 1964, 16,374 taang[5] and for 1965, 12,132
taang.   This is a reduction of 25 per cent.   For a population living in
very difficult circumstances this fall must have represented considerable
hardship.   The situation was made worse by the fact that the drop in
production was unevenly distributed.   Five residents of South Village
share-cropped wet-rice fields in the North Village section, which suffered
neither from floods nor from caterpillars.   Moreover, it did not seem to
be affected by water rationing.   Outputs from these fields rose from
1784 taang in 1964 to 1828 taang in 1965, an increase of 2.5 per cent.

Bad years have occurred before and there have been disputes about
the apportioning of work on the irrigation system.   In 1965-6 however,
all cultivators, both owners and tenants, gave the impression that some
sort of crisis had been reached.   They realised that once the plans for
State irrigation in the area were completed, many of their present problems would disappear - but that was many years in the future.   The
specific plans that would affect South Village were the construction of
the Küt reservoir (Fig. 4.1) and the digging of a feeder canal from the

_____
5   A taang is a northern measure of volume, reckoned by the villagers
to be roughly 30 litres;   to be distinguished from the thang which is
20 litres.

reservoir to supplement water provided by the Mae Faek dam for Amphoe San
Sai.   This canal would also irrigate South Village fields, and presumably
allow a considerable extent of upper terrace to be brought under cultivation.   All this gave prospects for a rosy future, but the problems of the
immediate present had first to be overcome.   The majority of cultivators
had little choice.   They were share-croppers and stood little chance of
getting contracts anywhere else.   Owners could easily find other tenants
if they gave up their tenancies.   Owner-cultivators were in a different
position: wisely or not, they could sell up and find themselves land
elsewhere.   In 1966 it seemed that the process had started.   One of the
most successful owner-cultivators in South Village had found a buyer and
was preparing to move when I left Thailand in August 1966.

     The movement of rural folk in Northern Thailand is nothing new.
South Village has traditionally absorbed migrants.   Its proximity to
forest makes swiddening possible, as well as such activities as timber
cutting and charcoal burning which cannot be carried on with impunity in
other areas.   There has apparently been a migratory drift northwards for
many years, largely it seems, as a consequence of population pressure on
rice land and more recently the result of irrigation expansion.   Very
often compensation for loss of land is said to have been insufficient to
allow similar or adequate land to be acquired in the same area.   Recent
migrants into the area (though not into South Village) appear to have
been in this position (cf. Kingshill, 1965:19).   Since the construction
of the Rangsit scheme, it has been reported that modern irrigation systems
have adversely affected traditional rice-farming communities (Thompson,
1967:518).   It would of course, be quite wrong to suggest that all loss
of land, sale of land and movement of agriculturalists into less favourable areas is a consequence of irrigation expansion.

     As far as the North is concerned both ecological and social factors
are responsible for a high level of movement.   Northern farms are small
by comparison with other areas of Thailand (Wijeyewardene, 1967:78).
This is a consequence of ecology and technology.   Because they are small
and because labour input is intensified, farming is more susceptible to
population pressure.   With an expanding population and the nature of
Thai inheritance, a limited resource such as wet-rice land is liable to
be divided into smaller and smaller holdings.   The only mechanism which

prevents holdings becoming uneconomic is the sale of land.   Most of the
land sold in South Village has gone to cultivators - but a substantial
portion in recent years has gone to one man, a reputedly wealthy ex-
teacher.   Because of his interest in the area, it is likely that since
1966 most land sold has gone to him.   This is only one individual operating in a restricted area, but it is the circumstances that are important.
In South Village the price of land has risen so that it is beyond the
reach of most cultivators.   In 1966 wet-rice land cost about 2500 baht
per _rai_ (US$751.20 per hectare).   With an expected return of 40 _taang_
of padi per _rai_ and a value of 10 baht per _taang_ this gives a return of
about seven per cent per annum.   Such land prices are not exorbitant,
but it is very difficult for a tenant farmer to raise that kind of money.
Consequently rice land must pass slowly into the hands of non-cultivators.
One of the immediate results of irrigation development is to hasten this
process.

To what extent has this process been unambiguously identified in
the South Village area, and what is its incidence in the rest of the
country?   I cannot answer the first question with absolute certainty.
The little evidence I have suggests that to some extent land is moving
into the hands, not necessarily of bureaucrats, but into a class which
is very heavily dominated by them.   The actual proportion may be very
small; but in a situation where the state will control more and more of
the most productive land through its control of irrigation, any movement
of land into the hands of those who control or work directly for the state
must, I think be considered significant.

This paper is not an attack on Thai irrigation policy, nor on the
Thai bureaucracy.   My concern has been to look at a largely unconsidered
aspect of a theory of political development, that is, the influence of
irrigation on the development of political systems.   In certain circumstances that effect may be overriden by other factors so that it becomes
insignificant.   As the theory of hydraulic society stands today, Thailand,
as well as many other countries, does not have the overriding factors
mentioned in the theory.   Looking at the history of irrigation in Thailand
has convinced me that the country today is much more a hydraulic society
than in the past.   I am less certain about the implications of this fact
for her socio-political present or future.

REFERENCES

Broman, Barry M., 1968. Prehistory and sociopolitical institutions of
        the Thai, unpublished (mimeo).

Caldwell, J.C., 1967. 'The demographic structure', in Silcock, 1967:27-64.

Coedes, G., 1966. The making of South East Asia, trans. from the French
        by H.M. Wright, Routledge and Kegan Paul, London.

Evers, H.D. and Silcock, T.H., 1967. 'Elites and selection', in Silcock,
        1967:84-104.

Food and Agricultural Organization, 1948. Report of the mission for Siam,
        Washington, D.C.

Kingshill, Konrad, 1965. Ku Daeng: the red tomb, revised edition,
        Bangkok Christian College, Bangkok.

Leach, E.R., 1954. Political systems of highland Burma, G. Bell and
        Sons, London.

Leach, E.R., 1959. 'Hydraulic society in Ceylon', Past and Present, 15,
        pp. 2-26.

Ministry of Agriculture, 1966. Agricultural statistics of Thailand 1964,
        Bangkok.

National Economic Development Board, 1964. The National Economic
        Development Plan 1961-1966: Second Phase 1964-1966, Bangkok.

National Statistical Office, 1965. Statistical yearbook, Bangkok.

National Statistical Office, 1967-9. Statistical yearbook, Bangkok.

Riggs, Fred W., 1966. Thailand: the modernization of a bureaucratic
        polity, East-West Center Press, Honolulu.

Siffin, William J., 1966. The Thai bureaucracy, East-West Center Press,
        Honolulu.

Silcock, T.H. (ed.) 1967. Thailand: social and economic studies in
        development, Australian National University Press, Canberra.

Silcock, T.H., 1970. The economic development of Thai agriculture,
        Australian National University Press, Canberra.

Skinner, G. William, 1958. Leadership and power in the Chinese community
        of Thailand, Cornell University Press, Ithaca.

Thompson, Virginia, 1967. Thailand: the new Siam, second edition,
        (original 1941), Paragon, New York.

Wales, H.G. Quaritch, 1965.   Ancient Siamese government and administration,
        (original 1937), Paragon, New York.

Wijeyewardene, G., 1967.   'Some aspects of rural life in Thailand', in
        Silcock, 1967:65-83.

Wijeyewardene, G., 1969.   'Taxation, inheritance and the structure of
        peasant communities: some thoughts on the manorial model',
        The Australian and New Zealand Journal of Sociology, 5,
        pp. 2-13.

Wittfogel, Karl, 1957.   Oriental despotism, Yale University Press, New
        Haven.

CHAPTER 5

THE POTENTIAL AND LIMITATIONS OF THAILAND'S
ENVIRONMENT FOR AGRICULTURAL PRODUCTION

M.J.T. Norman*

1. THE ENVIRONMENT

This paper reviews Thailand's present and potential agricultural production in relation to the advantages offered and restraints imposed by
the biological and physical environment of the kingdom.   To attempt a
thorough account of the agricultural potential of such a large and
environmentally variable country as Thailand in a short paper is clearly
impossible.   What follows is highly selective: emphasis has been placed
on crops or areas with potential for significant change, or with problems
demanding significant change.   There is also a personal bias: the
author is not familiar with southern Thailand nor with the major crops
grown there, and the agricultural production of this region is not dealt
with.

(i) Climate

     Most of Thailand experiences a tropical wet and dry or 'monsoon'
climate, with summer rainfall dominance; this is Aw in Trewartha's
classification (Trewartha, 1968).   The south, the west side of the
Peninsula and the eastern margin of the Gulf of Thailand (an area usually
included in the Centre for statistical purposes) show a similar pattern
but with higher rainfall and a shorter dry period.   On the other hand,
the east side of the Peninsula is subject to rain-bearing easterlies and
receives its maximum rainfall in early winter.   Mean monthly rainfall
data for selected sites are given in Table 5.1.

     The most important features of the rainfall pattern in relation to
agriculture are:-

Dr M.J.T. Norman is Professor of Agronomy in the University of Sydney.

Table 5.1: Monthly rainfall at selected stations (mm)

| | North | Northeast | Centre | South | | |
| | | | | E. Gulf | E. Penin. | W. Penin. |
	Chiang Mai (18°47'N)	Roi Et (16°03'N)	Chai Nat (15°15'N)	Chanthaburi (12°37'N)	Songkhla (7°13'N)	Phuket (7°58'N)
January	5	7	6	48	170	25
February	10	25	19	46	61	33
March	13	46	37	76	64	61
April	51	119	95	117	71	168
May	127	180	135	325	107	330
June	132	193	134	498	99	315
July	198	203	140	444	84	302
August	231	175	166	439	76	259
September	290	257	297	478	109	333
October	130	68	160	231	263	409
November	46	2	33	74	579	201
December	10	–	4	15	460	71
Total	1243	1275	1226	2791	2143	2507

Source: Chai Nat – Department of External Affairs, 1968.
Remainder – Nuttonson, 1963.

(a)   The natural division between the typical 'monsoon' environments
       with at least five consecutive dry months each with less than
       100 mm of rain, which include most of the Central, North and
       Northeast regions,and the southern environments, which approach
       the wet tropical Ar climate.   The former support an agriculture
       based almost wholly on seed-bearing annuals, while in the latter
       tree crops form a major component of agriculture.

(b)   The generally high rainfall even in the driest parts of the 'monsoon'
       zone.   None of the Central, North or Northeast rainfall stations
       listed by Nuttonson (1963) or in Thailand agricultural statistics
       (Ministry of Agriculture, 1966) receives less than 1000 mm a year.
       All have at least six consecutive months each with an average of
       at least 100 mm, and the general range of annual rainfall is from
       1100 to 1600 mm.   Hence there is no moisture limitation to annual
       cropping anywhere in Thailand.

(c)   The relatively low variability of annual rainfall. Table 5.2 gives
       a measure of variation for 20 selected rainfall stations, five in
       each region.   Mean annual deviation from the mean, over a period
       of 11 years, ranges from only 7 to 21 per cent.   The table also
       suggests that the variability of rainfall in the Northeast has been
       over-stressed.

       Temperature ranges are what one would expect in Aw and Ar climates
where there is no major altitudinal effect (Table 5.3).   With increasing
latitude and altitude there is a greater range between summer and winter
temperatures, but this does not exceed the diurnal range.   None of the
temperature differences between regions in the summer growing season is
of any agricultural significance, but regional differences in winter
temperature help determine to some degree the crops grown under irrigation
in the dry season.   More important, however, is the general fact that
winter temperatures are high enough to permit the growing of what are loosely
termed 'summer' crops, (e.g. tobacco, maize, peanuts, mungbeans) in all
areas where irrigation water is available.

(ii)   Soils and topography

       The soils of Thailand have been described and classified broadly by

Table 5.2:   Mean annual rainfall (mm) and mean deviation
             from the mean (%) for 20 rainfall stations
             (1955-1965).

Region and Station	Mean rainfall	Mean deviation from mean
NORTH		
Chiang Rai	1653	10.6
Chiang Mai	1186	11.6
Nan	1299	10.1
Uttaradit	1392	9.3
Lampang	1041	10.7
NORTHEAST		
Udon Thani	1457	7.6
Roi Et	1410	13.3
Ubon Ratchathani	1528	17.3
Nakhon Ratchasima	1216	11.0
Surin	1288	7.2
CENTRAL		
Nakhon Sawan	1144	13.7
Lop Buri	1379	12.2
Bangkok	1539	12.0
Nakhon Pathom	1243	21.3
Phetchaburi	1046	15.9
SOUTH		
Chumphon	2033	16.5
Songkhla	1985	13.8
Phuket	2024	18.4
Narathiwat	2581	14.0
Surat Thani	1703	16.0

Source: Ministry of Agriculture, 1966.

Pendleton (1962); more detailed studies of specific areas are available.
Topographic factors are of equal importance in determining agricultural
potential: this is particularly true in Thailand not merely because of
the large proportion of land of rugged relief, but also because of the
dependence upon irrigation in the flat areas.   The types of soil and topographic limitation differ from region to region.

(a)   The Central Plain

Major differences in soil physical properties and quite minor

Table 5.3: Mean monthly temperature at selected stations
(°C)

Region	North	Northeast	Centre	South
Station	Chiang Mai	Nakhon Ratchasima	Chai Nat	Phuket
Latitude	18°47'N	15°48'N	15°15'N	7°58'N
Altitude	314 m	171 m	15 m	10 m
January	21.4	23.9	25.0	27.5
February	23.2	26.9	27.7	28.1
March	25.9	29.1	30.0	28.6
April	28.3	29.9	31.2	28.6
May	28.6	29.1	30.6	28.0
June	27.9	28.7	29.4	27.9
July	27.4	28.3	28.9	27.6
August	27.0	28.1	28.5	27.6
September	26.9	27.6	28.1	26.8
October	26.1	26.7	27.7	27.0
November	24.6	25.2	26.3	27.1
December	21.9	23.1	24.0	27.2

Sources: Chai Nat - Department of External Affairs, 1968.
Remainder - Nuttonson, 1963.

differences in level, which govern the movement of flood, irrigation and drainage water, have a profound influence on the potential of the Central Plain area for cropping. Van der Kevie's classification (1969) into areas suitable for non-irrigated upland crops, for double cropping with rice and winter irrigated upland crops, for double cropping with rice only, and for single summer cropping with rice is a useful categorisation. Most soils are nitrogen-deficient and some are also phosphate-deficient. The acid-sulphate soils of the eastern plain present particular chemical problems.

(b)   The Northeast

In general, the sandy loams of the undulating upland areas between the shallow valleys are of low nutrient status and low waterholding capacity, though they have few topographic limitations to cultivation. The run-on areas in the valleys are dominated by more retentive clay soils, but there are major problems in water control.

(c)   The North

The main limitation in this region is topography.   The areas of
valley bottom soils, irrigated or with irrigation potential, are
very limited.   Agricultural expansion is largely determined by
the extent and topographic characteristics of the terrace lands
between the valley bottoms and the rugged montane regions (Chapman,
1967).

(d)   The South

This region (which includes the eastern margin of the Gulf) is of
great pedologic and topographic diversity, with well-distributed
loam and sandy soils.   Although the region is rugged, the ratio
of population to potentially cultivable land is substantially lower
than in the North.

2.   AGRICULTURAL HOLDINGS AND CROP PRODUCTION

In one sense a division of the total land area into 'farm holdings' and
the remainder has a more precise ecological meaning in Thailand than it
has, say, in Australia;   in another sense it has less.   In the virtual
absence of controlled paddock grazing of stock on land of varying degrees
of 'improvement', there is a sharp distinction between a holding, used
intensively for crop production, and the remainder.   On the other hand,
the statistics are often misleading, particularly in forest areas, because
a variable but significant proportion of the land classified as not being
in farm holdings is cropped, under shifting cultivation and without title.

Table 5.4 gives some of the characteristics of agricultural holdings
by regions.   The low percentage area in farm holdings in the North
reflects the rugged topography of the region and its constricted valley
bottoms.   The average area per farm holding in the North is also substantially smaller than in other regions.   Furthermore, the broad
statistical divisions mask the fact that, in the nine far northern provinces, the average farm holding is only 1.16 hectares (Ministry of
Agriculture, 1966).   This subregion and its problems have been analysed
in detail by Chapman (1967).   With these exceptions, however, the average
size of holding tends to range from two to five hectares and land area is
not a major limiting factor to family subsistence.

Table 5.4 also shows the effect of climate on the types of crop grown.   The percentage of farm holding area under tree crops in the 'monsoon' zone is low, but in the south, in the transition to the wet tropics, it is over 50 per cent.   Table 5.5 gives recent production data for 11 of the major field crops of Thailand.

Table 5.4:   The structure of farm holdings, by regions

	North	Northeast	Centre	South	Kingdom
Area in farm holdings (1000 ha)	2009	4227	3101	1812	11150
Area in farm holdings as % of total land area	11.8	24.8	29.9	25.8	21.7
Number of farm households (1000)	778	1220	723	493	3214
Area per farm household (ha)	2.58	3.46	4.29	3.67	3.47
Percentage of farm holding area					
(a) under crops other than tree crops	81.5	73.8	79.5	29.7	69.6
(b) under tree crops	3.6	2.1	7.9	52.5	12.2
(c) in pasture, fallow or woodland	14.9	24.1	12.6	17.8	18.2

Source: Ministry of Agriculture, 1966.

(i)   Rice

Thailand's national average yield of rice has been rising steadily since the mid-1950s, in spite of a steady increase in the area planted.[1] The current figure of 1600-1700 kg/ha is close to the average of the top ten tropical rice-producing nations, all of whom are growing local indica varieties with little or no fertiliser input.   Of the rice area of South and Southeast Asia, 92 per cent is still sown to such varieties (Anon., 1971).

1 See Silcock (1970:58-9) for data by regions from 1947.

Table 5.5: Production data for important field crops

	Year	Area (1000 ha)	Production (1000 tonnes)	Yield (100 kg/ha)
Rice (padi)	1966	6949	11975	17.2
	1967	5601	9595	17.1
	1968	6799	10895	16.0
	Mean	6450	10822	16.8
Maize	1966	590	1122	19.0
	1967	683	1242	18.2
	1968	670	1350	20.1
	Mean	648	1238	19.1
Cassava (undried)	1966	129	1892	147
	1967	124	1774	143
	1968	135	2000	148
	Mean	129	1889	146
Bananas[a] (excluding plantains)	1964	101	743	74
	1965	179	1173	66
	1966	182	1274	70
	Mean	154	1063	70
Peanuts (in shell)	1966	154	217	14.1
	1967	101	128	12.6
	1968	101	149	14.7
	Mean	119	165	13.8
Soybeans	1966	66	58	8.8
	1967	57	51	9.0
	1968	57	51	8.9
	Mean	60	53	8.9
Mungbeans[a] (all dry Phaseolus spp.)	1964	100	110	11.1
	1965	118	126	10.6
	1966	131	132	10.0
	Mean	116	123	10.6
Kenaf	1966	498	661	13.3
	1967	343	421	12.3
	1968	112	140	12.5
	Mean	318	407	12.7
Cotton (lint)	1966	79	30	3.8
	1967	88	27	3.1
	1968	81	30	3.7
	Mean	83	29	3.5
Tobacco (local and Virginia)	1966	83	880	10.6
	1967	62	700	11.4
	1968	83	900	10.8
	Mean	76	827	10.9
Sugarcane	1966	123	3829	310
	1967	124	4017	324
	1968	158	5200	329
	Mean	135	4349	321

Source: FAO, 1969.

a Data given for 1964-1966 because figures for 1967 and 1968 have the appearance of guesswork.

As yet the new developments in rice varieties initiated by the International Rice Research Institute in the Philippines have not had a substantial effect on commercial rice production in Thailand. A joint rice-breeding programme by the Rice Department (Ministry of Agriculture), Rockefeller, and Kasetsart University is operating at Bang Khen, but the first varieties from this source have only recently been named and released (Jackson, Panichapat and Awakul, 1969).

They are RD1, RD2, and RD3; RD1 and RD3 are non-glutinous varieties selected from crosses between IR8 and the Thai _indica_ variety Leuang Tawng. They combine the stiff straw, response to nitrogen and high yield potential of IR8 with the high quality of traditional Thai rice. RD2 is a glutinous variety originating from Gam Pai 15 and Taichung Native 1, the latter variety being from Taiwan. All are daylength-neutral and of medium maturity (120-130 days). It is also understood that the selection of an improved floating rice variety, suitable for the southern Central Plain region which is liable to deep and sudden flooding, is well advanced.

What could be the impact of these varieties on Thailand's rice production? We are not here concerned with the social and economic consequences of a local 'green revolution', though these will be far-reaching and incalculable, but with biological potential. Yield data from research stations are of little value, but a study made in Laguna province, Philippines, gives some indication of the likely increases in yield with the adoption of IRRI varieties and appropriate levels of fertilisation (International Rice Research Institute, 1968). The average yield of local varieties (92 farms) was 2320 kg/ha; the average yield of IR8 (106 farms) was 4490 kg/ha. With reference to Thailand's RD varieties, Jackson, Panichapat and Awakul suggest that '...rice growers can expect yield increases ranging from 50 to 100 per cent over the present varieties depending on the cultural conditions under which they are grown' (1969:91).

Regional yield data (Silcock, 1970:58-9) suggest the Central Plain and the Northern valleys are the most favourable regions for growing rice and that the Northeast is the least suitable (Table 5.6).

Table 5.6: Average rice yields by region, 1947-1964

Region	kg/ha
North	1894
Central	1662
South	1500
Northeast	1038

Source: Silcock, 1970:58-9.

The difference between North and Central may be partially due to inherent soil fertility differences, but it is also probable that the shortage of padi land in relation to population in the North encourages higher management inputs. The reduced yield in the Northeast and the South are related more to radiation and water supply.

Although rice is thought of as the cereal for the wet tropics, it would be more accurate to term it the only cereal of the wet tropics. The former appellation suggests that it is ecologically best adapted to a wet tropical climate, which is not the case. All four of the major rice-producing deltas of Southeast Asia - the Irrawaddy, the Chao Phraya, the Mekong and the Gulf of Tonkin - have Aw, not Ar, climates, and have at least five consecutive months each with less than 100 mm of rain. The advantages of the clear-cut dry season are twofold: harvesting is easier in the dry early winter, and the higher radiation associated with the fairly abrupt end of the rains (see Table 5.1) in October-November is physiologically advantageous. A major proportion of the yield of rice is contributed by photosynthesis after flowering, and a linear relation between yield and radiation in the last 60 days of growth has been established for IR8 (Owen, 1967). The wet season provides the water; the dry season provides adequate radiation at the critical time.

Given the appropriate radiation, the adequacy and reliability of water overwhelmingly influence rice yield. For this reason, extensive rice production in the Northeast is an ecological anomaly. The high variability of rice production in the region (both in the ratio of area harvested to area planted, and in yield per harvested hectare), and the resulting social and economic consequences, have given the agricultural potential of the Northeast an undeservedly poor reputation. Although all

areas in the region receive at least 1000 mm of rain, on free draining
soils of low fertility and with poor topography for impounding water
even 1100-1600 mm of rain does not provide a good environment for growing
rice.   The core of the problem is soil porosity coupled with the relatively early end of the rainy season.   However, given moderate fertiliser
applications and the appropriate crops, with a proportion of legumes in
the rotation, such an environment is a reasonably good one for subsistence
and cash crop agriculture.   Extensive regions in India and in sub-
Saharan Africa with a similar environment support high population
densities, but the types of crop grown are pearl millet, sorghum,
peanuts and cowpeas, all with a much lower water requirement than rice.
It was unfortunate that the Thai were already a rice-eating people by
the time they colonised the Northeast.

A reduction in rice-growing in the Northeast, if accompanied by
the development of other more dependable forms of crop production, would
represent an efficient reallocation of Thailand's resources.   There has
been, however, no reduction in the area sown to rice, though the figure
has remained relatively static from 1959 to 1965 (Silcock, 1970:58).

There are other ways of reducing the variability in rice production
and increasing average yield apart from contracting rice-growing to the
more favoured areas.   Improved water control and supply projects are outside the scope of this paper, but a partial agronomic solution, the
classic response to a situation of unreliable water supply, is to breed
varieties of a shorter maturation period.   A glutinous day-neutral
variety of 100 days maturity would be of great benefit to the region.
Even if yield potential (relative to RD1-3) had to be sacrificed to attain
this early maturity, this would be more than compensated for by the increased probability of having enough water to mature the crop.

(ii)   Other grains

The area planted to maize in Thailand has increased dramatically
over the past decade, largely owing to increases in the northern part of
the Central Plain under dryland conditions.   The economic spur has been
the strong export demand for coarse grains, particularly from Japan.   At
the same time yield has risen steadily, and the national average yield
is one of the highest among tropical nations.   It is, for example, almost

double that of India, Indonesia, Nigeria or Tanzania.   This is presumably
because in Thailand it is a commodity and not a subsistence crop and
there is little compulsion to grow it under poor conditions.

The basis of improved maize genotypes in Thailand is the group of
tropical varieties originally bred in Central America.   Further selection
has been made in Thailand and the current recommended variety is Improved
Guatemala P.B.5.   An intensive breeding programme is in progress at Pak
Chong with Rockefeller support, with special emphasis on pest and disease
resistance, since maize is grown largely as a wet-season upland crop.

Hybrid maize varieties from warm temperate regions like the United
States and Australia, though potentially capable of higher yields than
the current tropical synthetics, are more susceptible to pests and
diseases.   Furthermore, a decision was made to concentrate in Thailand
on true-breeding varieties, rather than hybrids, to simplify seed production.   However, workers at Chai Nat have found that typical Australian
and United States hybrids give very high yields in the dry season under
irrigation and heavy fertilisation (Department of External Affairs, 1968).

There is considerable scope for increased maize area, both as a wet
season upland crop and, in the Central Plain particularly, as a dry season
irrigated crop.   However, although research station data suggest the
possibility of much higher yields with adequate fertilisation, it is
difficult to visualise the national average yield increasing rapidly
beyond the present relatively high figure.   Even Taiwan, often a useful
pointer towards improved practices in underdeveloped countries, averaged
only 2480 kg/ha over the period 1966-68 (FAO, 1969).

Silcock (1970:86-7) lists the 10 provinces leading in maize production for 1951 and 1965.   In 1951, five out of the 10 were in the Northeast, the remainder being in the Central Plain.   By 1965, eight out of
the 10 were in the Central Plain (five in the northern part) and only one
was in the Northeast.   This represents a fairly rapid shift in production
to areas ecologically more suitable because of either greater rainfall
reliability, or soils with better water holding capacity.   Such a rapid
shift could only occur because maize is an opportunity cash crop and not
the basis of the farmer's subsistence and culture.

Sorghum is not at present an important crop in Thailand. However, it is more tolerant of intermittent within-season periods of moisture stress than maize, and varieties of shorter maturation period than those of tropical maize varieties are available. For these reasons it is more suitable than maize as a coarse grain crop for the Northeast and other areas of uncertain water supply. A breeding programme based on open-pollinated varieties of the Hegari type is in progress. The national average yield (c. 2000 kg/ha) is relatively high, again presumably a reflection of its status as a cash rather than a subsistence crop.

(iii) Oil and protein crops

This category includes peanuts, soybeans, mungbeans and sesame. They are all short-season annuals adapted to a 'monsoon' climate (though the adaptation of soybeans to the tropics is a relatively recent crop evolution). They may be grown in Thailand as wet-season upland unirrigated crops (i.e. in the North, Northeast and north Central regions), or as dry-season irrigated crops in association with wet-season rice, as in northern valleys. Quick-maturing varieties of mungbeans and sesame can also be sown as catch crops - for example, after rice, using residual moisture under lowland conditions, or in combination with peanuts or upland rice in two-crop wet-season unirrigated systems. Furthermore, three out of the four are legumes, eliminating the need for nitrogen fertiliser inputs. Finally, while they have an internal market they are also world market commodities currently in fairly strong demand. They are crops of great potential importance as components of any diversification programme.

There is little doubt that, for the reasons listed above, there is a large potential for expansion in these crops, linked with the potential for clearing further areas of land for wet-season dryland cropping and with the provision of irrigation water for winter cropping. Furthermore, their low fertiliser requirements, their versatility, and the existence of both local and export markets should make it relatively easy for the farmer to move into production without major outlay or major risk.

The area under soybeans (often grown as a vegetable) has increased from between 20,000 and 30,000 hectares before 1966 to 60,000 hectares in 1968. The mungbean area has quadrupled in the last decade from

approximately 30,000 to 130,000 hectares, the increase being almost
exclusively in the northern part of the Central Plain (Silcock, 1970:92).
The increase in peanut area has been less marked, but that of sesame
has doubled in four years, from 16,000 hectares in 1964 to 33,000 in
1968.

The standard soybean varieties Sojo 1, 2 and 3 were selected from
local material at Chiang Mai. A programme of introduction and selection
by the Department of Agriculture, with Japanese support, is in progress.
Higher yields may be obtained under irrigation in the dry season than
in the wet season, but shattering at maturity is more of a problem.
Hitherto, soybeans have not been an important crop in the tropics,
except in Indonesia, so yield comparisons are not particularly helpful.
Thailand's national average of about 900 kg/ha is about the same as
that of Nigeria, above that of Indonesia, but well below that of Taiwan
(1100-1400 kg/ha).

There are a number of good local varieties of peanuts in Thailand,
and new types have recently been imported. Selection is in progress
at Lampang, under the Thai-Australian Land Development Project. The
average Thailand yield (1200-1400 kg/ha) is high for the tropics, ranking
with that of Brazil and Indonesia and well above that of India and West
Africa. On the lighter Central Plain soils at Chai Nat, peanuts have
been very successful as a dry-season irrigated crop, as they are in the
northern valleys.

Both soybeans and peanuts have been subjected to modern crop improvement techniques (though more in temperate than in tropical regions):
mungbeans and sesame, on the other hand, are relatively unimproved crops.
Mungbean is a term loosely applied to at least two species of Phaseolus,
and within Thailand there is a very wide range of types. Selection
programmes are in progress at various centres, including both Lampang
and Chai Nat. There is also a range of sesame varieties which would
repay breeding and selection work. Both crops show harvesting deficiencies as they ripen over an extended period and tend to shatter.

(iv) Process field crops

The term 'process' has been used to designate those crops whose

primary product has to undergo some major form of processing before
marketing: examples are the crushing of sugarcane, the curing of tobacco
leaf, starch-extracting from cassava tubers, the ginning of seed cotton
and the retting of kenaf stems.   Because of the necessity for processing
in some type of factory, the growing and harvesting of such crops is
normally subjected to a degree of control to ensure a standard product
and a rational flow of material for processing.   Kenaf is the exception
here, since retting need not be done at a central point.

Thailand is the seventh largest tropical sugar producer in terms of
area, but because of its low average yield (only a little over 3000 kg/ha
raw sugar) total production is low.   Production is centred on provinces
flanking the Central Plain to the west, southwest and southeast.   Silcock
(1970:94-5) briefly summarises the economic vicissitudes of the industry
since the Second World War.

The best environment for sugarcane is a free-draining soil in a
region with a rainy season of some seven or eight months, dry weather
with high radiation for the remainder of the year, with supplementary
irrigation available during this period so that the accumulation of sugar
and the growth process can be manipulated.   The isthmus region between
the Central Plain and the South, which is partially subject to the early
winter easterlies and has in consequence a longer wet season, is probably
the most favourable area, and there have been recent increases in production in this region and the provinces immediately north of it (Wu, 1967 -
quoted by Silcock, 1970:95).   There is no reason, of course, why any
valley region in the monsoon zone of Thailand with well-drained soils and
a reliable supply of dry-season irrigation water could not be developed
for sugarcane, but water requirement is high and efficiency of irrigation
water use would have to be evaluated against that of short-season winter
crops.

Cassava is a source of subsistence carbohydrate, tapioca and, to a
growing extent, animal feed and industrial starch.   There is some production for local consumption in the South, but for historical reasons
commercial production is concentrated in the east Gulf region, with more
than half coming from the province of Chon Buri, where the original factories were set up (Silcock, 1970:93-4).   Thailand's national average

yield is high;   slightly less than that of Malaysia, but twice that of
Indonesia.

There is no ecological reason for such localisation of production.
There is a very wide range of maturity types in cassava adapted to Aw and
Ar climates with annual rainfalls ranging from 500-2000 mm.   Furthermore,
apart from the need for free drainage, cassava is undemanding in its soil
requirements and will produce a crop on soils of extremely low fertility.
Only the low winter temperatures of the North and Northeast would appear
to limit climatically its distribution.   As a producer of carbohydrate
per unit area it is unrivalled (Coursey and Haynes, 1970).

Thailand's area under cotton has been expanding steadily since
the mid 1950s, and is now about 80,000 hectares.   Much of the crop is grown
under dryland conditions in the north Central region.   The average yield
of about 350 kg/ha lint, although low by western standards, is as high as
any other major tropical producer with the exception of Mexico and the
Sudan, where it is grown largely under irrigation.   Cotton is also grown
as a dryland cash crop in the northern valleys, much of it on land of unsuitable topography.   It is hard to think of an annual crop that provides
better conditions for soil erosion.

The Department of Agriculture, with French assistance, has bred
medium-long staple varieties for Thailand;   Reba B50, which has been a
standard for some time, is being superseded.   One of the major joint
limitations to the production of maize and cotton is that some important
pests, e.g. Heliothis, are common to both crops.   Recent work at Chai
Nat is of interest: under irrigation in the winter (December-June), crops
of over 1000 kg/ha lint have been obtained experimentally using standard
United States upland varieties (R. Ferraris, pers.comm.).   Agronomically,
cotton is adapted to these conditions;   the main problem to be resolved
is the economics of insect control.   The trend in cotton production
throughout the developed world has been towards the stability and control
provided by irrigation;   it will be interesting to see whether the same
happens in Thailand.

Table 5.5 shows the precipitous decline in kenaf production from the
peak area of 498,000 hectares in 1966.   Recent events in Bangla Desh and

consequent disruption of the jute industry may revive kenaf growing, but we are not concerned here with economic forecasts. Although kenaf is more properly a subtropical crop, it provides a good short-season summer cash crop adapted to the free-draining soils of the Northeast, where 99 per cent of the kingdom's production is concentrated. Its major disadvantage is that it is exhaustive of soil nutrients. Doubts have been cast on the profitability of fertiliser application to kenaf (Silcock, 1970:80). The suggestions put forward later in this paper concerning cropping systems for the Northeast would go a long way towards increasing and stabilising yield per unit area without major fertiliser inputs.

(v)   Tree crops

It is not possible in an account of the agriculture of Thailand to ignore entirely rubber and coconuts. Thailand is the world's third largest producer of natural rubber, and is also an important copra producer. However, the kingdom has lagged behind its major competitors in the technology of growing both crops. This backwardness is associated primarily with the organisation of production into a large number of small holdings instead of in plantations, but the overriding factor in recent years has been the social instability of the far southern provinces in which the two crops are largely grown.

The pressure on land for food production in this region is not excessive. There are a number of areas into which rubber or coconut production could expand, and there is no doubt of the suitability of the climate for the crops. However, in the current social and political context, the biological potential of the far South for these or any other crops is very much a secondary factor in predicting how the region will develop.

3.   ANIMAL PRODUCTION IN THE NORTHEAST

The Northeast has for long been regarded as Thailand's problem area. It is difficult to maintain a stable crop economy based on subsistence rice for a dense population in a region of free-draining, relatively infertile soils, and where rainfall is insufficient for rice-growing without water

storage and control.   The emphasis in research and development projects
to alleviate this unbalanced situation has been largely directed towards
better water control to stabilise rice production, and towards diversification in annual cropping.

The Northeast is also the major region in Thailand for raising
cattle and buffalo.   In 1965 there were over 5,000,000 cattle and nearly
7,000,000 buffalo in Thailand (Ministry of Agriculture, 1966).   About
half the cattle and half the buffalo are in the Northeast, which produces
a surplus of animals, draft and meat, for other regions, particularly
the Central Plain and Bangkok.

Though farmers may raise both cattle and subsistence or cash crops,
there is little integration of the animal and crop enterprises.   Cattle
and buffalo are grazed in the secondary forest and savannah upland country;
they may benefit from some crop residues such as rice straw but there is
virtually no attempt at forage crop or sown pasture production.   Traditionally, cattle and buffalo are regarded by the farmer not merely as a
source of income but as a form of capital, to be built up in good times
and realised in poor times.   They are an economic buffer to the variability of crop production.   There are thus good reasons for encouraging
the development of mixed farms based on sown pastures if they are technically feasible.

Research and development studies with sown pasture species are being
undertaken by the Department of Land Development with New Zealand assistance.   It is clear from the work in progress that pastures established
on cleared upland and based on introduced pasture legumes are productive.
The absence of any reported complex nutrient deficiencies, the gentle
topography, the high rainfall of normal variability extending over at
least six summer months, makes the Northeast plateau a region of great
promise for sown legume pastures.   Certainly it is far more attractive
than the Cape York Peninsula or the Top End of the Northern Territory,
where land is being developed for pastures at an increasing rate.

The productivity of such pastures has not been widely tested, and
detailed regional studies could reveal complex limitations due to nutrient
deficiencies, soil water characteristics, or salinity.   However, except
in the zones of quartzitic and siliceous sandstone hills (Pendleton, 1962),

which could prove to have soils too shallow, and in zones subject to periodic flooding, there would seem to be no major environmental reason why most of the plateau could not grow productive pastures if the secondary forest were cleared and fertiliser applied.

The species likely to prove successful are the legumes Townsville stylo (Stylosanthes humilis), stylo (Stylosanthes guyanensis) and Siratro (Phaseolus atropurpureus).   There is a wide range of grasses from the genera Panicum, Chloris, Setaria and Urochloa that might find a place as companion species.   The recent introduction to Australia of a number of new perennial species of Stylosanthes from Central and South America could well provide further adapted legumes for the region.

However, unless there has been a recent change in outlook, it appears that the problems of annual crop production and cattle production from pastures are being tackled separately with little regard for the immense advantages that could accrue from a combined approach.   There is every reason to believe that sown pastures based on introduced pasture legumes could be readily integrated in a ley system with annual cropping in such an environment.   For example, at Katherine, in the Northern Territory, ley systems of Townsville stylo pastures and periodic annual crops (Fisher and Phillips, 1970) have been evolved and are being put into practice commercially in a 900 mm rainfall zone with a seven month dry season.

In a sense a ley system involving the alternation of one or more years of sown pasture with one or two years of annual arable cropping represents a controlled and substantially more productive form of shifting cultivation.   Instead of an extremely slow restoration of surface soil fertility by the cycling of plant nutrients through a forest recovering from slash-and-burn, the leguminous sown pasture is building up soil nitrogen (at rates of 50-100 kg/ha/year) for use by the subsequent annual crops, and at the same time fattening cattle and buffalo.   The primary additional capital input is the bulldozer to get rid of most of the trees and scrub, and the additional annual input is fertiliser.

The year-round animal carrying capacity even of good sown pastures on cleared land in such a rainfall zone is unlikely to exceed two full-grown beast equivalents per hectare.   Hence the scale of farm, in terms

of area and capital input, required to provide a living from cattle alone
is well beyond the normal range of Thai peasant agriculture.   On the
other hand, integration of cash and subsistence cropping with cattle or
buffalo raising on sown pastures would permit the setting up of a much
larger number of economically stable farms per unit land area or per
unit of land clearance capital.   The mixed farmer would be content to
derive only part of his income from livestock: his animals would be the
capital buffer, the pastures on which they grazed the biological buffer,
against the potential variability of the annual crop component of his
system.   The annual crops could be both subsistence, (e.g. upland rice,
peanuts, mungbeans) or cash crops (e.g. kenaf).   It is unlikely that
lowland rice could be incorporated into such a rotation because of the
need to confine it to areas topographically suitable for the impounding
of water.

4.   THAILAND'S CROPPING SYSTEMS

There are three elements of annual cropping systems in Thailand: wet-
season lowland rice cropping, wet-season non-irrigated upland cropping,
and dry-season irrigated cropping.   Rice may figure as a crop in all
three elements.

The three components may be found singly, or in all combinations
except one (there are no systems based solely on dry-season irrigated
crop production which do not also include wet-season rice growing).
Thus a major proportion of the Central Plain farmers grow only wet-
season lowland rice; tribesmen of the northern hills grow only non-
irrigated upland crops; farmers in the valleys favoured with a good dry-
season water supply (e.g. the Ping) grow rice and dry-season irrigated
crops; farmers in valleys without dry-season water may grow wet-season
rice and also upland non-irrigated crops under shifting cultivation (as
in the Nan and other northern valleys); and some may develop systems
involving all three components.

In what way have recent technical factors influenced, or are likely
to influence, these three components in Thailand's agricultural structure?
Since the end of the Second World War, there have been five technical

developments exerting major pressures, or potentially able to exert such pressures.   They are:-

(a)   The developments in river control engineering works, particularly the Chai Nat-Yanhee-Phasom complex in the Chao Phraya basin.

(b)   The massive efforts in tropical crop breeding, exemplified by the work of the International Rice Research Institute.

(c)   Improvements in fertiliser manufacture technology, particularly in relation to nitrogen.

(d)   The development of heavy equipment for land clearance and earth-moving.

(e)   Advances in tropical pasture technology (particularly in Australia).

In respect of the first element in Thai cropping systems, wet-season lowland rice, the most striking change has been the increase in the yield potential for tropical rice consequent upon the efforts of IRRI.   To-gether with application of adequate fertiliser and good water, pest and insect control, this could well result in a doubling of rice yields throughout tropical rice-growing areas.   The effect of this on world rice production and hence on export prices is already causing Thailand great concern.   These are detrimental secondary effects, but we must remember that for a large number of Thai farmers living in the poorer areas of the North and Northeast such a change would be an unmixed blessing.   In the North, for example, it could relieve many of the valley-dwellers who have been forced to become supplementary shifting cultivators of much of the need for this relatively inefficient form of cropping at some distance from their homes.   In the Northeast it would permit the contraction of rice-growing to those fields topographically and edaphically more suited to a stable yield year in and year out.   It would seem important to Thailand to bring the technological 'package' of improved rice varieties, fertiliser, insecticide and herbicide to these groups of farmers first.

The factor having the greatest impact on the dry-season irrigated cropping is, of course, the major developments in water control engineering, and it is in the middle and upper areas of the Central Plain that the greatest changes are likely.   However, 'second cropping' cannot be grafted on to a well-established system of wet-season rice growing, even at the technical

level, merely by the provision of dry-season irrigation water.   Where
the second crops are legumes such as peanuts or mungbeans the annual
nutrient cycle will be little changed, or if changed will be for the
better.   On the other hand, if maize or other non-leguminous crops are
to be grown the nitrogen economy of the system is completely transformed.
In addition, there is, as always, the possibility of salinisation of the
surface soils when upland irrigated crops are grown.   Long-term fertility and salinity studies are needed in all areas formerly growing only
rice but likely to develop towards second cropping;   some have already
been initiated at Chai Nat (Department of External Affairs, 1970).   It
must also be borne in mind that the development of dry-season irrigated
cropping is not necessarily dependent upon large-scale engineering.   As
Chapman (1969) points out in relation to the Nan valley, there are also
opportunities for small scale pumping from rivers and from field wells.

Whatever the means of irrigation, however, the prospects of
agricultural expansion and diversification through 'second cropping'
are good.   The winter climate throughout 'monsoon' Thailand is warm
enough to grow a very wide range of what are normally regarded as 'summer'
crops.   These include maize, cotton, soybeans, peanuts, sesame and others.
The inputs required will be higher than when they are grown as unirrigated
wet-season crops, but output should be higher and more dependable.   Some
of the major expansion may come from the extension of second cropping to
soils formerly considered to be suitable only for rice-growing, as in
the Chai Nat area (Department of External Affairs, 1968, 1970).

One of the greatest potential problems of Thailand's agriculture
is that associated with the third cropping system element,   wet-season
unirrigated cropping.   It is likely to prove particularly acute in
Northern Thailand, as a result of critical pressure on land resources
through sharp increases in population.   There are two main production
systems involved: upland cropping alone, under shifting cultivation, and
upland cropping associated with lowland rice production, where the upland
crops may be grown under conditions which may range from shifting cultivation to what is virtually an irregular permanent-field system.

Upland cropping alone under shifting cultivation is confined mainly
to middle and high altitudes in hilly country (500-1500 m) and is practised

largely by non-Thai peoples.   Examples are the Lua and Karen systems of
upland rice-growing and the Meo maize-opium system (Land Development Department,
1970).   Upland cropping supplementary to lowland rice production is confined to lower altitudes, in valley terrace lands within walking distance
of the lowland villages.   It is with the latter system that the Thai-
Australian Land Development Project is concerned.

In both instances, the problem is essentially the same; that of
contraction of the fallow period in the shifting cultivation rotation
below the point giving a sustained average crop yield and a stable
ecological situation.   Characteristics of this instability include declining crop yield through nutrient rundown, soil erosion, and invasion
by Imperata cylindrica, which renders land useless for further cropping.

The approach in the Thai-Australian Land Development pilot project
is to use heavy equipment to clear secondary forest land for permanent
unirrigated upland crop production.   The major technical problem is that
of maintaining chemical and physical soil stability under annual cropping.
Provided adequate soil conservation measures are taken it should prove
possible to control erosion if clearing is confined to relatively level
sites, but the maintenance of soil organic matter and available nutrient
status on these sandy loam or loamy upland soils under continuous cultivation must still be regarded as a problem (McGarity and Charley, 1969;
Charley and McGarity, 1970).   In the Northeast, where a tradition of
animal production exists, there is, as we have seen, the possibility of
achieving stability through ley-farming systems with short-term pastures
for cattle and buffalo raising alternating with annual cropping.   Whether
such a system would be economically and socially feasible elsewhere
deserves further study.   Certainly the inclusion of pasture in upland
crop rotations would give far greater flexibility and stability.

In the high-altitude areas the technical problem is even more acute
because of the absence of level land.   The choice may develop into one
of shifting the people to lower altitudes or of shifting soil in major
earthmoving schemes to create terraced arable land in favoured locations
(e.g. small high valleys).   The change from shifting cultivation to
permanent cultivation on terraces has been going on steadily for a long

time in hilly regions of Southeast Asia under pressure of increasing
population (Spencer, 1966); the challenge should not prove too great
now that we have soil conservation technology and the bulldozer.

In conclusion, although it may appear that attention has been concentrated at times more upon the limitations than on the potential of
Thailand's agricultural environment, it must be recalled that the kingdom
has a climatic pattern, particularly with respect to rainfall, that gives
great scope for diversified agricultural production.   Though Thailand
has not been blessed with soils of high fertility, soil nutrients
represent that component of the crop's environment that can most readily
be rectified.   Furthermore, the potential of the physical environment
for diversified cropping is capable of being realised because overall
population density is still sufficiently low to allow flexibility in
the development of new production systems.

REFERENCES

Anon., 1971.   'Behind the rice market changes', Ceres, 4, No.2, pp. 15-17.

Chapman, E.C., 1967.   'An appraisal of recent agricultural changes in the
        northern valleys of Thailand', 6th Academic Conference, Agri-
        cultural Economics Society of Thailand, Kasetsart University,
        Bangkok (mimeo).

Chapman, E.C., 1969.   'The Thai-Australian Land Development Project,
        1967-69: an outline of its socio-economic setting, field
        operations and results', ANZAAS, Section 21, Adelaide (mimeo).

Charley, J.L. and McGarity, J.W., 1970.   'Problems of nutrient rundown
        and structural changes on soils used for shifting cultivation...',
        in Land Development Department, 1970:358-82.

Coursey, D.G. and Haynes, P.H., 1970.   'Root crops and their potential as
        food for the tropics', World Crops, 22, pp. 261-5.

Department of External Afffairs, Australia, 1968.   Thai-Australian Chao
        Phya Research Project. First Report to the Ministry of
        Agriculture of the Kingdom of Thailand, Part A, Canberra.

Department of External Affairs, Australia, 1970.   Thai-Australian Chao
        Phya Research Project. Second Report to the Ministry of
        Agriculture of the Kingdom of Thailand, Part A, Canberra.

Fisher, M.J. and Phillips, L.J., 1970.   'The establishment and yield of
        fodder crops grown in Townsville stylo (Stylosanthes humilis)
        leys at Katherine, N.T.', Australian Journal of Experimental
        Agriculture and Animal Husbandry, 10, pp. 755-62.

Food and Agriculture Organisation, 1969.   Production Year Book, 23, Rome.

International Rice Research Institute, 1968.   Annual Report for 1967.
        Los Banos.

Jackson, B.R., Panichapat, W., and Awakul, S., 1969.   'Breeding perfor-
        mance and characteristics of dwarf photoperiod non-sensitive
        rice varieties for Thailand', Thai Journal of Agricultural
        Science, 2, pp. 83-92.

Kunstadter, P. and Chapman, E.C., 1970.   'Shifting cultivation and
        economic development in northern Thailand', Seminar at Chiang
        Mai, January 1970 (mimeo).

Land Development Department, 1970.   Proceedings of a seminar on shifting
        cultivation and economic development in northern Thailand,
        Bangkok.

McGarity, J.W. and Charley, J.C., 1969.   'Soil types and nutrient problems
        on the middle terrace of the Nan valley in northern Thailand',
        ANZAAS, Section 21, Adelaide (mimeo).

Ministry of Agriculture, Thailand, 1966.   Thailand agricultural
            statistics,   Bulletin produced for First Asian Inter-
            national Trade Fair, Bangkok.

Nuttonson, M.Y., 1963.   'The physical environment and agriculture of
            Thailand', American Institute of Crop Ecology, Washington,
            D.C. Study No. 27.

Owen, P.C., 1967.   'The climate of the sub-coastal plains of Northern
            Australia. A comparison with those of other rice-growing
            areas', Journal of the Australian Institute of Agricul-
            tural Science, 33, 247-253.

Pendleton, R.L., 1962.   Thailand: aspects of land and life, American
            Geographical Society Handbook, Duell, Sloan and Pearce,
            New York.

Silcock, T.H., 1970.   The economic development of Thai agriculture,
            Australian National University Press, Canberra.

Spencer, J.E., 1966.   'Shifting cultivation in southeastern Asia',
            University of California Publications in Geography,
            Volume 19.

Trewartha, G.T., 1968.   An introduction to climate, McGraw Hill, New
            York (4th edn).

Van der Kevie, W., 1969.   'A summary of soil survey data in the Central
            Plain and discussion of potential land use', Seminar on
            Technical Aspects of the Development of the Central Plains,
            Chai Nat (mimeo).

Wu, H.S., 1967.   Report and project for rationalisation and modernisation
            of Thailand sugar industry, Bangkok (quoted by Silcock, 1970).

CHAPTER 6

IRRIGATED AGRICULTURE IN THE CENTRAL PLAIN OF THAILAND

Philip Judd*

1. INTRODUCTION

The Central Plain is the most important agricultural region in Thailand.
By comparison with other areas, it is well watered, is reasonably fertile
and has good access to markets through the road systems and waterways
connecting it to Bangkok.   For many years it has supported a rice mono-
culture based on wet season monsoon rains and the flood waters of the
Chao Phraya river system.   It is the major area of surplus rice production and supplies both domestic and overseas markets.

The main problems restricting production in the past have been
lack of water control in the wet season and lack of water in the dry
season.   Because of its strategic position and importance to the
economy, efforts have been made since the late 19th century to improve
water control and stabilise wet season rice production.   In the post-
war period these efforts have been expanded to include water storage
and hydro-electric power production which has made dry season irrigated
cropping and crop diversification possible.   The overall development
programme, the Greater Chao Phraya Basin Development Project, is one
of the larger and more important development projects being undertaken
by the Kingdom of Thailand.

At present, Thailand is facing economic difficulties which are
related to uncertain markets and prices for rice, an imbalance in overseas trading and a rapid increase in population.   In the agricultural
sector the current five-year economic development plan calls for an
increase in agricultural production, and diversification to reduce
reliance on rice as a major source of revenue.   In the past, these

---

* Mr Judd was Leader of the Thai-Australia Research Project, Chai Nat,
until 1971.   He is now a private consultant on irrigation development
projects.

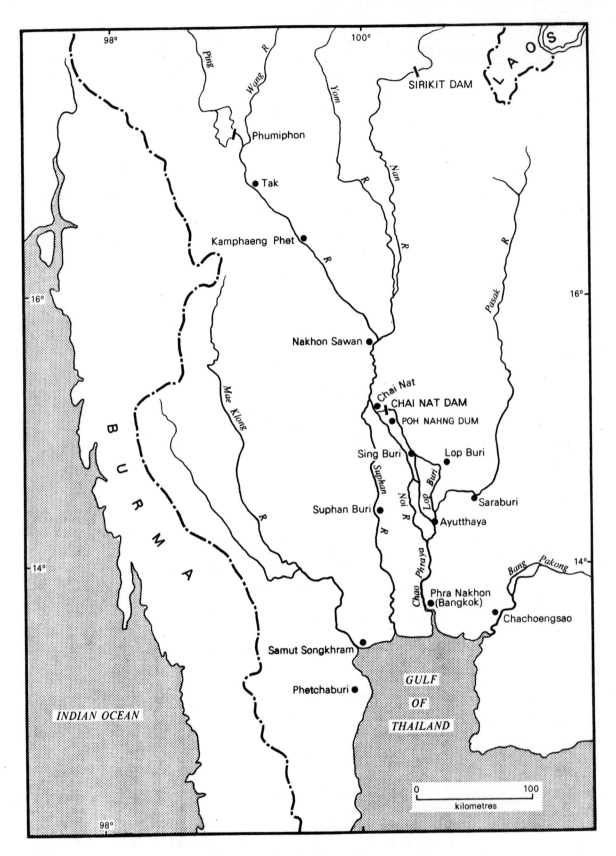

Fig. 6.1 Sketch map of the Chao Phraya river system.

objectives have been largely met by opening up new land, but Welsch
(1971) points out that opportunities for this type of development are
rapidly declining.   In the near future agricultural production targets
will need to be met by the development and application of new technology and revised government policies in existing agricultural areas.

2.   THE CENTRAL PLAIN

Since the Central Plain is strategically situated, and considerable
investment has already been made in water control, this paper examines
its potential role in contributing towards national objectives.   A
brief description of the area and the Greater Chao Phraya Development
Project is followed by a discussion of some of the technical difficulties associated with irrigated cropping and some of the problems
arising from the programme.   The extent to which production in the
Plain can be increased and diversified and areas where efforts should
be concentrated are indicated.

(i)   Location and drainage

It is important to differentiate between the administrative Central
region of Thailand and the Central Plain.   Whereas the Central region
extends from Uttaradit Province in the north to Prachuap Khiri Khan in
the south, the Central Plain, or lower delta of the Chao Phraya river
system, extends from Chai Nat province to the Gulf of Thailand, or from
15°20'N to 13°30'N (Fig. 6.1).   The area covers about 37,400 square km
or a little over seven per cent of the country.   The Central Plain is
fed from the north by the Ping, Wang, Yom and Nan rivers.   These
converge at Nakhon Sawan to form the Chao Phraya river system, which is
the largest and most important river system within Thailand.   The total
catchment of the system is estimated at 169,500 square km.

Immediately south of Nakhon Sawan the valley of the Chao Phraya river
is restricted to the east and west by elevated land but widens in Chai Nat
province to form the apex of the lower delta.   Once the river enters the
delta its course divides into four main channels, the Chao Phraya proper,

Table 6.1: Long term climatic data for Chai Nat, Thailand

Observations	Rainfall mm 1931-60	No. of Rainy days 1931-60	Max.Temp. oC 1951-60	Min.Temp. oC 1951-64	Av.Temp. oC 1951-60	Av% Rel.Hum. 1951-60
January	6.4	0.2	32.4	17.5	25.0	66.8
February	19.3	0.9	34.5	20.7	27.7	65.4
March	37.2	1.5	36.6	23.3	30.0	64.6
April	95.0	3.5	37.5	24.9	31.2	65.1
May	134.9	5.1	36.3	24.8	30.6	71.1
June	133.5	7.2	34.4	24.4	29.4	75.3
July	139.4	8.1	33.8	24.0	28.9	77.4
August	165.9	9.0	32.9	23.9	28.5	83.3
September	297.4	11.4	32.2	24.3	28.1	82.4
October	160.0	6.6	31.7	23.6	27.7	79.8
November	33.4	2.1	31.6	21.1	26.3	74.6
December	3.5	0.1	30.8	17.5	24.0	69.4
Year	1225.9	55.7	33.7	22.5	28.1	72.9

Source: Data from Division of Climatology, Meteorological Department, 1965: Mimeo notes, Feb. 4, B.E. 2508, Office of the Prime Minister, Bangkok.

the Suphan, the Noi and the Lop Buri rivers.   The Suphan flows into the
Gulf of Thailand at Samut Sakhon, but the other branches rejoin the Chao
Phraya before it reaches Ayutthaya where the Pa Sak river, the main tri-
butary, also joins the system.   Below Ayutthaya, the main stream flows
south, meanders through Bangkok, and empties into the Gulf at Samut
Prakan.   The delta is extended to the east by the flood plain of the
Bang Pakong river and to the west by the flood plains of the Mae Klong
and Phetchaburi rivers.

The delta is very flat, with a grade of 1:10,000 in the centre.
The northern part has been shaped by rivers to form a series of north-
south levees with depressions between.   Since the discharge capacity
of the Chao Phraya is too small to carry the wet season flow, the system
floods; water collects in the depressions and moves slowly south.   In
the southern portion, where there are depressions below the 4.5 m M.S.L.
contour, and where high tides in the Gulf slow down natural drainage,
water accumulates to a depth of 2-3 m in some areas.

(ii) Climate

The Central Plain is a relatively homogeneous climatological unit
with a tropical savannah climate characterised by a distinct wet season
(May-October) and a distinct dry season (November-April).   Long term
climatological data for Chai Nat are set out in Table 6.1.   A more
detailed description of the climatic conditions may be found in Nuttonson
(1963).

The climate is suitable for the production of a wide range of crops
throughout the year, given adequate water supplies, but warm humid conditions in the wet season lead to a high incidence of plant disease and
insect attack.   In the absence of irrigation or water control measures,
rainfall is the main factor affecting production.   In the dry season,
rainfall is inadequate to support crop production, and in the wet season
the level of rice production is largely determined by rainfall and the
size of the flood.   The average rainfall during the rice growing season
is about 900 mm, whereas the requirements of the short duration varieties
approximate 1000 mm and are much higher for the late maturing native
varieties (140-180 day duration) grown in the deep water areas.   The

annual flood plays an important role in making up the deficit.   Of course,
in the years of heavy rainfall and large floods, crops in the lower areas
may be wiped out, or yields considerably reduced.   Over the long term,
lack of adequate rainfall at critical times restricts yields of wet season
rice.

(iii) Soils and land use

The Central Plain has been the subject of several soil investigations.
Van der Kevie (1970) has recently reviewed available soil survey data and
the following summary is based on his paper.   He divides the Plain into
seven broad soil landscapes based on age, parent material, soil development,
physiography, vegetation and cultivation pattern (see Table 6.2 and Fig.
6.2).   Only the more important groups will be referred to here.

Table 6.2:   Soils of the Central Plain

Group	Area '000 ha.	Percentage of area
1. Soils on recent river alluvium	192	9
2. Soils on semi-recent river alluvium	352	17
3. Soils on marls and marl derived clays	110	5
4. Soils on brackish water alluvium	800	39
5. Soils on marine alluvium	368	17
6. Soils on low terraces and alluvial fans	272	13

Source: van der Kevie, 1970.

(a)   Soils on marine deposits, covering about 368,000 hectares, occur in
a band along the coast.   These are mostly fertile non-acid soils, with
the exception of a narrow band of saline soils adjacent to the coast.
They have poor drainage characteristics and are best suited to rice production.   Most of these soils are in fact used for wet season rice, with
a limited area of dry season rice grown by pumping water from the canals.
In Thon Buri, Nakhon Chaisi, Damnoen Saduak, and Chachoengsao districts,
farmers have developed a 'rung-type' system of irrigation and successfully produce fruit and vegetables on raised beds for the Bangkok market.
Deep ditches between the beds provide drainage and a source of water for
irrigation.   Silt accumulating in the channels is used to topdress the
beds.

(b)   Soils on brackish water alluvium lie in a broad band between Bangkok and Ayutthaya, the earlier capital of Siam.   These cover about 800,000 hectares and constitute the major soil group in the Plain.   They are predominantly heavy clay acid-sulphate soils, characterised by an acid subsoil high in sulphides which, if exposed to air, oxidise to produce extremely acid non-fertile conditions which are not suitable for crop production.   These soils are only suitable for rice in their natural condition.

(c)   Soils on recent and semi-recent alluvia are found in the northern portion of the Plain, between Ayutthaya and Chai Nat, and offer some potential for crop diversification and dry season irrigation cropping. They cover an area of about 544,000 hectares.   Although the semi-recent soils are older and are situated on slightly higher land between the Suphan and Noi rivers, from a land use point of view the semi-recent and recent alluvia are similar.   On both alluvia five toposequential soil series can be recognised.   In general terms, there are two soil series on the old river levees which are relatively well drained and well suited to dry season irrigated crop production.   Then follows a transitional zone on the levee slopes where the soils are generally heavier silty clays and have poor drainage characteristics.   These merge into the heavier flood plain silt clays with poor drainage, and finally into the swamp soils in the depressions which rarely dry out.

The majority of the good well-drained levee soils have been utilised already for housing, and for tree and vegetable production, since they are free from flooding in most years.   The transitional soils are normally used for transplanted rice, since there is reasonable water control on the slopes.   The flood plain soils are used for broadcast rice.

(iv) Traditional agricultural system

In the wet season, over 90 per cent of the Central Plain is planted to long grained indica rice, since flooding largely precludes the use of alternative crops.   There is a wide range of native rice varieties which vary in quality, time to maturity, straw length and ability to withstand rising flood waters.   This allows selection to suit local circumstances and the choice of variety and method of planting are largely determined by the depth and duration of flood waters.   On higher ground, or where

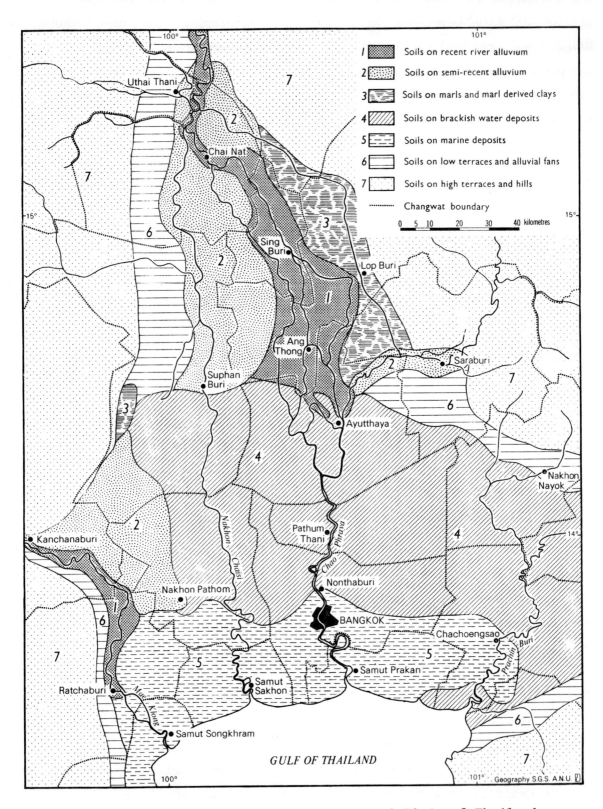

Fig. 6.2 Soil landscapes in the Central Plain of Thailand
          (after van der Kevie, 1970).

water control is adequate, the shorter-maturing varieties are used and
are normally transplanted in the period June-August.   In lower areas, or
where water control is poor, the rice is normally broadcast on ploughed
ground prior to the heavy monsoon rains, in May-June.   Varieties are
selected whose maturity will correspond with the time that flood waters
can be expected to recede.

In the deep-water areas, 'floating' rice varieties are used.   These
will grow up to 5 cm a day to cope with rising flood water and can withstand depths of 2-3 m.   While reliable statistics are not available, it
appears that about 50 per cent of the plain is under broadcast
rice.

There is little use of fertiliser, agricultural chemicals or
fertiliser-responsive varieties in much of the area, and most of the
field work is still carried out by buffalo and hand labour.   The only
concessions to modern technology are the use of tractors for initial
ploughing, and spot-spraying with phenoxy acetic herbicides to control
weeds in broadcast rice.

Harvesting commences in late November or early December in the
better drained transplanted areas, and continues through to late January
in the deep water areas.   All rice is cut by hand, bundled and carried
to the homestead for threshing.   Threshing is still carried out by
walking a buffalo, or running a tractor over the rice on a prepared
earthen threshing floor.   The rough rice is winnowed by hand or with a
locally manufactured winnower, and the bulk of it is delivered to the
rice mill or merchant.   Enough is normally retained for seed and domestic
consumption.

Traditionally, the dry season has been a time for fishing and fes-
tivities.   Until recently, lack of water precluded any cropping activity
except in areas adjacent to waterways and borrowpits.   Here, the more
enterprising people pump water for a second crop of rice, or raise vegetables.   In some areas an attempt is made to obtain a quick cash crop
in the period March-June by planting with the 'mango rains' which precede
the monsoon.   However, only a small percentage of the plain is cropped
in the dry season.

Surveys carried out by the Department of Land Development in five provinces in the Central Plain (Land Development Department, 1965) showed that about 41 per cent of the farmers were landowners, 29 per cent were tenants, and 27 per cent were part-owners who rented more land than they owned.   Farm size fell largely within the range 3.20 - 6.24 hectares. While the situation appears fairly stable, the report emphasised the relatively harsh and insecure tenancy terms and indicated that there was little prospect for the tenant farmer to become a landowner.   Incomes were also low, especially among tenant farmers, and there was little incentive for them to invest in farm and crop improvement.   Yields of rice by zone are shown in Figure 6.3, based on data computed by Fukui (1968).   These largely reflect the absence of new technology and also the effect of water control and land tenure.   For example, the poor yields in the Ayutthaya area can largely be attributed to poor water control and a high percentage of tenant farmers.

Apart from low yields, the farmer has faced a relatively low and fluctuating return for his rice.   While the marketing system for rice is well developed, the farmer has little bargaining power, the rather poor standard of milling leads to excess wastage, and until recently the imposition of the export tax or rice premium has kept the domestic price of rice at an unrealistically low level.

In summary, wet season rice production, which is still the main source of income for the rural community in the Central Plain, has been a relatively high-risk, low-profit-margin enterprise.   The farmers have responded by adopting a low input-low risk-low output approach.

3.   THE GREATER CHAO PHRAYA BASIN DEVELOPMENT PROJECT

It is against the background outlined above that attempts are being made to increase and diversify agricultural production, and to raise farm income, through the implementation of the Greater Chao Phraya Basin Development Project.

(i)   Brief history

Water control was recognised as the basic requirement for increasing and stabilising wet season rice production in the late 19th century.

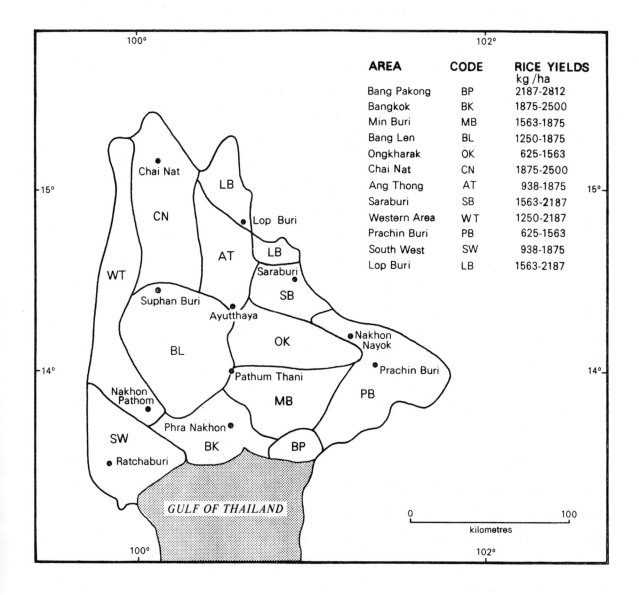

Fig. 6.3 Wet season rice yields by zone, Central Plain of Thailand
          (after Fukui, 1968).

His proposal was accepted, and what has now developed into the Greater
Chao Phraya Development Project was initiated.   An Irrigation Department was set up in 1914, and the first water control project was established on the Pa Sak river in the period 1915-1924.   By 1950, 700,000
hectares were served by a reasonable canal system, although flood control
and water supply were far from satisfactory.

In 1949, the Royal Irrigation Department (RID) prepared a proposal
for the construction of the Chai Nat Diversion Dam (RID, 1949), originally
proposed by van der Heide.   The main purpose of the dam was to raise the
river level at Chai Nat and to spread flood waters more equably over the
plain through existing waterways and additional distribution canals.
This scheme was approved and the dam was completed in 1957 with a
US$18,000,000 loan from the International Bank for Reconstruction and
Development (IBRD).   Water distribution canals were completed in 1964.
Since this was not a water storage dam, it did not have much effect on
the seasonal flow of water and could not supply much water for dry season
irrigation.   The increasing demand for power, and the need to further
improve water control, led to proposals for the Yanhee or Bhumiphol Dam,
the Phasom or Sirikit Dam, and the Ditches and Dykes Project (RID, 1961,
1962, 1964).   These, together with the Chai Nat Diversion Dam, constitute
the major water control and distribution systems under the development
programme (Figs 6.1 and 6.4).

The Bhumiphol Dam, situated at Tak on the Ping river, was designed
as a multi-purpose project to store water, generate power and provide
water for irrigation throughout the year.   The project was completed in
1964 with the assistance of a US$66,000,000 loan from IBRD.   Although
a multi-purpose project, its first objectives were power generation and
improved flood control.   It could not support an appreciable area of
dry season irrigation, nor alleviate flood problems in the Nan river valley.
Consequently, plans were pushed ahead to construct the Sirikit Dam on the
Nan river.   The main objectives of this project are to improve dry season
water supply to the potential dry season irrigation areas in the Central
Plain and Nan valley, to reduce the risk of flood damage, and to generate
power. This dam is currently being constructed with the assistance of an IBR

loan of US$26,000,000 and will be completed by 1973.   The combined
'active water storage' and generating capacity of the two dams will
be 16.2 x 10^8 cubic m and 1,160,000 kw respectively.

The Ditches and Dykes Project was initiated in 1962 with the
assistance of a US$5,600,000 loan.   Its purposes were the improvement
of water distribution on 800,000 hectares in the northern portion of the
Plain, the construction of 'feeder' roads, and the establishment of
research and extension services to assist the farmers to master the
techniques of irrigated cropping,   The proposals envisaged up to
100,000 hectares of dry season irrigated upland crops such as peanuts,
soya beans and mung bean, as opposed to the lowland crop, rice.

(ii)   Agencies responsible for the development programme

Two ministries carry the main responsibility for the development
programme - the Ministry of National Development and the Ministry of
Agriculture.   The Ministry of Interior is involved to a lesser extent
through local government at the provincial level, and the Ministry of
Economic Affairs is involved with marketing and price support for produce.
A list of participating agencies is shown in Table 6.3.

The main agencies are the Royal Irrigation Department and the Ministry of Agriculture.   The Royal Irrigation Department is responsible for
feasibility studies, design, construction, operation and maintenance of
all irrigation and drainage works.   It has received technical assistance
from the United States Bureau of Reclamation and from the Food and Agriculture Organization (FAO);   it is currently employing Dutch consultants
to improve water distribution, transport and drainage systems, with a
view to improving facilities to allow better water control and dry season
irrigated cropping.   It has recently established a 700 hectare Pilot
Land Consolidation project on the better soils lying between the Noi and
Suphan rivers, to develop land for year-round irrigated cropping.

The Ministry of Agriculture has overall responsibility for agricultural research and extension.   Its main effort has been the establishment
of a Central Region Agricultural Centre at Chai Nat, adjacent to the
diversion dam.   Formerly called the Chao Phraya Research Project, it was
set up in 1966 specifically to investigate problems of introducing dry

Table 6.3: Technical agencies participating in the
development programme

Agency	Function
Ministry of National Development	
Royal Irrigation Department	Construction, operation, maintenance of irrigation development works
Netherlands Engineering consultants	Consultants to RID on irrigation development and land consolidation
Department of Land Development	Soil survey, land use, land tenure
FAO	Advisors, soil survey, land classification
Land Department	Cadastral survey, land titles
Department Land Co-operatives	Promotion of development through multi-purpose farm co-operatives
Chinese Technical Mission	Advisors to Dept. Land Co-operatives
Ministry of Agriculture	
Under Secretary's Department	Co-ordination and administration of Chai Nat Centre and agricultural development activities
Rice Department	Research and development of rice
Agriculture Department	Research and development, upland crops
Agricultural Economics Division	Development planning, marketing, farm management, cost of production
Department of Livestock	Research and development of livestock and fodder production
Department of Fisheries	Research, development, freshwater fish
Department of Forestry	Research, development, silviculture
Australian Colombo Plan Team	Advisors on development, research and training, Chai Nat Agricultural Centre
UNDP Soil Fertility Project	Regional assessment, fertiliser requirements
Rockefeller Foundation	Advisors, corn, sorghum, rice breeding
Kasetsart University	Co-operative projects with other government departments
Rockefeller Foundation	Advisor, Agricultural Economics
Applied Scientific Research Council	Co-operative projects with government agencies, e.g. Chai Nat research projects.

season irrigated cropping into the plain, by using water from the storage
dams.   This project has been supported by the Australian Government
through the Colombo Plan since 1966-67.

A basic research team comprising a crop agronomist, soil chemist,
and soil physicist has been assisting with the development of the research
centre and the research programme, and at the same time training Thai
counterpart staff to take over the programme.   In 1969 a Farm Projects
advisor was appointed to the team to assist with the evaluation of research results on a 50-hectare farmers' project at Poh Nahng Dum, 25 km
south of Chai Nat.   In addition to providing technical advisors, the
Australian Government has donated specific items of equipment, and awards
Colombo Plan scholarships to promising counterpart staff for more advanced
training in Australia.   The project is given technical support by an
honorary Commonwealth Scientific and Industrial Research Organization
advisory committee.   Much of the technical discussion on agricultural
aspects of the development programme is based on research carried out
by Thai and Australian personnel at the Chai Nat Agricultural Centre
(Department of External Affairs, 1969, 1970; Ministry of Agriculture,
1970).

4.   TECHNICAL ASPECTS OF INCREASING AND DIVERSIFYING PRODUCTION IN THE WET SEASON

(i)   Drainage and water control

The amounts of water received in the catchment area of the Chao Phraya
river system are so large that the completion of the Sirikit Dam, while
reducing flood levels, will not solve wet season drainage problems.   The
Dutch consultants (RID, 1970a) report that it will still be necessary to
divert flood waters into the irrigation system, regardless of farmers'
requirements.   With the exception of a limited area of higher land,
farmers will not be able to take water and drain it off their land as
required, and the lower areas will still fill with water.   Because of the
large quantities of water involved, and the limited discharge capacity of
the river system, they suggest that the only practical solution to providing proper water control throughout the area would be the construction
of a large canal to take water from the northern section of the plain

directly to the Gulf.   They point out that this would involve heavy
investment and require careful planning.

On the credit side, water control and drainage measures at present
being taken should enable a greater percentage of farmers to obtain irrigation water in the early part of the wet season, when rainfall is least
reliable, and also to reduce crop losses due to excessive flooding.   However, as most of the plain will continue to be inundated for the greater
part of the wet season, there is little scope for diversification, and
rice will continue to be the major wet season crop.

(ii)   Prospects for more efficient rice production

In examining the prospects for more efficient rice production, one
must separate the broadcast rice areas with poor water control, and the
transplanted areas with reasonable water control, as their problems and
potentials are different.   In the transplanted areas, the most spectacular break-through in the past five years has been the development of
two non-photosensitive hybrid varieties bred by the Rice Department at
Bang Khen (Jackson et al., 1969).   The hybrids, RDI and RD3, based on
IR8 and Leuang Tawng, a local long grained non-photosensitive Thai
variety, are short strawed, nitrogen responsive and have good grain
characteristics acceptable to the Thai market.   They have resistance
to the green leaf hopper (Nephotettis bipunctus F.), and the 'tungro'
or yellow-orange virus which in the past has seriously reduced the yield
of native varieties in some years.   They mature within a 120-130 day
period and are well suited to a year-round cropping programme.   Given
adequate water supplies and water control, it would be technically possible to grow three crops per year.

Rice research work at Chai Nat has focussed on the agronomy of
the new varieties, and to date most of the results obtained are favourable (Department of External Affairs, 1969, 1970; Ministry of Agriculture, 1970).   Good yields have been obtained regardless of the date of
planting, although the highest yields are obtained with March-April
planting.

Linear responses to nitrogen can be expected up to an application
of about 80 kg N per hectare.   Under reasonable management conditions,
yields of 5000-6000 kg per hectare are obtained consistently both on the

Research Centre and by farmers in the Poh Nahng Dum Farmers' Project area. This is about double the yield obtained by farmers using native varieties and methods, and is in general agreement with the data of Kluen et al. (1969), who compared new and old varieties at seven representative sites throughout the Central Plain.

Weed control is not a major problem if the new varieties are transplanted and proper attention is given to land preparation and water control. As with all rice varieties, stem borer may reduce yields appreciably, especially in the dry season when the area of rice available for insect attack is restricted, but this problem can be controlled economically with B.H.C. granules broadcast into the rice field.

Plant breeders are not satisfied with the disease resistance of the new varieties, but at Chai Nat the only diseases of economic importance recorded to date are bacterial leaf streak and bacterial blight. These occur predominantly on the wet season crop grown under high levels of nitrogen. Recent results indicate that the incidence of the disease may be reduced by transplanting younger seedlings, which are less vulnerable to disease attack, since there is less root and top damage during planting.

Research to find less labour intensive methods of planting the new varieties has given promising results. Chauviroj et al. (1969) report that seeded and broadcast rice may give yields which are comparable to or higher than transplanted rice. However, more work is required on the problems of land grading, water control and weed control before new techniques can be introduced commercially.

While the varieties and technology are available to double rice yields and increase production efficiency, it must be stressed that the adoption of these techniques is only possible in areas where water control is good. No reliable data are available with regard to the area of the plain that could benefit, and this is obviously one topic requiring study.

In the broadcast rice areas there are no immediate prospects of markedly increasing rice yields commercially. However, rice breeders are currently working on the improvement of 'floating rice' varieties (Yantasast et al., 1970) and attempting to breed stem elongation characteristics into improved varieties. This work shows promise.

In the deep water areas, depth of water and water movement pose problems in terms of applying fertiliser, insecticide and weedicide, while management practices normally used with a high yielding variety may not apply. Research to develop improved management techniques for these areas is needed so that the full benefit of the new varieties being bred can be realised.

In summary, from a technical point of view, the potential for crop diversification in the wet season is poor, but there are good prospects of increasing rice yields and improving the efficiency of production immediately, in the better drained transplanted areas. The prospects of improving yield and efficiency in the broadcast areas are promising, provided more research effort is put into management techniques for the new varieties being developed.

5.   TECHNICAL ASPECTS OF INCREASING AND DIVERSIFYING CROP PRODUCTION IN THE DRY SEASON

(i)   Water supply

The quality of the Chao Phraya river water is excellent, and imposes no limitations on the types of crop that can be grown under irrigation in the dry season. The limitations are the total amount of water available and the reliability of the distribution system and both have restricted irrigation development until recently.

The distribution system was originally designed to distribute flood waters for the wet season rice crop by continuous flows. This poses several technical problems if the system is to be used for intermittent irrigation of dry season irrigated crops (FAO, 1968; RID, 1968). More regulating structures are required and modified methods of distribution need to be introduced to ensure reliability of supply. Partly because of the unreliability of dry season water supply, farmers have not maintained the ditches and dykes installed by the Royal Irrigation Department, and have made little attempt to extend water supplies to individual farms. The wide distribution of irrigated areas has led to water wastage and has increased problems of control. In fairness to those concerned, it was pointed out (FAO, 1968) that only about US$138 per hectare had then been invested in irrigation works in the northern section of the plain, whereas experience in other countries indicated that a minimum of $250 per hectare was required to install an efficient system.

To add to these problems, there was a shortage of water until 1970, due to a run of dry seasons, competition between agriculture and power generation requirements, and the need to release water from the Chai Nat Diversion Dam to control salinity in the lower reaches of the Chao Phraya. The need for salinity control led to a breakdown of the gravity irrigation system on several occasions. With the completion of the Sirikit Dam, adequate water should be available to irrigate 200,000-300,000 hectares, but further work will be required to bring the distribution system up to standard.

The exact amounts of water that will be available for irrigation when the Sirikit Dam comes into operation are still not determined, but the Royal Irrigation Department has a phased programme to upgrade the distribution system in the northern section of the plain to provide a gravity supply to 200,000 hectares by 1975.

(ii) Availability of soils

As already indicated, dry season irrigation will be largely restricted to the semi-recent and recent alluvial soils in the northern portion of the plain. Van der Kevie (1970) reports that most of these soils are well suited to irrigated rice grown in the dry season, except for some of the levee soils. However, only the soils on the levees and slopes show potential for irrigated upland crops. These amount to an area of about 257,000 hectares, but a high percentage of the levee soils are either already utilised for housing or other purposes, or cannot be readily irrigated by gravity. In practice, most of the dry season irrigation will be restricted to the heavier, less well drained silt clays on the slopes. An independent land classification by the Royal Irrigation Department (1970b) indicated that only 140,000 hectares could be rated as having a potential for growing upland crops, thus limiting the scope for diversification in the dry season.

(iii) Suitability of the slope soils for upland crops

The Chai Nat Agricultural Centre is situated on recent alluvium,

most of which is fairly typical of the slope or transitional soils
lying between the levee soils and the soils of the flood plains. They
may have slightly poorer drainage characteristics than their counterparts on the semi-recent alluvium, but there are no marked differences.
From experience to date, they are ideal for dry season irrigated rice
but pose management problems for upland crops because of their poor
physical properties (Department of External Affairs, 1969, 1970). They
have poor structure, which makes good seed bed preparation difficult and
restricts the intake of irrigation water. Further, many of them have a
heavy subsoil with low permeability within 30 cm of the surface, creating
water logging which seriously restricts the free downward drainage of
excess irrigation water and rainfall. A high correlation between
permeability of the subsoil and corn yield shows the former to be the
major physical soil factor affecting upland crop yields.

Finally, these soils are highly variable in terms of textural change
through the profile and drainage characteristics, over quite small distances. This makes it difficult to assess accurately the total area
suited to upland crops, and necessitates detailed soil surveys to determine desirable cropping patterns within an irrigation project area.

It is a long term and difficult task to achieve permanent improvements in the physical conditions of these soils, especially when soil
management practices for the wet season rice crop, e.g. wet cultivation
and puddling, are contrary to the basic rules for improving physical
conditions. A number of techniques are under test at Chai Nat, but it
is unlikely that any will prove spectacular or offer a rapid or easy
method of improving the soil.

The immediate solution lies in a high standard of water management.
Here techniques developed at Chai Nat have proved successful. They
involve careful grading to a slope of 0.10 - 0.15 per cent, the use of
crop ridges spaced at 75 cm, ponding of the water in the furrows to achieve
adequate water penetration, followed by rapid drainage to remove excess
surface water, and a 7-10 day irrigation cycle. The application of this
system to small peasant farmers at reasonable cost calls for co-operative
farm development to allow land clearing, land grading, the installation
of access roads and a farm irrigation and drainage system. Estimates
based on the Poh Nahng Dum Farmers' Project and the Dutch Land Consolidation

Project indicate a total development cost of about US$250 per hectare, using large machinery and local contract rates.

It is unfortunate that a less costly and less sophisticated answer is not available for upland crop production on these soils. However, experience with the farmers' project has demonstrated that farmers are capable of handling the relatively sophisticated planting and water management techniques, and that increased farm production, following development, could service a development loan (Judd et al., 1971).

On the well drained levee soils, the traditional methods of ploughing land and broadcasting seed, or planting seed in the wet season rice stubble, can give good results. While these simple low input techniques are better adapted to the local farming scene, they can only be applied successfully to a relatively small percentage of the potential irrigation area. Attempts to grow upland crops on the heavier soils on the fringes of the flood plain usually result in low yields, even when good soil and water management techniques are used. Further, there is evidence to suggest that intermittent irrigation and upland crops bring salts to the surface.

(iv) Soil fertility and nutrient requirements

At Chai Nat, no responses have been recorded to phosphate, potassium or trace elements on rice or upland crops. Nitrogen is the immediate nutrient requirement and research efforts have been largely focussed on this element.

Studies on form, rate and method of application on irrigated upland crops have shown that sulphate of ammonia is the most efficient carrier, and that banding all the fertiliser in the side of the crop ridge at planting is the best method of application. Similar studies on the new varieties of rice have shown little difference between urea and sulphate of ammonia as carriers. Deep placement or incorporation of fertiliser into the soil prior to transplanting, and splitting application between planting and primordia initiation, have given the best yield responses and nitrogen recoveries.

Linear yield responses are obtained with rice, hybrid corn and sorghum up to an application of about 100 kg N per hectare. Economic analysis of data from the Chai Nat Centre indicates that 90 kg N per hectare is close to an optimal application. Bearing in mind seasonal variations, falling rice prices and the management factor, analyses of longer term farm data are likely to give a lower figure, e.g. 60–70 kg N per hectare.

Preliminary studies of crop sequences indicate that there is little or no carry-over of applied nitrogen from one crop to the next, so in a non-legume rotation it would be necessary to apply the prescribed amount of nitrogen to each crop. Unfortunately, nitrogen costs US$0.37 per kg in Thailand, which is about twice the world price, due to protection of a rather inefficient local industry. Further, the ratio of nitrogen cost to crop price is also unfavourable, being about 7:1 for corn and 10:1 for rice. Under these circumstances, it is essential to have a reliable irrigation and drainage system and a good standard of management to minimise risks, and to utilise legumes and native sources of nitrogen where possible.

The prospects of using legumes in the dry season in rotation with wet season are good. Soybean, mungbean (Phaseolus aureus) and peanut are well adapted, nodulate well without inoculation, and are capable of fixing up to about 100 kg N per hectare. However, the extent to which they could reduce the need for applied nitrogen in a rice-legume rotation has still to be established. With regard to other natural sources of nitrogen, it has been found that unfertilised native rice varieties have consistently produced 2000 kg of padi per hectare – and removed about 40 kg N per hectare for many years without any sign of yields or of fertility declining. Only about 12 kg of this nitrogen can be accounted for, and it appears that 28 kg/ha is being contributed from unknown sources such as non-symbiotic nitrogen fixation.

Another interesting feature is that unfertilised dry season corn only takes up 25 kg N per hectare compared to 40–50 kg N hectare for irrigated rice grown on the same soil and in the same period. This again suggests that non-symbiotic nitrogen fixation could be an important feature of rice production, and that nitrogen transformation processes may be more

Table 6.4: Crops with potential for dry season production

Crop	Variety	Time of planting	Crop duration days	Method of planting	Fertiliser requirement kg/ha	Potential yields kg/ha	Gross[a] returns, US\$/ha
Rice	R.D.1 R.D.3	Feb.-Mar.	125	Transplant	60-80 N	5000 to 6000	200 to 300
Peanut	Local or Tainan 6	Jan.	110-120	75 cm ridge	Nil	2000 to 2500	280 to 375
Mungbean	Local	Jan.	90-100	75 cm ridge	Nil	1200 to 2000	150 to 250
Soybean	Sojo II	Jan.-Feb.	90-100	75 cm ridge	Nil	1500 to 2500	188 to 312
Grain corn	Hybrid -	Jan.	100	75 cm ridge	80-100 N	5000 to 6000	200 to 240
	Local -					4000 to 5000	160 to 200
Sweet corn	Hawaiian sugar	Jan.	70	75 cm ridge	80-100 N	-	300 to 450
Sorghum	Texas 610	Jan.	90-100	75 cm ridge	80-100 N	4000 to 6000	120 to 180
Sesame	Local	Jan.	90-100	75 cm ridge	50 N	300 to 500	55 to 95

a   Based on average farm gate prices.

efficient under submerged conditions.   Whatever the explanation, it
means that a farmer is getting about 30 kg of free nitrogen per hectare
every time he grows a rice crop.   This warrants serious consideration
when nitrogen prices are so high.

Long term experiments are required to determine the impact of
more intensive crop production and alternative cropping systems on soil
fertility.   The majority of the experiments on crop systems at Chai Nat
have been running for only two or three years.   In a comparison of rice-
fallow, rice-rice, rice-corn and rice-legume rotations, there was no
evidence of a decline in fertility after two years of continuous cropping.   On the other hand, in an experiment where three rice crops are
being grown per year under high levels of nitrogen, with total annual
production approaching 15,000 kg padi per hectare per year, rice yields
began to decline after the fifth consecutive crop.   A run-down in phosphate is suspected.

The available evidence suggests that there are no major soil
fertility problems preventing the adoption of more intensive cropping
on the traditional zone soils, and that nitrogen is the key nutrient
requirement.   Responses to phosphate can be anticipated in the future,
and work should commence now to determine likely maintenance requirements for alternative cropping systems on representative soil types in
the project area.

(v)   Crops with potential for the dry season

Crop research at Chai Nat has emphasised non-perishable field crops
that can be readily marketed and grown on a large scale.   If a crop is
well adapted to the environment and suitable for inclusion in a rotation
involving wet season rice and a dry season irrigated crop, more detailed
research is then carried out to establish the best cultural techniques.
Successful crops and techniques are evaluated at the Poh Nahng Dum
Farmers' Project to assess profitability and acceptance at the farm level.
The crops showing most promise at this stage are rice, peanut, mungbean,
soybean,   corn, sorghum and sesame (Table 6.4).

All these crops will mature within 90-120 days, which enables them
to be harvested before the onset of monsoonal rains in early May.   For

the majority, time of planting studies have shown that January planting
is close to optimum.   On the heavier transitional soils, planting of
upland crops on ridges spaced at 75 cm has proved the most satisfactory
means of avoiding drainage problems, and usually gives an appreciably
higher yield than flat planting.   The agronomy of most of the crops
listed is now fairly well understood and suitable cultural techniques
have been developed for rice, peanut, mungbean, soybean and corn.
Further work is required on sesame and sorghum.

     Reasonably satisfactory varieties of rice, peanut and soybean
are now available, but further selection and breeding work is required
on corn, sorghum, mungbean and sesame.   Peanuts are better adapted to
the lighter, better drained soils, but satisfactory yields are obtained
on moderately heavy soils.   The main problem here is separating the
nuts from the soil at harvest.   Irrigation just before harvest, and
washing the nuts in the irrigation channel prior to sun drying, is a
technique which the farmers are prepared to adopt, and a sound practice
if varieties are used which do not germinate at the pre-harvest irrigation.   Varieties in use are reasonably satisfactory from this point of
view.

     Technically, the prospect for mungbeans is quite good, but prices
fluctuate widely and it is not a profitable crop in years of low prices
unless yields are high.   Wide adoption of the crop and market expansion
are dependent upon obtaining consistently high yields of quality beans.
Cultural techniques are adequate and most progress will be from variety
selection and breeding.   The highest yielding lines have small rough
seeds which are not popular on the market, whereas the smooth, larger-
seeded lines give lower yields.   There appear to be good prospects of
combining yield with quality, and this is currently being examined by
a Thai counterpart worker at the University of Queensland.

     Soybean is reasonably tolerant of heavy soil conditions, and with
high plant populations (i.e. 400,000 plants per hectare) an experimental
yield of 2800 kg/ha was achieved in 1971.   Currently, more enterprising
farmers are selling the green beans on the stalk as a vegetable and
obtain up to US$468 per hectare.   This market will have to be saturated
before farmers turn to grain production.

A great deal of work has been carried out on grain corn at Chai Nat, and its agronomy is now well documented. Very good yields have been obtained with adequate nitrogen application and good water management, but there are three problems which will slow down widespread adoption of this crop. First, it is susceptible to poor drainage and is not well suited to heavier soils except under a high standard of management. Second, high yields have only been obtained with American hybrids, e.g. Pioneer 309B, and hybrid seed is not obtainable in Thailand. A locally produced variety to match its performance has still to be found. Third, it is a relatively high input crop in terms of fertiliser.

Sweet corn, on the other hand, is a very popular crop by virtue of its high returns, and because it matures in 60-70 days. This would allow two crops to be grown in the one dry season if it were planted early; the green residue is also a useful animal feed. Unfortunately, there is a limited market for fresh sweet corn, and appreciable expansion of acreage would depend on the provision of canning facilities and the development of miniature corn production.

Sorghum is well adapted to most of the area available for irrigated cropping since it is tolerant of a fairly wide range of soil conditions. It brings a lower price than corn, and good yields would be necessary to make it attractive. Yields of 5000-6000 kg/ha are possible experimentally from the hybrid Texas 610, but it has not been tested commercially. The local cultivar, TSP 750, is not well adapted to irrigated production, and seed is not available for the hybrid. There is still a need to find a suitable variety for commercial production. Birds are a problem on small plantings, but bird damage could be minimised by organising block plantings and by using sprays or bird-resistant varieties.

Sesame has been grown as a catch-crop for a number of years by broadcasting seed on to roughly ploughed land with the March rains, but yields were very poor. Yields of over 1200 kg/ha have been achieved at Chai Nat by planting a local selection on ridges and applying 50 kg N per hectare. Yields of this order would make it an attractive crop, but results have not been consistent. While the local 'Black Nakorn-sawan' line has outyielded all introductions, it is highly variable. New lines are being selected and further studies are being made on methods of planting and plant population, in an effort to obtain consistently high yields.

Other crops under test include cotton and sunflower. Yields of 2700 kg seed cotton per hectare have been achieved with the variety Rex with a December-January planting, 100-150 kg N per hectare, and a plant population of 40,000 per hectare. Ginning out-turn and lint quality were excellent but planting must be early to prevent monsoon rains seriously affecting quality. Insects are a major problem, especially the spiny bollworm, and cheaper methods of control must be found. The crop requires a high standard of management and relatively high inputs. These factors detract from cotton as a dry season crop under present circumstances, although it could well have a place in the future as the standard of agriculture rises and farmers build up financial reserves and gain more expertise.

Sunflower and tobacco are new crops in the research programme and more work is planned in the 1972 research programme. There is a good market for certain types of Thai tobacco and the crop, which is quite well adapted to the Central Plain, could offer much higher profits than some of those already tested.

Of the crops showing potential, rice, peanut, mungbean, soybean, and sweet corn are likely to form the basis for the development of irrigated upland cropping. Potential returns from rice make it attractive even with lower prices. Because of high returns, sweet corn and vegetable soybean will be popular with farmers until the local market is satisfied. Peanut, mungbean and soybean are attractive because they require little or no fertiliser and relatively low inputs.

(vi)   Weed and pest control problems

With the exception of cotton, pest control has not been a major problem on upland crops. Most pests are readily controlled with standard chemicals and it is largely a question of rapid identification and spraying with the appropriate chemical. No serious plant diseases have been encountered. However, there is little doubt that if the area of upland crops expands appreciably, both insects and disease will present bigger problems. It will be important to step up research in these fields to

formulate cheaper methods of control, set up an identification service
and train extension personnel in identification and control techniques.

Apart from sesame, weed control is only a problem during the first
few weeks of growth.   Most crops can compete effectively after this
stage.   Nevertheless, it is difficult to get farmers to weed.   First,
it is an unattractive job and it is difficult to show spectacular increases in yield in demonstration plots.   Secondly, on farms growing
both dry season rice and upland crops, rice transplanting competes with
labour for weeding upland crops.   Fortunately, a number of pre-emergence
herbicides are now giving promising results at Chai Nat (e.g. Lasso and
Planavin) and relatively cheap methods of weed control should soon be
available to the farmers.

Rats have been a serious threat to upland crops in some areas during
the last two years.   The damage is particularly noticeable now because the
areas of upland crop are quite small.   Planned programmes of rat control
will be necessary, especially in developing areas, to avoid serious crop
losses.

(vii) _Seasonal labour requirements and mechanisation_

In a simple year-round cropping programme, wet season rice will be
grown in the July-November period.   Following harvest, the land will be
prepared for January planting of the dry season upland crop.   The upland
crop will be harvested in April and the land prepared for rice transplanting in July.   At present all operations, with the exception of initial
ploughing for the wet season rice crop, are carried out by hand and
buffalo.   It is already evident that some degree of mechanisation will
be required to reduce labour requirements at peak periods and to allow
crops to be planted on time.   The major bottlenecks will occur when one
crop is being harvested and land must be prepared for the next crop.   In
the case of wet season rice, the first priority is the introduction of
portable threshing machines which can be carried to the rice field.
This could probably halve the labour requirement for processing the wet
season rice crop and allow dry season crops to be planted on time in mid-
January.

Using traditional methods, labour is committed to cutting, carting,
threshing and winnowing the wet season rice crop for between four and six

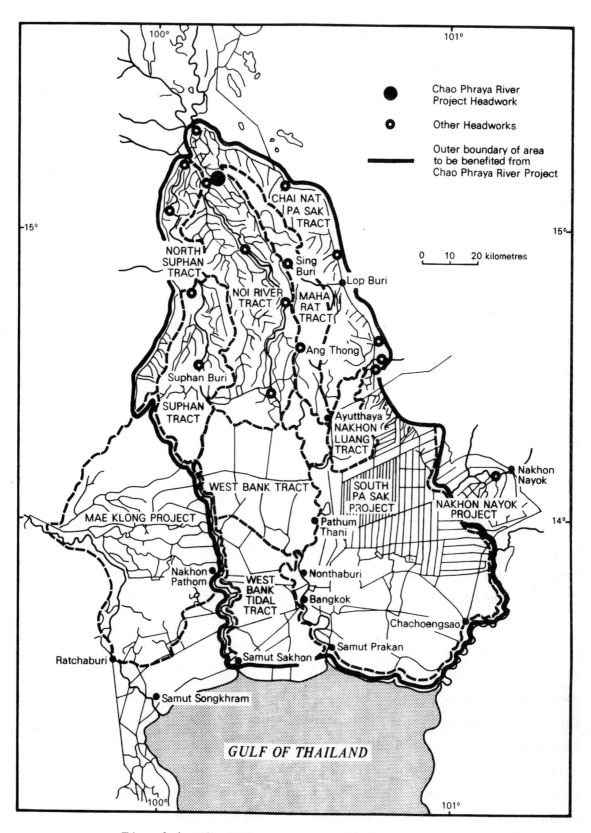

Fig. 6.4 Chao Phraya irrigation projects.

weeks, and the planting of second crops is delayed.   Late planting of
upland crops often leads to lower yields, harvesting difficulties, and
problems in persuading the custom ploughing service to plough water-
logged fields for the wet season rice crop.

Harvesting and threshing dry season upland crops is also time consuming and often leads to delays in clearing the fields ready for ploughing.   Here, the introduction of peanut lifters and a small multiple-
purpose thresher that could handle a wide range of crops is desirable.
Small portable rice threshing units are already in use in Japan, Taiwan,
and the Philippines, and there is a wide range of small threshing equipment available which should be suitable for handling upland crops.

While it is practicable to use the buffalo and walking tractor to
make crop ridges, farmers will need access to a custom service that can
prepare land for irrigated crops.   A large number of tractors are already available in the region, and it is largely a question of educating
contractors in land preparation techniques and encouraging them to purchase the appropriate equipment.   This development cannot take place
until there is sufficient irrigated area to support the contractors, and
government agencies charge realistic prices for the use of their equipment.

6.   SOME SOCIAL, ECONOMIC AND INSTITUTIONAL ASPECTS
OF DEVELOPMENT

In general, the Chao Phraya Basin Development Project has not made a large
impact on agricultural production in the region to date.   This has caused
disappointment and lack of confidence in some circles, and unfortunately
attempts have been made to find a scapegoat.   This attitude has not
helped the various agencies concerned to co-ordinate their efforts or to
work harmoniously together.   Looking at the situation objectively, the
poor results cannot fairly be attributed to one agency or group, but
rather to a combination of technical, social, economic and institutional
factors.   From the technical discussion it will be evident that reliability of water supply and drainage, water control on the farm and the
lack of farm development for irrigation are the key constraints. Assuming
these problems are solved, what will be the next constraint to dry season
cropping?

(i)   The farmers

The fact that the farmer is poor and uneducated is one of the more common reasons put forward for the slow adoption of new technology.   It is true that he has limited financial resources and a low standard of education, but this does not necessarily imply low intelligence or the lack of will to work.   Because he is working on a narrow profit margin and has limited reserves, he is justifiably cautious.   For the same reason he is shrewd, has a very good instinct for recognising new innovations that will increase income without large risks, and is quite ingenious at adapting new techniques to his own environment.

Experience at the Poh Nahng Dum Farmers' Project has shown that the farmer is not a major limiting factor, provided the new technology is sound, the economic incentives are there, the risks are reasonable and he has access to the required inputs and technical support system.

(ii) Economic incentives

While preliminary data from the Poh Nahng Dum Farmers' Project indicate that new methods of rice and peanut production are profitable and can support a substantial investment for farm development and cash inputs (Judd et al., 1971), profits are not high enough in relation to risks, to encourage rapid large scale adoption of new techniques.   Technically, yields achieved to date are good and there is little prospect of increasing them dramatically in the near future, although some gains can be expected from breeding and selection, especially in terms of quality and disease resistance.

The obvious avenue for increasing profit and minimising risk is the reduction of production costs and increasing and stabilising farm prices for produce.   There are several opportunities for the government to take ameliorative action to increase production.   These include the removal of taxes on equipment and materials used for agriculture, providing the farmer with ready access to fertiliser and chemicals at prevailing world prices, and establishing an agricultural credit service which offers longer term development loans at lower interest rates.   At present the rate of interest is 12 per cent and the maximum term is three years.

In the absence of a well organised marketing system for upland crops
in the potential irrigation area, unstable prices are the major obstacle
in the immediate future.   The relatively small volume of produce is also
a problem.   There is a long chain of small middlemen, and market intelligence and prices are poor at the village level.   There appears to be a
reasonable demand for most crops from Bangkok merchants, who could handle
any increases in production likely to take place within the next five years.
The need for a rational marketing system to link the farmer more directly
with the Bangkok merchant is clear.   It should be possible to solve this
problem through co-operation between the government and the trade.

Much emphasis is placed on the development of co-operatives in Thailand, to solve the economic problems of farmers, but they are not necessarily the best answer to the farmers' present difficulties.   First, co-
operative effort is not a strong characteristic of Thai farmers.   Secondly,
co-operatives encroach upon the preserves of a very strong and well
established marketing system run by private enterprise.   Finally, there
is a lack of skilled management personnel to run them efficiently.

(iii) Support services for the rural community

The development of an efficient irrigated agriculture calls for the
combined skills of many disciplines.   This is particularly so in a
situation where the system is starting from small beginnings and embraces
all aspects from farm development, through agricultural credit and seed
production, to agricultural extension and marketing.   At present, neither
government services nor the private sector are organised to provide the
complete basic services required by the farmer in the Central Plain.
This is undoubtedly the major obstacle to rapid development once irrigation water supply and drainage are reliable.

In the government sector, relevant expertise and resources are
dispersed among many agencies.   For administrative and other reasons it
is difficult to set up a combined budget, pool resources from the various
agencies and execute a co-ordinated programme.   Until this is done, progress may be slow, since the expertise and services offered by each agency
are complementary.   The lack of even one or two key support services can
expose the farmer to high risk and could mean economic disaster.   There

is already a lack of rapport between the farmer and the government official, and it is essential that a development programme be well planned
and successful so that the confidence of the farmer is restored.

On paper, there appears to be a reasonable amount of finance and
manpower to carry out the programme, but most government agencies are
faced with a shortage of well-trained personnel, especially in the lower
ranks located in the rural districts.   This has serious implications at
the district level, especially in the fields of agricultural extension.

The private sector has already demonstrated its ability to provide
services in response to development, as it has done for the expansion of
corn production in the past eight years.   However, there does not appear
to be a close working relationship between government agencies and private
enterprise in agricultural development.   In view of the considerable
resources and business expertise in the private sector, there could be
advantages in bringing them into development programmes at the planning
stage.

7.   CONCLUSIONS

The Central Plain offers good potential for increased agricultural production.   Unfortunately, limitations imposed by water control and drainage
problems allow little scope for crop diversification in the wet season.
Present evidence indicates that crop diversification will be limited to
a relatively small area of irrigated upland crops in the dry season in
the northern sector.   The main potential is for increased rice production.   While this may seem an embarrassment in the light of falling
prices and shrinking markets, several factors have to be considered.
First, the technical difficulties and cost of trying to replace rice as
the major crop would be enormous.   Secondly, it will be several years
before the impact of new varieties and technology make themselves felt
in terms of a large increase in production.   Thirdly, Thailand's population is still growing at a rate in excess of three per cent per annum and
domestic requirements will increase.   Finally, the Central Plain is
admirably suited to rice production, and with proper management should be
able to hold its own with any other rice growing area in the world, in
terms of cost of production and quality.

Crop diversification under irrigation in the dry season in favoured portions of the northern plain is technically sound, but to be successful it will require further investment to upgrade irrigation and drainage systems to the necessary standards of reliability. Further, a government-assisted scheme to facilitate land grading, and the installation of efficient farm irrigation and drainage systems will be necessary to allow the high standards of water management required.

It should be re-emphasised that in relation to many other irrigation schemes, the amount of money invested to date in the water distribution system and land development is small. The partial failures of the past are largely due to a lack of planning and to inadequate funds. Farmers do not have the resources or the expertise to bring water from the main channels to their farms or to lay out their land properly for irrigation in a difficult soil situation.

However, farmers' attitudes are not a major obstacle to implementing programmes for crop diversification and increased production, if the environment is right. Sufficient technical information is now available to launch a programme on a reasonably sound basis, although there are still gaps in the information, especially in the economic field. The key problems are poor economic incentives, inadequate support services, and shortages of well trained men in the country to run them. These problems are beyond the scope of the technician or individual government agency and are a matter of government policy.

ACKNOWLEDGEMENTS

I would like to thank Dr D.E. Welsch of Kasetsaart University; Dr Siri-bongse Boon-Long and Dr Saroj Montrakul of the Ministry of Agriculture; Dr Chaiyong Chuchart and Mr Charin Attayothin of the Ministry of National Development; and Mr Small, post-graduate economics student of Cornell University, for their help with the first draft of this paper. I would particularly like to thank Mr L.F. Myers for editing the final draft and for his support and valuable advice during the period of my assignment in Thailand. Finally, I would like to thank Thai and Australian colleagues with whom I have worked at Chai Nat and whose research efforts form the basis of discussion on the technical problems of second cropping. I take full responsibility for any errors of fact or of interpretation.

REFERENCES

Chauviroj, M. et al., 1969.   'Agro-economic studies of production
          systems for rice', Proceedings, seminar on aspects of develop-
          ment of the Central Plain, Part A, Ministry of Agriculture,
          Bangkok.

Chuchart, C. and Sopin, T., 1965.   The determination and analysis of
          policies to support and stabilise agricultural prices and
          incomes of the Thai farmers, Land Development Department,
          Bangkok.

Department of External Affairs, 1969.   First report to the Ministry of
          Agriculture, Parts A and B, Thai-Australian Chao Phraya Research
          Project, Canberra.

Department of External Affairs, 1970.   Second report to the Ministry of
          Agriculture, Parts A and B, Thai-Australian Chao Phraya Research
          Project, Canberra.

FAO/UNDP, 1968.   Report to the United Nations Development Programme
          (4th February to 30th April 1968), Survey Mission for the Chao
          Phraya Delta, Thailand, Rome.

Fukui, H., 1968.   Rice culture in the Central Plain, Part 1, Kyoto
          University, Kyoto.

Jackson, B.R. et al., 1969.   'Breeding performance and characteristics
          of dwarf photoperiod non-sensitive rice varieties for Thailand',
          Thai Journal of Agricultural Science, 2, No. 2; pp. 83-92.

Judd, P. et al., 1971.   An approach to farm development in the Northern
          Chao Phraya basin project area, Central Regional Agricultural
          Centre, Chai Nat, Ministry of Agriculture, Bangkok.

Kluen, T. et al., 1969.   'Report on field test on the yield of non-
          photosensitive varieties under farm conditions in the dry
          season 1969', Rice Department, Ministry of Agriculture, Bangkok.

Land Development Department, 1965.   'Relationship between land tenure and
          rice production in five Central provinces', Land Economic
          Report No.1, Bangkok.

Ministry of Agriculture, 1970.   Preliminary report on the Chao Phraya
          Research Project, dry season 1970, Bangkok.

Nuttonson, N.Y., 1963.   The physical environment and agriculture of
          Thailand, American Institute of Crop Ecology, Washington, D.C.

Royal Irrigation Department, 1949.   Report on irrigation and drainage
          and water communications project of the Chao Phraya river plain,
          Bangkok.

Royal Irrigation Department, 1961.   Ditches and dykes project, additional
        information to be included in the Revised Project Report sub-
        mitted on August 7, 1961, Bangkok.

Royal Irrigation Department, 1962.   Yanhee multi-purpose project,
        Bhoumiphol Dam, Thailand, Bangkok.

Royal Irrigation Department, 1964.   Nan River Project, Thailand multi-
        purpose project, irrigation, power, flood control and navigation
        feasibility report,   Engineering Consultants Inc., Denver,
        Colorado.

Royal Irrigation Department, 1968.   Report on the feasibility of land
        consolidation,   Netherlands Development Co., Bangkok.

Royal Irrigation Department, 1970a.   Northern Chao Phraya Study,
        Netherlands Development Co., Bangkok.

Royal Irrigation Department, 1970b.   Feasibility report on the semi-
        detailed land classification of Greater Chao Phraya project,
        LCR 7, Bangkok.

van der Kevie, W., 1970.   'Soil landscapes and potential landuse in the
        Central Plain',   Thai Journal of Agricultural Science, v.3,
        No. 1:1-12.

Welsch, D.E., 1971.   'Agricultural problems in Thailand: some policy
        alternatives',   Bangkok Bank Monthly Review, v.12, No. 3:89-104.

Yantasast, A. et al., 1970.   'Breeding dwarf varieties of rice for
        tolerance to deep water',   Thai Journal of Agricultural
        Science, v.3, No. 1:119-133.

CHAPTER 7

SOCIAL AND ECONOMIC DETERMINANTS IN RICE CULTIVATION IN NORTHEAST THAILAND

Ronald C.Y. Ng*

Much is known about the physical conditions that govern the yield of rice, and knowledge of the technical aspects of rice production is continually increasing.   However, it has been observed that even in relatively homogenous areas, rice yields can show marked differences.   These variations can be explained only in terms of social and economic determinants which can vary even between adjacent fields operated by different farmers. This paper examines in depth some of the data recently collected by the Mekong Committee in a bench-mark study of 15 Northeast Thai villages (Tothong, 1969) in an attempt to show how rice production can be affected by the social background, economic aspirations and cultivation performance of the farmers concerned.

1. BACKGROUND

Thailand is a predominantly agricultural country, with rice as the main staple food crop and chief export commodity.   In the Northeast, 85 per cent of the population resides in the rural areas and nearly 80 per cent of the cultivated area is devoted to glutinous rice.   Rice cultivation has a special significance in the Northeast where it has several inherent advantages over alternative crops which, despite government encouragement, are unlikely to make much impact in the near future.   Rice is the best low risk, drought and flood resistant crop for the local environment where much of the annual rainfall of 1250-1500 mm is concentrated in five summer months.   As the staple crop, it does not need to go through the elaborate processes of the modern market economy before satisfying the basic requirements of the family.   As only relatively small surpluses

---

* Dr Ng is Lecturer in the Department of Geography, School of Oriental and African Studies, University of London.

periodically find their way into commercial channels, rice is sheltered
from the wide fluctuations in market prices which are often associated
with cash crops.   Furthermore, the lack of credit and of marketing
facilities effectively prevents a rapid transformation of these self-
subsistent peasants to highly commercialised farmers.   By producing
his own seeds, contributing his and his family's labour and consuming
his produce, the farmer is in fact providing much of his own production
and subsistence credit between harvests (Peters, 1966).

At present, practically the entire rice crop is raised under rainfed conditions, as the peasants have almost no water control measures,
and by antiquated farming techniques.   Yields fluctuate markedly according to the variations in both the amount and the distribution of annual
rainfall.   Indeed, with an average of 1.16 tonnes per hectare over the
past decade, yields in the Northeast remain the lowest in the country.
Production, on the other hand, has been able to keep pace with rapid
population growth, not by the adoption of any modern agricultural techniques or of any of the improved rice varieties recently introduced into
the country, but by extending the cultivated area onto marginal land
(Nakajud, 1957).

Northeast Thailand is at the crossroads now.   The small surpluses
of normal years are likely to be dissipated within the next few years as
the population is expected to grow at the current rate of about three
per cent per annum (Charsombuti and Wagner, 1969). The scope for expanding
the cultivated acreage is limited.   The Northeast cannot expect to aug-
ment its food supplies by importing the kind of glutinous rice which its
population prefers from other regions of Thailand, or from nearby countries.
In addition, land will have to be found within the existing farm holding
areas to accommodate newly introduced commercial crops, which are the
only means of increasing family incomes (Ng, 1970).   It is imperative,
therefore, that all production factors, both physical and human, be understood so that an appropriate strategy for economic development of the
region can be devised.

2. THE SURVEY AREA

The area chosen for the comprehensive socio-economic survey is part of
the Muang district of Khon Kaen changwat (province), located east of the
Nakhon Ratchasima-Udon Thani Highway.   It extends southwards from the
Nong Wai diversion weir to the outskirts of Khon Kaen town (Fig. 7.1) and
covers roughly 15,000 hectares of agricultural land to be served by the
Right Main Canal of the Nong Wai Irrigation Project which is now under
construction.

With average slopes ranging from two to four per cent, the area is
typical of rice growing terrain in the region.   The major soils are the
Ratchaburi series of acidic clays and clayey loams which are commonly
found on the lower terraces on the banks of the Nam Pong, a major right-
hand tributary of the Lam Chi.   On the slightly higher middle terraces,
surface soils grade to the more sandy Roi-et series which are underlain
by clayey loam of older alluvium.   Together, these two series cover
roughly two-thirds of the survey area.   They are generally favourable
soils for rice cultivation and have potential yield capacities of 2 to
3.5 tonnes of padi per hectare.   The remaining soils are more complex.
On slightly steeper slopes, the Korat sandy loam series is found, occupying about six per cent of the total area.   This soil is used generally
for limited plantings of upland crops like kenaf.   On the natural levees
of the Nam Pong, an increasing amount of land is being reclaimed for
market gardening crops which are traditionally grown on the exposed banks
of the stream in its lower reaches.   The completion of the Ubonratana
Dam has exposed further tracts of such land and also reduced flood
hazards in downstream areas, allowing an expansion of this new form of
land use and increasing the income of local villagers.

The Nong Wai survey area is representative of the Upper Chi - Nam
Pong subregion of the Northeast.   The main socio-economic characteristics of this area are:-

(a)   A reasonable availability of infrastructural facilities, including
      the various aspects of communications, education, health and elec-
      tricity supply.

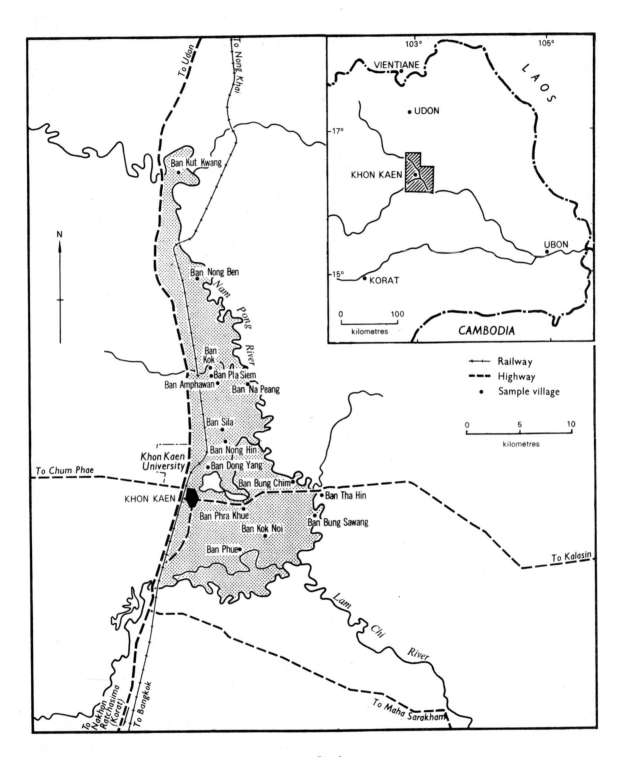

Fig. 7.1 Sketch map of the survey area.

(b)   Relative centrality to the larger towns of the Northeast including
      Khon Kaen, Udon Thani and Maha Sarakham, whose sizeable urban
      markets can absorb the market gardening produce of the area.

(c)   A moderate degree of population pressure on farm land, with farm
      size and family income being close to averages for the region.

(d)   An almost universal absence of tenancy.

(e)   A fairly high proportion of cultivable land currently planted in
      rice.

(f)   A mature social landscape which has not experienced any significant
      migration of population recently.

Fifteen villages were selected randomly from a total of approximately 48 in the area and 20 per cent of the households in these sample
villages, comprising 317 families in all, were interviewed (Table 7.1).
The total farm area reported by these households was 1184 hectares,
giving an average farm size of 3.7 hectares. Although this figure is
almost the same as the regional average, 60 per cent of the interviewees

Table 7.1: Salient features of settlement and land use
of the sample villages

Village	Cultivated area (ha)	Uncultivated area (ha)	Padi (ha)	Households	Average farm size (ha)
Na Pieng	110	30	104	35	4.0
Pla Siem	234	75	193	59	5.2
Ban Kok	628	157	588	131	6.0
Amphawan	357	37	346	79	5.0
Nong Ben	320	165	288	95	5.1
Kut Kwang	196	26	191	74	3.0
Phra Khue	1013	222	965	285	4.3
Kok Noi	316	157	293	106	4.5
Bung Chim	363	73	352	94	4.7
Tha Hin	237	72	237	105	3.0
Bung Kwang	210	81	210	52	5.6
Ban Phue	299	104	281	103	3.9
Don Yang	337	27	318	119	3.1
Sila	629	121	614	145	5.5
Nong Hin	432	23	409	102	4.5

Source: Field survey.

indicated that additional farm land was desirable.   Another 20 per cent
wished to hire some labour if they could afford to do so, in spite of the
fact that the average nucleated family consisted of about seven members.
The predominant form of land utilisation is rice which occupied more than
90 per cent of the total planted area in 1969.   The two other common
crops were kenaf and vegetables which made up no more than five per cent
of the cultivated area.

3.   PRODUCTIVITY OF PADI

One of the aims of the survey was to collect information on the economics
of rice production in the context of rainfed agriculture.   As might be
expected of any subsistence economy in Nong Wai, most of the cost of production was in kind, of which the bulk was composed of the labour contributed by the farmer and his family.   The calculation of labour costs in
areas where hired farm labour is virtually unknown has always presented
problems and, in this case, it was decided that it should be related to
estimated opportunity costs according to the locality.   The general wage
rate of daily casual labour in the wet season of 1969 was 10 bahts per day
(US$0.48), but in the villages near Khon Kaen town, a higher rate of 12
bahts (US$0.58) was obtainable.   The total imputed expenditure on each
planted hectare of padi, including a small amount of cash inputs, was
found to be 1229 bahts (US$59.09), corresponding to a cost per tonne of
1024 bahts or US$49.23 (Table 7.2).   The market price of padi in 1969
was 1100 bahts (US$52.88) per tonne, yielding a profit margin of 7.4 per
cent on total investments but excluding the opportunity cost of land which

Table 7.2:   Cost of production of transplanted padi in the survey area of
Nong Wai, Changwat Khon Kaen, 1969

	Cost per ha baht	Cost per tonne baht	Percentage
Seed bed preparation	69	57	5.68
Land preparation	685	571	55.60
Fertilisation	16	13	1.30
Water control	50	42	4.06
Harvest	398	332	32.47
Others	11	9	0.89
Total	1229	1024	100.00

Source: Field survey.

the farmers owned.   But 1969 was a favourable year both in terms of
yields and prices.   In the years subsequent to the survey the price
of padi has dropped by almost 40 per cent while wage labour rates have
appreciated by between 50 and 70 per cent.   Returns from padi production
have therefore worsened substantially (Business in Thailand, 1971).   In
spite of this, rice cultivation is, and will remain, the predominant form
of land utilisation in this area as elsewhere in the Northeast.

Agricultural productivity can be expressed in several ways.   Conventionally, output per capita and output per unit land area are used.
However, it was realised that although productivity on a per capita basis
is a good measurement of the nutritional situation, it fails to reflect
the vital consideration of the varying demographic structure of the
villages and to recognise the importance of the family as the basic production unit.   Thus, villages with very similar average outputs per
capita, as in the cases of Ban Kok Noi, Ban Phra Khue and Ban Don Yang,
had very different values for output per adult and output per family.
Similarly, almost identical output per adult, as in Bung Kwang and Ban
Phue, does not necessarily mean that output per family will be the same.
To maintain these significant differences the analyses presented subsequently in this paper utilise all four measures of productivity.

The survey data reveal that the average output of padi per capita
for the area was 387.4 kg.   As weather conditions in the 1969 growing
season were particularly favourable, this level of production was 39.4
per cent higher than the 285 kg per capita estimated as necessary for
food and seed requirements.   Table 7.3 shows that in four of the sample
villages, production failed to reach this critical value.   However, it
was established in the field that all villages could manage to obtain
enough rice for subsistence averaging over a few years.   The average
output per adult between the age of 15 and 64 was 723.1 kg, and returns
from rice cultivation were more rewarding in, say, Ban Amphawan than in
Ban Sila or Ban Kut Kwang.   Output of padi per family also reflects
similar patterns among the sample villages.   It is particularly interesting to note that the range of fluctuations for output of padi per family
is much less than the per capita or the per adult measurements.   This
observation lends weight to the conviction that the family is the basic

Table 7.3:   Production of padi in 15 sample Northeast villages

Village	kg/capita	kg/adult	kg/family	kg/rai	kg/ha
Na Pieng	228.5	391.8	1567.2	168.8	1055.0
Pla Siem	274.2	430.9	1580.0	107.1	669.4
Ban Kok	448.1	791.8	3380.4	193.6	1210.0
Amphawan	594.0	1013.4	3863.8	205.4	1283.8
Nong Ben	301.2	400.1	1769.0	141.8	886.3
Kut Kwang	206.3	365.6	1486.7	134.3	839.4
Phra Khue	491.1	532.9	1953.9	138.7	866.9
Kok Noi	496.3	992.5	3166.7	262.9	1643.1
Bung Chim	433.4	894.7	3531.6	244.9	1530.6
Tha Hin	328.1	589.2	2048.1	259.1	1619.4
Bung Kwang	385.7	780.1	3120.0	238.2	1488.8
Ban Phue	465.9	786.3	2733.4	205.7	1285.6
Dong Yang	492.3	989.9	3258.3	301.9	1886.9
Sila	218.6	387.3	1508.9	113.4	708.8
Nong Hin	283.2	548.1	2110.0	120.6	753.8
Average	397.4	723.1	2725.7	200.7	1254.4

Source: Field survey.

decision-making unit in an optimisation approach to farm production.   Thus, the head of a household cannot afford to mobilise fewer resources than those required to provide sufficient food for the family;   nor can he produce surpluses that the market cannot afford.

However the absence of any significant relationships between yields per hectare on the one hand and the per capita, per adult and per family outputs on the other, raises a whole series of questions concerning the rural economy of the Northeast.   For example, are variations in yield conditioned by physical factors, or are they derived from differences in the social setting?   These questions cannot be answered exhaustively, and the present exercise makes no attempt to provide definitive answers. However by analysing some of the fundamental socio-economic information recently collected, it may contribute to the designing of more precise questionnaires to reveal the true nature of subsistence rice farming in similar contexts.

4.   THE ANALYSIS

The survey provided much information concerning the social and economic background of the sample villagers, in addition to the detailed data on

expenditure and returns of rice cultivation.   From an initial total of
43 items of quantifiable data, 27 that were thought to be relevant to padi
production were selected subjectively.   These were then tested for inter-
correlation, as several different expressions might reflect the same
measurement.   The reduced data matrix, containing 12 variables, was then
regressed against each of the four productivity measurements used earlier,
using a modified series of computer programs and sub-programs from the IBM
Scientific Subroutine Package.   It was found that level of explanation in
each case was not significantly inferior to the results obtained by using
all 27 initial variables, and furthermore, that each of the coefficients
of multiple correlation was significant at the 0.01 level after adjusting
for the degrees of freedom.

These 12 final variables can be divided into two broad groups, one
pertaining to the background governing production decisions, or the social
complex, and the other describing how the total cost (consisting mostly of
labour) and its structure are manipulated by the farmer to obtain the level
of production actually achieved.   This second group is termed the
'Economic Complex'.   The variables, their mean values and standard devia-
tions are presented in Table 7.4.

Table 7.4:   The socio-economic variables

Variable		Mean	Standard Deviation
Social complex:			
X_a	Percentage of cultivated area planted to rice	89.07	7.64
X_b	Income from padi as percentage of total farm income	50.95	12.08
X_c	Income from padi as percentage of total family income	29.95	9.11
X_d	Percentage of farm land not cultivated	19.96	8.49
X_e	Number of adults per rai of padi	0.30	0.07
X_f	Percentage of population as dependents	45.50	6.32
Economic complex:			
X_g	Cost of rice production, in bahts per rai	204.28	40.43
X_h	Cash inputs as percentage of total inputs	0.80	0.05
X_i	Cost of nursery preparation in bahts per rai	11.37	2.16
X_j	Cost of land preparation in bahts per rai	113.45	21.16
X_k	Cost of fertilisers, insecticides, etc. in bahts per rai	12.40	4.89
X_l	Cost of harvesting rice, in bahts per rai	65.90	20.13

Source: Based on field data.

The results of multiple regression analysis indicate two interesting
intermediate conclusions.   First, the background or 'Social Complex'
variables are strongly correlated collectively, but not individually, with
the productivity measurements.   In other words, production per capita,
per adult, per family and even per unit area can be explained to a large
extent by variations in such considerations as the farmer's dependence on
rice as a source of income, the degree of specialism in rice cultivation,
the size of his farm holding, (as expressed by the number of adults per
rai of padi), and his environmental constraints (expressed by the percentage of the farm holding which is not cultivable).   Secondly, although
the variables in the 'Economic Complex' such as total cost of production
and costs of the main cultural processes, are not as efficient in explaining the productivity variations, they alone determine over 60 per cent of
the variations in yields of the 15 sample villages (Table 7.5).   The
physical or environmental constraints, which are not considered in the
present context, can at best explain less than 40 per cent of the local
variations in yield.

Table 7.5: Percentage of variations in padi productivity explained by
            the social and economic variables by multiple correlation
            analysis

	Social Complex	Economic Complex
Production per capita	65.19*	51.02
Production per adult	71.28*	46.63
Production per family	67.86*	44.57
Production per unit area	59.77*	61.50*

* Corresponding coefficient of multiple correlation significant at the
   0.01 level.

It is obvious that the two groups of variables are not mutually
exclusive or conceptually distinct from one another.   For example, the
amount of labour a farmer and his family can contribute, as indirectly
measured by total cost of production, is conditioned by the resources at
his disposal;   similarly, the number of adults in a farm household often
sets an upper limit to the costs of land preparation and harvesting.   So,
in the final stage of the analysis, all the 12 socio-economic variables

were entered into a <u>stepwise</u> multiple regression analysis; by minimising
the number of independent variables and by maximising the level of explanation, it was hoped to identify the most significant variables.

The final models for padi production per capita, per adult, per
family and per unit area contain no more than four independent variables
and are capable of explaining 80 per cent of the observed variations, with
corresponding coefficients of multiple correlation exceeding 0.8995.
These are:-

$$Y_c = -857.4 + 12.13\ X_c - 884.03\ X_e + 1422.65\ X_h$$

$$Y_a = -1415.7 + 28.09\ X_c - 10.98\ X_d + 2150.51\ X_h - 885.68\ X_e$$

$$Y_f = -4747.52 + 94.39\ X_c - 36.62\ X_d + 7803.77\ X_h - 3695.34\ X_e$$

$$Y_r = -603.63 + 0.87\ X_g + 0.79\ X_j + 666.43\ X_h + 4.11\ X_c$$

where Y_c is production of padi per capita, in kg,

   Y_a is production of padi per adult, in kg,

   Y_f is production of padi per family, in kg,

   Y_r is production of padi per <u>rai</u>, in kg;

and X_c is income from padi as percentage of total family income,

   X_d is percentage of farm land not cultivated,

   X_e is number of adults per <u>rai</u> of padi,

   X_g is cost of rice production, in bahts per <u>rai</u>,

   X_h is cash inputs as percentage of total inputs,

   X_j is cost of land preparation in bahts per <u>rai</u>.

These models show that income from padi as a percentage of total
family income figures significantly. In three of the models it is the
first variable that was entered by the analysis, explaining the bulk of
the variations. The direct relationship and positive value of the cash
input variable support the thesis that one way of increasing production
is to utilise more modern inputs. It can also be seen that the really
significant variables in the models number no more than six, equally
divided between the social and economic complexes. Whereas all the
three social background variables are represented in the production per

adult and per family and to some extent in the production per capita
models, the yield model (Yr) is much more strongly influenced by economic
variables.

5.   CONCLUSIONS

The result of the final analysis permits us to draw some important conclusions about rice production in the Northeast.   In all models, the
most important independent variable is that showing income from padi as
a percentage of total family income, X_c.   Changes in values of X_c will
directly and to a large extent determine variations in padi production
(Y_c, Y_a and Y_f).   It has been found for almost all the villages studied
that levels of production are much higher than those estimated as required
for subsistence.   Hence this variable includes an aspirational element
of income from commercial sales.   In other words, although the farmers
of the Northeast are basically subsistence-oriented, they also strive to
achieve a rice surplus for earning cash incomes.   Thus, the recent slump
in the price of Thai rice on the international market may have more
serious repercussions in the Northeast than commonly acknowledged.   This
may induce farmers to devote less human resources, namely cost of production which is composed mainly of imputed labour expenditure, to rice
cultivation.   The effect would be detrimental to padi production in the
region as suggested by model Y_r, production of padi per _rai_, in which
both cost of rice production and cost of land preparation have significant
and positive coefficients.

The fact that rice responds well to better cultural techniques and
labour intensiveness as suggested by the prominent positions occupied by
variables X_g (cost of production), and X_1 (cost of land preparation), has
been demonstrated by model Y_r.   If padi production is so strongly influenced by these variables, then there might be a good opportunity for
solving the problem of chronic low income levels characteristic of the
Northeastern farmers.   In short, if farmers can be persuaded to concentrate that part of inputs traditionally allocated to rice cultivation on
a smaller proportion of their farms and at the same time achieve higher
production per unit area, then the remainder of the farm holding can be
used for cultivating more cash crops which may bring a higher income when
the marketing situation is improved.

A common feature of the three models of production of padi on a
demographic basis (Y_c, Y_a, Y_f) is the negative coefficients for independent
variables X_d, percentage of farm land not cultivated, and X_e, the number
of adults per <u>rai</u> of padi.   The former can be regarded as an indirect
expression of the unfavourable environmental conditions, the latter, an
inferred measurement of population pressure.   As these two factors are
clearly related in a conceptual sense, an improvement of environmental
conditions, particularly of water supply, should reduce the proportion
of land not cultivated and in turn lower the values for number of adults
per planted <u>rai</u> of padi.   The net effect will be a substantial increase
in the regressed values for production of padi per capita, per adult and
per family.   A transformation from present rainfed agriculture to supplementary irrigation for the main rice cultivating season should remove one
of the most serious constraints in what is now an unsatisfactory production function.

Perhaps the most encouraging note in all the four models is the
important role played by variable X_h (cash inputs as percentage of total
inputs) which enters as the first significant variable in the production
of padi per <u>rai</u> model and third in the other three.   The positive regression coefficients with which this variable is associated imply that
when cash inputs form a higher percentage of the total cost of production,
there is a corresponding increase in the production of rice.   It suggests
that there will be general acceptance of modern cultural techniques such
as the use of fertilisers and insecticides if local demand calls for
higher production.

The survey area itself will soon be provided with a functioning
modern water control system and institutional support under the current
Five-year Social and Economic Plan (National Economic Development Board,
1970).   One is confident that the inherent strengths of the production
functions will be exploited and many of the bottlenecks will be removed,
to rationalise   rice cultivation and diversify the land use pattern.
It would be interesting and useful to repeat this exercise at an advanced
stage of the Plan to examine and compare both the aspirational and performance aspects involved in the cultivation of rice in the region.

REFERENCES

Business in Thailand, 1971.   'The harvest of no return',   Business in
        Thailand, June, Bangkok.

Charsombuti Pradit and Wagner, Melvin M., 1969.   Estimates of the Thai
        population, 1947-1976, and some agricultural implications,
        Kasetsart Economic Report, No. 31, Bangkok.

Nakajud, Arb, 1957.   Agricultural production, productivity and measures
        for promoting productivity in Thailand,   Department of
        Agricultural Economics, Kasetsart University, Bangkok.

National Economic Development Board, 1970.   Agricultural development
        strategy in the Third Economic and Social Development
        Plan, B.E. 2515-2519, Bangkok, (mimeo).

Ng, R.C.Y., 1970.   'Some land use problems of Northeast Thailand',
        Modern Asian Studies, 4, pp. 23-42.

Peters, C.W., 1966.   Agricultural credit and marketing in Northeast
        Thailand, U.S.A.I.D., Bangkok, (mimeo).

Tothong Chamlong, 1969.   Report on bench mark socio-economic survey of
        Nong Wai, Mekong Committee, E.C.A.F.E., Bangkok.

CHAPTER 8

VILLAGERS AS CLIENTS : A STUDY OF LAND DEVELOPMENT IN

NORTHERN THAILAND

E.C. Chapman*

1.   INTRODUCTION

It now seems clear that the late 1960s marked a major turning-point in
Thailand's agricultural development.   Between 1967 and 1971 expansion
of the cultivated area slowed almost to a halt, as discussed in Chapter 1,
and Thailand entered the period of the Third Plan (1971-76) recognising
that immediate agricultural objectives could only be achieved by rapid
improvements in yields.   Unfortunately, agricultural planning was not
ready for the change.   In Thailand, as Welsch has pointed out, agricultural policies aimed at increasing yields have for too long been based on
'conventional wisdom, opinion and rhetoric' (Welsch, 1971:95).   Faced
with the prospect of a gradual crisis in agricultural production during
the 1970s, and with the need for agricultural planning to be based on
facts rather than attractive assumptions, the Ministry of Agriculture is
now strengthening its policy-oriented research at existing regional
agricultural centres (Khon Kaen and Chai Nat), at numerous research stations,
and in feasibility projects such as the Thai-Australian Land Development
(TALD) Project, discussed in this paper.

The TALD Project is concerned with the improvement of crop yields
(mainly upland rice, mungbeans and peanuts) on villagers' small-holdings
in the upper Nan valley of North Thailand, where sandy soils low in plant
nutrients have been brought under intensive cultivation for upland crops
during the past 20 to 30 years.   The two Project Areas and the research
station near Sa Town (Nan Province) have been developed since 1967 on

---

* Mr Chapman is Reader in Geography, School of General Studies, in the
Australian National University.   Since 1967 he has been leader of the
Australian advisory team (Colombo Plan) for the TALD Project.

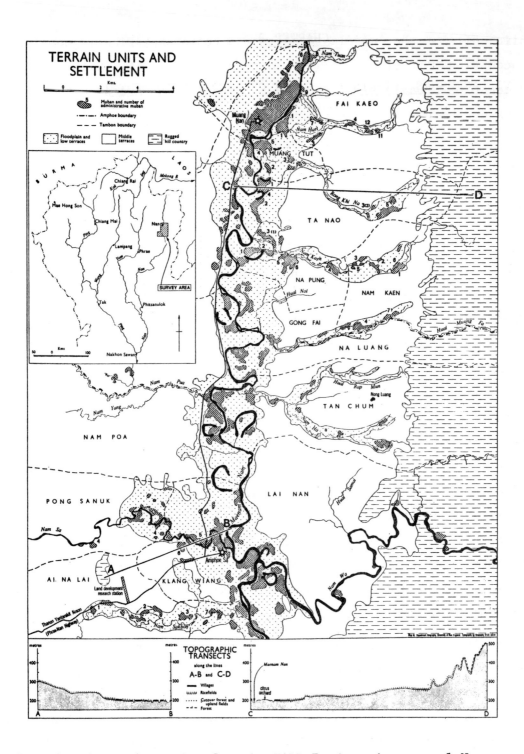

Fig. 8.1 The physical setting for the TALD Project in central Nan.
Project Area No.1, begun in 1968, occupies the middle-terrace terrain west
and southwest of Sa Town (Amphoe is used to refer to either the district,
or the administrative centre); Project Area No.2, begun in 1970, occupies
similar terrain in Tambon (Sub-district) Na Pung, east of the Nan River.
Villages (muban) are numbered within the sub-districts adjoining the two
Project Areas.

Source: Sheet 5166 I, Map Series L708 (1:50,000), 1960, and aerial photographs taken in 1954.

podzolic soils of the 'middle terraces', a geomorphologically complex
area occupying most of the valley floor, as shown in Fig. 8.1. Similar
soils occur on broadly similar terrace terrain, though less extensively,
in other northern valleys. Consequently, the TALD Project Areas can be
seen as representative of much low-yielding 'upland' which has been
brought within the cultivated area relatively recently, in response to
population pressure, and now poses serious policy problems for agricultural development.

Can the yields of rice and upland crops be improved significantly
in these areas, despite the constraints of poor soils and an uncertain
rainfall characteristic of the wet-and-dry tropics, and at costs which
are acceptable to the Thai government and the subsistence-oriented farmers
in the northern valleys? The answer to these questions depends, initially
at least, on the determination of an appropriate package programme involving
improved cultivation techniques, fertilisers, better seed and easier access
to rural credit, in much the same way as the High Yielding Varieties
Programme (HVP) was developed in India during the 1960s. The outstanding
contrast, of course, is that the HVP was explicitly concentrated on areas
possessing initial advantages in water supply and agricultural organisation,
while any upland programme in Thailand will be concentrating on areas
generally deprived of water for irrigation. This difference apart,
Indian experience in the attempted transformation of traditional agriculture during the past decade is perhaps most relevant to Thailand in having
demonstrated that farmers' responses to new opportunities are slow, highly
variable and related closely to the particular constraints affecting
individual villagers (Harriss, 1972; Lipton, 1968:116-17).

The TALD Project is still a very modest venture which in four years
to the end of 1971 was responsible for land-clearing and improved cultivation on 1095 ha (878 farm holdings) and in the period 1972-75 is expected
to increase at a rate of about 1000 ha (800 holdings) annually. The
Project is still in the process of establishing the various components of
its technical 'package', through agronomic research and equipment trials,
but equally it is concerned at this stage with the responses of farmers to
the opportunities for higher yields now available through improved cultivation of the terrace soils. The preliminary results discussed in this

paper demonstrate a diversity of 'farmer response' and the need to probe
its causes, as in India, if the expected benefits of development are to
be obtained by the villagers who most require government help.

2.   BACKGROUND TO DEVELOPMENT

Changwat Nan can claim the dubious distinction of being probably the most
poverty-stricken province in Thailand.   At the time of the Agricultural
Census in 1963 more than nine-tenths of its population lived in agricultural households and 55 per cent of farm holdings were smaller than 6.0
rai (0.96 ha);   average rice production per holding in 1962 was only 1715
kg, the lowest production level in all the provinces of north and northeast
Thailand, despite rice yields which are much higher than the kingdom average
(Chapman, 1967).

The reasons for Nan's plight and for the expansion of intensive
swidden cultivation on the low-yielding terrace land during recent decades
have been discussed in detail elsewhere (Chapman, 1970).   The fundamental
difficulty is a drastic imbalance of man and land, particularly in the
central part of the province, where more than 100,000 people are concentrated in the towns (Nan and Sa) and the villages near the Nan River
(Fig. 8.1).   In fact, urban and village expansion is steadily encroaching
on the very limited area of irrigated rice-fields, helping to force land
values as high as bahts 5000 per rai (US$1563 per hectare), for rice-fields
which normally yield one crop each year, worth about $188 per hectare at
harvest.   Only about half the province's requirements of rice are now met
by local production.

The serious over-population of Nan Province has not developed
suddenly and might have been avoided by greater out-migration, particularly north-westwards to Chiang Rai.   However, net out-migration was
small, at least until 1960, and the Nan population preferred to purchase
glutinous rice imports, mainly from Chiang Rai, by cash earned from limited
dry-season cropping (mainly tobacco and peanuts), from tangerine orchards,
and from wage labour.   Much of the employment is found in other northern
provinces, such as Phitsanulok and Sukhothai, and is strongly seasonal.
In the dry season there is a large outflow of men from villages in Nan

every year for two or three months before Songkhran (Buddhist New Year
in mid-April).   They often go to make charcoal from illegal timber-
cutting.

In the wet-rice areas bordering the Nan River the process of
agricultural involution has already had considerable effect.   Fields
are exceptionally small (commonly about 0.03 ha) compared with central
Thailand.   This allows more effective irrigation and drainage during
the rainy season but the difficulties of lifting water from the Nan River
have hindered the extension of cultivated land by multiple cropping.   As
a result, the lowland rice-fields are mostly unused during the seven
months dry season, from November to May (Chapman, 1970).

With irrigation limited at the present time to the narrow alluvial
margins bordering the Nan River and its main tributaries, the easiest
opportunities for extending the cultivated land over the past 20 to 30
years were found on the extensive river terraces, standing 30 to 40 metres
above the bottomland.   Here the outstanding handicap is the porosity of
the podzolic soils.   Their low capacity for moisture retention prevents
wet-rice cultivation and adds greatly to the risks of an upland rice crop
grown during the rainy season.   The soils dry rapidly once the rains
have stopped in October, often affecting maturing crops of late-planted
rice which may not be ready for harvest until three or four weeks after
the last useful rain.   Furthermore, without irrigation to drown the weeds
each rainy season, upland fields established by the usual slash-and-burn
methods are soon invaded by weeds and Imperata cylindrica ('lalang' or
'cogon grass').   The weed and grass infestation, as much as decline in
soil fertility after one or two crops, compels farmers to cut new areas
of the depleted scrub-forest and regrowth on the terraces.   Normally this
is done every year.

Yields of upland rice on the middle-terrace swiddens are reported
by farmers to be generally 30 to 40 per cent of the yields obtained in the
wet-rice fields in the same year.   Despite such low yields and even
lower relative returns on labour, a marked expansion of swidden cultivation
has taken place.   Increase in the demand for swiddens within easy walking
distance of villages, up to a distance of 4 km, has led to a gradual
shortening of the swidden cycle to one cropping season in two or three

years; in some areas it has also led to gradual changes from usufruct
occupation to formal land sub-division under the direction of the kamnan
(head of a tambon, or sub-district) and amphoe teedin (District land
officer).   In Project Area No. 1 at Sa, for example, the terrace land
immediately south of the Phrae-Nan highway and southeast from the land
development research station was subdivided into individual holdings of
4 or 5 rai (0.6 to 0.8 ha) during the 1950s, while usufructuary arrangements continued to operate in most of the block north of the highway which
was up to 3 km from the nearest villages (Fig. 8.1).

The importance of the middle terraces in the rural economy of central
Nan is exemplified in the 13 villages in Project Areas 1 and 2 (Table 8.1).
In the villages of Tambon Na Pung and the four tambon west of Sa Town,
two-fifths of the total households were involved in swiddening in 1966-67,
with the proportion rising away from the main lowland areas near the Nan
River.   In these two areas, 76 per cent of the swidden households combined upland and lowland fields in a supplementary swidden system;   the
remaining households had no land, other than their swiddens on the middle
terraces.   This highlights the fact that swidden cultivation has played
a major role as a safety-valve in Nan, providing land for villagers who
would otherwise be landless.

Table 8.1 provides evidence of the low yields and poor returns on
farm labour from the main swidden crops of upland rice and peanuts.   The
figures are based on results from benchmark surveys carried out in TALD
Project Areas in 1967.   The average gross returns on farm labour from
the upland swiddens were so consistently low in all 13 villages, that
the cultivation of such unrewarding crops seems totally irrational, until
we take into account that the opportunity cost of swidden labour is
virtually zero in most instances.   Most of the dry-season work in swiddens
(slashing, burning) is done either before men leave the village for out-of-
province employment, or by household members who would otherwise be idle;
and in the rainy season the need of the swidden crops for labour (planting,
weeding) is usually given a low priority if a farmer's irrigated rice-
fields require attention, or if there are chance opportunities for off-
farm employment.

Table 8.1: Average crop yields and returns on farm labour for 'swidden
            households' surveyed in Changwat Nan, 1967

Sub-district and village No.		Swidden households No.	Yields (kg/ha)			Gross returns Bahts per day worked		
			L.R.	U.R.[a]	P[a]	L.R.	U.R.	P
AREA 1								
Ai Na Lai	1	20	2000	1000	919	17	6	9
	2	63	2056	463	800	16	2	7
	3	5	1562	394	?	10	2	?
San	7	11	2293	320	475	17	6	4
Klang Wiang	3	62	2800	875	856	23	5	8
	4	38	2375	881	788	21	4	6
	5	50	2600	694	506	22	3	4
	6	32	2631	600	488	19	4	4
Pong Sanuk	4	34	2456	931	565	18	4	6
AREA 2								
Na Pung	1	49	2113	937	565	19	4	6
	2	73	2763	1119	919	26	5	8
	3	99	2763	1006	875	26	5	8
	4	56	1969	731	681	17	3	5

a L.R.: lowland rice; U.R.: upland rice; P: peanuts. The location of
   villages within each of the sub-districts is shown (by numbers) on
   Fig. 8.1.

Note: Data were obtained from householders by questionnaire interviews
       in February, March and April 1967. The yield data depend upon
       householders' assessments of area planted and the volume at harvest
       for each crop, and should be regarded as suggestive rather than
       definitive statements of yields.

Source: Recalculated from a series of tables in an earlier paper (Chapman,
         1970).

Taking into account the low yields from upland fields, and yet the
high proportion of village households cultivating middle-terrace farms,
it is not surprising that farmers and village headmen were keen for Thai
government help to remove trees and stumps, in order to bring upland fields
under plough cultivation. On the other hand, tractor-clearing and
efficient cultivation of the kind now provided for farmers in TALD Project
areas is likely to bring only short-term benefits unless the higher yields
can be maintained. To do this, fertilisers and more intensive cultivation will be needed, requiring higher cash and labour inputs than in the

past; if improved seed varieties, simple mechanisation and recommended
changes in cropping patterns are also introduced, the total effect will
be a drastic transformation of the farming system on the holdings which
adopt these innovations.   At the same time there will remain in the
background, affecting farmers' decisions, the traditional village assessment of the middle-terrace upland as low-yielding farmland of little
value: an area of rough commonage, providing meagre crops, wood for
houses and charcoal, bamboo shoots, fungi, nuts, and other important
food supplements which are particularly important in the 'starvation
months' before the rice harvest begins in September.   How long will
this traditional image last and affect the attitude of villagers, in
their response to new farming opportunities on this land?

3. PROJECT-VILLAGER RELATIONS

The technical aspects of land development on the middle-terrace farmland
are simple and sequential, requiring only rigorous timing and careful
organisation of heavy equipment and personnel so that the entire field
operations can be carried through between the end of one wet season
(October) and the early weeks of the next wet season, in May-June.   On
the other hand, sensitivity, to a degree unusual in Thailand, has been
needed for routine land development operations in this particular cultural
milieu, so that villagers' interests can be safeguarded and their cooperation obtained.

One soon realises, when beginning an agricultural development programme at village level in North Thailand, that mutual confidence between
villagers and government officials is rare.   Characteristically, most
government officers who visit villagers promising development benefits
are viewed with some scepticism, since the village has depended upon self-
help for major improvements in the past.   For their part, the government
officers often complain that villagers are unreliable, lazy and all too
ready to grasp any government assistance while doing little in return.
The situation which Moerman described so succinctly for a Thai-Lue village
in a remote lowland district of Chiang Rai Province is gradually changing,
but certainly in the mid-1960s it rang true for many villages in central
Nan:

...'villagers rarely use government services.   They send and
receive no letters, receive no meaningful agricultural extension,
know little of public health measures, ridicule community
development, and are ambivalent toward public education. Their
most conspicuous contacts with the government consist of donating
labor, paying taxes, fees and occasional bribes, and receiving
orders and vague exhortations' (Moerman, 1969:536).

In this situation, where the two parties participating in a proposed
development programme are clustered initially around widely separate poles,
the headman and schoolteacher(s) are usually the only 'brokers' to bridge
the gap to any extent; in Rogers' terms (1969:127), these are 'the marginal
men who stand with one foot in the village and the other in a wider sphere'.
For development operations to succeed this small intermediate group must
be augmented by officers who can identify with the interests of the
villages where they work.   The TALD operations have gained immensely, in
the five years to the end of 1971, from the gradual growth of rapport
between young officers trained in Bangkok, but with no initial knowledge
of the Nan dialect of Caa Muang (the northern Thai language), and village
leaders and farmers.   Some have married local girls, but the fact that
they live in the village, travel only occasionally to Bangkok, and become
full participants in village social life, has meant a great deal in filling
the traditional vacuum between 'Government' and village.

Early in 1967, as a first step towards improvement of terrace farming,
the Department of Land Development obtained possession of an area of 200
rai (32 ha), not already under land title, for the Sa research station
(Figs 8.1 and 8.2).   About one-quarter of this small area was cleared
for four farm households who grew crops under supervision in the rainy
seasons of 1967 and 1968.   Overall, the yields were highly satisfactory
in demonstrating to nearby villagers what might be achieved once the
stumps and roots were removed from former swiddens, but of course the
farmer variable precluded the possibility of these results being considered
as significant research.   After 1969, with its initial demonstration role
completed, the 'Sa Centre' has functioned as the nucleus for the land-
clearing operations on adjoining 'Farmers' Blocks' shown in Fig. 8.2, as
well as being an agronomic research station and repair depot for field
equipment used at Sa (Project Area No. 1) and, after September 1970, at
Tambon Na Pung, Tambon Nam Kaen and Tambon Na Luang (Project Area No. 2)
to the east of the Nan River.

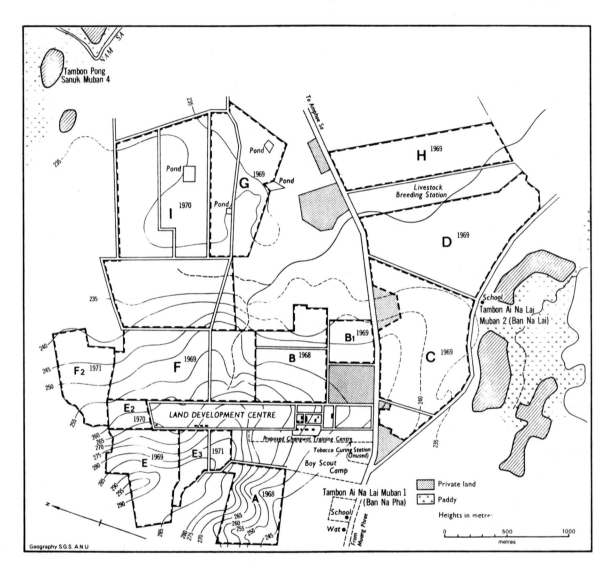

Fig. 8.2   Farmers' Blocks, TALD Project Area No.1, Sa (Nan).

When the Project's bulldozers began clearing the Farmers' Blocks
adjoining Sa Centre in 1968 and 1969, they also opened up a highly sensitive area in Project-villager relations.   The most obvious problem was the
the timing of field operations: since farmers are still using their
swidden land until harvest in October or November, and must have control
of their newly ploughed fields by the early weeks of the next rainy season,
the period for land development operations is restricted to eight months
from October to May or early June.   Land-clearing, the surveying and
allocation of small holdings (when not already held under title), root-
ripping and ploughing, must all be accomplished during the one dry season.
A tight schedule has to be followed, beginning with pre-development surveys
well before the October swidden harvest.   Tractor-clearing and cadastral
mapping then follow as soon as initial clearing of the bamboo scrub allows
a survey team to operate.   The contribution of small-holders is critical,
as trees and roots must be burned after removal by crawler tractors.   Although the same job could probably be done more quickly by machinery, this
would add substantially to the cash costs involved in the land-clearing
operations.   Furthermore, as the farmers are not required to pay for the
field operations on their holdings, the farmers' participation is a substantial contribution in kind;   at the same time, it reduces the capital-
intensive characteristic of land development operations.

Land tenure issues are fundamental, in any agricultural development
programme.   Very fortunately, there is little farm tenancy or farm fragmentation in Nan and household use-rights to the middle terrace farmland
are traditionally respected, despite the absence of written titles.
Village territorial claims are equally known and respected, although
boundaries through the scrub-forest and swidden regrowth on the terraces
are seldom marked.   In fact they have not mattered much in the past, but
once land-clearing began the precise location of village boundaries assumed
a new importance.   It became an important issue to villagers, for example,
that all the new holdings on Block B should be allocated to households
from Ban Na Lai (Tambon Ai Na Lai, Village No. 2) and not to the adjoining
Ban Na Pha (Village No. 1), shown in Fig. 8.2, because the former village
regarded Block B as part of its traditional area.   Subsequently, in order
to accommodate nearly 100 households from Ban Na Pha who claimed to have
used land on the south-eastern side of Sa Centre in the past, Blocks A and E

were cleared on steep slopes of up to 7 degrees, requiring a close spacing
of contour banks to prevent erosion losses.

At the level of individual households, land tenure issues associated
with the TALD Project have been considerably more intricate.   Traditionally, the use of middle-terrace land was through a form of communal
tenure under which use-rights to swiddens could not be inherited.   Subsequently population pressure and the greater demand for farmland has
sometimes led to formal subdivision by government officials and village
headmen.   Under these arrangements, over the past 20 years in parts of
central Nan, households have obtained individual parcels of land under
preliminary title (Nor Sor Song) which requires a farmer to establish
his right to permanent ownership by continuous occupation during three
years.   Understandably, in a socio-political situation where Thai villagers and officials consider the present trend towards private ownership
of land as normal and advantageous, it has not been possible to turn the
clock back to a system of communal land tenure, despite the attractiveness
of such a system.   Where land was not already held under private ownership with title, the central issue in 1968 and 1969 in Project Area No. 1
at Sa was the size of holdings.   This applied to Blocks A, B, E, F, G and
I at Sa, on the northern side of the Phrae-Nan highway.   Blocks C, D and H
had previously been subdivided.   In the six Blocks north of the highway,
holdings are generally 6, 8 or 10 rai in area (0.96 to 1.60 ha), the allocation for a particular household being decided in accordance with the farmer's
wishes and his household's labour supply.

Inevitably, as the population of each household changes, there will
be powerful pressures for change in the sizes of holdings.   Initially
the pressures may be towards subdivision, in order to create more holdings,
but in the more distant future much larger upland farms may result from
amalgamation of the existing small-holdings.   Until the distant day arrives
when urban employment opportunities have developed so significantly that
rapid rural-urban migration can take place, probably the most important
tenure consideration in TALD Project Areas will be to prevent the growth
of farm tenancy and landlordism which is risked with the establishment of
a farming system requiring higher cash inputs for fertilisers, contract
ploughing and simple farm machinery.

It might be argued that the concern for villagers' interests was
excessive, in the execution of a relatively uncomplicated land development operation.   Certainly, the total time involved in cadastral mapping, individual household consultations and subsequent year-by-year
monitoring of land use and farm yields is very considerable indeed, and
it may be that a larger-scale land development operation could not be
based on this model, geared as it is to the individual holding.   However,
it is all too easy to be fascinated by the noise, dust and vigorous action
of large-scale land development, without due appreciation of the fact that,
after the dust settles, the effectiveness of field operations will be
determined by the attitudes of farmers and their individual responses to
new opportunities.

4. THE FARMERS' RESPONSE

The immediate effects of bringing former swidden land on the middle terraces
at Sa into permanent-field cultivation, with effective ploughing for the
first time, were high rice yields (by standards in Nan) and a spectacular
return on the development investment.   The costs of field operations, as
discussed in the concluding section of this chapter, can be recovered from
the greater productivity of the cropland during the first three seasons,
but the direct benefits to the farmers are immensely more spectacular.
Since the individual holdings are two or three times as large as the
swidden area previously cultivated in a single year, households growing
only upland rice have obtained bumper harvests, as a compound of both
higher yield and the larger crop area.   This increased production has
been obtained without drawing upon paid farm labour.   Many farms in the
Sa Blocks, for example, averaged 1600 kg/ha of padi from 6 rai (0.96 ha)
during the first three years beginning in 1969.   Their domestic rice
production on the former swidden land jumped from an annual harvest of
about 450 kg, on 0.48 ha under crop, to more than 1500 kg from 0.96 ha.

The spectacular improvements in rice production have been matched
by a remarkable household elasticity of demand for rice in the years
immediately after the higher yields were obtained.   Before the TALD
operations began, most households in the villages of Project Areas 1 and
2 in Nan were grossly rice-deficient, to the extent of buying rice for

more than half the year and normally living on the brink of famine in the
few months before harvest.   Their former plight obviously helps to explain how many households have readily absorbed an increase of 200 per
cent in annual rice production, with only the addition of temporary household granaries.   Little surplus rice is sold, but domestic rice shortages
have been overcome and a gradual change in land-use away from the dominance
of rice, and towards cash crops, can be expected.

Substantial inter-block differences in the cropping patterns of the
Sa farms, shown in Fig. 8.3, reflect the preferences for rice and peanuts
inherited from the swidden farming system.   In Blocks A, B and E rice
occupied almost all the planted area in 1970.   Here the majority of
farmers, living in Ban Ai Na Lai or Ban Ai Na Pha, had no lowland fields
and were then entirely dependent upon their upland holdings for domestic
food production.   On the other hand, in Blocks F, G and I the proportion
of rice in the total planted area was only 48.6 per cent, 43.5 per cent
and 48.0 per cent respectively, in a much more mixed pattern of land-use
which reflects the fact that farmers in these three areas live in villages
near the Sa River, where a high proportion of 'swidden households' have
lowland fields as well.   Increasing diversity of cropping patterns can
be expected in the short-term on all these blocks, as less land is needed
to meet domestic rice requirements and correspondingly larger areas are
devoted to cash crops, such as peanuts and mungbeans.

The companion map of rice yields in 1970 (Fig. 8.4) shows a very
different pattern.   Here the outstanding feature is the common occurrence
of short-distance yield variations between farm holdings on the same block.
The mean padi yield for 235 holdings in the 6 blocks was 1530 kg/ha and
the standard deviation (709 kg/ha) was surprisingly large in a year when
growing conditions for rice at Sa were generally favourable, land preparation was approximately uniform over the whole area, and no fertilisers
were used by farmers.   The 1971 rainy season, by comparison, favoured
early plantings when dry weather in October affected crops planted after
mid-June;   and in 1971 the mean padi yield from 241 holdings in the 6
blocks was 1594 kg/ha (standard deviation, 1047 kg/ha), reflecting an even
more spectacular variation of yields within a very small farming area.

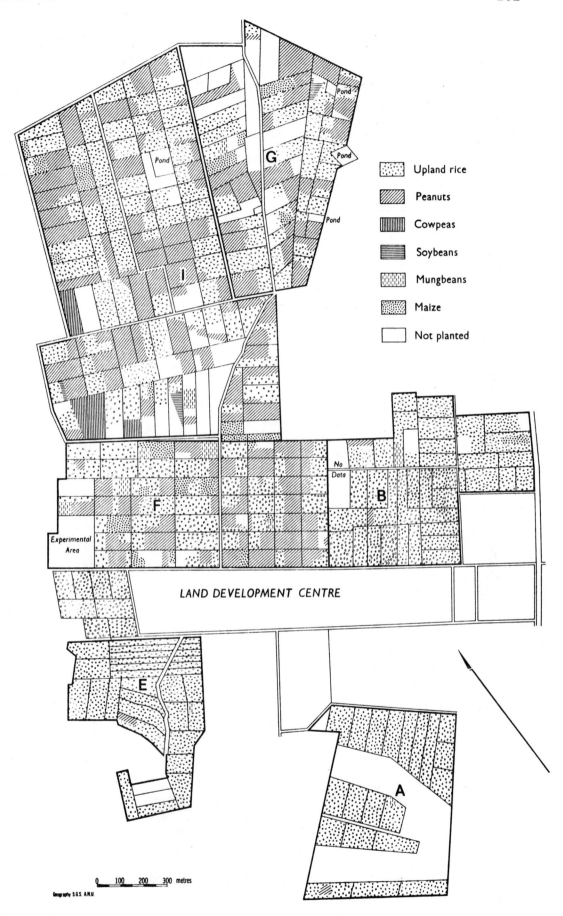

Fig. 8.3 Land use on Farmers' Blocks, Sa Project Area, 1970
(main rainy season crops).

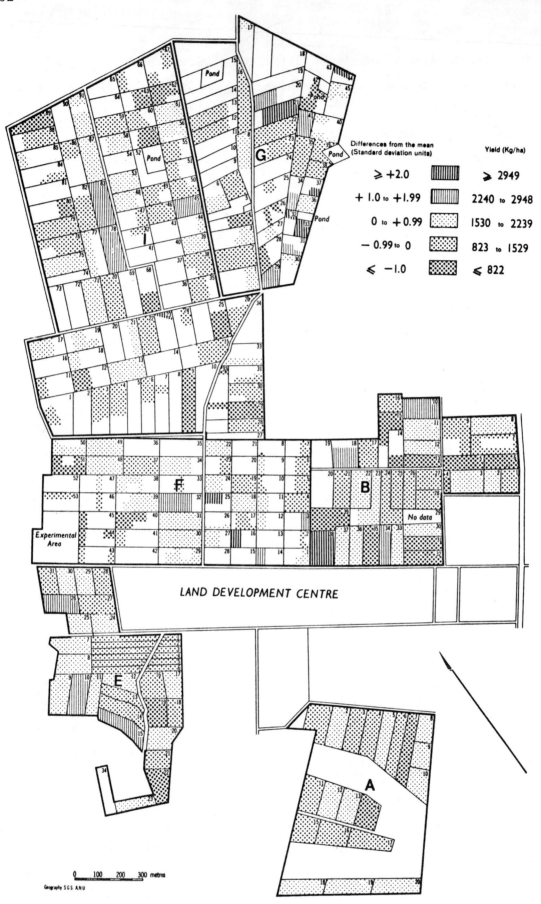

Fig. 8.4   Yields of upland rice on farmers' holdings in the six Farmers'
           Blocks, Sa Project Area, 1970. The mean yield was 1530 kg/ha
           and the standard deviation was 709 kg/ha. Holding yields are
           shown in standard deviation intervals above and below the mean.

Source: Harvest surveys, October-November 1970.

An understanding of why such different yields are obtained, often on adjacent farm holdings using the same soil series, is probably the most critical need for the future success of the TALD Project. As an initial step towards such an understanding, all households in the Project Area at Sa were interviewed soon after the 1970 harvest. Data from this survey are set out in Table 8.2, for one small area in Block B, comprising 10 holdings (Numbers 30-39, shown in Fig. 8.4). The salient fact which emerges is not variation in the available farm labour per household, which might have affected time-of-planting and weeding, but rather the extent to which different households received off-farm income during 1970. Although all 10 heads-of-household described their main occupation as 'farmer', actual farm income amounted to less than 50 per cent of gross household income in five out of the 10 instances; in the four instances where farm income exceeded 80 per cent of gross household income, the padi yields were outstandingly good, approaching or exceeding the research station's yield (2725 kg/ha) obtained on the same soil series (Yasothon Series), on the other side of the fence. From this preliminary considera- tion, it appears that rice yields obtained by this small group of 'farmers' are inversely related to off-farm income, with one exception (No. 30) among the 10 households. In sum, the evidence leads to the truism that good yields are obtained by the earnest farmers; the households whose basic needs were met by off-farm employment during the dry season before rice planting, obtained much lower yields in most instances, perhaps because they could afford to be more casual in their approach to early planting and weeding.

What are the implications of these large yield differences? First, it seems certain that as more innovations are offered to upland farmers in TALD Project areas, the specialist farmers who are already obtaining the relatively high yields will be the early adopters, thereby further in- creasing the yield disparities. In 1969, 1970 and 1971 all farmers in the Sa blocks had the benefit of good land preparation, carried out with Project equipment, together with the strong recommendation for early planting of rice in the rainy season; in 1972, many accepted the recom- mendation for the application of sulphate of ammonia on rice fields, at a minimum rate of 15 kg per rai (93.8 kg/ha); in 1973, higher-yielding

Table 8.2: Upland rice yields, available farm labour and sources of gross
            annual income for 10 households with adjoining holdings,
            Block B, 1970

Holding No.	Upland rice yield (kg/ha)	Cultivated area (ha)	Available labour (persons/ha)	Gross income per capita (bahts)	Sources of gross household income % farm	% non-farm
30	1750	1.60[a]	3.1	1057	27.8	72.2
31	706	1.92[a]	2.6	314	71.7	28.3
32	688	0.96	3.1	330	49.5	50.5
33	1563	0.96	4.1	338	44.4	55.6
34	2563	0.96	3.1	608	100.0	–
35	794	0.96	3.1	602	30.9	69.1
36	2125	0.96	3.1	318	86.9	13.1
37	2081	0.96	2.1	915	100.0	–
38	3344	1.44	2.8	514	84.7	15.3
39	750	0.96	2.1	275	41.9	58.1

a Includes a small area of lowland fields, assumed to have the same labour
   requirements as the upland fields.

Note: The size of the households varies between 4 and 10 persons, but in
       calculating 'available farm labour' only those members aged 13 to 59
       have been included, with deductions for household members permanently
       employed off the farm. The estimates of gross household income
       include all cash income and the value of domestic production consumed
       in the household, mainly rice valued at 8 bahts per tang (10 kg), at
       harvest.

Source: Survey of farm households, February–March 1971.

mungbean seed will be available at low cost; and in 1974, or later, recommendations are expected to be made on the cooperative purchase of better
cultivation equipment, such as a low-cost animal drawn toolbar, and on the
use of herbicides. Secondly, if experience with the adoption of innovations in the Indian wheatlands during the 1960s can be taken as a general
guide (Harriss, 1972:75), the farmers with more mixed cropping systems and
more varied sources of income will be slow to adopt the recommendations for
yield improvement.

        Thirdly, an intensive advisory programme is clearly needed if produc-
tion is to be increased from the large 'middle group' of holdings with yields
occurring within one standard deviation of the mean. This group had increased in 1971, compared with 1970, from 74 per cent to 83 per cent of all
holdings growing rice; unfortunately, the main change from 1970 to 1971 was

an increase from 39 per cent to 54 per cent in the holdings falling within
one standard deviation <u>below</u> the mean.   The adoption of recommended practices by these households, such as early planting and more intensive weeding
at particular stages in crop growth, will almost certainly be difficult to
achieve.   The poorer farmers among the 10 discussed in relation to Block B
yields already recognise why Nai Srilai, the owner of Holding No. 38,
obtains such good crops year after year; but as Lipton has pointed out in
relation to recent Indian experience, various farmers in the same village
and having adjacent holdings often have very different 'survival algorithms -
a set of rules of farming that ensure a tolerable minimum output' (Lipton,
1968:116).   In the Sa Project Area many farmers in households where there
is substantial cash income from off-farm work before the rainy season will
probably not see the need, or the desirability, of following Nai Srilai's
example when so much more effort is required.   Of course, they may be
influenced much more by the decision-making of Nai Suan Kuenpetr, the owner
of Holding No. 30, towards optimal production and income objectives rather
than towards income maximisation from agriculture.   If this happens, the
improvement of yields on the poorest holdings could still be very substantial
indeed.

Whether or not a major advisory programme is successful, it seems
certain that the yield disparities evident in these early years will lead
to major changes.   As the new potential of the middle-terrace uplands is
more widely appreciated, it is likely that pressures will mount for the
amalgamation of low-yielding farms into larger, more productive units owned
or managed by the more successful farmers.   Unless these pressures develop
concurrently with a marked increase in rural-urban migration, the ironic
situation may result where land development on the middle-terrace country
has actually increased farm tenancy and the growth of the landless group
whom it was intended to help.

5.   A PERMANENT FARMING SYSTEM?

The very uneven response of farmers to opportunities for higher yields can
be added to the difficulties which are inherent in the changeover from a
swidden farming system to permanent-field cultivation.   The characteristic
ecological problems of this change are the depletion of soil nutrients and

possible deterioration of soil structure, once continuous cultivation has replaced the 'bush fallow' system.

The likelihood of rapid nutrient decline in the middle-terrace soils of both Project Areas in Nan has been recognised from the outset.   For this reason a substantial agronomic research programme has been developed, first at Sa Centre and after 1970 at the Project's second research station in Lampang Province, dealing with other middle-terrace soils.   The research programme has concentrated on fertiliser trials and on the establishment of a rice-legume rotation designed to maintain nitrogen levels biologically, as far as possible, in order to reduce the inputs of purchased fertilisers. At the same time a long-term study of soil nutrition has been developed, with the particular objective of recording changes in the nitrogen and organic carbon status of soils used for repeated cultivation.

Overall, the early results have been encouraging.   They indicate that soil nitrogen levels have been lowered only marginally during two or three years of cultivation without the addition of nitrogenous fertilisers. On the other hand, the addition of nitrogen in the form of ammonium sulphate has resulted in a small increase in organic carbon levels while at the same time lowering pH in terrace soils which are initially acid anyway, to levels where symptoms of manganese toxicity in peanuts and mungbeans have become more widespread than is usually the case (J.L. Charley, 1972: personal communication).   Fortunately, the adverse effects of ammonium sulphate on soil acidity can be remedied easily and cheaply, by the application of lime, or by changing to other sources of nitrogen such as urea.

The most important results of the agronomic research programme so far have been the encouraging responses of local rice varieties grown on the two main terrace soils at Sa Centre, to applications of nitrogen in ammonium sulphate.   Yields on Yasothon series (a red latosol) and San Patong series (a grey podzolic soil) in the first, second or third year of cultivation are shown in Fig. 8.5, with the dotted lines indicating the expected yield responses at low rates of fertiliser application.   On the basis of these results it has been estimated that, at current local costs for ammonium sulphate, the use of fertiliser on Yasothon soils will be justified while padi can be sold or valued for subsistence at prices exceeding bahts 3.00 per tang (bucket containing approximately 10 kg). In recent years the price at harvest in Nan has been bahts 8.00 per tang.

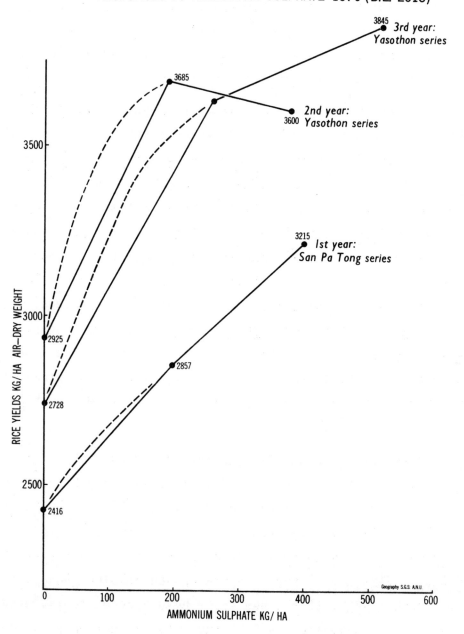

Fig. 8.5 Experimental yields of upland rice on the two main soil series, Sa Centre (Nan Province) in the rainy season of 1970.

Source: Mr I.M. Wood, Tropical Crop Agronomist, TALD Project.

Further research since 1970 on the selection of improved varieties of upland rice, peanuts and mungbeans offers the prospect of increased yields without the addition of substantial costs to the farmers.   The most important results have been with mungbeans, where higher-yielding varieties introduced from the University of Queensland have yielded up to 100 per cent above the local varieties used by farmers in Sa and Lampang.   A small quantity of seed of these varieties will be released to farmers in the Nan Project Areas during 1973, to be followed by a larger seed distribution programme involving both rice and mungbeans, as soon as seed-drying and storage facilities have been completed.

Although the expected problems of maintaining yields and avoiding rapid nutrient depletion are receding as research progresses, there are still long-term hazards of structural deterioration of the terrace soils and the cumulative effect of erosion losses.   A critical consideration in the long term may be the willingness of farmers to follow recommendations designed to reduce structural deterioration.   It is expected, for example, that a useful increment of organic matter can be obtained if farmers are prepared to return peanut plants to the fields, after threshing.   A much more drastic recommendation, hopefully to be avoided, would involve the planting of pastures or cover crops as part of a crop-pasture rotation.   A major difficulty standing in the way of such a land-use system, at the present time, is that many farmers involved in farming the terraces do not have buffaloes or cattle which could utilise the upland pastures.

Within the next few years the new farming system in TALD Project areas seems certain to come under stress of a different kind arising from the continued demand for land.   In the Sa area alone, 28 per cent of the population in 1970 was in the group aged 10-19.   As this group and older members of the same households marry, and later set up separate households, the pressures for subdivision of the existing upland holdings seem certain to become very strong indeed, if the new farms have become stable, productive units.   What this emphasises is that the intensification of land-use being achieved by the TALD Project on middle-terrace terrain must be matched in the lowlands as soon as possible.   With this end in view, investigations of underground water are now beginning in central Nan, in

the hope that a substantial increase in dry-season cultivation will be
possible there by pumping from shallow-depth aquifers.

6.   RETROSPECT AND PROSPECT

Looking back from the ploughed fields of upland holdings at Sa to the
short-cycle swidden system of the recent past, it is apparent that the
TALD Project has been primarily important in smoothing the transition
to permanent-field farming.   So far the chief impact of the project,
on the households involved, has been to increase domestic rice production so dramatically that the need for rice purchases in the months before
harvest has almost been eliminated.   While this change allows part of
the households' cash income to be deployed in other ways, the farmers are
still practising a subsistence-oriented farming system.   When the maintenance of higher rice yields on the better-managed holdings allows more
land to be released from subsistence production, the need for alternative
and profitable cropping systems will be acute.   So far only mungbeans
can be recommended, as the research results with peanuts have been just
as disappointing as the current yields on farmers' holdings.

In this and other respects the project is now entering a critical
stage.   In the four years since field operations began in 1968, most
attention has been given to the logistics of land development operations
and to creating an experienced field unit for work on the middle-terraces.
Careful costing of field operations in Nan in 1971 and 1972 has shown
that the immediate costs amount to approximately bahts 300-320 per rai
(US$93.75-100.00 per hectare), including all tractor operations, repairs,
maintenance and depreciation.   These costs can be compared with the
increase in production which has been estimated, on the basis of harvest
surveys, at about bahts 120 per rai (US$37.50 per hectare) each year in
the three years after land-clearing was carried out.   On this basis,
development costs can be recovered in the first three years.   If the
Thai government chooses to expand this work beyond the small initial
scope of the TALD Project, the decision will have to be made as to whether
costs are to be borne by the government (as a transfer of funds to poor
farming areas), or by the villagers involved, perhaps by loans through
the Bank for Agriculture and Cooperatives.

Although much has been learnt over the past few years about land development costs and farmers' responses to the new opportunities in central Nan, it would be wrong to begin immediate expansion of the existing project into a much larger operation.   Critical agronomic information is still needed, notably on ways to improve the yields of peanuts; further, the evidence of marked differences in the responses of farmers demonstrates the need for an effective agricultural extension programme to be established, to match the physical activities in land-clearing.

By mid-1975, if possible, the TALD Project should have established a comprehensive basis for a major development programme on low-yielding middle-terrace terrain in northern Thailand.   When that goal is reached, one important source of strength for future operations will be the rapport which has developed in TALD Project areas between unofficial leaders within the groups of farmers and many officers of the Department of Land Development.   Young Thai officers who have lived in rural areas of central Nan for the past few years now identify themselves with the local community and display an empathy with villagers which is remarkable for Thai government officers.   Placed in a wider context, this augurs well for the success of recent proposals which advocate a marked strengthening of agricultural extension in Thailand, to include recruitment of men from villages as 'extension assistants' (Report of the working group on rural manpower and employment, 1971; Fuhs and Vingerhoets, 1972:125-7).   These men may become a strong force of 'agricultural brokers', linking village farmers with government technical services and filling a vacuum which currently acts as a major handicap to agricultural development in Thailand.

Finally, it has to be recognised that development of the middle-terrace uplands, as outlined in this study of central Nan, is clearly only a limited palliative to the population problem which threatens many parts of northern Thailand.   Immense opportunities remain unexplored for intensification of land-use on lowland fields, by improvement of rainy season production and by further extension of irrigation for dry season cultivation.   All these opportunities for agricultural development need to be investigated systematically, and programmes integrated in a comprehensive schema for the Northern Region, if economic conditions in the

poorer rural areas are to withstand the stress of population pressure
within the next few decades.

ACKNOWLEDGEMENTS

The author is indebted to many Thai and Australian colleagues who have
worked on the Thai-Australian Land Development Project, for contributing
to his appreciation of the problems encountered.   In particular, grateful thanks for their help are due to Dr Chaiyong Chuchart, Khun Praiwan
Resanond and Khun Sawasdi Pongsuwan of the Department of Land Development, and to Dr J.L. Charley, Associate Professor J.W. McGarity and
Mr I.M. Wood of the Australian Colombo Plan Team.

REFERENCES

Chapman, E.C., 1967.   'An appraisal of recent agricultural changes in
             the northern valleys of Thailand', 6th Academic Conference,
             Agricultural Economics Society of Thailand, Kasetsart
             University, Bangkok (mimeo).

Chapman, E.C., 1970.   'Shifting cultivation and economic development in
             the lowlands of northern Thailand', in Land Development
             Department, 1970, Proceedings of a seminar on shifting
             cultivation and economic development in northern Thailand,
             Bangkok, pp. 226-50.

Fuhs, F.W. and Vingerhoets, J., 1972.   Rural manpower, rural institutions
             and rural employment in Thailand, Manpower Planning
             Division, National Economic Development Board, Bangkok.

Harriss, B., 1972.   'Innovation adoption in Indian agriculture - the
             high yielding varieties programme', Modern Asian Studies, 6,
             pp. 71-98.

Lipton, M., 1968.   'Strategy for agriculture:urban bias and rural planning'
             in Streeten, P. and Lipton, M. (eds), The crisis of Indian
             planning, Oxford University Press, London, pp. 83-147.

Moerman, M., 1969.   'A Thai village headman as a synaptic leader',
             Journal of Asian Studies, 28, pp. 535-49.

Report of the working group on rural manpower and development, 1971.
             National Economic Development Board, Bangkok (mimeo).

Rogers, E.M., 1969.   'Motivations, values and attitudes of subsistence
             farmers : towards a subculture of peasantry', in Wharton,
             C.R. (ed.), Subsistence agriculture and economic development,
             Aldine, Chicago, pp. 111-35.

Welsch, D.E., 1971.   'Agricultural problems in Thailand - some policy
             alternatives', Bangkok Bank Monthly Review, 12, pp. 89-104.

CHAPTER 9

THE OPIUM PROBLEM IN NORTHERN THAILAND

W.R. Geddes*

1. INTRODUCTION

Opium production is one of the most serious problems faced by Thailand.
It endangers the nation's reputation, saps its political strength and
injures a vast number of its people.

Neither in its origins nor in its current dimensions is it essentially a 'Thai Problem'. To a large extent it is one brought upon the
country by foreigners and maintained by foreign appetites. In an
article written in 1965 I stated: 'The real culprits in the opium trade
of Thailand are the consumers in Sydney, New York, London and all the
other places where the drug is used'.[1] The producers are all hill
tribesmen originating from China where they developed an economy
depending upon opium as a result of the influence of foreign traders.

Much of the criticism directed at Thailand because of the problem
is unfair on several counts. First, its origins, as a major problem,
lie outside Thailand. Secondly, it is an international problem which
can only be combatted by international efforts. It would be both unreasonable and impractical to expect Thailand to deal with it alone from
its own resources in the interests of the world community. Thirdly,
Thailand has made considerable efforts to tackle the problem, cooperating
with international bodies to an extent unprecedented in Southeast Asia.

In some respects the efforts the Thailand government has made have
compounded the problem for it, especially the declaration of opium
production as illegal. It increases the difficulty of maintaining
standards of honesty in the civil service. Illegal opium and corruption inevitably coexist, just as illegal alcohol and corruption coexisted
in America. The profits are so enourmous, the temptation so great, the

---

* Dr Geddes is Professor of Anthropology in the University of Sydney.
1 Quoted by Prasit Disawat in Ministry of the Interior, 1966:38.

need for concealment so conducive to dishonesty.   Narcotics inject a
poison into the veins of officialdom wherever they go.   Considering the
extent of the traffic which passes through Thailand the poison is less
than might be expected and the face of the government as a whole is
strongly set against it.

The efforts of Thailand are handicapped by two other factors.
The first is the attitudes of neighbouring governments.   In parts of
Burma and in Laos production is still legal and it is not wholly proscribed
in southern China.   Much of the opium grown in these countries passes
into Thailand.   The second factor is the tolerance shown to the hill
tribes.   They have been permitted to continue growing opium until such
time as replacement crops can be introduced.   Their persistence with an
illegal crop at the same time as they are subjected to propaganda against
it and interference with their trade outlets causes tension between the
tribes and the government to the political disadvantage of the government.

In the international perspective in which the opium problem must be
viewed, Thailand is a victim rather than a cause.   The extent to which
it is a victim and the degree of its self-interest in working towards a
reduction of the problem has only recently been fully recognised.

2.   THAI ATTITUDES TOWARDS OPIUM

Concern regarding opium consumption goes back at least 600 years in Thai
history.   A King of Ayudhya in his wars with Sukothai in the fourteenth
century A.D. became aware that opium smoking was sapping the physical
strength of his soldiers and enacted a law whereby drug addicts and pedlars
could be imprisoned and their property seized.   Succeeding kings passed
further legislation to suppress opium smoking.   The extent of it greatly
increased when Chinese began entering the country in large numbers during
the reign of King Rama III (1824-1851).   In 1839 an endeavour was made
to enforce the existing laws against opium smoking but it failed because
the Chinese traders formed secret societies to protect their activities.
In 1852 King Rama IV, recognising that opium smoking could not be suppressed by force, legalised it, but only for Chinese.   Sales of opium
were taxed and by 1907 the government had created a monopoly, although
undoubtedly illegal sales continued outside it.   In 1913 an opium refinery

was established and the opium was sold by distributing firms under special
licence.

The monopoly was valuable to the government; it produced a revenue
in 1950 for instance, of more than US$5,500,000.   Both sales and produc-
tion were officially under government control.   The Opium Act B.E. 2472
(1929) states: 'Article 5. It shall be unlawful to cultivate the opium
poppy, or to possess opium seeds, except under a licence granted by the
Government'.   This article, which has been reiterated in subsequent legislation, is still in force.

Despite the revenue benefit, the Thailand government became more and
more concerned in recent years about the adverse social consequences of
the availability of opium, particularly the spread of drug taking to the
Thai people and the increasing use of the powerful opium derivatives,
morphine and heroin.

In 1955 the government issued a proclamation stating that the sale of
opium would be outlawed from the 1st January, 1956.   On the 9th December
1958 the 37th Proclamation of the Revolutionary Party made the sale and
smoking of opium illegal throughout the Kingdom and seven months later the
paraphernalia of the opium dens were publicly destroyed in a huge bonfire
in Bangkok.

Opium production was dealt with by Section 20 of the Harmful Habit-
Forming Drugs Act (No. 3) B.E. 2502 (1959) which states: 'Whoever grows,
produces, imports or exports ...   any type of harmful habit-forming drug...
shall be liable to a term of imprisonment of six months to ten years and a
fine equal to ten times the value of such drug but not less than three
thousand baht'.   The complete prohibition of opium consumption was motivated by the realisation of the spread of the habit amongst the Thai people,
whereas in earlier years it had been largely confined to the Chinese.

Although the prohibition was effective in largely eliminating opium
smoking in the towns, the total number of addicts to the drug has continued
to increase.   At the end of 1958 there were 70,980 registered opium smokers.
To this figure should be added the number of unregistered smokers and morphine and heroin consumers, but it is doubtful if the total number reached
more than at most 150,000 addicts.   Following the ban on opium smoking,

the use of heroin, which is much more easily concealed, increased greatly. Dr Prayoon Norakarnphadung, the Director of Thanyarak Hospital for Addicts, estimated 400,000 heroin users in 1963.   Although this figure may be too high, few observers would place the number of addicts at less than 250,000. The Report of the United Nations Survey Team to Thailand in 1967 stated: 'United Nations sources, concurrent with those of the World Health Organi- sation, suggest that 1.6 per cent of the population is certainly affected by the use of narcotic drugs, with the main incidence falling, after the abolition of opium smoking, on the working age population' (U.N. Survey Team, 1967:66).

Not all the users of opiates are 'hard-core' addicts.   The heroin generally sold in Bangkok appears to be weaker in morphine content than forms sold in Hong Kong and elsewhere, and is therefore less strongly addic- tive.   Nevertheless, the extent of drug use is a serious problem for the country.   In contrast to opium smoking, heroin affects more Thai than Chinese, the urban workers more than agricultural workers and the younger age groups rather than the older.   It is closely related to criminality. In 1960 about 59 per cent of all arrested persons appeared to be drug users.

Measures against heroin use being taken by the Thailand government include education, treatment of addicts and law enforcement.   The most effective measure, however, would be the elimination of the supply.   The first step in this would be to determine the source of heroin, or the opium from which it is made.   Some certainly comes from neighbouring countries and some is produced in Thailand.   Only by knowing how much is so pro- duced can the size of Thailand's problem in eliminating the source of supply be known.

3.   ESTIMATES OF OPIUM PRODUCTION

For the 1967 United Nations Survey I analysed estimates of opium production stated or implied in relevant reports on the Hill Tribes.   The analysis is given in detail in Chapter V of the Report published by the Thailand govern- ment in Bangkok in 1967 (U.N. Survey Team, 1967).   Here I shall only summarise it.

The first account studied was that by Gordon Young.   In fact the
whole analysis was stimulated by a statement made to myself and separately
to the other members of the United Nations Team by Mr Young to the effect
that in his opinion the amount of opium production probably did not exceed
four tonnes. It was clear that he had not fully considered the conclusions
which could be drawn from statements in his own excellent pioneering study
of the Hill Tribes (Young, 1962).

Young estimated the relative importance of opium production in the
economies of the various tribes.   He also gave estimates of population
and of average incomes for the tribes.   By collating these several estimates I concluded that: 'If we accept its validity, Young's report shows
that in 1960 opium production for all the tribes could not have been under
thirty tons.   The figure could have been very much greater, but it certainly could not have been less' (U.N. Survey Team, 1967:4).

The second report analysed was that of the socio-economic survey
carried out by the Department of Public Welfare in 1962, with the advice
of Dr Hans Manndorf, a United Nations anthropological expert provided under
the programme for technical assistance in narcotics control (Report...1964).
This was the first fully systematic survey made in tribal areas.   Eighteen
villages were selected in the provinces of Tak, Chiang Mai and Chiang Rai.
The tribes covered in the selection were the Meo, the Yao, the Lisu, the Lahu
and the Akha.   These tribes were chosen because it was believed that they
were the main, if not the only, opium growers.

Preliminary study led to the conclusion that 0.5 _rai_ of land (0.08
ha) intensively cultivated or one _rai_ (0.16 ha) of land less intensively
cultivated, yielded about 1 kg of opium.   Each family in the opium growing
tribes cultivated three to four _rai_ and therefore produced about 4 kg of
opium.   A cross-check was made by considering the tribal incomes.   It was
estimated that the average family income in the tribes concerned was approximately 3200 to 3600 baht (US$153.85 to 173.08).   The price of opium was
800 to 900 baht per kg (US$38.46 to 43.27).   Therefore, if all the income
came from selling opium the figures would again indicate a production of
4 kg of opium per family.   The preliminary conclusions were confirmed by
detailed studies of the selected villages.

Utilising Young's report, Manndorf and his associates then assessed the total population of the five tribes as 133,550 in northern Thailand. This figure, they said, indicated that there were approximately 18,925 families.   At a production rate of 4 kg of opium per family per annum, the total annual production of the tribes must be approximately 75,700 kg.

When this figure was published doubt was expressed as to its accuracy. Many persons felt that the production could not be nearly so great.   The validity of the calculations was called into question.   The most serious criticism which could be made of this report was that, owing to limited resources, the samples were too small.   The figure of approximately 76 tonnes could have erred on either the high or the low side.

Because of the uncertainty which continued to exist both as to the demographic situation in the tribal areas and as to the quantity of opium produced, the government decided to carry out a preliminary survey of population and production during the opium season 1965-6.

It was planned to determine the actual number of all hill tribes living in the northern part of Thailand, to obtain data on some of their demographic characteristics and to collect data on crops and livestock and on the quantity of opium produced.

Field work for the survey was conducted during the period from 15 December 1965 to 31 March 1966.   A sampling method employing three types of samples was used:

(1) The A-type sample.   From a total of 1200 areas covering the entire northern region defined by aerial photographs taken in 1961, each area being approximately 90 square kilometres, 200 areas were selected. Survey teams of the Royal Thai Survey Department were sent into each of these areas to conduct a simple count of Hill Tribe households and inhabitants, classified by tribe and sex, as a basis for arriving at an estimate of the total populations of the tribes.

(2) The B-type sample.   This comprised 100 of the areas in the 200 constituting the A-type sample.   These B-type sample areas were re-photographed from an altitude of 10,000 feet (3048 m), to produce aerial photographs on a scale of 1:20,000.   The purpose of this sample was to determine the areas of land under various crops, especially opium, and the

photographs were intended to assist the field workers in locating sites
of crops by ground survey and to facilitate measurement of areas under
the various crops.   Unfortunately, owing to difficulties of weather and
other factors, in many cases the photographs could not be taken until
after the survey teams had been through the areas.   The field staff
were the Royal Thai Survey Department teams who were carrying out the
broader sampling throughout the A-type sample.

(3) The C-type sample.   This sample comprised 50 of the areas in
the 100 constituting the B-type sample.   The purpose of this sample was
to obtain detailed demographic and socio-economic information by means of
household interviews.

Two methods were used in the Survey to obtain information on the
extent of opium production.   One was to ask the villagers directly how
much they produced.   This method gave a total for all the tribal areas
of 38,600.44 kg.   The organisers of the Survey did not expect this method
to yield highly reliable results.   There is an understandable reluctance
on the part of tribespeople to reveal facts about opium.   Even when no
official action has been taken against growers they are aware of its
illegality.   Secondly, opium is, in effect, money to the tribesmen.   If
the amount they have of it is known their positions in trading and social
exchanges may be weakened.   At times, too, various persons within their
tribe, or from outside, may make requests or demands for a proportion of
their crop and therefore it is advantageous to the tribesmen to make the
amount appear as small as possible.

The second method was to measure the area of land growing poppy and
to calculate its yield from production averages which had been previously
determined.   By this method the total area of poppy land in 1965/6 was
estimated to be 112,000 _rai_ (17,920 ha).   Previously Dr Krui Punyasingh,
Agricultural Adviser to the Ministry of the Interior, had conducted extensive crop-cutting tests as the result of which he concluded that the
average yield of opium per _rai_ was 1.3 kg.   Therefore, calculating on
this basis, the production of opium in the 1965/6 season was 145,600 kg.

When this figure was revealed it was received with considerable
surprise because few people had suspected that local production was anywhere near as great as 146 tonnes.   But it could fit in with other known

facts.   An addicted opium smoker is said to consume on average about 1.3
kg per year.   The consumption, therefore of the registered opium smokers
in 1958 could have been 92 tonnes and it is probable that there were at
least twice as many actual smokers in the country as a whole.   Since 1958
the consumption of the drug, through expansion of heroin use, must have increased greatly.   Therefore even if local production is as high as 146
tonnes annually it still means that Thailand is a receiving rather than
a donor country in terms of world opium supply.

If this reasoning is correct the export which probably does occur
from Thailand must be the result of transit trade rather than of primary
production, although the actual opium which is exported may or may not
be locally produced.   It seems to me that this is an important fact to
recognise.   Critics of Thailand may suggest that the country profits
from opium.   This is highly doubtful.   Individuals may enrich themselves through trade but on balance there is probably a loss of foreign
exchange.   Even if there were a slight monetary balance in favour of
Thailand it must be more than offset by the weakening of the labour force
through addiction.

The only real gain which Thailand gets through local production is
the negative one of preventing a greater drain on exchange through more
buying from outside.   Thailand may suffer a disadvantage if efforts to
reduce production are not made on a regional basis.   It is to its credit,
therefore, that it is prepared to risk this disadvantage by presenting
itself as an example.

Some of the surprise at the figure which emerged from the 1965/6
survey was due to the fact that it was so much higher than estimates from
earlier surveys.   It was, for instance, almost double that of the estimate
made by the Department of Public Welfare as the result of its 1962 survey.
Probably the earlier estimates were too low.   But it is also possible
that production increased in the intervening years.

The Hill Tribe population, especially amongst the China-originating
major opium growing tribes, has been steadily expanding through immigration
and natural increase.   Also higher-yielding strains of opium poppy have
replaced earlier lower-yielding strains.   It is improbable, however, that

this process will continue.   The indications are that due to increasing
pressure on available land resources opium production has now passed its
peak in Thailand.   Not only government propaganda but shortage of suitable land are forcing more and more tribesmen to seek alternatives.

Was the figure of approximately 146 tonnes an accurate assessment?
There are many possibilities of error and therefore it should not be
taken as an absolute figure.   In the light of further experience I would
now incline to a lower estimate of somewhere in excess of 100 tonnes.
The significance of the 1965-6 survey lay in the fact that it did indicate that production was considerable and that therefore its elimination
was a major problem.   My own researches, limited in scope but intensive
in a small area, confirm this general picture.

The Meo village of Meto in Amphoe Hot of Chiang Mai province was
studied in detail by Khun Nusit Chindarsi of the Tribal Research Centre
and myself.   In 1965 it had a population of 570 persons in 71 households.
The total area of poppy cultivations was 1301.3 rai, or 209.55 hectares.
The people were asked how much opium they produced in that year.   The
total according to their own declarations was 604.46 kg.   We may safely
accept this as a minimum figure but it was almost certainly too low.   The
average yield worked out at only 0.53 kg per rai (0.08 kg/ha).   Actual
measurement of the harvest from a portion of one field gave a yield of
2.128 kg per rai (0.34 kg/ha).   No doubt the yield over-all was less
than this but not as low as the above figure.   There were several reasons
why the people probably underestimated their production to us.   Some have
already been mentioned but a more important reason was that opium fields,
as distinct from padi fields, are often not owned conjointly by a whole
household but by different individuals or families within it.   Thus the
head of the household from whom the declaration of total yield was usually
obtained may not have been aware of the full extent of household production.
If we assume that average production was between 1.0 and 1.3 kg per rai -
a conservative estimate - then the total opium production of Meto in
1965-6 was between 1.3 and 1.6 tonnes.

The most striking feature of Meto was the dominance of opium production in the economy.   Approximately four-fifths of the cultivated land
was devoted to it and one-third of the households had no padi fields at all.

For their subsistence they had to rely on sales of opium.   This exempli-
fies the dependence upon opium of the principal opium producing tribes.

4.   THE DEPENDENCE OF TRIBAL PEOPLE ON OPIUM

In northern Thailand the opium poppy does not grow well at heights below
900 metres and groups living at lower altitudes - mainly the Lua', the
Shan, the Khmu, and most of the Karen and Akha - are not usually poppy
cultivators.   The groups who generally live above this level, namely
the Meo, the Yao, the Lahu and the Lisu, are the principal opium producers.

The populations of these latter groups were estimated by the 1965/6
survey as follows:

Meo	53,031
Lahu	15,994
Yao	16,110
Lisu	9,440

Thus in terms of numbers and also probably in terms of opium production per head the Meo are the most important group.   Because of this fact
and because they are the people I know best the following discussion will
deal specifically with them but much of what is said probably applies also
to many of the other opium producing groups.

The Meo came into Thailand mainly within the last half-century with
a tradition of poppy cultivation and they seek the land best suited for it.
The first criterion is altitude.   Other things being equal, the higher
the better.   There is very little usable land above 1600 metres and most
Meo villages will be found between that height and 1000 metres, with a
median height of about 1200 metres.   The second criterion is a suitable
land configuration.   If possible the slopes should not be severe.   If
steep slopes must be used, growers prefer them to be near the tops of the
hills where erosion is least.   The third criterion is soil quality which
is judged by type of vegetation and the appearance and feel of the soil.

Areas of land which fulfil these criteria are generally small.
Usually within a few years of first settlement they acquire a high density
of population.   The main reason for this, other than their small size, is
that the Meo prefer to congregate in fairly large groups for reasons

connected with their social structure and religion, for security, for the
pleasures of a wider social life and for the prestige of a large village.
The density in the Meto area was 46.5 persons per square kilometre.
Because of excessive steepness much of the land was unsuitable for cultivation.   The density on the cultivable land was approximately 70
persons per square kilometre.

The density of population combined with the large size of household
poppy cultivations means that a large proportion of the available land is
under cultivation each year.   At Meto the average area of poppy cultivation per head was 2.4 rai (0.38 ha).   The average household size was
eight persons, giving an average household cultivation of 19 rai (3.04 ha).
In 1965 between 30 per cent and 40 per cent of the cultivable land available to the people was under cultivation.

Such a high degree of land use makes impossible a rotational system
of swiddening such as is practised by the non-opium growing tribes.   The
Meo can maintain themselves on their present system only by continuous
cultivation of the same areas of land.   Poppy allows them to do this
because it can be grown season after season continuously for periods of
five to 20 years depending upon the quality of the soil.   It is frequently
associated with a between-seasons crop of maize which is used mainly for
pig and fowl raising.

Inevitably, however, there is a limit to the time the people can so
maintain themselves in an area.   Thus opium often forces the Meo to a
migratory way of life.   This way remains viable either if there are
unexploited areas for them to move to, or if the total population remains
so light that although all areas have been previously exploited there are
enough areas abandoned sufficiently long to allow re-exploitation.   Both
conditions appear to be disappearing in northern Thailand.   Therefore
the Meo are facing a crisis.

What are the alternatives for them?   Theoretically, even in Meto,
it might seem possible for them to change to a rotational system of dry
rice cultivation.   If all the land were used for rice, each household
might have available to it about eight rai (1.28 ha) of land each year on
a seven year cycle.   But practically this would be impossible because much

of the land has already been used for poppy for several years and has lost
its fertility for rice.   Thus the adoption of rice cultivation as the basic
means of subsistence would only be possible in new areas and such areas are
far too few to accommodate the Meo population.

It would also be extremely difficult culturally, and economically
depressing for the Meo to make such a change.   Their social life and their
demographic pattern is adapted to a cash economy.   In relation to other
non-opium producing tribes their standard of living has been comparatively
high.   A subsistence economy on the land likely to be available to them
would place them probably at the lowest level.

Another alternative is for them to change to crops which will provide
a livelihood from smaller areas of cultivation.   The practicality of this
is also highly doubtful as a solution for all the Meo, especially as
incipient welfare measures appear to be accentuating their increase in
population.   But it is a possibility of providing relief for some of the
Meo and it has the added advantage of replacing opium with other cash crops
which, rightly chosen, could enrich the Thai economy.   It would be the
easiest alternative for the Meo to adopt and could utilise their experience
with cash-cropping.   It is the course which certain Thai agencies, including the King's Programme, have been following and which has been
advocated in a United Nations plan discussed below.

5.   UNITED NATIONS PROPOSALS FOR OPIUM REPLACEMENT

There have been two United Nations missions to Thailand in connection with
the opium problem, on both of which I served.   The first mission in 1967
surveyed the economic and social needs of the opium-producing tribes and
produced a general report.   Significant aspects of its conclusions were
that opium was a basic feature of the economies of some of the largest
tribes;   its elimination would be a long term process;   and forcible
measures should be avoided, with the emphasis placed upon a programme of
crop replacement.

A further mission was sent to Thailand in 1970 and one of its tasks
was to recommend a pilot project for the replacement of opium in a selected
area or areas.   It was in Thailand from October 1st until December 10th,
1970.   Both missions were supplemented by high-level Thai teams which

provided basic information and much of the advice leading to the final
conclusions.

The Report of the 1970 mission has not yet been officially published.
What follows therefore is my own personal assessment of the situation which
was incorporated in this Report and endorsed by the other members of the
mission.

Plans for economic change have to pay first regard to the existing
reality.   Each of the opium-growing tribes has its distinctive socio-
cultural system embodying customs, religious beliefs and social inter-
relationships founded in tradition, moulded by history and generally
adapted to present circumstances.   Through their socio-cultural systems
the tribes find their group organisation and their personal security.   If
the systems were to be broken down completely, community cooperation would
collapse causing demoralisation.   Replacement with another system from
a state of complete breakdown would mean building anew that which has
taken many generations to create.   Therefore change should be construc-
tive not destructive, supplementing or modifying what is already there,
proceeding through the will of the people themselves.   The conclusion
from this is that development measures should be implemented as far as
possible through the existing social system and only at the wish of the
people.

After recommending assistance to Thai government programmes which
are already in action and proposing the establishment of a Highland Agricultural Research and Production Station, the mission proceeded to consider a project for crop replacement in selected villages observing the
principles stated above.

From a list of six villages which the government thought might be
suitable for the pilot project two were selected.   One was Meto,
already mentioned, and the other was Pa Khia in Chiang Dao district of
Chiang Mai province.   They were the two largest on the government list
and presented a range of land types and conditions which appeared to cover
most of those in the opium region.

Both villages were Meo but even at the outset of the project other
tribes would be influenced.   Meto is set amongst Karen communities,
the nearest of which is little more than one kilometre from some of the

Meo houses.   Poppy cultivation has been spreading from the Meo to the
Karen.   Numbers of Karen work on Meo fields and because of the availability of opium in the area and its use as a currency many Karen have
become addicted to the drug.   At Pa Khia there are Lahu and Lisu communities in the neighbourhood.   Any successful change in the crop production
of the Meo would be quickly followed by these other tribal groups and it
should not be difficult to extend to them the supply and market facilities
instituted in Pa Khia.   Meto has the added interest of the presence of
11 Yannanese trading stores depending partially on opium.   It may be that
events since 1970 have made one or both of these village unsuitable for
the project.   The general lines of the scheme, however, should be appli-
cable wherever it is instituted.

The first step suggested was the election of a Community Council.
Its exact structure would depend upon the social structure of the village
concerned but it was suggested that at Meto it might comprise the headman,
two nominees of the headman (one who would normally be his assistant and
one a leading shaman) and one representative for every clan in the village.
It should be mentioned that this proposal for Meto was developed in discussion with the villagers.   All suggestions for development would be
submitted to the Council for debate and action would depend on its approval.
Meetings would be held publicly.

It would be necessary to have some outside personnel at the start to
introduce new techniques and to teach in the proposed school.   It was
recommended that the number of outsiders be kept as small as possible in
order to preserve a 'low-profile' approach which would not undermine Meo
initiative, leadership and self-respect.

It was suggested that at Meto there should be two positions filled
initially by outsiders, probably Thai government personnel.   The first,
an organiser, would coordinate the project and be both the consultant
and servant of the Community Council.   As his behaviour might well
be the key to the success of the whole project, he should be a person with
sympathy for the hill tribes, an ability to live with them on equal terms
and a readiness to learn language and customs as quickly as possible.   He
would live in the village and therefore care would have to be taken by the
agency employing him to ensure that he obtained full credit for his work
and did not miss out on chances of promotion.   It was felt he should be

given a salary supplement in recognition of the pioneering importance, difficulty and self-effacing quality of his work.

The second would be an agricultural advisor who would discuss agricultural matters with the villagers, advise them on new crops and planting techniques, help them in obtaining seed and generally assist them in all efforts to replace opium and improve production of other crops. He would act as a medium between the Highland Research and Production Station and the village, seeking advice from experts there on problems which arose, translating advice from visiting experts to the villagers, obtaining supplies of plant material and arranging for the training of persons from the village. My own feeling was that because of the qualities required for the job - agricultural knowledge, self-reliance, enterprise and fluency in English to enable him to deal with foreign experts - the advisor should be a graduate in agriculture.

In addition it was proposed that a villager be recruited to serve as an agricultural assistant and another as a storekeeper. They would be sent to the Highland Research and Production Station for preliminary training.

The agricultural programme would involve first of all a classification of the land to determine its suitability for particular crops. This could be carried out in two stages. In Stage 1 an immediate survey would be made to decide the best areas in each farmer's land for the new crops which that farmer elected to plant. In Stage 2 a complete survey of all village land would classify it in terms of its best long term use.

There were two reasons for suggesting that the land classification be in two stages. The first was the desire to make an immediate attack on opium production, as this was a United Nations charge to the mission. The complete survey would take a long time. In the first planting season the Meo would be encouraged to plant potatoes and beans on land which they would otherwise use for poppy. This might not be the best long term use of the land and in that case the aim would be to convert it to more suitable uses when these were indicated by the second stage of classification.

The second reason for proceeding with the classification in two stages was to avoid frightening the Meo. They are aware of the tenuous nature of their land holding and their dealings with officials in the past have often

been delicate.   It would be easy to under-estimate the extent of suspicion,
because it would probably not be openly expressed, and then be surprised at
resistance, unexplained lack of cooperation, or people moving out of the
project area.

When the second stage is reached, it would be made clear to the
people through prior discussion that the survey was to help them make the
best use of their land by telling what crops were likely to yield the greatest profit.   It would have to be explained that there was no intention to
usurp their land ownership.   Agreement would be sought first with the
Community Council and then with the individual owners concerned to make
some land available for general project purposes, such as demonstration
plots, nurseries and sites for buildings, and owners should be compensated
for land they yielded.   There might be other areas unclaimed because
owners had left, or which were no longer considered suitable for production, which the people might agree could be classified into a common pool
for distribution to persons short of land or to those who would agree to
use it for a designated purpose.   It was proposed that the government consider granting full land rights to farmers who eliminated opium.

It is not possible in the space of this short paper to discuss details
of the planting programme and the other economic developments which might
be instituted in the village area.   Suggestions for profitable plant
sequences, the introduction of tree crops and new enterprises such as seri-
culture and fish breeding are included in the mission's report and it is
also proposed that expert advice be available from consultants, mainly Thai
but also including some foreign experts.

Great importance was also given in the proposals to the provision of
community medical, educational and recreational facilities, for three
reasons.   First, they would improve the interest and quality of life.
Secondly, they would support the economic aspect of the project by encouraging the people to remain settled in order to enjoy the facilities.
Thirdly, the people's capacity to manage their own affairs would be improved
by education and their efficiency by better health.

It was hoped that in the operation of the facilities attention would
be paid to the maintenance of tribal identity, on the grounds that loss of
self-respect might cause demoralisation and so undermine the project.   For

instance, it was recommended that school-teachers and dispensers, as well
as agricultural assistants, should if possible be Meo and that, although
Thai would be the basic language of senior classes in the school, the
children should also become literate in Meo. It was suggested, too,
that the pupils be encouraged to take pride in Meo costumes. It was expected that a degree of assimilation would occur and no impediment would
be put in the way of any who wished to change their cultural identity,
but the project itself would do nothing to devalue Meo customs or values.

In all the proposals emphasis was placed on the necessity of keeping
the cost low by utilising local resources and materials in order to preserve the 'low-profile' approach, to maintain the autonomy of the community and to establish the scheme on a basis which could be maintained by
local resources after the initial outside support had been withdrawn.

(i)   New crops and markets

Replacement crops would have little appeal to the villagers unless
they could be sold, preferably at a price as profitable as that of opium.
This requires the right choice of crops and the right marketing organisation.

The following categories of crops appear suitable:

(a) Crops which grow better in the highlands than in the lowlands.
The most promising appear to be tree crops, such as coffee, tea and
various fruits.   The King's Programme of assistance to the hill tribes
has done a great deal of work in developing better strains of peaches and
is experimenting with apples.

(b) Crops which can be grown in the highlands when they are in short
supply in the lowlands. Most vegetable crop production would fit into
this category.   These are also the crops which can most easily replace
opium because it, and the maize which precedes it, are grown during the
wet season when vegetables such as cabbages, potatoes and beans are in
short supply in the lowlands.

In all cases it would be necessary to avoid over-supply. Sometimes
the hope has been expressed that a single miracle crop will be found to
replace opium.   This is highly unlikely.   The topography of the hill

tribe area probably will preclude its developing any kind of extensive
export agriculture.   Although there may be a possibility of some green
vegetable export to Malaya, generally production must be for purely local
markets which have limited absorptive capacity.   Therefore the introduction of new crops should be diversified according to a planned pattern.
The fact that little attention has been given to diversification in plans
so far may be justified in the early stages of new crop introduction, but
the need for it is becoming apparent.   Failure to recognise the need soon
enough could result in serious discouragement of tribal communities who
may produce in a mood of optimism only to have their hopes dashed by
inability to sell at adequate prices.

Diversification according to market potentiality requires good
market knowledge.   Marketing organisation is also necessary if the tribal
producers are to gain the most from the markets which do exist.   Therefore it was recommended that, as a necessary supplement to the crop replacement project, a marketing organisation be set up.   It was proposed:

(a)   that a Marketing Expert be supplied by the United Nations
       to study Thailand conditions and give advice.   He would
       be attached to the Highland Research and Production Station.

(b)   that producers' cooperative stores be established in the
       villages in the project area.

(c)   that a Marketing Organiser be appointed who would arrange
       for the collection and sale of produce bought by the
       village stores; supervise a produce depot in Chiang Mai;
       study market conditions constantly and seek new outlets
       for tribal products; and visit the villages in the project
       area periodically to advise on market conditions, modes of
       storage, etc.

(ii)   Price support scheme

Considerable debate occurred over a proposal to establish a guaranteed minimum price for crops which villagers in the project area might be
induced to plant in place of opium.   Some of the objections to it were
powerful, such as the argument that it would create a precedent for a
measure which the government would find impossible to finance in other
communities which might then request it.   Nevertheless my own view is
that it is probably essential for the success of the project.

Two reasons are generally given for the opium-growing tribes' attachment to opium as a cash crop.   The first is its ease of transport.   One

kilogram of opium is worth as much as about 750 kg of padi.   Fruit and
vegetables, too, have a vastly higher ratio of bulk to value than opium.

The second reason is the high price of opium.   This, however, can
easily be overstated.   The great profits from opium are made by traders
and increase in ratio the further the opium travels.   For hill tribe producers it is often only marginally more profitable in terms of labour
input than other products such as vegetables.   Sometimes it is less so.
This may be true even when the labour of transporting the other products
to market is included.

The above two factors, therefore, are not sufficient to explain the
tribal attachment to opium.   Although both are influential, they are less
important, in my opinion, than a third factor which has not been fully
recognised.   This is the certainty and stability of the market for opium.

Opium has in fact a guaranteed price.   Of all the crops of Southeast
Asia its price has been the most stable.   During the 12 years I have been
familiar with the Meo the price has always been between 750 and 1000 baht
per kg depending upon the time of the year it is sold.

Markets for alternative crops likely to be produced in the first
phases of a crop replacement project show wide variation.   The price of
potatoes, for instance, varies from 1.50 to 11.00 baht per kg, the fluctuations being partly due to seasonal factors and partly due to manipulations
by traders.

It was therefore proposed that a produce-purchasing scheme, including
credit facilities and associated with the marketing organisation mentioned
above, be established in the project villages.   To encourage confidence in
the scheme it was recommended that guaranteed minimum prices be offered for
major products at least for the first two years.

The minimum prices would be effective only when market prices had
sunk so low that growers could not obtain those prices otherwise, through
cooperative selling or by private sales.   The stores would seek to avoid
loss by storing the produce until prices rose, or by having their own established outlets.   When general market prices were above the minimum levels
the stores would pay higher prices determined by the amounts they expected
to recoup.   The guaranteed price, it was felt, would be a major stimulus
to the elimination of opium.

As guaranteed minimum prices would be realistically adjusted to expected market prices, and only potentially profitable crops would be introduced, the sum required to operate the scheme would not have to be great and once a new crop pattern was established in a village the resources of the fund could be utilised elsewhere.

6.   CONCLUSION

I began this paper by arguing that the problem faced by Thailand was not of its own making and not maintained by its own venality.   And although in these days it appears easier to gain popularity in the West by criticising established Southeast Asian governments, I shall end on the same note.   There is a real danger, I think, that if the problem is not recognised as a world problem with world responsibility for its solution the government may relax its efforts in money and manpower to reduce opium production and trade, although the growing realisation of the extent to which the Thai people themselves are suffering from drug abuse may persuade it otherwise.

The motivation for United Nations schemes comes basically from countries which are recipients of opium and opium derivatives.   If the schemes proposed for Thailand follow the normal procedure of the United Nations Technical Assistance Programme, the Thailand government must bear a proportion of the cost itself and the schemes will not begin until it agrees to do so.   In the case of most United Nations schemes there is sound reason for this requirement as the gain is normally in terms of the country's own welfare.   But this case is different.   The main gain is expected to be extra-territorial.   At least until neighbouring countries engage in similar efforts the work which Thailand is called upon to do will profit it only minimally and cost it trouble.   Even the effort is in a sense extra-territorial because it means interfering with the economies of tribes which in the present delicate strategic situation it would be more politic not to disturb.   Therefore my own view is that in the case of the hill tribe opium replacement scheme United Nations assistance should be given without insistence on Thai counterpart funds.

The Thailand government is in fact in an unenviable middle position. It receives criticism both from the outside world and from the tribes – in the one case because it does not do enough to restrain the flow of opium and in the other case because it does too much.   We have suggested why the first criticism is largely unfair and we shall now suggest why the second one is also.

One cannot expect illiterate tribal people isolated from the wider world to understand so complicated a matter.   All they know is that a traditional product is now condemned.   Yet in truth the illegality of opium, which earns the government so much censure in tribal minds, is the very source of its profitability to them.   Nothing would end opium production in the hills of Thailand more quickly than to remove all restrictions on opium production and trade.   The tribal producers could not possibly compete with cheaper sources of supply elsewhere.

REFERENCES

Ministry of the Interior, 1966.   The report of the preliminary socio-
        economic survey of the Hill Tribes 1965-66, Ministry of the
        Interior, Bangkok.

Report...., 1964.   Report on the socio-economic survey of the Hill Tribes
        in Northern Thailand, Department of Public Welfare (mimeo).
        A shorter version of this Report which does not give details
        of opium production was published under the same title by the
        Ministry of the Interior, Bangkok, 1966.

U.N. Survey Team, 1967.   Report of the United Nations Survey Team on the
        economic and social needs of the opium-producing areas in
        Thailand, Thailand Government, Bangkok.

Young, G., 1962.   The Hill Tribes of Northern Thailand, Siam Society,
        Bangkok, 1962.

CHAPTER 10

POPULATION DYNAMICS AND DISPERSAL TRENDS
AMONG THE KAREN OF NORTHERN THAILAND

Peter Hinton*

1.   INTRODUCTION

Unlike other ethnic groups of shifting cultivators in northern Thailand,
the Karen are concentrated in one large area between the Sittang River in
Burma and the Ping River in Thailand.   The other groups are widely dispersed, occupying small pockets of country over the whole of north Thailand,
north Burma, Laos and southern China.   The wide dispersal of these peoples
reflects their greater mobility when compared with the Karen, who prefer
sedentary residence.   In this paper I will demonstrate how this pattern
has developed, and show how it ill serves the Karen when population increases
rapidly.   I shall first of all document demographic and migratory trends
among the Karen and then discuss this material in the light of data relating
to the Meo, Yao and Lahu peoples in Thailand.

2.   THE KAREN DATA

The Karen are the largest ethnic group inhabiting the uplands of Thailand,
where they form about 44 per cent of the total population; but with only
about 250,000 people, they represent an insignificant section of the
32,000,000 or so Thai.   In Burma, there are about 2,000,000 Karen and they
are second only to the Burmese in numbers (Tadaw, 1961).

Most Karen are concentrated on the eastern watershed of the Sittang
River, and on the eastern and western watersheds of the Salween.   The
latter region extends across the Burmese frontier into Thailand, where
settlements can be found as far east as the Ping River valley and as far
south as Pran Buri.   A handful of long-established villages can be found
east of the Ping valley (Fig. 10.1).   Thus in north Thailand and Burma,
large tracts of contiguous country are largely or exclusively inhabited by

_____

* Mr Hinton is Lecturer in the Department of Anthropology, University of
Sydney.

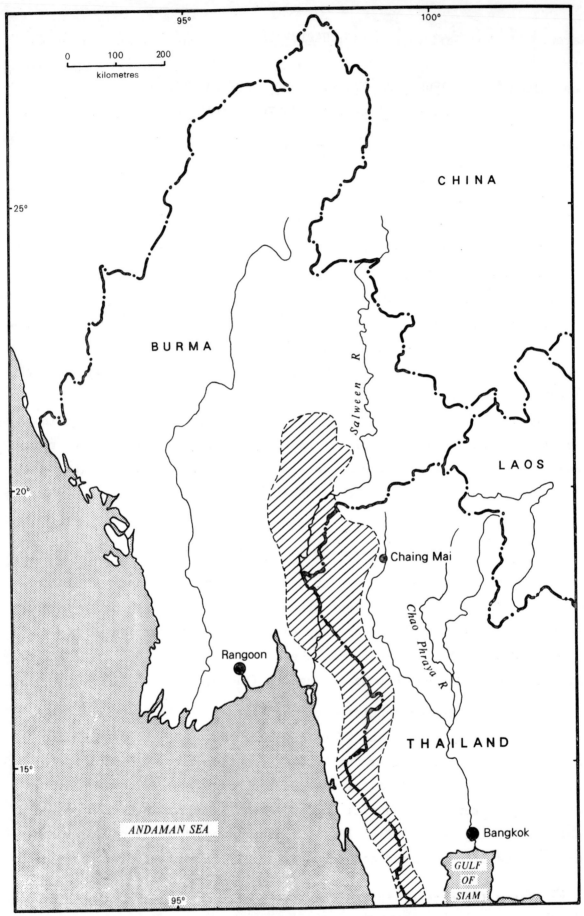

Fig. 10.1 Main area of population.
Source: Lebar, Hickey and Musgrave, 1964.

Karen.   In Mae Sariang district, which contains the heaviest concentration of Karen in Thailand, it is possible to walk for several days and
see only Karen.

According to Marshall (1922), a Baptist missionary whose book
remains the only detailed account of Karen culture, many Karen in Burma
cultivated irrigated riceland in the plains of the Sittang, Salween and
their tributaries.   Others mixed irrigated terrace cultivation with
swidden practices in the uplands.   In Thailand most Karen fell into the
latter category, although many villages depended entirely on swidden rice.
Their economy operated typically on a subsistence basis, although small
quantities of marketable commodities such as sesame seed, tobacco, forest
products and livestock, were also produced.

My field investigation concerned four major villages, three of which
had one or more satellite hamlets.[1]   As each major village farmed a recognised territory in common with its satellites, I regard each complex
of communities as an entity (Fig. 10.2).   The area of 33.4 square kilometres claimed by the four villages lay about 20 miles southeast of the
town of Mae Sariang.   Nevertheless, contacts between the people of these
villages and lowlanders, or even with upland dwellers of non-Karen ex-
traction, was most infrequent.

The terrain was rough and generally suitable only for swidden cultivation, although some creek valleys could be used for small scale construction of irrigated terraces.   The mean altitude of the villages was about
900 metres, which was unsuitable for opium poppy cropping.

The area was not pioneered by Karen.   Until about 1800 it was the
scene of fairly extensive Lua' settlement, relics of which can be found to
the present day in the form of potsherds and discarded implements scattered
over former village sites.   In about 1800 the dispersed Lua' villages
contracted, to form much larger and more easily fortifiable settlements
(Kunstadter, 1967:641).   The cause of this radical change in Lua' distribution appears to have been the aggressive expansion of the Kayah (Karenni),
whose traditional territory lay to the northwest (Mangrai, 1965: ch.8).
The Kayah terrorised isolated Lua' villages, but did not stay in the area.

---

1 Fieldwork was carried out in 1968-69 over a period of 18 months while
Advisor to the Tribal Research Centre, Chiang Mai.

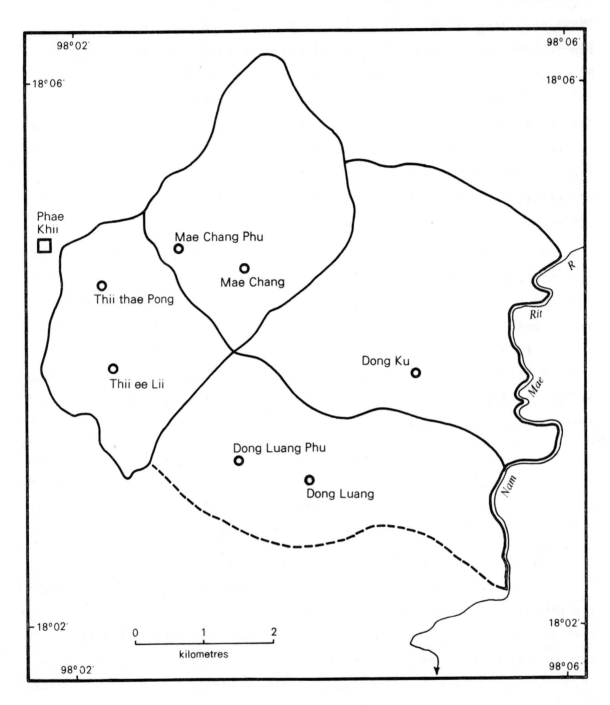

Fig. 10.2   Territorial boundaries of study villages.
            An unbroken line denotes a recognised territorial
            boundary.   A dotted line indicates an indefinite
            boundary.

Source: Sheet 4665 III, Series L708, 1:50,000, U.S. Army Map
            Service, Edition 1-AMS, 1962.

Their interest was in booty, not in territorial conquest.

A few decades after these events, the Karen began to move into
Thailand in fairly large numbers.   Their migration was prompted by a
resurgence of Burmese military power, which was used to subdue Karen in
areas which had resisted the assertion of Burmese hegemony.   Large numbers
of Karen began to move into Thailand about 150 years ago, occupying land
left by the departing Lua'.

At first the villages appear to have been widely separated, but as
the population of each expanded, satellites split off and all swidden land
was claimed by one community or another.   Of the four villages surveyed
in detail, Thii ee Lii was the oldest; but the oldest village in the area,
evidently first established by migrants direct from Burma, was Phae Khii,
a large village lying a few kilometres to the west (Fig. 10.2).   As the
population of Thii ee Lii grew, it in turn gave rise to a satellite settlement which ultimately claimed its autonomy by delineating a separate territory, and asserting its independence in ritual matters.   This new village
became known as Mae Chang.   After a further passage of time, and by a
similar process, Dong Ku and Dong Luang, originally satellites of Mae
Chang, became autonomous communities.   This development occurred about 70
years ago.   In recent years, Dong Luang and Thii ee Lii and Mae Chang have
given issue to satellite hamlets, leaving Dong Ku as the only village of
the four to remain a single village community.

At first new settlements could be formed when members of large, well-
established villages who owned land towards the periphery of their village
territory, found it more convenient to build their homes close to their
swiddens, instead of commuting daily between farm and village.   Secondly,
villages divided by major factional disputes often split into two or more
discrete settlements.   Over the past 20 years or more the latter factor
has been the only cause of village fission, for villages have been so close
together that community members had no difficulty in quickly reaching all
arable land available to them.   The most recent satellite settlements to
form, those associated with Mae Chang and Dong Luang, are a consequence of
divisive quarrels within the parent villages.

I have said that one of the major causes of village fission was
population growth.   It is interesting to examine the nature of this growth,

and to determine to what extent it has been caused by natural growth as
opposed to in-migration.   To do this I shall trace the development of
Dong Luang and its satellite from a pioneering nucleus, to a fully
fledged village community.

The pioneering nucleus of Dong Luang consisted of three households,
two of which were connected by a sibling link.   (I should add here that
the Karen norm is for monogamous nuclear family households, and it is
uncommon for other relatives to be attached.)   The three pioneering
households were unusually large, with a total of 26 persons giving a
mean of 8.7 per household.   This compares with a mean of 4.5 per household, yielded by a survey of 166 domestic groups in 1969.   When they
established the settlement, none of the three married couples in the
pioneering households had completed their reproductive lives, so that
the number of persons who moved into the area was probably less than 26.

In 1969 there were 39 households and 179 individuals in Dong Luang
and its satellite villages.   Of these, members of 25 households (totalling 133 individuals, 64 per cent of households and 75 per cent of the
overall population), traced direct bilineal descent from the pioneering
group.   During the period elapsing between the foundation of the village
and my field survey, 38 marriages involving descendants of the pioneers
took place.   Of these, seven were between village members who stayed in
the village after marriage; 13 were between a community member and outsiders, and followed by residence in the outsider's village; and 18
were between a community member and an outsider, and were followed by
residence in Dong Luang.   Thus the net gain through outsiders marrying
into the community was only five persons, whom I shall ignore to simplify
calculation.   On this basis, the population directly descended from the
pioneering group increased by 411 per cent, or at a rate of 2.35 per cent
per annum over 70 years.

What of the 14 households and 46 individuals at Dong Luang who were
not bilineally descended from the pioneering group?   The major contribution to this section of the population was made by a household which
moved from Dong Luang to Thii ee Lii, about 10 to 20 years after the new
village was established.   By the end of its reproductive life this household totalled eight persons.   In 1969 its living descendants totalled 21

individuals and accounted for seven households.   The balance (six households and 25 individuals) were people, or descendants of people, who
became attached to the village at various times over the 50 years;   all
were able to trace some kind of cognatic link with existing members of
the community.   The two conclusions indicated are: first, over the past
half century or so, population accretions have occurred primarily by
natural increase and migration into the area has been of little significance;   secondly, the rate of this population increase, insofar as the
Dong Luang case reflects the study area as a whole, was extremely rapid.

Brief consideration of the present age structure of all villages
in the area indicates the probability that the past rate of increase will
be sustained.   The median age for the total population was only 18.2
years, reflecting a population which had a high potential growth rate
(Fig. 10.3).   There is no doubt that the birth rate would have been even
higher had not several limiting factors operated.   First, the age of
marriage was usually quite late.   I estimate that the average age for
men was 24 years, and for women 22 years.   Pre-marital intercourse was
frowned upon, and was believed to bring supernatural punishment not only
for the couple, but for the whole community concerned.   Elaborate and
expensive rites were necessary to placate the spirits if fornication was
revealed.   The illegitimacy rate was extremely low: in Dong Luang, for
instance, only one woman had an illegitimate child.

Secondly, serial marriage was not generally permitted, and although
I recorded three cases of widows or widowers remarrying at Dong Luang,
most were compelled to rear their children without the aid of a spouse.

Thirdly, the people of the area had no access to modern drugs or
medical treatment, nor did they show any inclination to seek such attention at Mae Sariang or elsewhere.[2]   This factor had two consequences;

---

2 Although there were no medical services - either prophylactic or
curative - of significance available to the people of the study area,
it may well be that the control of disease by health authorities in the
lowlands prevented the spread of epidemics from the more populous areas
to the sparsely inhabited uplands.   Smallpox epidemics, for example,
have occurred within living memory, but no longer happen.   Epidemic
control measures in the lowlands may thus have indirectly influenced
population trends in the uplands.

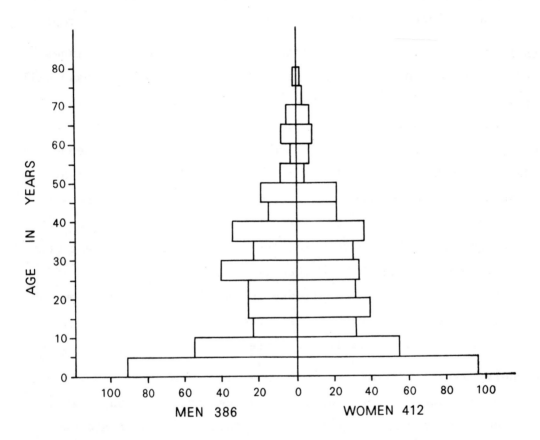

Fig. 10.3 Age-sex pyramid for the seven villages surveyed.

Note: The Karen have no way of reckoning the ages of persons.
       These figures are estimated.

Source: Field data.

a very high rate of maternal and infant mortality and a life expectancy
reduced considerably by the possibility of death through untreated ill-
nesses or accidents.   It was difficult to obtain figures of infant and
maternal mortality for a wide sample, owing to the reticence of Karen
women in talking about such things, but I did collect information which
I consider to be reliable from 12 women of completed fertility, and
this gives some indication of prevailing mortality rates.   The 12 women
had had a mean of 9.6 live births each;   of these a mean of 4.4 babies
failed to survive infancy.

Fourthly, the Karen knew of no herb or device which could be used
for contraceptive purposes.   They identified a root which they claimed
was an effective abortifacient used sometimes by girls who conceived
before marriage.   I know nothing of the effectiveness of this plant,
nor of the frequency with which it was used.

Fifthly, infanticide was unknown among the Karen, although I
observed one case where a couple who already had three children and
felt that a fourth would be a burden beyond their capacity, allowed a
new-born infant to die.   Karen values did not condone the purposeful
killing of the child, but when it caught a minor infection, the parents
did not hold the appropriate rites or use herbal treatments.   The infection soon developed into pneumonia and the child died when it was a few
weeks old.   I have reason to believe that similar cases have occurred,
possibly contributing to the high infant mortality rate, and possibly
reflecting concern about the consequences of population pressure.

As I have noted elsewhere (Hinton, 1970) such concern was justified,
for the population of the study area in 1968-69 was already placing severe
stresses on the land available for swidden farming.   Provisional calculations indicate that the physiologic density of the region may have been in
excess of 50 persons per square kilometre.   This high density compelled
farmers to operate on a mean fallow cycle of 5.6 years - compared with a
desirable minimum of at least 12 years for most soils and vegetation types
encountered.   Productivity per head had, as a consequence, fallen to a
level where many could not grow enough rice for their annual requirements.

Provisional calculations using Carneiro's formula[3] have shown the carrying capacity of Dong Luang village territory to have been 153 persons under a purely swidden regime. The present population is 179 persons. If population continues to increase, as I have suggested that it will, the position of these people will be quite untenable before very long.

These calculations present a slightly pessimistic view, for the Karen did have supplementary means of livelihood. As I noted earlier in the paper, some households farmed irrigated terraces. These were being extended year by year as time and other demands on labour permitted. Nevertheless, the nature of the terrain will place a definite limit on the extent of terrace development for wet rice production. Livestock - oxen, buffalo and elephants - raised for investment purposes and sold for cash income, were another source of livelihood for some, but the limited area of grazing land will prevent pastoral production becoming an important alternative to the subsistence production of rice. Wage labour in the lowlands, particularly in the vicinity of Mae Sariang, was another source of cash income which was used to purchase rice, but the absence of opportunities for long term and financially rewarding employment meant that only a few people working for short periods were able to gain from this source of income.

In my view, the Karen will continue to seek alternative means of livelihood to supplement the subsistence cultivation of swidden rice, but they will continue to derive their primary sustenance from this form of production. Thus terrace cultivation, livestock husbandry and wage labour will ameliorate conditions, but will not radically affect the final impact of an increasing population on land suited to swidden cultivation.

---

3 Carneiro (1960) suggests that:

$$P = \frac{\dfrac{T}{R + Y} \times Y}{A}$$

Where: P = population which may be supported
        T = total arable land
        R = length of fallow in years
        Y = length of cropping period in years
        A = area of cultivated land required to provide an average
            individual with the amount of food he ordinarily derives
            from cultivated plants in a year.

My study was confined to a limited area.   The question which
immediately arises is whether the situation I have described is typical
of the Karen elsewhere in Thailand.   Such discussion is hampered by the
absence of government census data, so I can only refer to my own observations in other areas, and then relate my findings to the evidence provided by Kunstadter's material (Kunstadter, 1969) from a locality about
30 miles north of Dong Luang.

My impression on visiting villages within a radius of two days'
walk of Dong Luang, was that population pressure was not restricted to
my study area.   This was a predictable finding, for Karen norms concerning residence after marriage tended to prevent purely local imbalances
from occurring.   There were no rules prescribing residence in either the
husband's or wife's village after marriage.   Theoretically, any person
who could trace cognatic kinship with any member of a village, could claim
a right to reside in that community;   in practice, one's residence was
determined by negotiation between leaders of the villages of the bride
and groom, and the main consideration was the relative availability of
land.   In other words, pragmatic assessment overrode strict jural considerations and this helped to insure an even spread of population in
relation to agrarian resources.

Kundstadter's material corroborates my own.   The median age for
Karen - and also Lua' - in the area he studied was even lower than the
figures yielded by my survey, and the number of live births registered
per woman of completed fertility, was higher than the mean I recorded.
Swidden land was scarce, due to pressure of population, but not as scarce
as in the Dong Luang area.   This was possibly because there was more
irrigable land, and also because surplus Lua' population tended to move
away to the lowlands.   Karen were much less inclined to take such a step,
preferring to acquire swidden land vacated by Lua' through purchase and
other means.   It seems reasonable, then, to conclude this analysis of the
Karen data by suggesting that rapid population growth and resulting land
scarcity were widespread phenomena.

3.   THE MEO, YAO AND LAHU DATA

Recent field research by Geddes (1970), D. Miles (private communication)
and Walker (1967; 1970), permits discussion of the Karen findings in a

broader perspective.   In this section, therefore, I suggest that the
mobility of these others prevents their population/land imbalances from
being more than local, short term occurrences, even when population expansion is comparable with that of the Karen.   In my conclusion I shall
try to throw light on factors which prompt these different mobility rates.

The relative stability of the Karen is reflected in a Thai government survey quoted by Geddes:

> 'The Miao stand out as the tribe least stable in their
> residential pattern.   According to the survey, 92.1 per
> cent of households have moved within a ten year period.
> Well beneath them on the scale are three tribes with figures
> closely approximating one another; Lahu (76.7 per cent),
> Lisu (75 per cent) and Yao (73.7 per cent)....at the bottom
> of the scale are the Karen with 24.4 per cent of movement
> reported within the ten year period'   (Geddes, 1970:2).

My findings suggest that the Karen may be more sedentary than the
cited figure (24.4 per cent) indicates, for in my sample, only 4.7 per
cent of households had changed residence after marriage.   The government
figure, however, may have been biased by the fact that Karen villages do
sometimes change sites for religious reasons, while remaining within the
small, strictly delineated territory of the community.

Geddes' data, gathered primarily in Meto village, Mae Sariang district, graphically illustrates the extreme mobility of the Meo.   The Meo
began moving into this area to cultivate opium, although they knew that
it had already been extensively subjected to swidden cultivation by Karen,
and that the area suitable for opium cropping was of no great extent.   The
first Meo arrived at Meto after 1958; by 1964 the population was at its
peak, yet by 1967 only a quarter of the peak population remained.   All
indications were that the area would soon be entirely vacated by Meo.

The imbalance between population and land suitable for opium cultivation at Meto, thus rapidly became acute.   Obviously this cannot be
attributed to natural population increases which could scarcely become
significant in the space of a mere 10 years.   The real cause was the rapid
congregation of Meo from villages over a wide area of Thailand, attracted
by the promise of bumper opium crops.   When these failed to materialise
the Meo dispersed from the Meto area.

The Yao of Phu Lang Kha in Chiang Rai province, like the Meto Meo, grew considerable quantities of opium but, unlike the Meo, they were self-sufficient in rice (Miles: private communication, 1971).   A major reason for this difference appears to have been that there was a great deal more arable land at Phu Lang Kha, in relation to population, than at Meto, when the population was at its peak.   The Yao achieved this balance by strict regulation of migration into the community.   According to Miles, the only way an outsider could join the community was by marrying one of its members.   Further, having regard to their long term needs, the Yao had done their best to prevent encroachment of non-Yao on land earmarked for future use.   This consideration may have motivated the government-appointed sub-district chief, himself a Yao, when he refused permission to Meo in a nearby village to expand into virgin jungle (Miles, private communication, 1971).

The data that Walker has published to date do not indicate whether or not the Lahu of Ban Pang Farn, Chiang Mai province, have placed restrictions on in-migration.   In any case, few migrants had taken up residence in the area in the period immediately preceding or during his field study (Snit Wongprasert, private communication, 1971), despite the availability of more swidden land than the community needed.   Like the Yao, the Lahu were self-sufficient in rice and also cultivate opium, although in smaller quantities than the Yao.   Lahu had been exploiting the Ban Pang Farn area for about 20 years.   There were two other Lahu villages near Ban Pang Farn, but otherwise the region appears to have been virtually uninhabited virgin forest.

Walker's demographic data indicates some of the same growth characteristics as I found among the Karen.   His population pyramid shows a low median age, and his calculation of the rate of natural increase was 2.2 per cent per annum (Walker, 1970:102).   Nevertheless, unless massive in-migration occurred, there was sufficient land to provide for many years, even given the high growth rate.

The points which can be drawn from these comparisons can now be summarised.   Of the four groups of shifting cultivators discussed, major imbalances in the man/land ratio were present among the Karen and Meo.

Imbalances among the Meo were temporary and localised, arising from the
high rate of mobility among the Meo.   Among the Karen, such imbalances
were general and of long standing, arising from natural population increases and the inclination towards sedentary residence.   Among the Yao,
imbalances did not occur because restrictions were placed on in-migration.
Among the Lahu, there is no evidence of the operation of such restrictions;
yet, for some reason, migrants were uninterested in the Ban Pang Farn area,
despite the availability of ample land.   In neither case did it seem
likely that natural population increases would cause severe pressure on
agrarian resources in the foreseeable future.

4.   CONCLUSION

Geddes explained the extreme mobility of the Meo in terms of their almost
complete commitment to opium cultivation.   Land suited for opium poppy
was of high altitude and of specific soil type.   This critical combination
of soil and altitude was found in comparatively few areas of Thailand, and
these were small and widely scattered.   Consequently, Meo had to be prepared to migrate once any given pocket of opium land became over-exploited.

In my view, this argument does not explain why Meo congregate so
quickly once a new opium area is pioneered.   On the contrary, one might
expect that like the Yao, the pioneers would discourage newcomers, so as
to allow themselves scope for longer term exploitation.   Perhaps these
considerations demonstrate the danger of purely ecological explanations of
mobility patterns among swidden cultivators;   there may be cultural factors
which differentiate the Yao from the Meo in this respect.

The relative stability of the Karen was, as Geddes suggests, partially
due to the stabilising influence of irrigated terrace ownership.   Terraces
required a considerable capital investment of labour, and owners were
naturally loath to leave fields which they had developed.   Nevertheless,
terrace ownership was only one stabilising factor, for many Karen villages
in Thailand relied entirely or largely on swidden cultivation, and these
appeared to be as sedentary as those which were dependent on wet rice.   It
was my observation that the Karen had strong preference for stable residence,
expressed in bi-annual offerings to the Lord of the Territory, with whom a
relationship favourable to Karen needs was built up over a period of years.

In the absence of data from Burma, my explanation of the origins of this deep-seated preference for stable residence, must remain tentative. But I suggest that these residential attitudes were a product of centuries of residence in Burma, where wet rice was of much greater consequence for them than it has been in Thailand.   When the Karen moved into Thailand, wet-rice land was already largely occupied by others and relatively small areas of irrigable land remained.   So swidden cultivation came to be of greater relative importance instead.

In normal circumstances, I suggest, the Karen would never have migrated east in the numbers that they did; but they were dislodged by the political developments described above.   In Mae Sariang district and neighbouring areas, they at first fanned out over the hills, settling in widely scattered villages established close to irrigable land.   But, as neither the irrigable nor the swidden land in the vicinity would support the growing population of the parent villages, satellite villages claimed outlying land and became independent.   As satellites were established in ever-widening circles from the parent communities, their territories began to abut those of satellites of other parent villages, until all available land was claimed by one settlement or another.

The situation of the more recent satellites differed considerably from that of the original villages.   By the time they were established, most irrigable land had been claimed, and often only swidden land could be found.   Yet the old preference for stable residence remained, and the Karen applied their traditional swidden techniques, using the methods of soil and forest conservation, which had enabled them to cultivate swiddens to supplement irrigated fields over extended periods; if wet-rice land had formerly committed them to residence in one place, their residence in one place had taught them that they could ill afford to be profligate with contiguous swidden land.

In my view, the rapid rise in population has precipitated a situation in which the villages farming primarily on a swidden basis are ill served by their preference for stable residence.   They would be better off pioneering territory like that occupied by the Ban Pang Farn Lahu, even if it lay some distance away from the present area of Karen occupation. But the Karen I knew were uninformed about the world beyond a day or two's

walk away from their village; they travelled little, sold no significant
cash crop which might have integrated them into a far flung trade network;
and most spoke no language other than their own.   So in a number of respects they were poorly equipped for pioneering excursions.   Nor did they
have the opportunistic inclinations which lead people like the Meo, Yao
and Lahu into new territory.

My impression was that the only factors compelling Karen mobility
were traumatic social and political developments, such as occurred in
Burma a century and a half ago.   It may well be that such developments
will be precipitated by the very overpopulation which I have been discussing in this paper.

REFERENCES

Carneiro, R.L., 1969.   'Slash and burn agriculture: a closer look at
        its implications for settlement patterns', in A.F.C. Wallace,
        ed., Men and cultures, University of Pennsylvania Press,
        Philadelphia, pp. 229-34.

Geddes, W.R., 1970.   'Opium and the Miao: a study in ecological adjust-
        ment', Oceania, 41, pp. 1-11.

Hinton, P., 1970.   'Swidden cultivation among the Pwo Karen of Northern
        Thailand, present practices and future prospects', in Land
        Development Department, Proceedings of a seminar on shifting
        agriculture and economic development in Northern Thailand,
        Bangkok.

Kunstadter, P., 1967.   'The Lua' and Skaw Karen in Maehongson province
        of north-western Thailand', in P. Kunstadter, ed., Southeast
        Asia tribes, minorities and nations, 2, pp. 639-74, Princeton
        University Press, Princeton.

Kunstadter, P., 1969.   Fertility, mortality and migration of hill and
        valley populations in northwestern Thailand. Paper presented
        to the 68th meeting of the American Anthropological Association,
        (mimeo).

Lebar, F.M., Hickey, G.C. and Musgrave, J.K., 1964.   Ethnic groups of
        mainland Southeast Asia, Human Relations Area Files Press,
        New Haven.

Marshall, H.I., 1922.   The Karen people of Burma, Ohio State University
        Bulletin 26, Columbus.

Mangrai, Sao Saimong, 1965.   The Shan States and the British annexation,
        Data Paper 57, Southeast Asia Program, Cornell University,
        Ithaca.

Tadaw, S.H., 1961.   'The Karens of Burma: a study in human geography',
        in Theodorson, G.A., Studies in human ecology, Row, Peterson,
        New York, pp. 496-508.

Walker, A.R., 1967.   'Red Lahu village society: an introductory survey',
        in P. Hinton, ed., Tribesmen and peasants in North Thailand,
        Tribal Research Centre, Bangkok, pp. 41-52.

Walker, A.R., 1970.   Lahu Nyi village society and economy in North Thailand,
        (2 vols) Tribal Research Centre (mimeo).

CHAPTER 11

SOME DEMOGRAPHIC IMPLICATIONS OF REGIONAL COMMERCE:

THE CASE OF NORTH THAILAND'S YAO MINORITY

Douglas Miles*

1. INTRODUCTION

My paper examines non-biological factors affecting the size of the Yao
domestic unit and is based on a study of Pulangka in the extreme north
of Thailand. This village comprises 19 houses which had a total population of 247 people in March, 1966. Peo is the Yao word for a collection
of people living under the same roof and having genealogical connections
with one another. I designate this as a 'dwelling-group'. It plays an
important role in the organisation of agriculture, religion and politics.
The belt of Yao villages contains about 16,000 people and lies for the
most part within 20 km of Thailand's northern border with Laos and Burma.

Pulangka village straddles a mountain ridge, at an elevation of
approximately 1000 metres, near the point where the boundary between Nan
and Chiang Rai provinces meets Thailand's international border with Laos.
Its agricultural economy is oriented to markets in valley towns such as
Pong, Nan, Chiang Kham, Chiang Rai, Phayao and Lampang. Until recently,
the network of regional commerce extended well beyond the immediate
locality in northern Thailand and brought Pulangka's villagers into
contact with traders operating from provincial towns in Laos, Burma and
China; the network also linked the Yao of Pulangka with other highland
communities, of Black and White Meo, Khmu, Akha, Lahu and Hill Tai (Htin,
PhuGo' and Khon Myang), as well as lowland Tai people[1] in the valleys
and metropolitan Chinese businessmen.

---

* Mr Miles is Lecturer in Anthropology in the University of Sydney.

1 I have used the word Tai as a general label for Theravada Buddhists in
Thailand and Laos, and for non-Buddhist speakers of their languages.

A striking feature of the Pulangka dwelling-groups is their marked
variation in size, ranging in membership from three to 57 individuals and
from one to 10 households.   Beginning with this fact, my aim in this
paper is to demonstrate the relationship between the success of Yao as
market producers and the size and sex components of each _peo_. Consequently,
the extent of Yao participation in commerce will be seen as a powerful
influence on the population of villages and the ethnic group as a whole.
My arguments stem from a consideration of the cost element in Yao marriage,
filiation and adoption.   Yao groups increase and diminish in size by
means other than natural reproduction.   They also acquire members by
purchase and, conversely, they retain those family members recruited
through birth only by forfeiting the monetary income that derives from
selling people.

2.   THE YAO AND THE PULANGKA ECONOMY

The Yao people are Sinitic in origin and in their cultural orientation.
Their main concentration of population is in the provinces of Kwantung,
Kwangsi and Kweichow of the Chinese Peoples' Republic where they number
almost 750,000.   Other Yao inhabit parts of North Vietnam, Laos and
Burma.   In Thailand, members of the Yao ethnic group are swiddeners of
three major crops: rice, opium poppy and maize.   Sometimes only one or
two of these crops are produced, but the Pulangka Yao cultivate and
market all three.

The Yao view all territory under virgin jungle as a gift of nature,
and all land under former swiddens as part of the estate of the community
to which the original cultivator belonged.   No person or corporation in
the village has permanent claim to a farmed tract.   Individual rights
lapse and revert to the common estate once fallow begins.   Because shifting cultivation is the exclusive system of agriculture (Miles, 1969),
such reversion is frequent.

The proportion of village land that any one Yao dwelling-group may
exploit during an agricultural cycle depends on the amount of labour that
it can devote to the task, and not on any pre-existing claim.   Hence a
unit with more workers has potential control over more land.   The unit

which decreases in size tends to have less land per cultivator, the
expanding dwelling-group more; there is a similar correlation with per
capita income (Miles, 1972a).

   None of the three crops requires continuous work throughout the
whole agricultural cycle, but the fact that they compete strongly for
labour during many months of the year creates a heavy strain on labour
resources and encourages cooperation between households (Miles, 1972a).
Furthermore, the crops of maize, poppy and rice require different soils
and altitudes; the fields where they grow are often separated by considerable distances, requiring up to 10 hours return travelling time.
This necessitates division of a family's workforce into dispersed gangs,
each specialising in one crop and combining only occasionally during
slack periods.   However, some peo are too small to be broken down into
different work gangs.   It is not surprising that Yao strategies for
profit accumulation give primacy to labour over land as the scarce
resource in agriculture.   Significantly, nobody buys land, but peo
obtain people from one another and from outsiders through marriage,
filiation and adoption, which are mechanisms to regulate competition
for workers.

3. MARRIAGE AND CHILD PURCHASE

(i)   Residence at marriage[2]

   The peo has two components: it focuses on a tso, a core of cognates who are the descendants of the same set of ancestors. A rigid
prohibition prevents marriage between such people.   The peo therefore
includes spouses that derive from other tso.   Each cognatic core has
affinal alliances with others.   I shall try to show that this fact
contributes to disparity in the size and scale of dwelling-groups.

   A tso resembles a lineage in that it recruits at birth male cognates' children whose mothers live virilocally.   I emphasise that it
may also include the offspring of female cognates who live natolocally
and whose husbands or paramours have not paid bridewealth.   Thus two

2 This discussion of peo recruitment and Figure 11.1 have been repro-
duced from my paper (Miles, 1972a) with the permission of the editors
of Mankind.

principles of recruitment to the core of the _peo_ operate simultaneously.
Married members of the exogamous unit may be of either sex; likewise
their spouses.

If Yao adhered to either one of these principles rather than the
other, exogamy would be conducive to an equitable distribution of
population amongst the various dwelling-groups.   Through strict
adherence to virilocality, _tso_ would acquire the filiation only of male
cognates' children and forfeit rights over sisters' and daughters' offspring to like units.   All female cognates would marry out; all in-
marrying spouses would be wives.

On the other hand, strict natolocality of women would entail the
tso's forfeiture of rights over the male cognates' progeny and complete
dependence on matrifiliation.   Men would marry out; all in-marrying
spouses would be husbands.   In both cases there would be reciprocity in
exchanges of spouses between _tso._

But in fact the two principles operate simultaneously and the
system exhibits a phenomenon which Levi-Strauss (1969:238) noted among
the Kachin: some descent groups come to corner a large proportion of the
spouses.   Their _peo_ recruit not only the wives and children of male
cognates but also the husbands and offspring of daughters and sisters.
The dwelling-groups of other _tso_ therefore lose the membership of male
cognates and depend on matrifiliation to persist in time.   The contra-
diction between the two principles results in three _de facto_ variants of
localised descent groups.   Figure 11.1 depicts the differences dia-
grammatically and illustrates the implications for dwelling-group size.

In order to hold demographic factors constant the models assume
that every reproductive couple in each type has a pair of children of
either sex.   In Types M and P one sibling marries out in each generation;
the other remains stationary.   In Type B both siblings remain stationary
and import spouses to the dwelling-group.   In three generations Type M
achieves a membership of three to six married people; Type P of six;
and Type B of six to 28.   I suggest then that principles of recruitment
to the _peo_ provide a structural foundation for the extreme disparity in
dwelling-group and scale that I encountered in Pulangka.   But why does
the phenomenon occur?   A key to the answer lies in an analysis of
child-purchase.

TYPE M

TYPE P

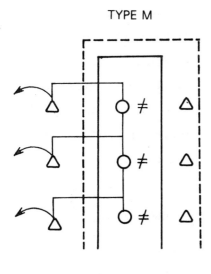

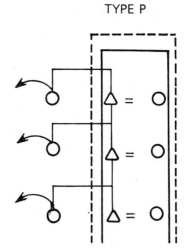

TYPE B

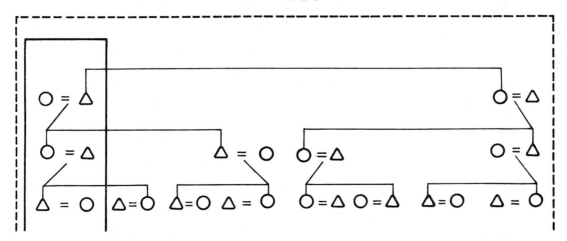

Fig. 11.1   Types of local units.

(ii)   Child purchase

Over 22 per cent of the Pulangka population under the age of 20 are adoptees.   Payment of money, goods and other types of compensation has almost invariably accompanied the transfer of rights from the biological parents of these people to the peo to which they now belong.   I emphasise the fact that the Yao regard children as saleable commodities but that while they frequently buy, they rarely sell.   Table 11.1 indicates that 87.5 per cent of adoptees in my Pulangka sample derive from other ethnic groups.   Only 12.5 per cent were born as Yao.   A brief account of extra-village relationships is essential to explain this situation.

4.   COMMERCE AND CONTACT BETWEEN ETHNIC GROUPS

Village territories of Yao, Meo, Khmu, Akha, Lahu and Hill Tai often interdigitate in the mountains of north Thailand and western Laos.   There is a Meo settlement within 15 minutes walk from Pulangka, a Tai village two hours away, and a Khmu community within a day's pony ride.   The farms of Pulangka's shifting cultivators often adjoin those of the Meo and Tai. Interaction with members of other ethnic groups is therefore frequent.

Table 11.1:   Origin of adoptees (under 20 years old) in Pulangka, 1967

Ethnic origin		Number	Percentage
Yao		4	12.5
Non-Yao:	Tai	19	59.4
	Khmu	5	15.6
	Meo	1	3.1
	Chinese	2	6.3
	Vietnamese	1	3.1
	Total	32	100.0

Source: Field data.

Paradoxically, the Yao have even closer ties with foreigners living in more distant places.   Because of the territorial dispersal of the ethnic group, travellers between Yao habitations often require accommodation en route.   The major mountain trails pass through the centres of settlements with various cultural identities.   Pulangka adults have long-established and even inherited connections with individuals among Black

and White Meo, Khmu, Lahu and Hill Tai.   They depend on such people for
horse feed, fresh ponies, meals and shelter.   The parties refer to each
other by various pronunciations of the Thai word 'sahai', qualifying the
term with first person possessive pronouns.   Sahai are the main contacts for economic dealings between villages.   Their visits usually
give rise to informal but bibulous festivity permeated with bonhomie.
The reciprocal relationship is highly valued and a source of prestige.
Formal occasions such as weddings and funerals in the mountains are often
cosmopolitan affairs where the sahai of the principal participants are
very prominent.

     The sahai with whom Yao have most dealings are Chinese shopkeepers
in the valley townships of north Thailand and western Laos.   All Pulangka
dwelling-groups accept credit from these traders or their itinerant representatives.   The hillmen purchase cloth, kerosene, lighting utensils,
cooking and eating equipment as well as tools, horseshoes, nails, patent
medicines, salt, dried fish and meats.   All Yao clothing has such derivation.   Male attire consists of ready-made black cotton 'pyjamas' or nylon
slacks and shirts; women buy cloth and cotton which they manufacture into
the trousers, tunics and head-dresses diacritical of the ethnic group.
The shopkeeper often advances payment for carpenters, house-builders,
coffinmakers, silversmiths and even the veterinary surgeons and doctors
whom the Yao consult in the towns or bring to the village.   The merchant
always has a ready-made stock of ceremonial paraphernalia such as card-
board replicas of houses and tinsel substitutes for gold and iron bars
which the Yao burn during rituals; rice paper for making imitation money;
and incense for offerings to the spirits.

     Communication between the Yao and the urban Chinese is by letter in
Mandarin script which most Pulangka elders can read and write.   The costs
of all transactions are debited to the account of the customer who pays
in primary produce at the end of harvests.   Pulangka Yao often make
these payments by providing maize to the merchant's other clients in the
hills.   For example, in June, Meo may promise that they will provide the
trader with opium in the following February, at the end of the tapping
season, and request his assistance to purchase maize for their horses.
The entrepreneur instructs his debtors in a Yao village to deliver a mule

or pony caravan of cobs to the Meo after the intervening maize harvest
in August.   Because of similar arrangements most Pulangka opium is
earmarked for customers of particular traders before it is even planted.

Some Yao produce enough opium to have quantities for direct deals
with consumers in lowland Tai villages.   Among the latter are landless
individuals and farmers who experience bad harvests that create lowland
demands for mountain rice surpluses.   Nearly all hill settlements in
the region participate in a complex network of debt and credit that
focuses on urban centres.   A market in children is part and parcel of
the system.

Chinese merchants in north Thailand and western Laos purchase
children in the same way as their counterparts did in pre-revolutionary
southeast China (Freedman, 1966:7).   The acquisition is usually an
aspect of the indebtedness of Tai peasant customers who forfiet rights
over their offspring to a foreclosing creditor.   But the practice is
not, as Goody (1969:6) suggests, an accommodation to conjugal barren-
ness and it accounts for more than the large size of Chinese merchant
families interested in expanding the territorial range of their operations,
which Freedman emphasises.

Children enter the market system as commodities for profitable re-
sale.   A parallel practice is debt-bondage by which an insolvent debtor
works for his creditor or provides a kinsman as a substitute.   Debt-
bondsmen are transferable.   A third party can pay what is owing, thus
gaining rights over the debtor.   I know of several Thai fathers who
have responded to foreclosure by providing nubile daughters to country
shopkeepers.   Some of the latter supply male and female bondsmen for
Bangkok and Vientiane businesses such as restaurants, brothels and
massage-parlours.

A triadic feature that some such dealings display is highly relevant to the argument developed later in this chapter.   A rural trader
always has accounts and debts with big urban merchants.   He can transfer
this debt to a peasant customer who settles with the payment of a human
being directly to a representative of the city merchant.   The shopkeeper
may in fact never see the child, girl or bondsman involved.   Part I of

Figure 11.3 illustrates the point: a single arrow indicates the direction
of credit; a double arrow the direction of payment.   However, I know of
no instance where Yao or Meo have sold infants to Chinese or become debt-
bondsmen and involuntary prostitutes.   This reflects the powerful position of opium growers in north Thai and western Laotian economics.   In
respect to the child trade, Yao are exclusively buyers.

Pulangka people purchased most of the adoptees in my sample through
urban Chinese shopkeepers (Table 11.1).   Eleven Tai and two Khmu were
living in the shops at the time.   Four Tai and two Khmu were residing
in their parents' villages when the parents disposed of their children
directly to the Yao, to settle their debts of opium and rice.   Both Chinese
adoptees in the table first arrived in Pulangka with itinerant opium buyers
plying mule caravans out of Luang Prabang.   The two boys were accepted by
different Pulangka _peo_ that promised to pay for them with opium at a later
date.   The sole Vietnamese had a similar origin.   He arrived with a
blacksmith who had obtained him in a village _en route_ from Vientiane.

(i)   External transactions in adoptees and brides

The case of a Chinese adoptee introduces the next phase in this
enquiry; namely, the relationship between child purchase and marriage.
This male became a member of a Pulangka _peo_ at the age of 10 around 1941.
The creditor did not re-visit Pulangka until 1949 when he wore the uniform
of one of Chiang Kai Chek's Kuomintang officers and was accompanied by
30 armed soldiers.   At first he demanded three times as much opium as
the amount originally stipulated.   The adopting _peo_ had however, fallen
on hard times and could not comply.   The fictive mother, now a deserted
wife, was highly reluctant to part with the youth who was the only male
member of the dwelling-group's work force.   She asked the village headman for opium.   Both of them then negotiated with the Kuomintang group,
which later left the village with the woman's 15 year-old daughter as
the wife of the commander.   The fact that soldiers caused the village
little trouble thereafter is incidental.   Of greater relevance is the
nature of the exchange.   The _peo_ acquired an adopted son in lieu of
bridewealth.

(ii) Bridewealth and commerce

A brief account of the economic transactions accompanying Yao
marriage is necessary before proceeding.   Bridewealth is the normal
counterprestation from the peo of a groom to the givers of a bride who
lives virilocally.   It usually consists of money calculated in terms
of the traditional Yao unit of ceremonial currency, a silver ingot
(ngantiu) weighing 365 grams.   In 1968, the average cash value of bridewealth transactions was 4000 baht or US$192.   The price changes with
fluctuations in the international silver market.   Thus commercial
phenomena determine the value of Yao brides.   The importance of viewing
Yao marriage prestation in the wider context of market economics is illustrated by the following incident:

> Pulangka's most flamboyant rake is a man with the Tai nickname
> Tongtong, a literal translation of which is 'the Golden Abdomen'.
> He bought a nylon shirt from a travelling hawker who was asked
> to debit the cost to the account of his natal peo.   But the
> members refused to pay on the grounds that the Golden Abdomen
> owed them money from a bridewealth transaction.   Several years
> before the unit had sponsored Tongton's virilocal marriage.
> Six months later he was dunned for a large debt accumulated
> over a long period of time with another trader.   Tongtong then
> allowed the merchant to marry his pregnant wife, in return for
> the cancellation of the debt plus a few hundred baht instead of
> bridewealth.   The members of the peo had since insisted that
> Golden Abdomen return to them a cash equivalent to the gross
> price at which the Chinese had valued the woman.

A number of generalisations arise from these observations.   From
the Yao point of view, brides as well as children have a monetary value
that is determined by the market, and both may substitute for goods and
cash.   Unlike members of other ethnic groups in the region, the Yao do
not sell their own infants to foreigners.   Their abhorrence of the notion
equals the horror they express at the idea of Yao girls becoming prostitutes.   But the Yao purchase children; they also sell and buy brides.
Since the value of both is determined in the same sphere of trade, brides
are easily exchanged for adoptees.   A woman is a valid alternative to

the money that an individual should present to the custodian of the child
he adopts.   The transfer of the bride creates ties of kinship and
affinity between relatives of both parties.   But it would be fanciful
to regard the transaction partly as a result of such a motive.   The
commercial aspects of the exchange should be stressed, and their implications will be examined for situations in which brides are exchanged for
brides.

5.   INTERNAL TRANSACTIONS IN ADOPTEES AND BRIDES

The cases described so far concern dealings between Yao and outsiders.
The Yao may provide brides to foreigners but I know of only one case in
which a Pulangka male has imported a foreign wife.   Members of this
community buy the offspring of parents who have different ethnic identity
from themselves but never allow foreigners to purchase Yao.   Thus while
they may give a Yao bride for a foreign adoptee, they never give away a
Yao child for a foreign bride.   It is only within the society that a
Yao becomes a substitute for bridewealth.   Again, however, the commercial aspect of the exchange is very marked.   Three cases in which Pulangka
people have adopted Yao are discussed below and illustrated in Figure 11.2.

(i)   Case 1

The first concerns the adoptee Liusin, an 18 year-old girl who since
the age of 10 has been recognised as the daughter of Fusin, her actual
mother's (Mooehgwek's) brother, with whose peo she resides and worships.
The parents of Mooehgwek migrated to Pulangka prior to Fusin's birth.
They had no relatives in the village.

A year later, smallpox killed Mooehgwek's father and her mother died
soon afterwards in giving birth to Fusin, who became a foster child in the
midwife's household.   Mooehgwek was 16 at the time and she stayed on in
her parents' house where her lover, Fumeng, also took up residence.   A
few months later the couple moved to Fumeng's village where his parents
sponsored their wedding.   There was no bridewealth payment at this
marriage because Fusin was too young to organise the negotiations and
there was no other surviving member of his peo.   At the age of 24, Fusin
had a wife, a son and a daughter.   Mooehgwek was then 40 and had six

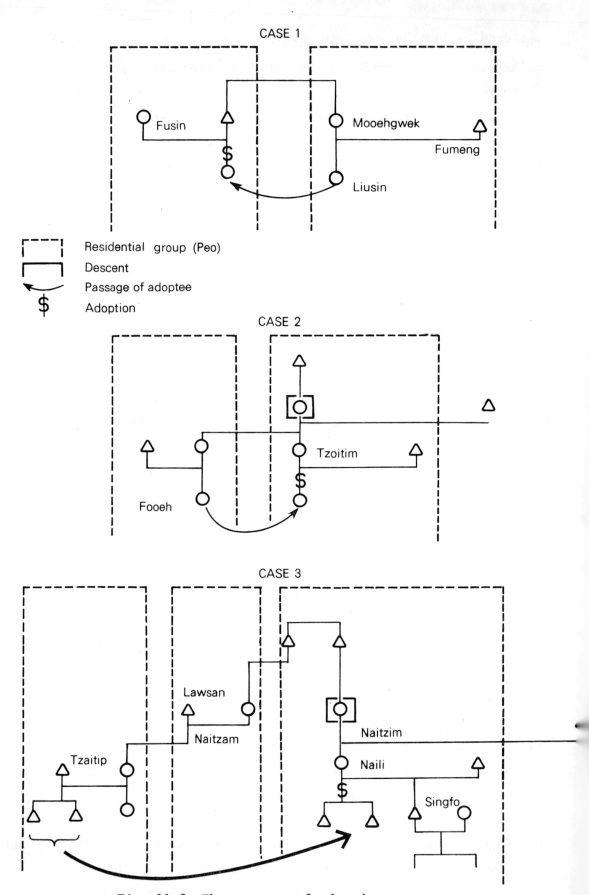

Fig. 11.2 Three cases of adoption.

children.   The last born was Liusin whom Fusin demanded in lieu of the
bridewealth which Fumeng owed his wife's natal peo for his virilocal
marriage.

Fusin's claim had nothing to do with the rights attaching to his
kinship status as a mother's brother.   Few Yao would have such privileges in respect to their sister's child.   The transaction rested wholly
on two principles: that the virilocal residence of a wife gives her peo
of derivation rights to compensation from her spouse's kin; and that an
adoptee is a legally valid substitute for bridewealth.

(ii)   Case 2

Fooeh is the fictive daughter of her natural mother's elder sister
Tzoitim.   Her biological father came from another village and was an
originally uxorilocal husband in Tzoitim's peo.   He paid no bridewealth.
This man took Tzoitim's sister home to his natal village when she was
pregnant with Fooeh, her first born child.   The then unmarried Tzoitim
claimed the baby immediately after weaning.   The fictive mother has
since had two other children by an uxorilocally resident husband; both
are matrifiliated.

(iii) Case 3

This case is an extreme example of how bridewealth debts may persist for more than one generation and be transferred.   Naili's mother,
Naitzim was born into the joint family of her father and his brother.
The peo then included Naitzim's parallel cousin, Naitzam who had a pre-
marital daughter called Tzaitip.   Naitzam married Lawsan who lived
uxorilocally for a time.   He then took his wife and stepdaughter to
reside permanently in his natal peo but paid no bridewealth.

Tzaitip had a pre-marital child and then married a man who had
recently acquired a Tai boy by cash purchase.   Her husband who never
lived uxorilocally agreed to forfeit both this boy and his first born
child by Tzaitip as substitute for the bridewealth he owed Lawsan.
Neither of these children ever saw Lawsan who had them delivered directly
to Naili; thus Lawsan paid for his wife and her child with the offspring
of his daughter's husband.

In sum then, just as Yao may use their women as brides to cancel commercial debts with outsiders, they can settle bridewealth debts amongst themselves by using their own or adopted children who thenceforth belong to the peo of the bridegivers.

(iv)   Adoption and matrifiliation

The same cases (Fig. 11.2) illustrate the next main point.   As stated earlier a priori or retrospective bridewealth payments in cash or human form, validate virilocal residence of a wife and patrifiliation of her children.   For example, Fusin (Case 1), has made the prestations in full and lives virilocally with his actual and patrifiliated offspring. Similarly, Naili's son Singfo (Case 3), has a virilocally resident wife and children who belong to the peo of his birth.   But why are Naili, Singfo and Tzoitim (Case 2) matrifiliated?

To answer the question, let us focus on Singfo (Case 3), whose father, Naili's husband, lives uxorilocally and has paid no bridewealth. In this respect he has many counterparts among other men in Pulangka genealogies.   But in contrast to some other husbands who were formerly uxorilocal, Naili's husband's marriage was celebrated by a wedding which the bride's peo sponsored, thus terminating the possibility of the son-in-law taking the wife to his natal peo and patrifiliating any of his children.   On the other hand, Lawsan (Case 3), and Fumeng (Case 1), never went through a wedding at the expense of their in-laws.   After a period of uxorilocal residence they withdrew their wives and later paid bridewealth in the form of adopted children.

Considering Naili and Tzoitim (Cases 2 and 3), it should be stressed that neither of these individuals are adoptees.   In contrast to Liusin (Case 1), and Fooeh (Case 2), they were not born in other tso and later transferred.   Like Singfo (Case 3), they were matrifiliated recruits by birth.   Their fathers lived for some years in the wife's peo and then became virilocal.   Naili and Tzoitim remained there when their parents shifted to reside virilocally.   The siblings of the two women are of interest.   Naili's father had to adopt her younger brother who was born before the move.   The siblings born afterwards belonged automatically to their patrilateral tso.   Tzoitim and her sister (Fooeh's mother of

Case 2) were born before their parents' departure, and their other siblings who are patrifiliated, later.

There is no doubt that the Yao regard the retention of Naili and Tzoitim by their matrilateral and natal tso as representing the cost of their fathers' virilocal marriages. In other words, matrifiliation of offspring is equivalent to adoption as a substitute for bridewealth. It is one explanation for the cases in which children reside apart from their living parents. Only by examining the phenomenon in relation to hill community trade can an observer understand this fact. It is incorrect to attribute the occurrence of matrifilial membership in tso to looseness in the implementation of agnatic recruitment principles, or to assume that bride-exchange between Yao tso is a matter of alliance obligations and the responsibilities of affinal relationship.

6.   COMMERCE AND BRIDE EXCHANGE

Pulangka fathers display great remorse in forfeiting rights over children who become adoptees and matrifiliates in other men's tso. They fear and abhor the situation in which a nubile daughter may be forced to marry against her own will, which sometimes occurs in bride-exchange. The Yao place great stress on the ideal that both sexes should have the freedom to chose their own conjugal partners. They encourage pre-marital sexual experience and other forms of experimentation in domesticity. What Westerners would call illegitimacy is condoned and often welcomed, and nubile girls frequently adopt children before marriage. Yet in some cases freedom is curtailed by prescriptive connubium. The explanation lies in bridewealth indebtedness. It is not an aspect of obligations attaching to kinship or affinal status.

Some years ago Africanists suppressed the term 'brideprice' because of its connotation that payment for wives is somewhat equivalent to slave purchase. Levi-Strauss (1969:238) also ridiculed the idea that where prestations of material goods accompany marriage, women are exchanged for things. His whole theory rests on the proposition that kin groups exchange brides to establish and perpetuate affinal alliances. In this viewpoint the economic aspects of the transaction are secondary, but I argue to the contrary.

268   THAILAND

When a female member of a Yao _tso_ chooses a husband whose _peo_
insists on virilocal residence and patrifiliation of children, the
bride receivers must indemnify the givers.   They may provide the payment in cash or other material valuables.   To accumulate the price,
Pulangka residents participate in regional commerce which, as we have
seen, entails debthood.   Some succeed in their enterprises, others
fail.   Entry into a trader-client relationship entails the understanding that the creditor may nominate the form in which the insolvent debtor
must settle.

Unindemnified wife-givers among the Yao are matrimonial counterparts to the Chinese trader who may force individuals into debt-bondage
or parents into forfeiture of rights over their children.   Some demand
matrifiliates or adoptees as substitutes for bridewealth;   others insist
that a female member of a debtor's _peo_ abrogate the right to marry
according to her own choice, resulting in bride-exchange.   Like matrifiliation it is an alternative to the material counterprestations with
which wife-receivers otherwise provide their affines.   The structure
of such exchange is shown by eight cases in which _tso_ of people living
in Pulangka exchanged brides directly.   In other words, a male member
of a girl's _tso_ gained a wife from the group into which she had married.
Whereas the first woman chose her own husband, the others had no option.
Each of these matches involved two descent groups only.   Four examples
were also recorded in which three descent groups participated in such
transactions.   Each is equivalent to circular connubium in that the
original matrimonial creditor (A) gained for one of its male members a
woman from the _tso_ of the _peo's_ affines' affines (III in Fig. 11.3).

Here _tso_ B has received a bride from A;   C from B.   B is in A's
debt, C in B's.   But instead of giving one of its own women to A, B
has demanded a bride from C not for itself, but for A.   B has thus
avoided forcing one of its own girls to marry against her will.   In
other words circular connubium occurs among the Yao in the absence of
alliance rules that it should do so.   The prescription is a matter of
debt and credit, not an expression of the rights and obligations associated with kinship status.   If C had the cash or other assets to pay B,
the latter could indemnify A and there would be no exchange of brides.

Parallels between other types of indirect exchange are illustrated in the other parts of Figure 11.3.

The country shopkeeper uses the girl he can demand from a peasant to settle his own debt with a metropolitan trader (I, Fig. 11.3). A man substitutes the two children that his daughter's affines owe for her marriage as retrospective payment to a third descent group from which his own wife and step-child derived (II, Fig. 11.3; see also Lawsan, Case 3, Fig. 11.2). An insolvent _tso_ abrogates the right to claim a wife from indebted affines to the group that it owes a bride (III, Fig. 11.3). In each case, the exchange involves a third party.

The phenomenon of circular connubium which Figure 11.3 illustrates has gained a century of attention in anthropological discussions about southeast Asians.[3] In at least one case its occurrence is an aspect of commerce, as shown by two other marriages in Pulangka. These are the cases of Gawsiau and Santjiau, two uxorilocal husbands who are male counterparts to the woman whom wife-giving _peo_ may demand from insolvent bride-receivers. Both examples conform to Part 3 of Figure 11.3. Each man was born into a _tso_ (C) which had received brides from B a generation before; C in turn owed bridewealth for virilocal women it has taken from A several generations earlier. A foreclosed by demanding human compensation from B's debtor C, but nominated husbands for its natolocal women not wives for virilocal male members. In short, the circle closed in the two cases through an exchange of a groom for a bride. The parallels between the parts of Figure 11.3 are more than mere analogies. They manifest the value which human beings have as commercial commodities in the market oriented economy to which Yao child-purchase and bridewealth are geared.

7.   CONCLUSION

This chapter began with the observation that Pulangka _peo_ exhibit much variation in the number of members they contain. This fact was related to structural differences between dwelling-groups and the extent to which

---

3 In a recently published paper I have re-examined classical examples of circular connubium in the light of variables emphasised in this discussion (Miles, 1972b).

PART 1

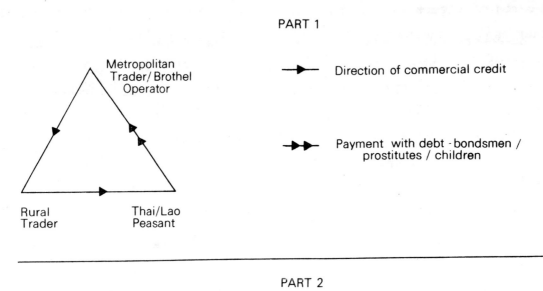

Metropolitan
Trader/Brothel
Operator

Rural
Trader

Thai/Lao
Peasant

→ Direction of commercial credit

▸▸ Payment with debt-bondsmen /
    prostitutes / children

PART 2

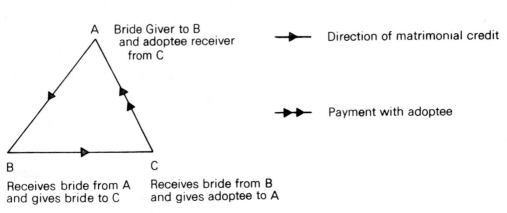

A Bride Giver to B
   and adoptee receiver
   from C

B
Receives bride from A
and gives bride to C

C
Receives bride from B
and gives adoptee to A

→ Direction of matrimonial credit

▸▸ Payment with adoptee

PART 3
CIRCULAR CONNUBIUM

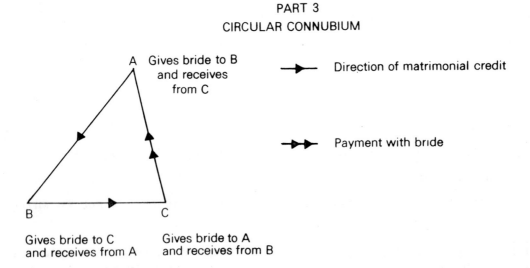

A Gives bride to B
   and receives
   from C

B
Gives bride to C
and receives from A

C
Gives bride to A
and receives from B

→ Direction of matrimonial credit

▸▸ Payment with bride

Fig. 11.3 Types of indirect exchange.

Yao adopt children.   The practice depends on commercial success or
failure which in turn determines whether Yao individuals acquire members
of other tso for their own peo or forfeit their own members as spouses,
adoptees and matrifiliates in other peoples' dwelling-groups.   Matrimonial credit may accumulate over many generations but foreclosure on
many debts takes place at one point in time.   The process operates
through direct spouse-exchange, circular connubium, adoption and matrifiliation.   Its result is extreme imbalance in the membership of
dwelling-groups during particular agricultural cycles.

     Underlying the phenomenon is disparity in the amount of labour that
different peo control.   Large work gangs have full annual self-employment,
curtailing the income-making opportunities of small groups in primary production.   Wealthy families are in a position to re-invest their surpluses by purchasing foreign children that others cannot afford.   In sum,
the commercial factor demands attention in any attempt to analyse population growth and decline of Yao domestic entities, settlements and the
ethnic group itself.

ACKNOWLEDGEMENT

The author and editors are indebted to the editors of Mankind for permission to reproduce a small part of the text and Figure 11.1 (see
footnote 2) which were previously published in a recent paper by the
same author (Miles, 1972a).

REFERENCES

Freedman, M., 1966.   Chinese lineage and society, LSE Monographs in
        Social Anthropology, No. 33, The Athlone Press, London.

Geertz, C., 1963.   Agricultural involution, University of California
        Press, Berkeley.

Goody, J., 1969.   'Adoption in cross-cultural perspective', Compara-
        tive Studies in Society and History, 11, pp. 55-78.

Levi-Strauss, C., 1969.   The elementary structures of kinship, Eyre
        and Spottiswoode, London.

Miles, Douglas, 1968.   'Filiation, wealth differentiation and marriage',
        Yao Project Series No. 3, Tribal Research Centre, Chiang
        Mai (mimeo).

Miles, Douglas, 1969.   'Shifting cultivation, threats and prospects',
        in Hinton, P., (ed), Tribesmen and Peasants in North
        Thailand, Tribal Research Centre, Chiang Mai.

Miles, Douglas, 1972a.   'Land, labour and kin groups among southeast
        Asian shifting cultivators', Mankind, 8, pp. 185-97.

Miles, Douglas, 1972b.   'Bride-exchange, matrifiliation and adoption',
        Bijdragen tot de Taal-, Land-en Volkenkunde, 128, pp. 99-117.

CHAPTER 12

INTER-CULTURAL MEDIATION IN SOUTH THAILAND

Elise Tugby and Donald Tugby*

1.   INTRODUCTION

The relationships between the Thai, Chinese and Malay cultural groups in
the provinces of Narathiwat, Yala, Pattani and Satun in South Thailand
(Fig. 12.1) are complex and this reflects the complexity of history, ecology and cultural patterns in the area.   In reality, the four southern
provinces are a cultural and political marchland between Buddhist and
Islamic nation-states: after about 500 years of Thai control, there
remains a marked dichotomy between the dominantly Thai-Buddhist towns
and the dominantly Muslim countryside, and the solidarity of the Thai-
Muslim group is reflected in the recurrence of insurrections by Thai-
Muslims against rule from Bangkok.   Inevitably and increasingly, however, a range of individual mediators and mediating agencies, including
Thai administrative and economic institutions, has endeavoured to bridge
the gap between the two cultural entities.   The role of these 'culture
brokers' and the success of related government activities in inter-
cultural mediation is a topic of critical importance for the future of
the region.

2.   HISTORY

The southern movement of the Thai into the peninsula began in the 14th
century but was held back by Malacca which controlled the peninsula as
far north as Pattani.   During the 15th century, when Malacca became the
leading maritime power in Southeast Asia and the centre for the diffusion
of Islam, the Malays of South Thailand were converted to Islam.   Following
the Portuguese conquest of Malacca in 1511 the sultanate of Pattani

---

* Dr Elise Tugby is Senior Lecturer in Geography and Dr Donald Tugby is
Reader in Anthropology and Sociology, University of Queensland.

gradually broke up and Tome Peres, writing in 1516, described Pattani as
belonging to the king of Siam.   However, Siamese control was not secure.
During the Ayutthaya period the provincial governor at Nakhon Si Thammarat rebelled against the central government on a number of occasions.
In 1692 the southern provinces were placed under the Kalahom (military)
division.   In the meantime Pattani developed as a port and was for a
time important as a European trading station.

     After the sack of Ayutthaya by the Burmese in 1767, and a brief
rebellion by the governor of Nakhon Si Thammarat, the area was again
administered by the Kalahom from Bangkok.   The Thais now set about expanding and more firmly controlling the outlying parts of their domain.
After a revolt in Pattani in 1790, neighbouring Songkhla was set up as
an administrative centre to control Pattani and Trengganu, while Kedah
and Kelantan remained under Nakhon.   Pattani was divided into seven
small states, six of which had a Malay ruler.   After the Sultan of Kedah
was forced to flee to Penang by Siamese invaders in 1821, attempts by his
supporters to retake Kedah twice sparked rebellions in the seven states.
In 1831 an army was sent from Bangkok;   the chief of Pattani fled to
Kelantan and the chiefs of Raman and Nong Chik towards Perak.   The chief
of Yala was captured and sent to Bangkok, the chief of Nong Chik was
killed and the chiefs of Raman, Rangae and Sai Buri gave themselves up
(Vella, 1957).

     Six years later there was another revolt.   This time the chiefs of
Pattani, Yiring and Sai Buri remained loyal and a siege of Songkhla was
raised by an army of about 5000 sent from Bangkok.   The leader of this
force remained for some months at Songkhla to settle Malay affairs.   A
threat to the newly-appointed and Thai-supported Sultan of Kelantan was
temporarily settled by forcing one disputant to flee to Trengganu and by
making the others take oaths of allegiance;   but it was finally resolved
in 1842 by appointing a brother of the former Sultan as chief of Nong Chik,
and a cousin as chief of Pattani.

     The consolidation and extension of Thai influence in the Malay
states was opposed and finally stopped by British interests.   In 1909
the present border was established by a Thai-British agreement which
forced Thailand to abandon all claims to Kelantan, Trengganu, Kedah and

Perlis; but it made the Seven States, by then reorganised under the new administrative system introduced by Rama V in 1899, part of the Kingdom of Thailand.

Thai expansion in the Malay states in the 19th century was characterised by features which have continued into the 20th century and which affect ecological and inter-cultural relations in contemporary South Thailand. In the first place the central government recognised the need to bring local officials under more direct control. Power was exerted at the local level by the dismemberment of local political units, and by the removal of local leaders to Bangkok and their replacement by Thai nominees. Whenever possible direct rule was substituted for indirect rule (as in Nakhon, Kedah and the Seven States). The armies lived off the land and powerfully affected the local economy. Large scale internal movements of the Malay population took place and many Malays were re-settled further north on the peninsula. Ethnic Thais moved southward and occupied land in the Malay areas and some Malay families were removed to Bangkok as war captives. Almost incidentally the Thais recognised and reinforced the close relationships between the Seven States and Kelantan by appointing members of the Kelantan elite to chieftainships in the Seven States.

The above account, which might be described as a Euro-American academic historian's account of events, differs substantially in emphasis from Malay oral tradition as collected in the Pattani area in 1956 (Fraser, 1960). This tradition emphasises the victories, rather than the defeats, of the Malays in their struggle against Thai domination. According to the Malay accounts, Pattani was economically important prior to Islamisation and prospered after conversion.[1] The Raja was succeeded by his sons Raja Tua and Raja Muda who ruled jointly. Raja Tua was invited to Bangkok to marry one of the daughters of the Thai king, but he was disrespectfully treated there and attacked and captured the king's palace. He later married the king's daughter and returned to Pattani when peace was established.

---

[1] A Moslem doctor is said to have converted the Raja, and his subjects followed him in the new faith.

In Raja Muda's reign the king of Thailand was refused the hand of
Raja Muda's sister. He attacked Pattani but the Malays defeated the
Thais by eating up their food supplies. Raja Muda was succeeded by his
three sisters, one of whom was requested in marriage by the Thai king.
She refused and married the Sultan of Johore. The Thai king tried to
attack Pattani but was again unsuccessful owing to food shortages. After
the death of this queen the succession lapsed and owing to the fragmentation of Pattani, the Thais were able to overcome the area.

A younger son of the Raja of Kelantan attempted to reorganise the
area after the Thai invasion but was never completely successful. The
fifth and last of this line, Raja Abdul Kadir, refused to submit to more
direct Thai administration in the 1890s and was forced to flee to Kelantan.

The picture of a prosperous independent Pattani which in the past
was capable of overcoming the Thais is clearly of some present political
importance. In the style of traditional Malay thought the prosperity
of the Malay polity is linked to the leadership of the Raja.

In recent years insurrection has been spasmodic. There were rebellions in 1947, 1950 and 1954 and in 1950 about 1000 people took to the
hills and guerilla activity persisted for two years. In September 1969,
the provinces of Pattani, Narathiwat, Yala and Satun were declared
terrorist-influenced areas, and the government subsequently sent army units
to combat the bandits. A recent estimate has put the number of Thai-Muslim
guerillas in the area at 500.

3. POPULATION AND HABITAT

In contemporary South Thailand about 70 per cent of the population are Thai-
Muslims.* Thai-Buddhists, some foreign Chinese and a few Indians make up
the remainder. The Thai-Buddhist group has accreted to itself Thai citi-
zens of Chinese ancestry who, their ethnic origins being well known to
people in the area, form a distinct group some of whose cultural activities
centre on the Chinese temple.

---

* Editorial note: The Malays of southern Thailand are officially called
Thai-Islam or Thai-Muslim. The latter term has been adopted throughout
this volume for consistency.

South Thailand has a varied terrain, with high forested interior ranges; extensive deltas on the South China Sea coast separated by sand dunes and clay swales and backed by hills; and a narrow west coast fringed by islands (Fig. 12.1). There is a wide variety of resources but a basic pattern of terrain types and land use is replicated throughout the southern provinces. A section through the Pattani and Yala provinces along the Pattani River shows a sequence of ten habitats:

(i) Thai-Muslim coastal fishing villages are sited on the dunes;

(ii) Thai-Buddhist charcoal makers site their huts near the fringing mangroves growing on the muds of the shallow Pattani estuary;

(iii) extensive shallow bays are used by part-time Thai-Muslim salt makers on the clay foreshores of the Pattani estuary;

(iv) Thai-Muslim villages on the banks of the Pattani River produce coconuts and fish;

(v) Pattani township itself, low-lying and inundated in part during frequent floods, serves as the provincial and district administrative headquarters, commercial and trading centre and higher education centre; the old central business district crowded with shops, stores, banks, cinemas, markets, bus depots and petrol stations has villages clustered around it which serve as dormitories for the townsfolk, but which are also the homes of people who fish and cultivate rice;

(vi) inland from Pattani delta-sited Thai-Muslim and Thai-Buddhist villages are functionally simpler, with wet-rice cultivation as the main activity; some land is under coconuts and on the river levees fruits such as rambutan are grown;

(vii) towards Yala, in the Yarang district, hilly land unsuited for wet-rice growing provides unflooded sites for Thai-Muslim and Thai-Buddhist rubber planters; there is an increase in the area of village lands under rubber and a decrease in the area planted to wet-rice as one moves upstream; however, wherever villages have access to land suitable for wet-rice it is planted; dry-rice is often planted on hill slopes to supplement wet-rice yields; dry-rice is also grown when a new rubber garden is started;

(viii) in valleys tributary to the Pattani River where valley floors are wide and carry detrital tin, there are settlements of Chinese and Thai-Buddhists of Chinese descent who are labourers in the tin mines and who are uninvolved in agricultural activities;

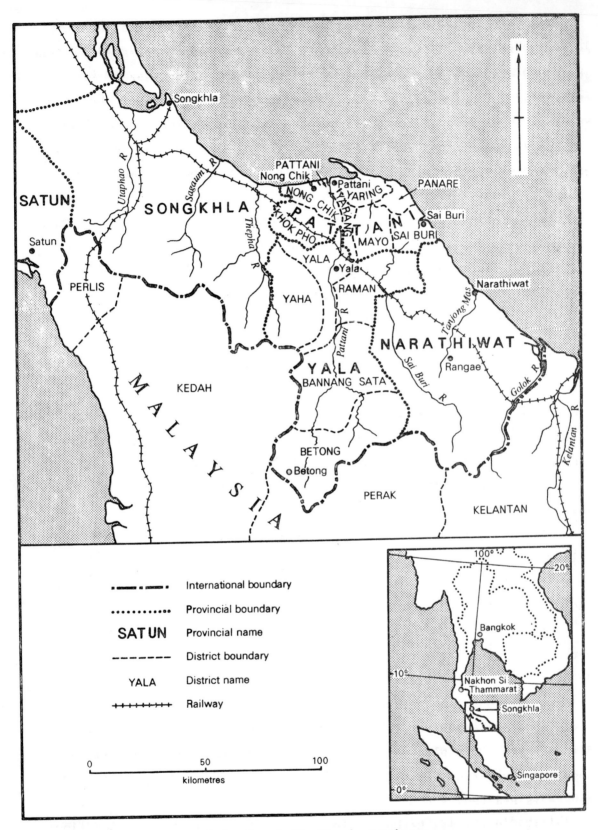

Fig. 12.1   South Thailand provinces.

(ix) in the mountainous headwaters of the Pattani River there are large rubber plantations in which the 'village' becomes a plantation-owned coolie line; each segment of a long building is occupied by a labourer and his family who are Chinese, or Thai-Buddhist of Chinese descent; and

(x) in the Betong area there are plantations, small rubber gardens and terraced wet-rice fields owned by Thai-Muslim and Thai-Buddhist villagers who also gather forest products.

Is there any association between the various land use activities and particular cultural groups?   In Yala and Pattani provinces Thai-Muslims are engaged in rural, near-subsistence activities such as wet-rice cultivation with some cash cropping of fruit and rubber.   On the coast, the Thai-Muslims fish as a subsistence and cash activity and their income may be supplemented by salt-making and coconuts.

The opportunities for such subsistence activities are greater in the province of Pattani where delta and beach occupy a large part of the total area.   About two-thirds of the total population of the two provinces is found in Pattani and of this about 78 per cent are Thai-Muslims. The percentage of Thai-Muslims in Yala province is about 61 per cent. The Betong area offers little opportunity for wet-rice growing and in the municipality the Thai-Muslims make up 30 per cent of the population, Thai-Buddhist 25 per cent and Chinese 40 per cent.   Only a few rural settlements in Yala and Pattani provinces are reported as Thai-Buddh st. Most Thai-Buddhists are employed in government service where they occupy almost all the positions.   Thus as a group they are town dwellers or live in nearby urbanised villages.   Most people in this group are not locally born.   The few who have resided in the area for some time have usually acquired small rubber plantations.

The Thai-Buddhists of Chinese descent are urban dwellers, but few are in government service.   This is the wealthiest cultural group and they own factories, petrol stations, and banks; have a monopoly on whisky distribution; and own rubber plantations.   Their fortunes have been established by their Chinese ancestors.   Members of this group marry Thai-Buddhists or Chinese but also within their own group.   Most live in the towns of Yala and Pattani, but some live in the main towns of the districts.

The Chinese group is small and made up of Chinese who have either
spent most of their lives in Thailand or are new, and in some cases,
illegal migrants.   The shop-owners, traders, rubber plantation owners
found in the major towns are wealthy - but the mine-workers, rubber-
tappers, and market gardeners of Yala province are poor.

Since it is apparent that few in the cultural groups share the
same social and economic milieu, how are the groups inter-related and
what keeps each in its own economic niche?   The Thai-Muslims have
little capital and cannot enter business in competition with the Thai-
Buddhists of Chinese descent.   The latter have no interest in putting
money into risky ventures such as salt making, rice growing (risky
because of poor drainage and frequent floods), the marketing of fruit
which cannot be stored, and bus transport in which there are high maintenance costs.   However they are interested in Thai-Muslim primary
produce such as rubber and fish which can be processed.   The Thai-
Buddhists of Chinese descent do not compete with Thai-Buddhists for
government positions - though the position is secure, the increment in
wealth is too small.   The Thai-Buddhists have no competitors for
government positions - the Thai-Muslims cannot get government jobs
because they do not have enough education.

The wealthy Chinese function like the wealthy Thai-Buddhists of
Chinese descent, but the poorer Chinese take few risks until they accumulate capital.   The Thai-Buddhists sell services to all those who need
them and hence advance themselves economically whenever the opportunity
presents itself without taking risks.

4.   THAI-MUSLIM CULTURE PATTERNS

The nuclear family household is the usual economic unit in Thai-Muslim
culture.   There is a clear-cut division of labour between the sexes, but
not much economic specialisation among men or women.   A man is held responsible for the maintenance of his wife and children in village sentiment and canon law but the nuclear family as such is not a potent source
of identity for men or women.   Rather, family identity is related to the
diffuse kinship network which characterises Malay culture.

On the other hand the village community is a potent source of identity with respect to economics, personal status and religion. Individual action is preferred in economic affairs, but for some forms of activity, such as working the larger fishing boats, co-ordinated action is necessary and the crew members of these boats often come from the same hamlet. Personal status can refer to both age and origin.   The individual passes through life's stages as a member of a community-bound association of peers among whom distinctions are sometimes made according to the position of one's male ancestors in the social hierarchy of Raja times.[2]   The village is bound to religion by the coincidence of community and congregation. The mosque, where community prayers are held every Friday, is the focus of community religious affairs and is supported by a village committee.   A community feast is held there at the most important festival of the year, the breaking of the fast.

The village is the largest visible political unit in the Thai-Muslim social world and its boundaries are visibly and symbolically manifested. It subsumes many activities and its existence is dramatised in the inter-village singing contests in which each side in turn sings derogatory songs about the other.

According to Thai-Buddhists in Bangkok, South Thailand is an area of sweet mandarins, dark-eyed girls and little hatchets.   All Thai-Muslim men carried small hatchets as weapons until they were banned in 1959. Sudden personal attacks with these weapons were not uncommon.   Violence occurs in sudden outbreaks which quickly release tension (this is similar to the classical pattern of amok).   Thai-Muslims also tend to be quarrelsome but most aggression finds an outlet in institutionalised covert form. Bull fights are popular.   Thai-Muslims like to give an appearance of independence and of not being beholden to anyone.   Male Thai-Muslims like to be 'big men' - to feel that they are of social importance and to have this made publicly manifest.   They like to wear the white hat of the hadji - a visible prestige symbol.   They like to be extravagant and will not argue overmuch about the price of goods sold to them for to do so is to lower their prestige.   In short, there is an accentuation of pride and self-esteem among them of which the sociological counterpart is an hierarchical social order.

---

2 There are four terms of address in Pattani, in descending order: Ku, Ni, Wan and Che.

Thai-Muslims avoid direct confrontation in an issue.   In the
village community they use behind-the-back criticism as a means of social
control and keep up a pretence of conformity to social rules.   There is
much public spitting during the fast.   This gives an appearance of homo-
geneity which disguises individual differences.   The more politically
sophisticated Thai-Muslims whose channels of communication reach beyond
the boundaries of village gossip to Kelantan and Kedah, see these real
differences themselves and speak of the ordinary villagers as bovine.

5.   THAI-BUDDHIST CULTURE PATTERNS

The Buddhist conception of the cosmic order is reflected in the social
order (Hanks, 1962).   All creatures are placed in a hierarchy of effectiveness in action which is related to the degree of freedom from selfish
ends.   Individual creatures move up or down this hierarchy according to
their gains and losses of merit.

Similarly in social life there are no fixed ranks;   an individual
maintains or improves his position in the hierarchy by giving benefits to
others.   The greater a person's resources, the more benefits he can give.
Benefit-giving is the basis for the formation of patron-client relationships, which are characterised by inequality.   Reciprocity is implied in
these relationships, but the relationship can be terminated when a person
sees no further benefit in it for himself.   Thus the working out of
Buddhist values in social process provides for both group formation and
idiosyncratic individual action.   The former yields what Hanks, in relation to economic affairs, has called the entourage (Hanks, 1966), an
association of persons related to a leader, each member of which occupies
a position in the organisation according to the contribution he makes.
Individualism in Thai-Buddhist village culture has been vividly demonstrated by Moerman in relation to the structure of knowledge: he relates
how a man with a knowledge of insecticides lived and farmed with his
father-in-law for 10 years without telling him anything about insecticides
(Moerman, 1961:9).

Thus in Thai-Buddhist behaviour violence is played down, sublimated
and balanced by making merit.   Control of anger is recognised as a virtue.

It is said that the question was put to Buddha 'What does it profit a man most to kill?'   The reply was 'To kill anger'.   Tolerance and compassion towards others contribute to making merit and individual advancement.   In looking at his reflection in the mirror of society the individual tries to accentuate internal harmony and balance.

6.   INTER-CULTURAL MEDIATION

(i)   In administration

The features of the structure and modus operandi of the Thai bureaucracy which affect inter-cultural mediation are paternalism, use of entourage relations and lack of efficient communication channels.

In the Sukhothai period (A.D. 1238-1317) all heads of areas (of whatever size) were called 'father' of their respective territory (Riggs, 1966: 79-80).   The integral relationship between a leader and his people for which this kinship-based imagery stood has long since ceased to characterise the relationships in reality.   There has been a differentiation into peasant mass and ruling elite and the relationship between ruler and ruled has been absorbed into the bureaucratic system.   Nevertheless paternalism persists although now in the form of a stern rather than a kind father. In the first place local officials feel themselves to be responsible for good order in their area;   secondly, they are enjoined to care for the people;   and thirdly, individual officers feel that they should exercise Buddhist compassion in playing out their roles.   For their part, Thai-Buddhist villagers take the opportunity to express their willingness to be ruled whenever they receive a ritual visit from the District Officer.

These experiences and attitudes condition the expectations of Thai-Buddhist administrators in their relations with Thai-Muslim villagers. Many of the latter however do not fulfil a basic Thai assumption, namely the recognition of the administrators as legitimate rulers.   As far as possible they lock up their affairs in the village community and sometimes conspicuously avoid using officially-provided resources.   Good clinics and other resources sometimes remain unused for this reason.   Thai-Muslims perceive individual officials in terms of their own criteria for personality assessment which vary around the notion of good-hearted (baik hati),

but their general judgment is that the Thai officials are weak (lemah).
The Thai-Muslims maintain the facade of conformity, but in practice avoid
Thai 'parental' control.

Entourage relations exist within the bureaucracy and in relationships between members of the bureaucracy and outsiders.   Officials
regard such relations as a part of the role they occupy - for the com-
passionate granting of a concession, tangible and intangible rewards
should be received.   Thai-Muslims find difficulty in entering into such
relations because they are afraid of the criticism of their fellows.
Their model of economic action is individualistic, not co-operative, and
they do not like to enter into relations which involve unspecified
reciprocity.   Thai-Buddhists of Chinese descent and Chinese proper enter
entourages readily and sometimes become members of a circle of officials.
The entourage functions as the main mediating mechanism between Chinese
culture and Thai culture, but the membership of any entourage changes
because most officials are moved every two or three years.

The lack of communication between Thai government departments in
Bangkok has been noted by Riggs (1966:351). In the provincial setting of
South Thailand where facilities must often be shared by members of
different departments, and there are friendship groups of men of similar
grade from different departments, there is more knowledge of what others
are doing.   However, regular avenues of communication between officials
and Thai-Muslims are limited to one or two official channels, because
most officials do not speak Malay and most Thai-Muslims do not speak Thai.
Village and hamlet headmen and medical assistants are called in regularly
to be paid and to be given official information to pass on to the
villagers.   Official parties occasionally turn up in villages for
special purposes, such as to collect money for a new police post.   The
only other avenue of communication is through paid official interpreters
attached to the courts, or clerks who act as unofficial ombudsmen for
the Thai-Muslims.

A sense of cultural superiority on the part of Thai-Buddhists is
partly responsible for lack of information about Islam which leads them
to offend Islamic susceptibilities.   When the central mosque was being
built in Pattani, the officials decided to have a foundation stone similar

to the lucky stone laid down for the building of a new wat (Buddhist
temple);   a Thai-Buddhist political figure from Bangkok was invited to
perform the ceremony, but only after representations were made by Muslims
in the area was an Islamic leader from Bangkok also invited. Occasionally a Thai official will wear a kopiah (a hat normally worn only by
Thai-Muslims) - but when a Thai official appears in a Chinese restaurant
in a kopiah (with the implication that he may be eating pork) this is regarded as an insult by the Muslims.   The officials attempt to integrate
Buddhist ceremonial with the Islamic religious cycle.   Following the
breaking of the fast there is a fair in Pattani.   Buddhist priests are
invited by the officials to participate in the opening ceremony. These
official attempts to communicate with the Thai-Muslims through ritual
integration are interpreted by the Muslims as signs of official insensi-
tivity to Islam.

Finally, the absence of efficient communication channels from Thai-
Muslims to officials leads to misinterpretation of what information does get
through.   It takes many years for an official to build up a personal
information filter which enables him to read the signs aright.

(ii)   Chinese cultural mediators

Chinese culture in South Thailand has the same characteristics as
elsewhere in Thailand, namely, it emphasises materialism and a concern
with wealth as a means for achieving upward mobility.   Status is defined
in terms of wealth and business leadership, and the Confucian family,
with its role sets determined by generation, age and sex, is the key
element in social organisation.   This culture pattern is shared by
persons identified as Chinese, who are mostly in lowly occupations, and
persons of Chinese descent who identify with the Thai-Buddhists.   There
is a greater percentage of persons who share Chinese culture patterns in
South Thailand than elsewhere in rural Thailand, but they are less
socially visible because the relationships between the politically dominant Thai-Buddhist and the numerous Thai-Muslims dominate the scene.   In
this relationship the Thai-Buddhists of Chinese descent have important
mediator roles.   They own and operate most of the tin mines, own the
factories, handle the export of rubber, the import and sale of consumer
goods, and act as money-lenders for the Thai-Muslims.   Thus they inter-
pose an economic shield between the two most visible groups, on the one

hand guarding the Thai-Buddhist administrators from charges of direct
economic exploitation and, on the other, shoring up the Thai-Muslim
peasant economy.

The more prosperous Thai-Buddhists of Chinese descent have lived
in the area for a long time, whereas the turn-over of ethnic Thai
administrators is fairly frequent.   The fact that there are relatively
few ethnic Thais in the area has maintained the ethnic purity of the
Thai-Buddhists of Chinese descent.

The Thai-Muslims perceive the Chinese in their role as traders.
From their point of view the Chinese are good-hearted because they do
not deceive the villagers.   It is possible to be in debt to a Chinese
for a considerable amount.   The Chinese will bargain with the Thai-Muslims
(in contrast to the ethnic Thais who demand goods at a fixed price).

(iii) Case studies

(a)   Thai-Muslim mediators

Thai-Muslims who occupy minor roles in the administration look like
the 'culture brokers' pictured by Wolf (1956), who operate at the levels
of both community and national interest.   At the same time they do not
change their overt cultural identity;   they reside in Thai-Muslim villages
or in Thai-Muslim areas of the town.   In the office they use Thai names
and official uniforms and speak Thai;   in the village they wear Malay
dress and speak Malay.   Their ambivalent position is shown up on extra-
office occasions: at official dinners they must either eat Thai food,
or sit at a separate table, or stay away.   On these occasions they usually
wear Malay dress.   Some of these minor officials try to play two roles
and drink with the Thais behind the scenes, but maintain a facade of conformity to Islamic regulation in public.

The tension which this ambivalence creates within a person usually
results in his criticising severely the Thai-Buddhists behind their backs.
This conforms with village practice and may be an attempt to maintain a
position in the village community.   Such persons keep their fellow Muslims
informed about the moves of the administration.   The administration
accepts such people with tolerance;   the Thai-Muslim see them as exploiting

the Thai-Buddhist for their own self interest.   Thai-Muslim minor
officials can operate in this way because Thai-Muslim society is acepha-
lous.   The demise of the Raja left Thai-Muslim society without political
representatives with an indigenous warrant.   Operating in this social
vacuum the broker lives off the ambiguity of his role (Press, 1969).

Some Islamic religious teachers are effective as another kind of
Thai-Muslim mediator because they have high prestige within their own
society.   They may sit on boards or collaborate with officials on ceremonial occasions and give credence to the notion that the Thai-Muslims
are part of the Thai nation.   (cf. the picture of the Javanese kijaji
as drawn by Geertz, 1959.)

Che Muktar is about 37;   he lived in Bangkok for some time.   He is
very obsequious towards officials.   He married a Buddhist who became a
Muslim.   His father was a strict Muslim.   He has two names, one Thai-
Buddhist and one Thai-Muslim.   He emphasises his Muslim identity by
wearing formal clothes when he goes to the mosque.   He drinks in private
rooms with the Buddhist officials.   During the last fasting month he
pleaded illness as an excuse for not fasting, but avoided meeting his
father face-to-face or letting his neighbours see him take food.   He is
on bad terms with his wife, whom he beat with a knuckle-duster because
he said that without telling him she had pawned some goods to help a
relative's son through school in Bangkok - a typical Thai-Buddhist action.
Within the house his actions are abnormal;   he hits the children and moves
and talks compulsively.   He shows such obvious signs of tension that even
his fellow Muslims regard him as abnormal.

Khun Mat shows another form of adaptation.   He is a Muslim police-
man aged about 30 and born in Bangkok.   He has relatives but no deep roots
in Pattani.   He is married to a Thai-Buddhist who became a Muslim and he
is anxious to get on in the service.   He functions adequately as a mediator
because in the villages he pretends to be a representative of modern Islam.
But in Buddhist style he displays an amused tolerance towards village
orthodoxy.   Among Thai-Buddhists he uses the Buddhist salute which is not
normally used by Thai-Muslims.   He says that according to modern Islamic
ideas in West Malaysia he can eat eggs and bacon for breakfast and so
suffers no pangs of conscience when eating Thai food.

Hadji Idris is an official advisor to the administration on religious issues.   He runs a private Muslim religious school and tolerant Buddhists pay the same respect to him as they would to any religious teacher.   He takes advantage of his official connections to act as an agent for a shipping company which carries pilgrims to Mecca.   Hadji Idris's position thus depends not on his fraternising with Buddhists but on remaining an orthodox Muslim.

(b)   Chinese mediator

Khun Tan is a Chinese merchant of Thai nationality who associates closely with Thai-Buddhist officials.   He is about 36.   His grandparents and his wife's parents are Thai-born Chinese.   He was educated in a Chinese school in Penang, but he acts like a very loyal Thai citizen.

He speaks Malay, Thai and several dialects of Chinese.   He says that when he was at school in Penang he moved his seat from time to time so that he could learn a new dialect from his neighbour.   In his basic aims he is both Chinese-like and Thai-like.   He is writing a patriotic book for school children, but the Thai-Muslim version displays an ignorance of Islamic practices.   He has already been decorated by the King for his gifts to schools.   At present he is undecided whether he should try to become a local political representative.   At the Chinese New Year, Khun Tan invites Buddhist monks to his house rather than going only to the joss house.   He attends impartially weddings, funerals and feasts of Thai-Buddhist, Thai-Muslim and Chinese.

To the Thai-Buddhists Khun Tan is known as a man who likes money, who eats little, wears old clothes, and whose servants are unpaid relatives. To the Thai-Muslim he is a reliable shopkeeper who never cheats and is willing to extend credit and give loans to Thai-Muslim coolies on his plantations.   Khun Tan is said to be the friend of all; he is polite to everyone, even to the missionaries who provide him with free English lessons.   The Thai-Buddhist officials who are his associates try to break down the armour of his good humour.   Khun Tan's only reply is an oblique dig at Thai-Buddhist beliefs in magic.

7. CONCLUSION

We might have expected, following Caldwell's sanguine view, that a decrease
in Thai-Muslim bitterness of the 1950s was partly a result of a successful
education programme (Caldwell, 1967:30) and that the Thai-Muslims would move
towards integration, but the evidence is to the contrary.   In spite of a
speed-up in the establishment of the South's university centred on Songkhla
and a considerable increase in security forces, the number of incidents
involving local bandits has risen sharply.   The persistence of insurrection,
or the threat of it, suggests that this social movement is a structural
phenomenon.

The need for man-made social change has been recognised by the Thai
government.   According to Etzioni, social change is a function of the
relationship between control processes and consensus formation processes
(1968a; 1968b).   On the face of it the Thai bureaucracy has a monopoly
of the instruments of control, yet it fails to have any part in the daily
direction and management of Thai-Muslim affairs.   The bureaucracy has
sufficient knowledge to bring economic change about, yet it cannot pass
this knowledge on to Thai-Muslims.   Decision-making is a monopoly of the
bureaucracy, but, as we have seen, there is no effective machinery for
'selling' decisions already made.   Consensus formation between Thai-Muslims
and the bureaucracy cannot come about because there are so few channels of
upward communication, and the balance of power is so heavily in favour of
the bureaucracy that the Thai-Muslims cannot be committed to bureaucratic
decisions.   In the struggle for the minds of the immobilised mass of Thai-
Muslim peasants the most effective mobilisers are clearly the religious
teachers who have the advantage of control over indigenous institutions.
In short, the possibility of a structural transformation of the total
society in South Thailand does not exist.

How can we account for the solidarity of the Thai-Muslims?   Some
hints of an answer have been given above, but before they are followed up
let us look at administration-peasant relations elsewhere in Thailand.
Overwhelmingly they were, and are characterised by the passivity of the
masses.   If the masses were wooed at all, it was in paternal or patronage
terms (Hindley, 1968).   Moerman recounts how in a village in the northern
district of Chiang Kham, an announcement by the District Officer of the new

government policy of friendship between villagers and officials was greeted
with laughter by villagers and officials alike (Moerman, 1964:40).   In
short, there is an expectation of great social distance between peasants
and officials.   In South Thailand there is a minority of peasants who are
Thai-Buddhists.   As a result of their different reaction to the administration and the absence of cross-cultural cues of similarity they do not make
common cause with the Thai-Muslim peasants.   The Thai-Muslims remain culturally isolated in spite of nationalistic propaganda aimed at forcing a
change of identity.   Normally in acculturation situations members of the
subordinate group come to value positively the norms of the dominant group
(Berreman, 1964).   But two conditions mitigate against this happening to
most Thai-Muslims in South Thailand.   First their group maintains its own
instruments of socialisation, and secondly the dominant group maintains
itself at a great social distance.   (In an official publication (Publicity
Committee, 1957:21) the main derivation of the Malay is said to be from
the Jakun, 'a primitive jungle tribe scattered through the peninsula' and
the Pattani Malays are said to be 'strongly mixed' with Semang, i.e.
Negritos.)   As we have seen, Thai-Buddhist officials do not give credence
to the viability of Islamic culture nor do they understand its functioning.
In accordance with Young's hypothesis the solidarity of the Thai-Muslim
is increased by the discrepancy between the differentiation of their social
system and the symbolic recognition which is accorded it by the incorporating system (Young, 1970).

These findings do not presage well for the future of relationships
between Thai-Muslims and the administration, but it is necessary to examine
briefly other factors in the situation.   Education is thought to be a potent
factor in Thai-isation, but its effect is limited by the need for continuity
in socialisation.   A school system should sustain the emotional values of
childhood and channel them into the societal values of adult roles (Kiefer,
1970).   But the school system in South Thailand cannot so function for the
Thai-Muslims because there is discontinuity of experience from family and
community to Thai school.   On the other hand the Islamic school (pondok),
which 80 per cent of Muslim boys in South Thailand attend, does reinforce
family and community values.   Rapid Thai-isation therefore cannot be expected from attendance at Thai schools.

Other factors stem from the possibilities for economic development. Wet-rice growing on the deltas and along the coast can be expanded and intensified without ecological breakdown, given capital inputs for irrigation and drainage. New rice varieties can be introduced and some small changes in technology brought about without social or economic disruption. Rubber growing on hills and mountains cannot, however, be greatly expanded by traditional slash and burn methods without serious soil degradation and an increase in silting and flooding. It is precisely in this field that the expectations of the administration for increasing the economic productivity of the area lie. The border settlement projects are intended to have the additional function of increasing the politically reliable Thai component of the population. Although most of the Thai-Muslims see the Thai administration as a colonial regime they might nevertheless feel less aggressive towards their masters if they were economically satisfied. Unfortunately the Thai-Muslim ethos lays no great stress on materialistic satisfaction at present, but consumer demand could rise to match that of Malays in neighbouring Malaysia. It remains to be seen whether the Thai economy can meet such rising economic expectations[3] without also having to meet political expectations. In this regard the presence of many Peace Corps personnel, USIS members and Green Beret United States advisers in South Thailand and the demonstration by a reported 1500 students in Kuala Lumpur against Thai mistreatment of Muslims (Canberra Times, 6 June 1971) are evidence that the inter-cultural situation in South Thailand is no longer simply a domestic Thai matter.

ACKNOWLEDGEMENTS

The authors wish to acknowledge the assistance of SEATO in providing funds for the fieldwork and to express their gratitude to the many Thai officials and villagers whose patience and willingness to help made it possible to carry out the project.

---

3 Some observers are not hopeful about the future of the economy (Cook, 1968; Solovyov, 1967).

REFERENCES

Berreman, G.C., 1964.   'Aleut reference group alienation, mobility, and
          acculturation', American Anthropologist, 66, pp. 231-50.

Caldwell, J.C., 1967.   'The demographic structure', in T.H. Silcock, ed.,
          Thailand, Australian National University Press, Canberra,
          pp. 27-64.

Cook, C., 1968.   'Thailand, problems for the future', Eastern World,
          Supplement, 22, pp. i-v.

Devahuti, D., 1965.   India and ancient Malaya, Eastern Universities
          Press, Singapore.

Etzioni, A., 1968a.   'Introduction', in J.P. Nettl and R. Robertson, 1968.
          International systems and the modernization of societies,
          Faber and Faber, London.

Etzioni, A., 1968b.   The active society: a theory of societal and
          political processes, The Free Press, New York.

Fraser, T.M., 1962.   Rusembilan, Cornell University, Ithaca.

Geertz, C., 1959.   'The Javanese kijaji: the changing role of a culture
          broker', Comparative Studies in Society and History, 2, pp. 228-49.

Hanks, L.M., 1962.   'Merit and power in the Thai social order', American
          Anthropologist, 64, pp. 1247-61.

Hanks, L.M., 1966.   'The corporation and the entourage: a comparison of
          Thai and American social organization', Catalyst, no. 2, pp. 55-63.

Hindley, D., 1968.   'Thailand: the politics of passivity', Pacific Affairs,
          41, pp. 355-71.

Kiefer, C.W., 1970.   'The psychological interdependence of family, school,
          and bureaucracy in Japan', American Anthropologist, 72, pp. 66-75.

Moerman, M.H., 1961.   A northern Thai village, South East Asia Survey
          Research Report, United States Information Service, Thailand.

Moerman, M.H., 1964.   'Western culture and the Thai way of life', Asia,
          no. 1, pp. 31-50.

Press, I., 1969.   'Ambiguity and innovation: implications for the genesis
          of the culture broker', American Anthropologist, 71, pp. 205-17.

Publicity Committee, 1957.   Thailand: past and present, Publicity Committee,
          Ninth Pacific Science Congress, Bangkok.

Riggs, F.W., 1966.   Thailand: the modernization of a bureaucratic polity, East-West Center Press, Honolulu.

Solovyov, B., 1967.   'Behind a prosperous facade', International Affairs, Moscow, no. 1, pp. 48-53.

Vella, W.F., 1957.   Siam under Rama III 1824-1851, J.J. Augustin, New York.

Young, F.W., 1970.   'Reactive subsystems', American Sociological Review, 35, pp. 297-307.

Wolf, E., 1956.   'Aspects of group relations in a complex society: Mexico', American Anthropologist, 58, pp. 1005-78.

CHAPTER 13

THE THAI-MUSLIM BORDER PROVINCES:
SOME NATIONAL SECURITY ASPECTS

Astri Suhrke*

1. INTRODUCTION

The four Thai-Muslim border provinces (Fig. 13.1) present a political
scenario which is far from unique to southern Thailand: an ethnic minority group is located in a border area which is regarded as 'sensitive'
by the government because of disorder, banditry and the activities of
various organised counter-elites. The relationship between the central
government and the Southern Muslims has a long history of fluctuations
between relative amity and relative hostility. The current phase appears
to be one of considerable tension due to intensified competition between
the government and the various counter-elites which operate in the area -
Muslim separatists, Malayan communists and Thai communists. The result
is that the alternatives presented to the minority group have been drawn
with greater clarity and the pressure to make a choice has correspondingly
increased. The purpose of this paper is to examine these alternatives,
the tactics employed by the various political groups, their relative
strengths, and insofar as possible, to assess the response of the Thai-
Muslim community.

Most of the material for this paper was collected during fieldwork
in Thailand in 1970 and 1971. I held a series of interviews with officials
in the central and local administration, parliamentarians, and representatives of the Thai-Muslim community both in the South and in Bangkok. In
addition, I was able to draw on unprocessed data and official publications
of the four changwat (province) administrations in the South, and from
regional administrative offices in Songkhla. On the basis of this information, I have tried to outline the major characteristics of the present

---

* Dr Suhrke is Assistant Professor of International Relations, School of
International Science, The American University, Washington, D.C.

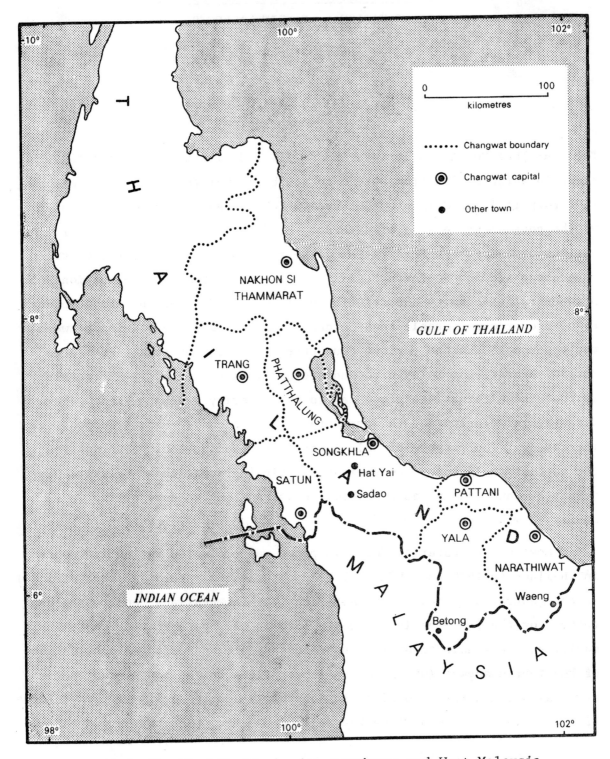

Fig. 13.1   The Thai-Muslim border provinces and West Malaysia.

situation.   The sensitivity of the topic has made it necessary to keep
the discussion at a fairly general level.

2.   BACKGROUND

The Thai-Muslim population in the South is concentrated in the four provinces of Pattani, Yala, Narathiwat and Satun (Fig. 13.1).   Altogether
it represents around 700,000 people or three per cent of the national
population according to the 1960 census.   In Pattani, Yala and Narathiwat,
the Thai-Muslims constitute between 70 and 80 per cent of the local population and are clearly demarcated as a distinct group.   They use Malay
as their daily language and only a small percentage (20-30 per cent) can
speak Thai.   They are all Muslims, maintain their traditional Malay dress
and customs and very rarely intermarry with Thai-Buddhists.   Officially
they are called Thai-Islam or Thai-Muslim, but Thai-Buddhists in the South
frequently refer to them as phuak khaek (khaek is a collective noun for
Malays, Indians, Arabs and Negroes; phuak means group).   The Thai-Muslims
in turn usually call themselves 'our group', sometimes Malay, Muslim or
Pattani-Muslim, but not Thai.   The term Thai in their usage always refers
to Thai-Buddhists.

Satun differs from the other Thai-Muslim provinces in that the majority of the population speaks Thai, mainly due to a longer history of close
administrative interaction with a Thai-Buddhist majority.   Satun is also
geographically separated from the other three provinces by a broad slice
of Thai-Buddhist territory in Songkhla province.   Partly for these reasons,
Satun does not have the history of separatist sentiment and political conflict with the central government which we find in Pattani, Yala and Narathiwat.   For all practical purposes, therefore, the Thai-Muslim minority
in the South appears as a political problem only in three provinces.   This
is acknowledged in the common practice of referring to them simply as saam
changwat (the three provinces).

In an earlier article I have discussed the history of intermittent
conflict between saam changwat and the central government, which partly
can be explained by events in neighbouring Malaya or seen as local response
to changes in the policy of the Thai government (Suhrke, 1970).   While
this may account for the timing of particular difficult periods, it is

obvious that such tension springs from a continued feeling in the three
provinces that its people constitute a distinct entity, and the refusal
of the Thai government to acknowledge or accept this.

History has produced its own legacy of mutual suspicion.   In its
extreme form, this means that the Thai government distrusts the political
loyalty of the Thai-Muslims and suspects that they regard themselves as
Malay rather than as Thai;   while the Thai-Muslims fear that the Thai
government is trying to assimilate them by changing their local customs,
institutions, language, and perhaps also religion.   The problem is thus
not so much one of a religious difference alone, but of religion tied up
with a concept of race based on language and custom.   Certain socio-
economic factors no doubt tend to preserve these attitudes.   The three
provinces are, generally speaking, rural and isolated communities.   There
are no large municipalities compared with those in the mid-southern provinces.   Movement of people tends to be within the three or four provinces and much less so between them and Thai-Buddhist provinces (Krom
Raengngaan, 1968-9).   Economic life is concentrated on rubber, and to
a lesser extent on coconut, rice and fruit production and fisheries, with
a prevailing pattern of small-holdings.   Except for Yala, none of the
provinces raises much local revenue as the volume of trade and commerce
is relatively small.   Village life is consequently changing at a very
slow pace, and traditionalist attitudes remain strong.   These include an
ordering of priorities whereby religious observance is considered more
important than material advancement, and studies of Islam, Arabic and
Malay take precedence over secular education.   Religious instruction is
offered by the village Pondok schools run by the community, while secular
education is represented by Thai-Buddhist government schools.   The distance between the two communities is further accentuated by the apparent
concentration of wealth among local Thai-Chinese businessmen and some local
government officials.   Most government officials in saam changwat are
Thai-Buddhists, and the distinction of people from government is thus
added to the other demarcation lines which separate a large part of the
Thai-Muslims from the Thai-Buddhists.

The importance of history and a rural environment in maintaining a
separatist notion among the Thai-Muslims in the South is demonstrated if
one considers the Thai-Muslims in the Central Region, particularly those

living in the Bangkok-Thon Buri metropolitan area.   The Thai-Muslims here
have integrated into social and political life in a manner similar to the
Chinese, although they usually retain the Islamic religion and customs.

     There are thus formidable obstacles to the government policy of
integrating the Thai-Muslims so as to eliminate most of the differences
except religion between the Thai-Muslims and the Thai-Buddhists in the
area.   'Policy' is perhaps too presumptuous a word.   Government action
has usually been ad hoc in response to national security considerations,
or part of country-wide development efforts.   Recent years have brought
increased concern, reflected among other things by the appearance in
Bangkok of several government and academic publications dealing with
conditions in the South (Panutcharoen, 1971; Krom Kaanpokkhrawng, 1967, 1969;
Sowannachawtechoeng, 1969; Siam Rath, 1971; Samantarit, 1970).   This
was partly due to the general political relaxations following the promul-
gation of the 1968 Constitution.   Political parties, individual parliamentarians, university spokesmen and the press seized upon a number of
issues, including the Thai-Muslims, to debate government policy.   This
in turn put some pressure on the government to control the alleged increase in banditry and subversion in the border provinces, and more determined suppression by government forces certainly contributed to the apparent
and actual escalation of activity.   It is also possible that growing
anxiety over pressures on the northeastern and northern boundaries spilled
over in the form of greater government concern with the southern border as
well.   Law and order problems were not, however, simply a product of increased awareness.

3.   NON-MUSLIM COUNTER-ELITES

It is of course difficult to distinguish between what the Thais call
political bandits (phuukawkaanraai) and ordinary bandits (phuuraai tham-
madaa).   The latter are widespread and often work together with political
groups in robbery, kidnapping and extortion.   It is clear, however, that
at least three counter-elites are found in the mid- and extreme South, each
operating in its own territory.   One group, directed or encouraged by Thai
communists, operates in the mid-southern provinces stretching north-south
from Nakhon Si Thammarat to Sadao in Songkhla province (Fig. 13.1).   Here

they meet the Malayan communists (The Malayan Peoples' Liberation Army
of the Malayan Communist Party) who are deployed along the Thai-Malayan
border to the eastern coast of the peninsula.   The southeastern end of
this triangle is Thai-Muslim territory and the base of at least one
revolutionary separatist organisation.   The major fear of the Thai
government at present is that either communist group will move into
this triangle and exploit the minority issue in a more consistent manner
than before.

(i)   The Thai communists

Thai government spokesmen tend to use the communist label somewhat
indiscrimately, but it appears that terrorist activity inspired by Thai
communist leadership is a relatively new phenomenon in the mid-southern
provinces, dating from the last four or five years.   Ambushes of police,
kidnapping or assassinations of government officials and agents are occurring more frequently, and a major permanent camp was recently discovered
in the mountain range between Phatthalung and Trang - complete with vegetable garden and training facilities.   There are obviously some links
between the Thai communists and their Malayan counterparts, both in information and training, and their camps are organised on a similar pattern.
Extensive cooperation is complicated by divergent aims and tactics.   The
Malayan communists use Thai territory as a sanctuary for their activity
in Malaya, and they have gone to some lengths to avoid conflict with the
Thai authorities.   The Thai communists, on the other hand, are local
people from the mid-southern provinces whose main concern is with local
recruitment and operations.   Mainly for these reasons, the two groups
have delineated their respective spheres of influence.

The local origin and outlook of the southern Thai communists partly
explain the weak links between them and the Muslim separatists in the
border provinces.   Although the programme of the Communist Party of Thailand includes a point on autonomy for nationalities within the country
(Weatherbee, 1970:66), similar references do not occur in local propaganda
sheets issued in the South, or among material found in the camps seized by
government forces.   The southern communists have shown no interest in
this doctrinal point, and the Thai-Muslim community on the whole appears
ignorant of communist propaganda regarding national minorities.   The links

which so far have been established with separatist organisations on the
Thai side are mainly technical, relating to information and supply of
weapons and ammunition.   Recent movements of Thai communists also show
a thrust northwest into Trang rather than towards the South.

(ii)   The Malayan communists

Until a couple of years ago, there seemed to be a tacit co-existence
between the Malayan communists and the Thai forces.   Neither side was
eager for a confrontation, although this was most pronounced on the MCP
side.   The Thai government recently decided to pursue the Malayan communists more vigorously for a number of reasons, including pressure from
the Malaysian government and increased Thai concern with conditions in
the South.   Early in 1970, for instance, two permanent camps in Sadao
and Betong districts were attacked and destroyed.   Joint Thai-Malaysian
regular patrols in the border area and specific operations have also
increased.   Simultaneously, the armed branch of the MCP stepped up its
activity in Malaya and was in mid-1971 striking as far south as the Ipoh
region.   Their tactics on the Thai side of the border, however, have
altered in only one respect.   Previously they avoided units of the Thai
Border Patrol Police, but now they attack when the BPP is on joint patrols
with Malaysian security forces.   Their major aim of retaining a safe
sanctuary on the Thai side seems unchanged.   They are mainly interested
in food, provisions and intelligence.   There are recruitment campaigns,
but as before these follow strictly ethnic lines.   The Malayan communists
have predominantly Chinese cadres in the middle and western section of the
border, and their greatest support points here are Betong and Sadao which
are heavily Chinese or Thai-Chinese.   The MCP is propagandising and re-
cruiting by emphasising firstly the Chinese identity, and secondly the
liberation of Malaya.   The Chinese are also the main victims of extortion,
while the Thai-Muslims in this area are virtually ignored.   Further east
the Malayan communists have a larger proportion of Malay activists, and
attempts to enlist support and manpower from among the Thai-Muslims have
been conducted from their traditional hideout in Waeng.

The picture so far is thus rather fragmented.   Ethnic divisions,
local concerns and divergent aims prevent the various groups from developing into a coherent organisation.   The variable most likely to change in

the near future is the extent of coordination between the Thai and Malayan
communists.   As the Thai and Malaysian governments intensify joint suppression efforts, the two counter-elites may find their previous conflict
of interest subsiding.   Furthermore, if recruitment and organisation
expand, some parochial concerns may be reduced pari passu.   This probably presumes a more advanced stage of operations and structure than is
at present apparent among the southern Thai communists, although less so
among the Malayans.   Coordination across ethnic lines is still possible,
but the significance of such divisions in the past makes it unlikely that
they will be completely erased.   More important, dissatisfied Thai-
Muslim elements which might have been a major recruitment ground for either
communist group have a strong parochial outlook which acts as an isolator.

4.   THAI-MUSLIM SEPARATISTS

It should be stressed that separatist thinking is nothing new in the border
provinces.   In its modern form, it dates from the turn of the century
when the local chao muang (provincial governors) were deprived of much
power and influence as part of the national administrative reorganisation.
Separatism has since flared up at intervals, but it has always been contained.

(i)   Organisations

An assessment of the present strength of separatist feeling in the
border provinces is difficult partly because there are several groups
involved.   Two movements are based in Kelantan and at least one is operating on the Thai side of the border.   This proliferation of groups has
occurred for a number of reasons, of which one is competition between
personalities and another a divergence of both aims and tactics.

A reformist school of thought maintains that the Thai-Muslims should
take advantage of all the opportunities offered for training and advancement under the present Thai administration in order to secure a better
bargaining position vis-à-vis the central government.   Ultimately it is
hoped that more local autonomy will be granted, perhaps in the form of a
separate administrative unit in federation with Thailand.   This idea seems
to have particular currency among the older generation who remembers
Pridi's concept of a federal constitution in the 1930s.   To advocate the

reformist view openly is impossible today.   Moreover, the historic response of Thai governments has been to tighten rather than loosen central
control over outlying provinces in periods of stress and uncertainty, and
there is no indication that the present administration is likely to reverse this trend.   This makes it difficult to maintain the reformist
position as a political alternative and plays into the hands of extreme
separatists who operate underground and claim that only full independence
through armed struggle is possible.

The revolutionary school of thought contains different ideological
nuances.   Some stress Pan-Islamic ties both before and after the projected independence, while others reject this in favour of a single, independent Republic of Pattani.   The idea of incorporation into Malaysia has
understandably disappeared.   This proved impossible when the Federation
of Malaya was formed after the war and when independence was granted in
1957, and the Thai-Muslims strongly doubt if either Malaysian governments
or state governments in Kelantan would give more than moral support to the
separatist movement.   Another problematic difference concerns the extent
of cooperation which should be sought with the communists.   One of the
Kelantan groups apparently favours considerable contacts, while the Thai-
based group is more sceptical about the possibility of establishing bene-
ficial links with Thai and/or Malayan communists.   This is partly a
function of the group's parochialism, which is both a strength and a
weakness.

Religious leaders and teachers have traditionally been suspected
by the Thai government of propagating separatist ideas.   Past disclosures
of attempted uprisings or separatist agitation have generally, but not
uniquely, involved such men.   There is no doubt that representatives of
this group are currently participating in the leadership of the Thai-based
revolutionary organisation.   They appear to be largely responsible for the
movement's political programme, but it is uncertain to what extent they
actually dominate the organisation.   These men are old and orthodox in
religion.   Islam is the focus of their political thinking.   Secular
education is rejected both because it takes time and attention away from
religious studies, and because it may attract the young people to Thai
ways and values.   Educational and employment opportunities offered by

the Thai-Buddhists are rejected for the same reasons.   Semi-governmental
positions such as phuuyaibaan and kamnan (village and commune headmen) are
regarded as devices for diluting Muslim tradition and the Malay community
by enticing Thai-Muslims to cooperate with the Thai government.   In other
words, they view the Thai administration as a colonial power with which no
compromise is possible.

The old revolutionaries stress that the Pattani-Muslims (as they call
themselves) must have full independence because they constitute a separate
race with their own religion.   Their future Republic of Pattani is to consist of the four border provinces plus a large part of the Thai-Buddhist
province of Songkhla in order to prevent Satun from being isolated.   Otherwise, there seems to be little consideration for the constitution or
economic organisation of the future republic.   The low revenue raising
capability of the Thai-Muslim provinces is a case in point.   Narathiwat,
which is not atypical, collected US$1,250,000 in local revenue in 1970,
while the changwat budget as subsidised by the central government totalled
US$5,870,000, excluding capital investment effected directly under central
administration offices (Changwat Narathiwat, 1970).   The orthodox religious
revolutionaries do not find this a major problem, however, because they
see religious needs and services as the primary concern of the community.

(ii)   The parochial factor

The casual attitude towards secular matters is paralleled by a feeling
of the uniqueness of the southern Thai-Muslim community - a notion which
has been sustained by the isolated and rural characteristics of the society.
An inward-looking orientation towards 'our group' has its counterpart in
distrust of other groups, or at least a feeling that outsiders cannot fully
understand nor fully help the community.   The history of intermittent
conflict with the only other group with which the Thai-Muslims have been
in daily contact, Thai government representatives, no doubt contributes to
such suspicions.   This parochialism appears to condition the views held
by the orthodox, old revolutionaries regarding cooperation with outside
groups.   They seem to distrust the Thai communists and the Thai government almost equally - neither speak Malay nor profess the Islamic religion.
Although the Malayan communists speak Malay, this is not sufficient to
establish a large measure of confidence.   There is also some reserve

towards other Muslim countries and Muslim groups.   Some are seen as
unorthodox (e.g. a number of Muslims in Malaysia), and some are regarded
as incapable of understanding the Pattani-Muslims (e.g. the Thai-Muslims
in the Central region).   In terms of the ultimate success of the movement, the exclusive belief in 'our group' is no doubt a weakness since
it limits the willingness to seek outside help and support.   Its strength
lies in its appeal to the Thai-Muslim community.   The traditionalists
represent values which still prevail in large sectors of the community,
by utilising the bonds of respect and authority between villagers and
their religious leaders.   The religious teachers, for instance, (toh
kroo or tok guru) live with their pupils in a boarding house arrangement
for several years under the old system of Pondok schools, and they remain
a source of authority and leadership.

The old revolutionaries admit that most of their support comes from
the poor and uneducated.   They claim a thousand activists (including the
guerilla section), and a reservoir of general sympathy among the villagers.   It is probable that most of the villagers have few conscious or
articulated political beliefs, but equally possible that sentiments of
belonging to the community and reverence for its religious leaders can
be converted by the latter into support for the separatist cause.   As
in the past, the movement's educational efforts stress the teaching of
Islamic religion, the history of the Muslim sultanates and Malay language - which is done openly and legally - and lead up to clandestine
propaganda concerning the present struggle and future aims.   There are
also leaflets in Jawi and, for outside consumption, in Thai and English.
In these public relations activities the group based on the Thai side
has an obvious advantage over those located in Kelantan.

(iii) The military section

There is a military section which organisationally appears somewhat
separate from the various political splinter groups, but which claims to
work for the revolutionary separatist cause.   This group seems to have
a fairly sophisticated structure and leadership.   The official leader
is Poh Yeh (alias Bapa Idris), but it is possible that he is merely a
figurehead.   The guerillas are predominantly located in Narathiwat and

Yala, and to a lesser extent in Pattani.   Some of the 'officers' have been trained in the Thai army and are familiar with guerilla methods from liberation fronts in Asia and the Middle East.   They also maintain some contacts with other counter-elites in the area such as through the supply line of weapons from Laos.   The guerillas are concerned to be recognised both domestically and internationally as a Muslim liberation front in order to counteract government claims that they are either bandits or communists.

The purpose of the military section is to train villagers in the use of weapons and guerilla tactics, whereupon they return to the vill-ages as 'reserves' until the time for revolt has come.   A relatively small force is thus kept in the jungle at any given time, and these units maintain a rather modest level of terrorist activity.   They occasionally ambush government forces to obtain weapons and sometimes use terrorism to impress both the villagers and the government of their existence, but routine operations seem confined to extortion and kidnapping to collect funds for further strengthening of the organisation.   In the latter respect they are evidently working with bandit gangs.

(iv)   Some future prospects

The separatists seem to envisage the day of uprising as quite far in the future.   They may have a better organisation than similar move-ments which have failed in the past, particularly in the military section, but in most other respects there is little difference.   The major excep-tion lies in one new development which may or may not work in favour of the separatists.   This is the increasing number of educated Thai-Muslims in the three provinces.   As part of its recent concern with conditions in the South, the Thai government has greatly expanded the number of primary schools and teachers in the last four years and relaxed entrance requirements to the university.   Initial statistics suggest that Thai-Muslim pupils are responding better to improved educational opportunities than the Thai-Buddhists in the area (Fig. 13.2), thus slowly altering the local pattern in which Thai-Muslims predominate in the lower grades while the Thai-Buddhists are a majority in the higher school levels (Khuhamuk, 1969).   Government policy presumes that political loyalty is a function

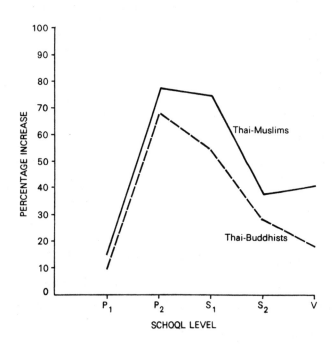

Fig. 13.2   Increase of pupils in Pattani, 1966-70

Note: The diagram shows the percentage increase of pupils divided into
        Thai-Muslims and Thai-Buddhists in the four-year period 1966-70.
        The figures include both government and private schools, but
        exclude _Pondoks_.

        P_1 = lower primary; P_2 = upper primary;
        S_1 = lower secondary; S_2 = upper secondary;
        V = vocational

Source: Based on figures compiled by the Education Division,
          Changwat Administration, Pattani.

of Thai education and the ability to speak Thai.   This is probably too
simplistic, but the fact that the revolutionary separatists attack the
education programme vigorously, kidnap government teachers and have been
fighting the conversion of _Pondok_ schools into private schools which
teach both standard curriculum and Islam, demonstrates their fear that
the government's educational policy will undermine their main source of
popular support.

The educated Thai-Muslims may still be a responsive audience to separatist arguments. Very little is known of the political attitudes and values of this group, and further research on such aspects as educational background and influences is needed. However, this is an extremely difficult subject to research for political reasons, and the population in question is still relatively small. Only preliminary suggestions are therefore possible at this stage.

Education may merely increase awareness of the standard difficulties which beset development administration and which are not peculiar to southern Thailand. In this region, however, inefficient and corrupt administration and economic hardships are often subsumed under the dichotomy of Thai-Buddhist rule over a Thai-Muslim people. The educated Thai-Muslim may simply interpret the local situation in coherent ultra-Malay or ultra-Muslim terms. It would seem that this tendency is more pronounced among the Thai-Muslims who are educated abroad than among those who receive local high school instruction or continue to Thai universities through the Islam College in Bangkok. There are no statistics on how many southern Thai-Muslims study abroad, but a not insignificant number is found in Malaysia, Egypt and Pakistan in both religious and secular institutions. On returning, the Thai government's reluctance to appoint them, or any qualified Thai-Muslim, to administrative positions in saam changwat creates furthur alienation. It is evident that several young, educated Thai-Muslims are currently exploring the extent of common sympathies between themselves and the older, orthodox revolutionaries. Active cooperation is, however, complicated by the difference in background and opposing views on secular education. It is here that the weakness of the separatists group is most apparent, as represented by the traditionalist and uncompromising views of the older leaders. The educated Thai-Muslim would also seem more attuned than the religious leaders to the economic problems of an independent Republic of Pattani. Whether or not it is a realistic proposition to oppose the military strength of the Thai government in an open conflict is debatable. It is noted that the government has problems of law, order and subversion in many parts of the country and must spread its military and economic resources accordingly. The Thai-Malaysian agreement concerning joint military operations on the border applies only to communist organisations, and will in all probability remain unaltered.

The major imponderable in the present situation is the link between the educated Thai-Muslims and the old orthodox leaders in the separatist movement.   If a merger between these two groups should take place, the organisation would probably be internally strengthened by having a broader appeal.   It might also be more open to the possibilities of cooperating with local communist groups or soliciting foreign assistance.   The parochial characteristics which tend to prevent the older leaders from seeking such a development seem much less apparent among the younger group with both religious and secular education.   In this case, the Thai government would have to face a much more serious separatist problem in the South than at any time in the past.

On the other hand, the educated Thai-Muslim may feel closer to the reformist who seeks a long term bargaining position with the Thai government (and probably welcomes the revolutionaries for their threatening background noises), and who, in the meantime, enjoys the material and social advantages offered him through education in the present administrative framework.   There is little employment discrimination in government or private institutions provided the Thai-Muslim is technically qualified;   only administrative positions in saam changwat are difficult to obtain.   The Thai-Muslim may also adopt a moderate viewpoint, often held by individuals belonging to a distinct community, and maintain that the only realistic option is to accept a policy of loose integration and merely seek better educational and economic opportunities for the Thai-Muslims on par with other Thais.

The result of expanded education for Thai-Muslims in the South will not become fully apparent for another five or ten years when the upper-primary and lower-secondary schools have a larger intake of the school population.   In the meantime, major changes seem unlikely.   Unrest and difficulties will no doubt continue, particularly with moral support from abroad such as the student demonstrations in Kuala Lumpur during Prime Minister Thanom's visit in June 1971.   Similarly, increased suppression of bandits-cum-separatists will inflame the conflict in the short run. Much recent bitterness and fear within the Thai-Muslim community stem from the application of the Revolutionary Proclamation concerning criminals (antaphaan) for detaining people suspected of aiding bandits and gangsters.

According to this proclamation, dating from the Sarit regime, a person
can be imprisoned for no less than one month, or no less than one year,
with no upper limit and no trial, only administrative reviews of the case.
Between 300 and 400 people were detained under this clause in saam changwat in the two years 1969 and 1970; the official figure for Pattani alone
is 110 (Changwat Pattani, 1970).   The proclamation was not used in neighbouring Thai-Buddhist provinces which also have widespread banditry.

5.   CONCLUSION

The separatist group maintains that the people will support them if they
are strong, but not if they are weak.   Although this begs the most important questions, it is a relevant assessment of the current situation.
The concern of the separatists, it sometimes seems, is not so much with
ultimate success at some point in the future, as with the moral imperative of carrying on the struggle.   It is an obligation with historical
and social roots, framed in racial and religious terms.   The movement
will probably follow the past pattern of unrest and futile uprisings,
which from a national point of view have been relatively minor, unless
the old leadership attracts and makes room for a sizable number of young,
educated Thai-Muslims.   This may also increase the willingness to
cooperate with other counter-elites in the area and develop in the
direction feared by the Thai government, i.e. that the southern triangle
becomes a coordinated entity.   Such an eventuality would seem to belong
to the intermediate rather than short or long term future.

REFERENCES

Changwat Narathiwat, 1970.   Hua khaw banyaaisarup khawng jangwat
        naraathiwaat. (Provincial Yearbook) Narathiwat, Sala Klang.

Changwat Pattani, 1970.   Khaw banyaaisarup saphaap khawng jangwat pattanii.
        (Provincial Yearbook) Pattani, Sala Klang.

Khuhamuk, Praphan, 1969.   An analysis of attitudes concerning the education
        of Thai-Islam students in education region 2.   General Education
        Development Center, Yala (typescript).

Krom Kaanpokkhrawng, 1967.   Ruang kiokap jangwat chaaidaen phaak taai.
        (Matters concerning the southern border provinces), Department
        of Local Administration, Ministry of Interior, Bangkok.

Krom Kaanpokkhrawng, 1969.   Sing thii naaruu kiokap jangwat chaaidaen
        phaak taai. (Things worth knowing about the southern border
        provinces), Department of Local Administration, Ministry of
        Interior, Bangkok.

Krom Raengngaan, 1968-9.   Saphaap khaw thetjing lae raengngaan nai paet
        jangwat phaak taai. (Conditions and facts about labour in
        eight southern provinces), Department of Labour, Ministry of
        Interior, Bangkok.

Panutcharoen, Chan, 1971.   Botbaat lae itthiphon khawng pondok taw
        kaansueksaa khawng yoowachon thai muslim nai jangwat chaaidaen
        phaak taai. (The role and influence of pondoks in the education
        of young Thai-Muslims in the southern border provinces) unpub-
        lished thesis, National Defense College, Bangkok (mimeo).

Samantarit, Termsakdi, 1970.   Khaw banyaaisarup sathaanakaan sii jangwat
        phaak taai. (An account of conditions in the four southern
        provinces), prepared for a seminar at the National Defense
        College, Narathiwat (mimeo).

Siam Rath, 1971.   'Report from a seminar on the Thai-Muslim border
        provinces held at Chulalongkorn University', Siam Rath, June 28,
        1971.

Sowannachawtechoeng, Mongkol, 1969.   Kaanphatthanaa jangwat chaaidaen phaak
        taai dooi khanakammakaan phatthanaa phaak taai nai raya saam pii.
        (Development in the southern border provinces by the Southern
        Development Committee in the three-year period 1964-1966),
        unpublished M.A. thesis, Thammasat University, Bangkok.

Suhrke, A., 1970.   'The Thai-Muslims: some aspects of minority integration',
        Pacific Affairs, 43, 531-47.

Weatherbee, D.E., 1970.   The United Front in Thailand. A documentary
        analysis, University of South Carolina, Columbia.

CHAPTER 14

FREIGHT TRANSPORT IN THAILAND

Peter J. Rimmer*

1.   INTRODUCTION

In contemporary Thailand, transport has been assigned a key role in
expanding the economy, equalising urban:rural incomes, and countering
insurgency.   The First Economic and Social Development Plan of 1961-66
devoted 26 per cent of total public expenditure to establish and improve
all-weather connections between all provincial capitals (Fig. 14.1).
Under the Second Plan for 1967-71, allocations for the same purpose rose
to nearly 30 per cent (National Economic Development Board, 1968:39).

A very high proportion of this investment has been directed towards
creating a national, all-weather network of roads between provincial
centres.   This policy conforms to advice from foreign military missions
and from international funding agencies;   it also satisfies the belief
held by many Thai government departments that any roads at all will bring
meaningful benefits.   This policy met the needs of the Thai economy of
the 1960s, which would otherwise have been hampered by the geographical
limitations and restricted services of the inland waterways, the State
Railway of Thailand (hereafter referred to as the Railway), and coastal
shipping (Fig. 14.2).   The improved road network also allowed more
efficient counter-insurgency measures, and stimulated additional economic
activity.   For example, the savings in distance and in time which the
Friendship Highway has brought between Bangkok, Nakhon Ratchasima and Nong
Khai have multiplied outputs of primary produce and increased the number
of ancillary enterprises much faster than comparable areas without all-
weather roads (Kasiraksa, 1963;   Jones, 1964;   Patapanich, 1964;   Wilson,
et al., 1966:18).   For these reasons, the Ministry of National Development
proposes to allocate 43 per cent out of a total of $154,000,000 allotted to
transport for further road construction in the Plan of Control and

_____

* Dr Rimmer is Senior Fellow in the Department of Human Geography,
Institute of Advanced Studies, Australian National University.

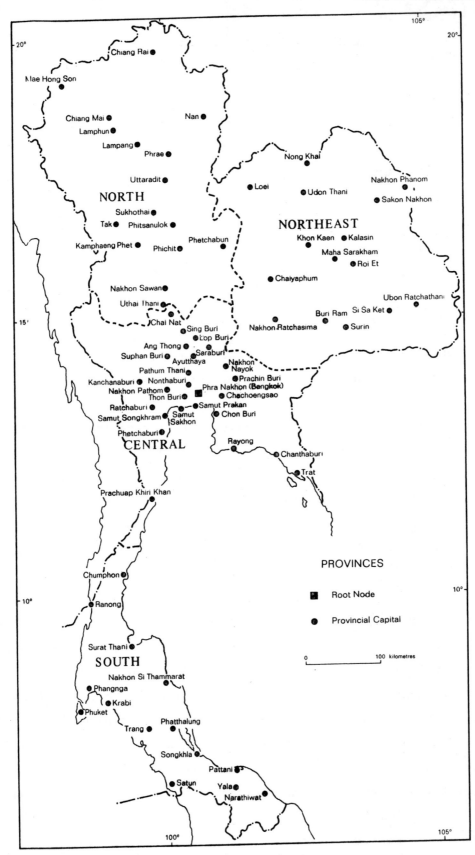

Fig. 14.1 Location of provincial capitals.

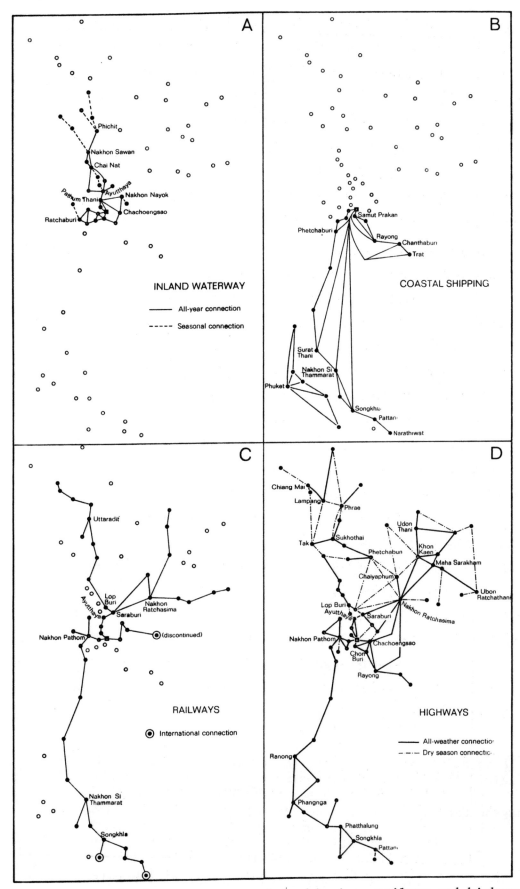

Fig. 14.2   Inland waterway, coastal shipping, railway and highway
            networks, 1970.

and Coordination for 1972-6.   This should provide for 5974 km of trunk
highways and 7430 km of provincial and rural roads.   The proposal has
been sent to the National Economic Development Board for approval (The
Investor, 3, 1971:395-8), but seems unlikely to go unchallenged as many
of the benefits anticipated from earlier road schemes have not been
fulfilled.   Some roads have expanded areas of subsistence activity,
while others have merely extended the scope for the activities of
corrupt officials.   Inadequate maintenance and gross over-loading of
trucks[1] have resulted in the premature break-up of roads.

Yet there is evidence that the daily traffic on some roads is well
below planned capacity.   If this situation continues the further extension of an under-utilised rural road system seems an unwarranted diversion
of resources at a time when Bangkok's traffic congestion and other problems
demand attention.   Thailand can ill afford the luxury of misallocating
its resources or duplicating its transport facilities.   The International
Bank for Reconstruction and Development considers that road transport is
underpriced and returning less than the Railway on adjusted fixed assets
(IBRD, 1966).   The main problem is to control the rate of road construction so that inland waterways, coastal shipping and the Railway do not
regress into the role of residual carriers operating below their optimal
capacity.   A succession of consultants has suggested that Western-style
devices such as vehicle licensing, set freight rates and user taxes could
be used to regulate transport in a national context (Transportation Consultants Inc., 1959;   IBRD, 1966).   The effects of such advice are difficult
to predict without an appreciation of the institutional environment in
which the Thai government operates, and a comparison of the freight role
performed by different transport systems.   An attempt has been made to
analyse transport decision-making in Thailand (Rimmer, 1971a), leaving the
assessment of truck competition on individual modes to be considered here.

---

1 It is difficult to estimate the extent of truck over-loading in Thailand.
Official figures for checking station Km.31 on Highway Route 1 (Bangkok-
Saraburi) for 1968 were 6.46 per cent;   for KM.97 on Highway Route 1
(Bangkok-Saraburi) 7.64 per cent;   and for Km.72 on Highway Route 3
(Bangkok-Si Racha) 4.33 per cent.   It is recognised by the Highway Department that these records may not give a true picture as many over-loaded
trucks do not pass through the checking stations.   The true percentages
are certainly higher than those given, but it is difficult to gauge by
how much.

To obtain basic data on national transport the Royal Thai government instituted surveys of the freight carrying activities of inland
waterways (Harbour Department et al., 1964), coastal shipping (Harbour
Department, 1969) and trucks (Ministry of Communications, 1969).   These
supplement annual statistics, dating from 1958, which give the origin
and destination of carload freight movements on the Railway.   The
adequacy of all these data is examined in the following section, which
analyses reciprocal freight movements between the provinces and Bangkok,
the root node in all networks.   However, it is possible only to infer
the degree of truck competition and to draw only a very general picture
of total freight movements because of the different time-spans of the
various surveys, varying commodity classifications, assorted sampling
designs and collection schema (Table 14.1).   Subsequent surveys should

Table 14.1:   Main sources of commodity flow data in Thailand

Mode	Date	Check points	Sample	Unit	Commodity classes	Notes
Inland waterway	1963-64[a]	20	3 rounds each of 10 days	Province	8	126 out of 236 routes covered
Coastal shipping	1964-65	18	3 rounds each of 10 days	Province	19	Local, fishing, and international vessels included in survey
Trucking	1966-67[b]	12[c]	Each round 7 days - 5 in Central, 3 in North and Northeast, 2 in South	Province	102	Also includes data on buses and taxis, make of vehicle, and number of wheels
Railway	Annual (since 1958)	576	Complete	Station	69	Data compiled from waybills

a   Under the direction of Professor L.A.P. Gosling, the Department of
Geography, University of Michigan, Ann Arbor, U.S.A. conducted surveys
on inland waterways in November 1966 and February 1967, but the results
have yet to be released.

b   A pilot study of motor vehicle traffic was conducted in 1966, the 1967
survey was repeated for 1968, and a study of intra-regional vehicle
movement instituted in 1969 - this last survey will miss the period
directly following the rice and maize harvest, but a repeat survey in
1970 should remedy this deficiency.

c   Checking stations in 1967 were located at Hinkong, Bang Pakong, Sam Yeak
Kia Chab (Central);   Amphoe Thoen, Kamphaeng Phet, Chai Nat (North);
Pak Chong, Borabu, Nakhon Nayok (Northeast);   and Chumphon, Huai Yot,
and Phatthalung (South).

be standardised to generate comparable data;   ideally, the size of each
region should be the smallest that will affect the transport decision, but
as indicated in Section 3, it is possible to simulate actual flows only
for zones embracing several provinces.   At such a gross level of aggrega-
tion, there is little point in deciding if such flows are efficient or
optimal, but casting the study in terms of a simulation model (the
rudiments of which were conceived by wargamers), does identify phenomena
of interest and allows recognition of the fundamental characteristics of
Thailand's transport system.   The simple simulation model employed may
help future studies of transport in Thailand.

2.   COMPETITION FOR BANGKOK'S FREIGHT

Information on reciprocal flows by all four modes between Bangkok and the
provinces provides the most comprehensive data set for examining the disruptive effect of the road construction programme since the completion of
the Friendship Highway in 1958 - the first of the new and upgraded undertakings.   At that time the role of road transport outside Bangkok was to
feed other modes of transport.   The capital-provincial movement of freight
was divided, with little contentious overlap, between inland waterways
(paramount within the Central Plain), coastal shipping (dominating the
South), and the Railway (figuring strongly in movements originating or
terminating in the Northeast, North, and South).   This 'steady state' has
been progressively eroded by a fast growing truck industry which has
captured freight from other modes and generated new cargo flows.   As data
inadequacies prevent a comparison of periodic changes in the modal split
of traffic, an indirect approach is applied to detect the effect of inter-
modal competition inherent in the volume of freight movements between
the provinces and Bangkok (Table 14.2).

The method of analysis for each separate mode-direction combination,
such as rail to the capital and rail ex-Bangkok, is to employ a three
variable multiple regression model $(log_e Y = a + blog_e X_1 + clog_e X_2)$.[2]

---

2   The model (1) $log_e Y = a + blog_e X_1 + clog_e X_2$ provided the best fit to the
data in an exercise which also employed (2) $Y = a + bX_1 + cX_2$ (3) $log_e Y = a + bX_1 + cX_2$ (4) $Y = a + blog_e X_1 + clog_e X_2$.

Table 14.2: Volume of reciprocal freight flows between Bangkok
             and the provinces by individual modes at specified
             dates

(thousand tonnes)

Mode	Survey date	To Bangkok	From Bangkok	Other inter-provincial (to and from)
Inland waterways	1964	5669	442	209
Coastal shipping	1965	129	263	156
Trucking	1967[a]	5409	3938	5485
Railway	1968[b]	1960	1006	3860

a Author's estimate.
b Carload freight only.

This single equation approach is used even though it is recognised that
sampling error and inbuilt correlation effects in both the dependent and
independent variables can undermine its efficiency (see King, 1969:135-64).
Though these problems can be very real in handling Thai data the method
is retained here because comparisons can be made with other flow studies
which have demonstrated that distance and population as independent
variables have had conspicuous success in accounting for much of the
explained variation in the dependent variable, volume (Gould, 1960;
Smith, 1962; Golledge, 1963).   'Shipment volume between two points is
a simultaneous function of both demand and distance considerations, so
that formulations involving both of these variables should be more powerful in identifying those flows that are greater or less than expected'
(Smith, 1970:407).   Such results prompted the choice of line haul distance
and estimated provincial populations as independent variables to account
for variations in modal flows to and from Bangkok.

A persistent theme in the analysis of commodity flows is the need
to eliminate the structural effects of distance and population before
examining the residuals (Simmons, 1970).   Thus, it is in the locational
arrangement of under-predicted and over-predicted standardised residual
values reflecting, in part, possible unexplained variation, that the
identification of the differing regional impact of truck competition is

sought.[3]   Standardised residuals, with the standard error of estimate
as the constant, are favoured for the mapping of positive and negative
residuals involved in this task as the values for a large number of
observations occur in approximately equal numbers. Values assume magni-
tudes ranging from -3.00 to +3.00 regardless of the range characteristics
of the data which facilitates comparability, and observed values are
known so that a magnitude equal to or greater than 1.0 will occur approximately 32 per cent of the time (Thomas, 1968).   A limitation in the use
of the standard error of estimate is that a few residuals may be expected
to lie at a distance of two, three, or more standard errors from the
regression plane irrespective of whether 15 per cent or 90 per cent of
the total variation is explained.   To forestall the charge that attention is focused on chance occurrences in terms of the percentage of total
variation that is being examined, other structural values, such as the
coefficient of multiple determination, R^2, are examined prior to the
separate analyses of residuals in flows to and from Bangkok which are
geared to detecting inter-modal competition.

(i)   Flows from the provinces to Bangkok

Distance to Bangkok contributes more in explanation than population
when an examination is made of the standard partial correlation coefficients stemming from the series of multiple regression analyses, where
the volume of freight carried by each mode is the dependent variable
(Table 14.3).[4]   Such a result is not surprising as population is a poor

---

3 The standardised residual value is defined by the expression $(log_e Y_{cn} - log_e Y_n)/K$ where $log_e Y_{cn} - log_e Y_n$ expresses the difference between the
observed value for the nth unit area and the value for that area as is
estimated from the regression equation. K is any selected constant.
In this study the standard error of estimate is used as the constant to
give the expression $(log_e Y_{cn} - bg_e Y_n)/S\ log_e Y_c$.   This expression gives
the magnitude of the difference between the estimated and observed value
for the nth unit area in terms of the standard error of estimate for the
set of observations (Thomas, 1968).

4 Where the partial regression coefficients cannot be compared directly
because of differing metrics they can be standardised and represented as
B_j's.   They are derived as follows: $B_j = b_j(s_j/s_o)$ where s_j is the
standard deviation of the independent variable and s_o is the standard
deviation of the dependent variable.   Since they are dimensionless terms,
the B_j's can be compared directly as measures of the relative importance
of the different independent variables in accounting for variation in the
dependent variable (King, 1969:139-41).

Table 14.3: Movements from the provinces to Bangkok
             Number of observations (N), standard partial regression
             coefficients for distance (B_1X_1) and population (B_2X_2),
             coefficients of multiple regression (R), and coefficients
             of multiple determination (R^2).

Mode	N	B_1X_1	B_2X_2	R	R^2
Inland waterways	20	−0.17	0.42	0.42	0.18
Coastal shipping	17	0.68[a]	0.17	0.68	0.47
Railway	41	0.56[a]	0.33[a]	0.63	0.39
Trucking	69	−0.52[a]	0.32[a]	0.57	0.32

a Significant at the 0.05 level (t test)

reflector of variations in volume shipments by comparison with differences
in land capability, land use, and geographical distributions of massive
freight generators, such as industrial raw materials.   There is, however,
a consistent though relatively weak, positive association between population and volume for all modes, whereas the correlation of distance and the
dependent variable is equivocal.   A distance decay function is present in
trucking and, only to a slight degree, in inland waterways, but coastal
shipping and the Railway carry an increasing volume of freight as distance
to Bangkok increases - an important distinction in delimiting the relative
strength of individual modes (Fig. 14.3A).

When distance and population are combined their joint explanatory
power given by the coefficient of multiple determination, R^2, ranges from
18 per cent to 47 per cent for the respective modes, but none are significant (Table 14.3).   A considerable amount of unexplained variation still
remains and the maps of standardised residuals from regression are examined
in turn for each method of transport to gauge if inter-modal competition
has resulted in some of the over-predicted and under-predicted values
(Fig. 14.4).

(a)   Inland waterways

The residuals for inland waterways provide few clues to the nature
of truck competition, except that the positive outlier at Phichit could
mirror the effect of poor highway connections which insulate the province.
The negative residuals at Nonthaburi, Nakhon Pathom, Samut Prakan and
Chachoengsao might be attributed to a switch to road transport.   There

322   THAILAND

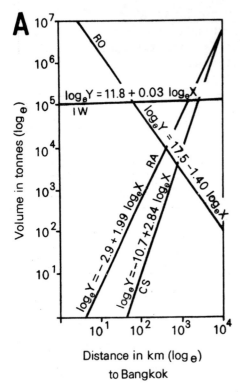

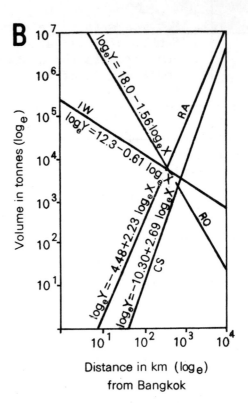

Fig. 14.3A Regression lines
for the relationship between
volume shipments and distance
to Bangkok for movements from
the provinces to the capital
by inland waterway (IW), coastal shipping (CS), the Railway
(RA), and road transport (RO).
The lines are taken from a
series of special regression
analyses employing the model
$log_e Y = a + log_e bX_1$.

Fig. 14.3B Regression lines
for the relationship between
volume shipments and distance
from Bangkok for movements from
the capital to the provinces by
inland waterway (IW), coastal
shipping (CS), the Railway (RA),
and road transport (RO). The
lines are taken from a series
of special regression analyses
employing the model
$log_e Y = a + log_e bX_1$.

is, however, an anomaly between the expected occurrence of truck competition and the distribution of positive residuals, presumably stemming from
the nature of the commodities shipped to Bangkok. Barges carrying sand
(from Pathum Thani, Ratchaburi, Samut Songkhram and Ayutthaya), maize
(especially in the main channel during the wet season from Lop Buri and
Saraburi), and miscellaneous foodstuffs (from Samut Sakhon) will mask the
increasing movement of padi and rice by road - a practice favoured by the
shift of new mills to highway sites and the storage of export rice within
12 hours journey from the capital to take advantage of price changes.

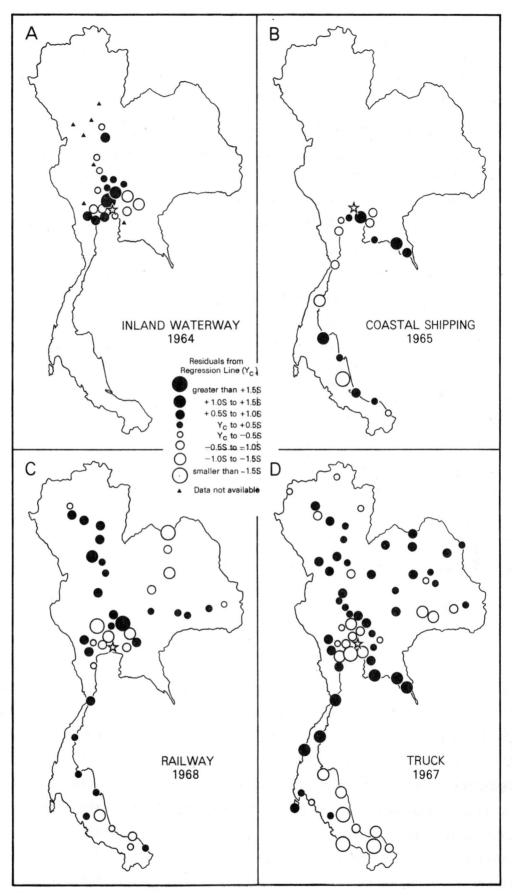

Fig. 14.4   Standardised residuals from regression for freight flows to Bangkok from the provinces by inland waterway, coastal shipping, railway, and truck for specified dates.

(b)   Coastal shipping

The selective impact of truck competition is also apparent in the residuals for coastal shipping in 1965 as, hypothetically, one would expect provinces north of Surat Thani to show negative values and those to the south positive.   High positive residuals in the northern areas closest to Bangkok stem from specific commodities with particular value-load characteristics that make long-distance trucking uneconomic.   For instance, the movement of timber (logs) is responsible for the strong positive showing of Chanthaburi and Trat while the more anomalous position of Samut Prakan reflects the surviving remnants of a presumably greater trade in the short haul of bulky items to the capital.   The negative residuals on the peninsula at Phetchaburi, Prachuap Khiri Khan, and, particularly, Chumphon would, however, mirror the anticipated effect of truck competition.   South of Chumphon the pattern of residuals – with strong positive showings at Surat Thani and Songkhla and a negative value at Phatthalung (without a port) – is as anticipated.   Shipments to Bangkok, comprised mainly of timber, rubber, coconut products (largely ex-Surat Thani), glass sand (ex-Songkhla), and 'other products' (chiefly empty returns), are protected from truck competition by the circuitous highway network.   Internal adjustments are occurring within the South as feeder roads permit the concentration of cargoes at main ports, but the Railway is the chief competitor for long-distance freight.

(c)   Railway

A preponderance of negative values in the South could indicate that the Railway is not doing so well vis-à-vis coastal shipping despite the absence of severe truck competition, but a more plausible explanation is that there is little cargo offering there compared with other parts of the Kingdom.   The main negative values occur in the immediate penumbral zone of Bangkok where road and inland waterway have time or cost advantages and in the northeast corridor to Nong Khai where road transport has captured the bulk of shipments to Bangkok following the extension of the Friendship Highway (Rimmer, 1971b).   Conversely, the main positive residuals occur on the northern line from Saraburi to Chiang Mai.   As this northern line is not paralleled by a highway the Railway is only susceptible to sporadic or incipient interference from road transport and

then only for a narrow range of commodities.   The stronger positive
showing of Saraburi stems from the heavy movement of cement to Bangkok,
while that of Sukhothai reflects large flows of maize.

(d)   Truck

Some confirmation of the suggested impact of road competition on
other modes is given by the residuals for trucking movements, though the
concentration of negative values around the capital arises from the under-
statement of commodity movements because the checking stations in this
area were so located as to record only a small proportion of cargo
originating and terminating there.   The negative values in the South,
Northeast, and North, except for Lamphun in the economic shadow of Chiang
Mai, reflect the protection afforded other modes by indirect and tortuous
road links, some of which are only usable in the dry season.   The strong
positive showings of Phuket and Ranong are not unexpected, as roads
provide the only direct links with Bangkok;   but those at Chumphon, and
Prachuap Khiri Khan in the South, Trat on the eastern littoral, Nong Khai
and Udon Thani in the Northeast, and Nakhon Sawan probably demonstrate
the growth of trucking at the expense of other modes.   It is possible
that this preference for trucks could be dictated by the cargo offering,
but this cannot be checked as the traffic survey does not give a breakdown of commodity flows from the provinces to Bangkok.

This analysis of freight flows from the provinces to Bangkok has
shown that it is possible, if only indirectly, to identify areas of
transport competition that would repay detailed field investigation.
As goods from Bangkok to the provinces are largely consumer items,
population estimates, as an indicator of demand, should with distance,
account for a higher proportion of the variance in the dependent variable
volume.

(ii)   Flows from Bangkok to the Provinces

Rather surprisingly the standard partial correlation coefficients
from the second set of multiple regression analyses undertaken for flows
ex-Bangkok indicate that distance contributes more to total explanation
and population contributes less compared with the first set (Table 14.4).
Again road and inland waterways recorded distance decay functions

Table 14.4:   Movements from Bangkok to the provinces
              Number of observations (N), standard partial regression
              coefficients for distance ($\beta_1 X_1$) and population ($\beta_2 X_2$),
              coefficients of multiple regression (R), and coefficients
              of multiple determination (R^2)

Mode	N	$\beta_1 X_1$	$\beta_2 X_2$	R	R^2
Inland waterways	20	-0.55^a	0.36	0.56^b	0.31^b
Coastal shipping	17	0.70^a	-0.11	0.70	0.49
Railway	41	0.62^a	0.30	0.68_b	0.47_b
Trucking	69	-0.56^a	0.38^a	0.61^b	0.38^b

a   Significant at the 0.05 level (t test)
b   Significant at the 0.05 level (F test)

(particularly marked for the latter mode) while coastal shipping and the
Railway showed a tendency to increase their share of freight with distance
from Bangkok (Fig. 14.3B).   Standard partial correlation coefficients for
population, in comparison, showed only a slight positive association for
inland waterways, the Railway, and trucks, and a slight negative one for
coastal shipping.

     The cumulative effect of these changes is represented in the respec-
tive coefficients of multiple determination, R^2, indicating the total
variance explained by the regression.   The range is narrower in this series
though inland waterways and coastal shipping with values of 31 per cent and
49 per cent respectively remain as the extreme values of R^2.   There is
still scope, therefore, by analysing each mode separately, for assessing
whether inter-modal competition over- or under-predicts each situation
(Fig. 14.5).   This also allows us to estimate whether the observations made
on flows from Bangkok hold for the reverse set of movements.

(a)   Inland waterways

     Inter-modal competition is difficult to detect in the disposition of
residuals for inland waterways in goods flows ex-Bangkok.   Positive values
are concentrated in the main channel of the Chao Phraya River and on the
Tachin and Mae Klong Rivers west of the capital, while high negative
residuals occur at Nakhon Nayok and Prachin Buri on the margins of the
inland waterway network - a reflection more of navigational hazards than
the effect of trucks soliciting traffic.   A breakdown of movements by

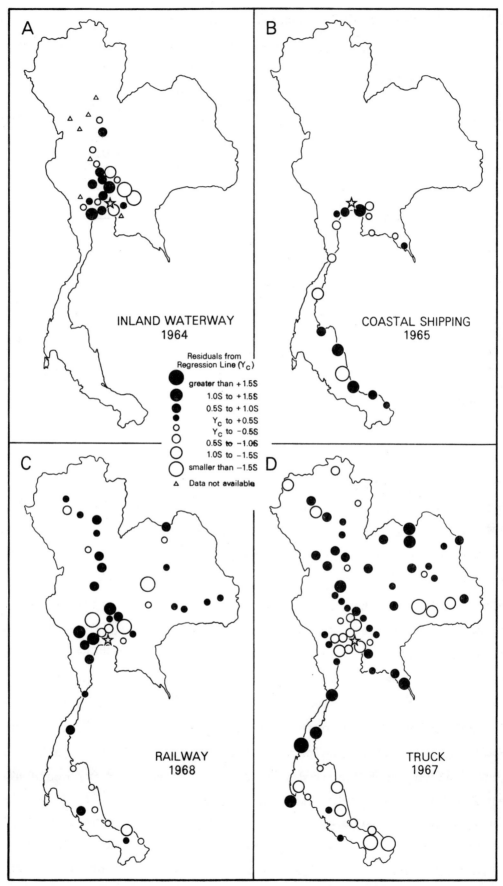

Fig. 14.5 Standardised residuals from regression for freight
flows from Bangkok to the provinces by inland waterway, coastal
shipping, railway, and truck for specified dates.

commodities, amounting to only eight per cent of out-bound flows,
suggests that through truck competition shipments are comprised largely
of low value/high bulk commodities such as fuel and raw materials,
though there is some transhipment of padi and rice to provinces west of
Bangkok.   Even the distribution of petroleum products is now performed
by road except where river-side service stations persist for the benefit
of the waterborne community; the high positive residuals at Ayutthaya
and Samut Songkhram, however, indicate the persistence of fuel movements by barge in 1964.   No doubt since the survey trucking companies
have made a determined effort to divest inland waterways of this
remaining traffic.   Such competition is effective as inland waterways
are handicapped by slow operating speeds - the journey Bangkok-Phichit
takes eight days at an average speed of 2.2 km per hour - a figure that
excludes time for loading, unloading, and repairs (Harbour Department,
et al., 1964).

(b)   Coastal shipping

It would appear from the preponderance of negative residuals north
of Surat Thani and Trat that road transport has been more successful in
depriving coastal shipping of short haul freight ex-Bangkok.   Positive
residuals at the head of the Gulf stem not from a large movement of cargo
but from a bias induced in the multiple regression analysis by retaining
Phetchaburi and Prachuap Khiri Khan in the input though they handled no
cargo in 1965.   Phatthalung received a token cargo and is the only
location in the South to record a negative residual.   Heavy shipments
ex-Bangkok of raw materials, construction materials, fuel and lubricating
oil, food (sugar), drink, and tobacco give Nakhon Si Thammarat, Surat Thani,
Songkhla, Pattani, and to a lesser extent, Narathiwat, strong positive
values.   The stronger showing of Songkhla in 1965 could be attributed to
roads enabling it to serve extra-territorial provinces such as Phatthalung
(without a port), and Satun (on the Andaman Sea).   Trade with Ranong,
Phangnga, and Phuket (without direct sea access to Bangkok) could also be
responsible for Surat Thani's marked positive residual, but field evidence
of such movements is slight.

(c)   Railway

Stronger inferences about the effects of inter-modal competition upon the Railway can be drawn from time series data for individual stations (Rimmer, 1971b).   The main negative values at Nakhon Nayok and Suphan Buri result from truck domination in the lower Central Plain. Those in the southern coastal provinces reflect high volumes of cargo from Bangkok carried by coastal shipping; however Trang and Yala, which have no direct access to the Gulf, recorded positive values.   The negative value found at Chaiyaphum in the Northeast results from truck competition, although the railway line was opened only in 1967. Finally, the negative value at Lamphun is the result of Chiang Mai's economic dominance.

Over-predicted residuals on the northern line between Nakhon Sawan-Chiang Mai and on the line from Nakhon Ratchasima-Buri Ram-Surin-Si Sa Ket-Ubon Ratchathani, indicate only incipient competition from trucks.   Those on the periphery of the Central Plain reflect a persistent movement by rail of certain commodities from Bangkok.   However, the importance of this group (Lop Buri, Nakhon Pathom and Kanchanaburi) is probably overstated by including in the input those provinces which have railway connections but no freight, such as Nakhon Nayok, Nonthaburi and Pathum Thani.

(d)   Truck

Further confirmation of the extent of road competition on freight flows ex-Bangkok is again sought in the trucking residuals.   As anticipated, negative values occur in the South, parts of the Northeast, and the North where the character of the road network precludes the effective operation of long-distance trucking fleets against other modes using road feeder services.   The location of checking stations employed in the survey accounts for the negative values among the provinces in the lower Central Plain.   The surrounding ring of small positive residuals can be attributed to the scope of the survey as checking stations split some provinces in two.

The highest residual values occur at Ranong and Phuket, which have no alternative methods of transport to Bangkok; Trat, where coastal

shipping is the only rival; Nong Khai, which serves as a transhipment
point for Laos; Udon Thani and other Northeast locations where freight
volumes are inflated by military cargoes; and Nakhon Sawan in the North
which also has a military installation attracting heavy inputs of munitions.
This pattern will probably be subject to considerable change with the
accelerated withdrawal of U.S. troops and with the construction of direct
road links between Chumphon-Surat Thani, Nakhon Ratchasima-Ubon Ratchathani, and Bangkok-Chiang Mai.

Transport competition and the nature of the commodity mix would,
therefore, seem to be potent factors accounting for the unexplained
variation in flows ex-Bangkok to the provinces. Their combined impact
may have been exaggerated firstly, by the absence of a more sensitive
gauge than unweighted population data as a measure of aggregate demand
and secondly, by employing line haul distance which neglects terminal and
delivery movements - time in transit may have been a more responsive
variable than distance. Anomalies arising from the conduct of the
separate surveys and incompatible commodity classifications handicap
attempts to introduce variables into the multiple regression analysis
that would reflect the relative degree of inter-modal competition and
differences in the commodity mix. The insertion of an estimate of
inbound/outbound provincial traffic by other modes (X_3) into the multiple
regression analysis ($log_e Y = a + b log_e X_1 + c log_e X_2 + d log_e X_3$) as an indicator of the strength of competing modes contributes very little to
additional explanation. In flows from the provinces to the capital
increases in the coefficient of multiple determination, R^2, are 1 per
cent for inland waterways, 8 per cent for coastal shipping, 1 per cent
for Railway, and 4 per cent for truck. In movements ex-Bangkok, gains
are 23 per cent for inland waterways and 1 per cent for coastal shipping.
The Railway and trucks experienced no change. Rather than pursue these
modal peculiarities further a more profitable approach is to amalgamate
the surveys by bringing them to a common base to give an overall view of
freight flows in Thailand and to see if population and distance perform
better as independent variables at an aggregate level.

(iii) <u>A composite view of capital-provincial movements</u>

Amalgamated values of flows to and from Bangkok are obtained by using the national traffic survey (Ministry of Communications) of 1967 as the base, and assuming that:-

(1) inland waterway flows (1964) to the capital from provinces with positive residuals increased by five per cent per annum, but those with negative residuals remained unchanged. This is not unreasonable given the heavy movement of raw materials from the provinces to Bangkok, while a much smaller outflow of commodities from the capital to the provinces has probably declined.

(2) coastal shipping flows (1965) between Bangkok and Surat Thani, Nakhon Si Thammarat, and Songkhla are conservatively assumed to have increased at two per cent per year; flows involving Pattani, Narathiwat, and ports north of Surat Thani are left unchanged.

(3) Railway movements (1968) are reduced to those prevailing in 1967.

Table 14.5: Composite inter-provincial movements to and from Bangkok Number of observations (N), standard partial correlation coefficients for distance ($\beta_1 X_1$) and population ($\beta_2 X_2$), coefficients of multiple regression (R), and coefficients of multiple determination (R^2)

Direction	N	$\beta_1 X_1$	$\beta_2 X_2$	R	R^2
To Bangkok	69	-0.61^a	0.58^a	0.71^b	0.50^b
From Bangkok	69	-0.50^a	0.61^a	0.68^b	0.46^b

a Significant at the 0.05 level (t test)
b Significant at the 0.05 level (F test)

When this composite figure is used in the multiple regression analysis the standard partial regression coefficients for distance and population are significant in the reciprocal flows between Bangkok and the provinces (Table 14.5). As anticipated earlier population performed better in flows ex-Bangkok, but only slightly so. Indeed, the coefficient of multiple determination, R^2, accounts for 46 per cent of the explained variation in outbound flows from the capital compared with 50 per cent for movements in the reverse direction and is significant in both cases. While a measure of confidence may have been restored in the use of population and distance as independent

variables such results must be viewed with extreme caution;   therefore
residuals for the individual provinces are not considered further in this
paper.

A less demanding use of the factored capital-provincial flow data
for 1967 (and provincial-provincial data) is to subtract the origin
statistics for all modes from the comparable set of destination data to
reveal sources and sinks.   Each negative and positive volume statistic
for provincial nodes is located by latitudinal and longitudinal co-ordinates
which can be logarithmically transformed to create a transport surface by:-

(1) superimposing a rectangular mesh on the map;

(2) relaxing the location of the volume statistic to the nearest
     mesh node where it represents the height of the surface at
     this point;

(3) increasing the fineness of the mesh by two dimensional inter-
     polation which results in a smoother surface;

(4) viewing the surface as an isometric projection.

The initial projection provides a normal view of the transport surface with
provincial sources as hillocks and sinks as hollows (Fig. 14.6A).   A
second projection reverses the initial surface so that the sinks are
hillocks and the sources hollows (Fig. 14.6B).[5]

The conventional view of freight movements in Thailand is of flows
moving from the North, Northeast, and parts of the Central Region to the
metropolitan area and the spill-over of some of these flows via Bangkok
into the deficit area of the South focused on Songkhla.   This impression
is only partly substantiated.   Comparison of the two projections of the
transport surface indicates:-

(1) the presence of pronounced sinks in the main export areas of
     Bangkok-Thon Buri and the South and a preponderance of sources
     in the North, Northeast, and Central Regions - particularly
     Ayutthaya, Saraburi, and Chon Buri;

(2) that the traditional pattern of freight movements is disrupted
     by sinks at Nong Khai (a transit base for Laos); Nakhon Sawan,
     Nakhon Ratchasima, Ubon Ratchathani, Nakhon Phanom, Udon Thani
     (all with U.S. military installations); and Chiang Mai (a
     heavy importer of petroleum products).

_____

5 The surfaces projected in this study were produced by J.A.B. Palmer,
Consultant Programmer, C.S.I.R.O. Computer Research Centre, Canberra.

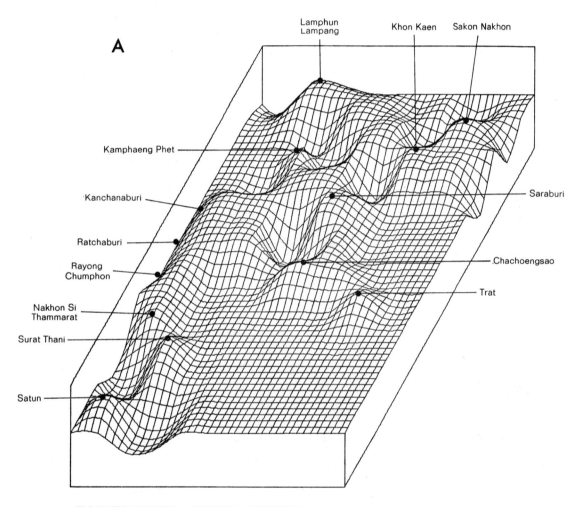

TRANSPØRT SURFACE – LØGARITHM TRANSFØRM

Fig. 14.6A Transport surface showing provinces with surplus freight
            as hillocks and those with net inflows over outflows as
            hollows.

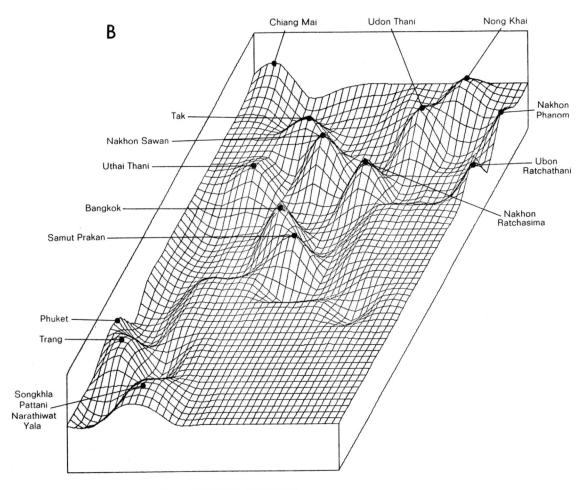

TRANSPØRT SURFACE – LØGARITHM TRANSFØRM

Fig. 14.6B Reversed transport surface showing provinces with deficits
as hillocks and those with a surplus as hollows.

While such surfaces provide a broad survey of freight movements in
Thailand it is necessary to decompose the total transport situation into
its components if the impact of capital investments in transport is to be
pinpointed. A simulation model is suggested for the purpose.

3. SIMULATING FREIGHT FLOWS IN THE NATIONAL TRANSPORT SYSTEM

A model simulating inter-provincial freight flows by all modes in Thailand
would be particularly apposite for gauging the competitive effects of new
highway links on the total transport system or for assessing the alternative strategies of making the Railway, inland waterways, or coastal shipping more efficient. The absence of comparable commodity data for all
modes in Thailand prevents such a study at the inter-provincial level.
Indeed, any attempt to simulate current transport movements from existing
survey data must use the zones delimited in the national highway survey
(Ministry of Communications, 1969), which encompass several provinces.
While these zones are not an ideal basis for transport decision-making
they can be employed in an initial simulation model to expose the broad
pattern of movement and the main lineaments of the total system.[6] The
model can be adjusted to accommodate origin and destination data on inter-
provincial movements when such data become available.

(i)   The network and the simulator

     The simulation network is constructed by representing each of the
twelve zones by a single node that is capable of being a source or sink
depending on whether supply is greater than consumption (Fig. 14.7).
Assuming adequate storage capacity, goods can flow from sources via
channels representing separate modal links (inland waterways, coastal
shipping, Railway and highway) to sinks for distribution (Fig. 14.8).
Each link has a set capacity specifying the tonnage that can pass through
in a unit of time. Such a network can be extended by adding new nodes
and links, as indicated in Fig. 14.8, to include port facilities (notorious
bottlenecks in Thailand), direct connections with adjacent countries (Laos

6 The basic structure of the model is derived from Hardiman and Stockton
(1967). Similar research has been undertaken by Ford and Fulkerson (1962).

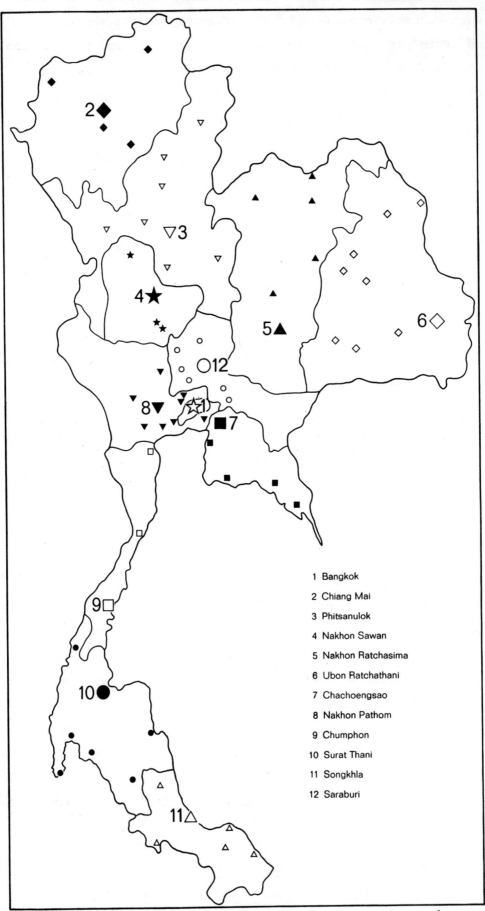

Fig. 14.7 Constituent provinces and representative nodes
for the twelve transport zones in Thailand.

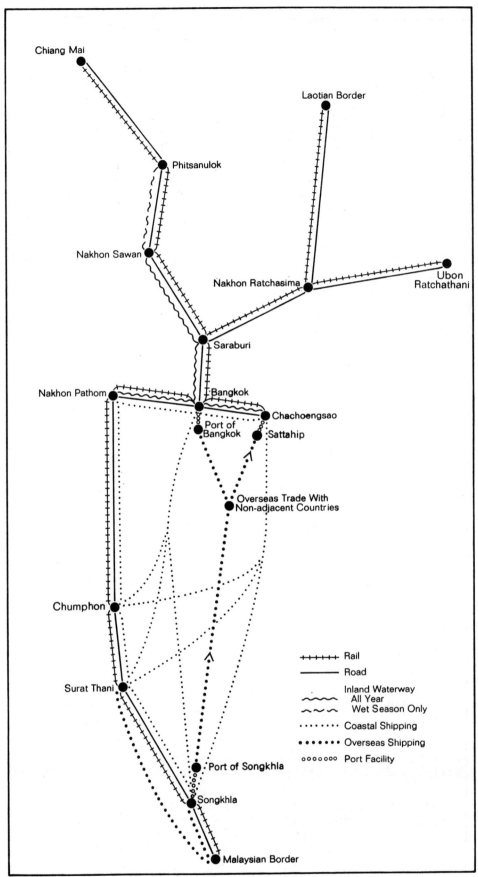

Fig. 14.8   A schematic representation of the main lineaments
            of Thailand's national transport system.

and Malaysia), and overseas trade with non-adjacent countries (including, for convenience in this study, Cambodia and Burma); however, only parts of the framework are employed here (Morlok, 1967).

Commodity flows between selected nodes are subject to the normal operating procedures of a transport system, i.e. sources have to be determined to see that their supply equals or is in excess of demand (considered to be constant over a period) and universally-applicable decision rules followed in the re-supply action have to be pre-set. Given the input parameters - number of time periods t_O, separate node requirements for each commodity, relative costs for transporting particular commodities between sources and sinks, link capacities,[7] and distances between nodes - the operating procedures of the transport system can be duplicated by programming the simulator (Fig. 14.9) to supply the periodic demand for a series of commodities ranked in order of priority (i index). A fixed series of steps is involved in the simulator which chooses:-

(1)   supply nodes for each destination-commodity combination by a random numbers generator as no fixed priority exists among transport users of different modes,

(2)   a route set for destination-commodity-node according to the shortest distance involved, and

(3)   modes for each destination-commodity-node-route by the least cost principle.

Results from the operation of the simulator are recorded on the commodity-node-link record file for each mode. Some indication of the source of data inputs is given in a sample run.

---

7   Locks limit inland waterway movements and calculations show, for example, that 2440 tonnes is the daily maximum flow that can be handled in any one direction between Nakhon Sawan and Bangkok; vessel size and type of cargo (dry/liquid) can be used to determine coastal shipping's capacity; the number of freight trains (eleven scheduled to and from Bangkok daily) and siding length (only 44 wagons can be handled, for instance, in the 322 m siding at Thung Song) can be employed to assess rail link capacity; and planned design standards and average daily traffic figures (published annually) can be made use of to gauge truck capabilities.

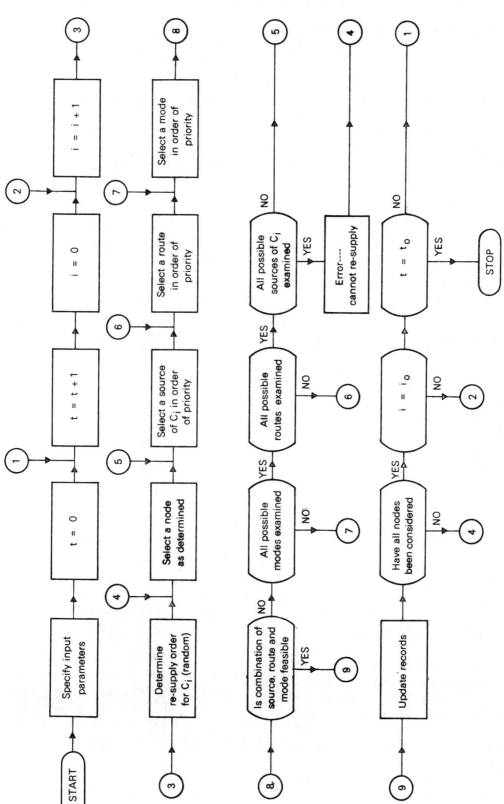

Fig. 14.9 Flow chart of the simulator (devised in association with Murray Ray, Joint Programming Section, R.S.Pac.S. and R.S.S.S., The Australian National University, Canberra). It reflects earlier work by Ford and Fulkerson (1962) and Hardiman and Stockton (1967).

(ii) <u>Sample run</u>

A sample run is undertaken manually for a single commodity –
petroleum products – for one time slot to gauge if the simulator would
give acceptable results.   Data inputs are drawn from the following
sources:-

(1)   Node requirements: data are available for civilian movements
      in 1970 from which it is possible to calculate surplus and
      deficit nodes (Table 14.6) – markets for individual products
      vary as, for instance, fuel oil and premium grade motor
      spirit are concentrated in the metropolitan area, but for
      this study they are grouped together as an undifferentiated
      item.

<u>Table 14.6</u>:   Sources and sinks for petroleum products in 1970

	Node	Source	Sink
1.	Bangkok	3489	–
2.	Chiang Mai	–	181
3.	Phitsanulok	–	174
4.	Nakhon Sawan	–	161
5.	Nakhon Ratchasima	–	222
6.	Ubon Ratchathani	–	349
7.	Chachoengsao	–	434
8.	Nakhon Pathom	–	913
9.	Chumphon	–	142
10.	Surat Thani	–	498
11.	Songkhla	–	217
12.	Saraburi	–	529
13.	Malaysian border	331	–

(2)   Route distances: data are available for the Railway in the
      rate books; road distances are taken from an oil company
      gazeteer; and coastal shipping distances are calculated from
      a map of Thailand and can be considered as rough approximations.

(3)   Unit costs for individual modes for each origin-destination
      combination: data are provided by the oil companies, but the
      figures quoted are approximate as contract rates operate through-
      out much of Thailand – a single figure is given for each origin-
      destination combination, but rates vary for regular and premium
      grade motor spirit, kerosene, gas oil, and diesel fuel.

(4)   Link capacity: data are not readily available without a
      detailed breakdown of vehicle capacity, but a statistic can be de-
      duced from the storage capacity of individual companies (Shell,
      Caltex, Esso, Summit, and the Oil and Fuel Organisation) which
      are road, rail, or sea-fed.

The results of employing these input parameters in the simulator seem reasonable (Table 14.7).   Indeed, the simulator offers scope for

Table 14.7: Link record of data inputs and resulting allocation schedule for petroleum products 1970

Source/sink	Mode	Estimated distance	Unit cost	Allocation
Bangkok/Chiang Mai	Road	809	38.5	–
/Chiang Mai	Rail	751	20.3	181
/Phitsanulok	Road	736	19.0	33
/Phitsanulok	Rail	389	14.8	141
/Nakhon Sawan	Road	341	14.5	56
/Nakhon Sawan	Rail	249	9.5	105
/Nakhon Ratchasima	Road	256	14.5	41
/Nakhon Ratchasima	Rail	264	13.5	181
/Ubon Ratchathani	Road	692	35.6	64
/Ubon Ratchathani	Rail	575	15.7	285
/Chachoengsao	Road	99	6.0	434
/Nakhon Pathom	Road	58	3.7	913
/Nakhon Pathom	Rail	64	8.9	–
/Chumphon	Road	508	24.7	–
/Chumphon	Rail	485	14.9	142
/Surat Thani	Road	923	29.1	–
/Surat Thani	Rail	651	17.6	–
/Surat Thani	Ship	616	7.0	193
/Songkhla	Road	1329	37.0	–
/Songkhla	Rail	974	26.3	172
/Songkhla	Ship	720	11.0	19
/Saraburi	Road	108	6.6	529
/Saraburi	Rail	113	6.8	–
Malaysia/Surat Thani	Ship	375	6.0	305
/Songkhla	Road	389	14.8	26

examining the effects at t_1 of the decision to use unit trains in the North and Northeast and to switch to tankers in serving Songkhla and Surat Thani ex-Bangkok and phase out Malaysian supplies, at t_2 the proposal for a pipeline from Si Racha on the eastern littoral to Nakhon Ratchasima, at t_3 the impact of a canal/pipeline across the Kra Isthmus, and at t_4 the discovery of crude oil in the Gulf of Thailand.   The computerised simulator is now available to cope with such scenarios and has already been tested using rice flows calculated from the survey data.   Even at such an aggregate level the simulator is extremely demanding of data and it is hoped that future transport surveys will bear its basic needs in mind.

4. CONCLUSION

For analytical purposes this study of freight transport in Thailand is separate from the examination of transport decision-making. There is a pressing need, however, to correlate the operations of individual transport networks. The production of unrelated modal surveys is symptomatic of the dissipation of transport decision-making among several rival agencies and the absence of a strong integrating body or of a national control system. Individual networks are planned in isolation resulting in unnecessary competition, little co-ordination, and much inter-agency conflict. The current economic situation of slow export growth and a decline in investment activity is likely to induce transport co-ordination, possibly through road user charges, as part of a critical review of current expenditure priorities. If such regulation is to be effective efforts need to be redirected from modal surveys to the generation of time series data on the total transport situation at several levels - metropolitan, inter-provincial, and intra-provincial (Hafner, 1969). Hopefully, such surveys will be part of a more concerted effort to produce reliable statistics for monitoring the impact of any redirection in government economic policy.

ACKNOWLEDGEMENTS

Grateful acknowledgement is made to The Australian National University for financing fieldwork in Thailand; the Applied Scientific Research Corporation of Thailand (especially, F.G. Nicholls, N.L. Wake, and Chirtsukdi Sornchai) for logistical support; and the Department of Geography, University of Michigan, Project 30 staff (especially G. Levine, Mit Pramuanvorachat, and Phaijoyont Uathavikul) for passing on their experience in the transport field. J. Heyward and K. Mitchell, Cartographic Section, Department of Human Geography, Research School of Pacific Studies, The Australian National University, drew the maps; Barbara M. Banks, Research Assistant, Department of Human Geography helped process some of the data; Murray Ray, Joint Schools Programming Service, The Australian National University devised the flow chart of the simulator and programmed it; and J.A.B. Palmer, Consultant Programmer, Computer Research Centre, C.S.I.R.O., Canberra projected the transport surfaces.

REFERENCES

Burns, R.E., 1969.   'Transport planning: selection of analytical techniques', Journal of Transport Economics and Policy, 3, pp. 306-21.

Ford, L.R. and Fulkerson, D.R., 1962.   Flows in networks, Princeton University Press, Princeton.

Golledge, R.G., 1963.   'A geographical analysis of Newcastle's rail freight traffic', Economic Geography, 39, pp. 60-73.

Gould, P.R., 1960.   The development of the transportation pattern in Ghana, Northwestern Studies in Geography No.5, Evanston, Illinois.

Hafner, J.A., 1969.   Research project no. 30/3 case study of competition between waterways, road and rail transport; Report No. 1, Transport development and geographic change in the Central Plain of Thailand, Applied Scientific Research Corporation of Thailand, Bangkok, (unpublished report).

Harbour Department (in co-operation with the National Economic Development Board and the National Statistical Office), 1964: Report: survey of inland water transportation - Central Rivers Basin, Bangkok.

Harbour Department, 1969.   Report: survey of coastal shipping, 1965. Unpublished MS, Bangkok, (mimeo).

Hardiman, R.R. and Stockton, R.G., 1967.   A first generation simulator of the Thailand transportation system, Monterey, (mimeo).

International Bank for Reconstruction and Development, 1966.   Transportation sector report No. FE 536, 2nd September 1966, Bangkok, (mimeo).

Investor, 1971.   The Investor, 3, Bangkok.

Jones, J.H., 1964.   Economic benefits from development roads in Thailand, SEATO Graduate School of Engineering (now Asian Institute of Technology), Technical Note No.15, Bangkok.

Kasiraksa, W., 1963.   Economic effects of the Friendship Highway, SEATO Graduate School of Engineering (now Asian Institute of Technology), Bangkok.

King, L.J., 1969.   Statistical analysis in geography, Prentice-Hall Inc., Englewood Cliffs, N.J.

Ministry of Communications, 1969.   Report: survey of road transport, 1967. Unpublished MS, Bangkok.

Morlok, E.K., 1967.   An analysis of transport technology and network
            structure, The Transportation Center, Northwestern
            University, Evanston, Illinois.

National Economic Development Board, 1968.   The second national
            economic and social development plan, Government Printer,
            Bangkok.

Patapanich, T., 1964.   Economic effects of the East West Highway, SEATO
            Graduate School of Engineering (now Asian Institute of
            Technology), Bangkok.

Rimmer, P.J., 1971a.   'Government influence on transport decision-
            making in Thailand', in G.J.R. Linge and P.J. Rimmer
            (eds.), Government influence and the location of economic
            activity, Department of Human Geography Publication HG/5,
            Research School of Pacific Studies, The Australian National
            University, Canberra, pp. 325-57.

Rimmer, P.J., 1971b.   Transport in Thailand: the railway decision,
            Department of Human Geography Publication HG/6, Research
            School of Pacific Studies, The Australian National
            University, Canberra.

Simmons, J.W., 1970.   Patterns of interaction within Ontario and Quebec,
            Centre for Urban and Community Studies, Research Paper No.
            41, University of Toronto, Toronto.

Smith, R.H.T., 1962.   Commodity movements in southern New South Wales,
            Department of Geography, Research School of Pacific Studies,
            The Australian National University, Canberra.

Smith, R.H.T., 1970.   'Concepts and methods in commodity flow analysis',
            Economic Geography, 46, pp. 404-16.

Thomas, E.N., 1968.   'Maps of residuals from regression', in B.J.L.
            Berry and D.F. Marble, Spatial analysis: a reader in
            statistical geography, Prentice-Hall Inc., Englewood
            Cliffs, N.J., pp. 326-52.

Transportation Consultants Inc., 1959.   A comprehensive evaluation of
            Thailand's transportation requirements, (3 vols), Washington,
            D.C.

Wilson, G.W. et al., 1966.   The impact of highway investment on
            development, Brookings Institution, Washington, D.C.

CHAPTER 15

BANGKOK 2000

Larry Sternstein*

1. INTRODUCTION

As in many 'developing' nations, Thailand is developing around a lone
large capital city.   Bangkok is a primate city, not only in size but
also in the complexity, the fearful interrelatedness, the damnable
immediacy, and the sheer number of problems wanting solution.[1]   Those
responsible for developing Bangkok reason that since the problems have
been imported so too should be the answers.   The foreign consultant is
invited to tackle the more troublesome of the symptoms of development
and while so engaged is expected to train promising nationals in his
ways.   Meanwhile, as many qualified Thai as possible are sent into the
developed camp to discover these ways first-hand.   It would be hyper-
critical to fault the leadership, but the danger is clear.   An adoption
or too simple adaptation of the mannerisms of the city of the 'developed'
world will harden Bangkok in a small mold, committing it to an existence
in mime.   Free of piled improvements and disjoined political units, the
city fathers are still so overwhelmed by the problems of growth that the
opportunity presented goes unrecognised, or seems instead a particularly
ill piece of ill-fortune.   The experts prescribe only well-tried
remedies and proffer plans that do little more than ameliorate present
difficulties.

2. ALTERNATIVE PLANS

A first master plan for Bangkok was submitted by American consultants in
August 1960 (Litchfield et al., 1960).   Based on less than three years

---

* Dr Sternstein is Senior Lecturer in the Department of Geography, School
of General Studies, Australian National University.

1 This discussion follows my critique (Sternstein, 1971:1-16) of recent
Thai plans for the Bangkok Metropolitan Area brought together in an
edited translation in Sternstein, 1971:17-218.   It also incorporates
material from another paper (Sternstein, 1972).

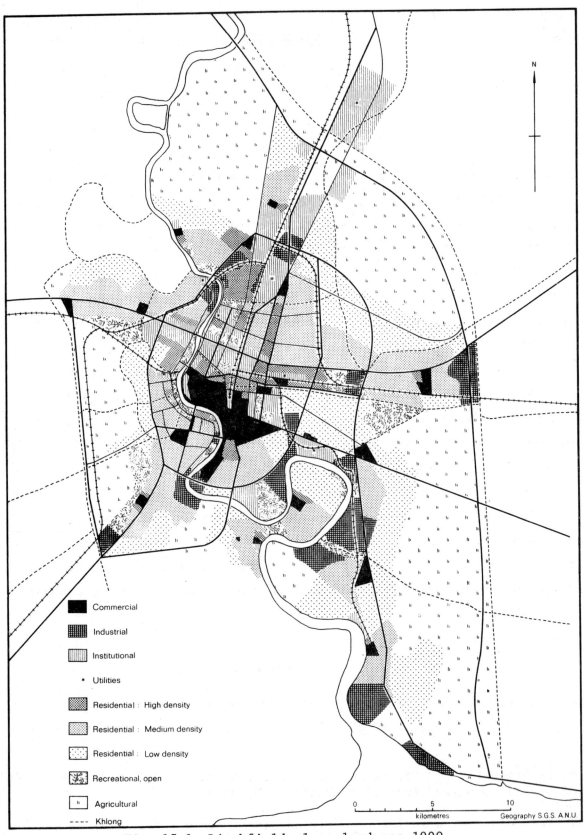

Fig. 15.1 Litchfield plan: land use 1990.

study, the Greater Bangkok plan 2533 (1990) was to be a guide for the next
30 years.   The plan is essentially a land use plan (Fig. 15.1) with
blocks of different uses separated by access ways producing a pleasant
mosaic-like structure to cater for anticipated industrial growth and
able in 1990 to accommodate 4,500,000 people with their attendant facilities.   In the absence of the necessary fiscal, legal and administrative
infrastructure, the plan has languished.   Thai authorities refer to it
when, by chance, a development project envisaged in the plan crops up in
the traditional ad hoc approach;   otherwise the plan is wisely ignored.

During the preparation of the plan a number of promising Thai were
seconded to the consultants and several were sent overseas to study different aspects of the planning process.   The Department of Town and
Country Planning was created in 1961 on the recommendation of the consultants.   Previously, separate, un-coordinated, and even opposed, developments had been pursued in the metropolitan area by a host of agencies
with equal, overlapping, or conflicting mandates.   City planning sections
in the Bangkok and Thon Buri municipalities had been established only in
1956 while the Town Planning Division of the Department of Public Works
had been re-established in 1953 after a spasmodic existence since about
1935.   The Department of Town and Country Planning assumed responsibility
for overall planning in the metropolitan area (and in up-country centres
as well) and brought together the small cadre of Thai planners.   Other
planning agencies were to plan only special projects consistent with the
policy of the Department.

Since 1961 the Greater Bangkok plan 2533 has been revised several
times by the City Planning Division in the Bangkok Municipality.   The
most recent and grandest is titled, engagingly, Memorandum describing
activities under the responsibility for planning and proffering advice
concerning the future of Bangkok - in brief, the Greater Bangkok plan
2543 [2000] (Chancharoensook, 1969).   In fact such activity is beyond
its scope, but the Division pleads the urgency of the situation and has
received a generally sympathetic hearing - except at the Department where,
officially, the effort is ignored.   So the Department's plan, dated
February 1971, is entitled Report on the first revision of the plan for
the metropolitan area (Department of Town and Country Planning, 1971).

This 'first' revision of the Greater Bangkok plan 2533 was necessitated, according to the Department, by the fact that the draft City Planning Law, then waiting approval, raised the possibility of a coordinated development provided there was a valid comprehensive plan.   As the advisors warned in proposing the creation of the Department of Town and Country Planning, two offices promoting two separate plans for the same city, cannot create intelligent growth (Nims, 1963).   Effective development stems from critical discussion and the airing of different views but it is irresponsible for two agencies of government which are legally and professionally affiliated and fully aware of (but not openly acknowledging) each other's activities to use nearly identical means to gain near-identical ends.   The Department of Town and Country Planning, as senior partner, should acknowledge the de facto planning by the City Planning Division, and incorporate that which is good in their de jure planning.

Both the First revised metropolitan plan and the Greater Bangkok plan 2533 are remarkable for their lack of reference to prior or continuing studies.   This is despite the fact that the Department should be vitally interested in the working of each of the many responsible agencies and must elicit opinion from them, if only to encourage that sense of interrelatedness necessary to coordinated effort.   Furthermore, one might expect that when a non-government authority is sufficiently concerned to present alternative strategies these should be seriously explored.   But the First revised metropolitan plan gives no consideration to Professor An Nimmanhaemindr's Solution to the traffic problem in Bangkok-Thon Buri and establishment of a new national administrative centre (Nimmanhaemindr, 1970).

The three studies noted, Report on the first revision of the plan for the metropolitan area, Memorandum describing activities under the responsibility for planning and proffering advice concerning the future of Bangkok and Solution to the traffic problem in Bangkok-Thon Buri and establishment of a new national administrative centre, represent authoritative Thai thinking on total city planning - they are the first and only such statements.

3.   FIRST REVISED METROPOLITAN PLAN

The Report on the first revision of the plan for the metropolitan area
attempts to confirm the Greater Bangkok plan 2533 despite the changed
condition of the metropolitan area and despite the fact that the future
must also be very different from that anticipated in the original plan.
In the main, parameters critical to the comprehensive plan are revised
from up-dated data and certain suggestions, some of them reasonable, are
reiterated from the Greater Bangkok plan 2533.   Basically the revision
stems from a very great difference in the population anticipated in the
metropolitan area in 1990;   6,500,000 in the First revised metropolitan
plan as against 4,500,000 in the original plan.   The Greater Bangkok
plan 2533 insisted on government limiting growth to 4,500,000 in 1990
in the belief that, failing this, population densities would deepen and
a huge financial outlay would be necessary to provide the public facilities required.   The authors of the First revised metropolitan plan doubt
the practicability of attempting to limit numbers in the metropolitan area
to 4,500,000 and suggest that government must find the means to provide
the necessary facilities.   The approach suggests a healthy pragmatism,
but the projections giving a population of 6,500,000 in 1990 are based on
questionable assumptions set in three suppositions which though duly
'tested' are not convincing.   The suppositions are:-

> 'Supposition 1.   The population in the Bangkok and Thon Buri
> municipalities will increase at a decreasing rate of 1.4 per
> cent each decade from the rate of 5.54 per cent in 1967.
>
> Supposition 2.   The population in the Bangkok and Thon Buri
> municipalities will increase at a decreasing rate of 0.04 per
> cent per year from the rate of 4.50 per cent in 1967.
>
> Supposition 3.   The population in the Bangkok and Thon Buri
> municipalities will increase in accordance with an increase
> in the proportion of the population of the nation in the metro-
> politan area at a rate of 0.18 per cent per year from the rate
> of 8.00 per cent in 1967.
>
> In attempting to arrive at the supposition most suitable we have
> found suppositions (1) and (2) equally appropriate and most
> probable, and so the Department of Town and Country Planning
> has chosen supposition (1) and, therefore, we expect that in
> 1990 the population in the metropolitan area will be 6,237,720.'
> (Department of Town and Country Planning, 1971.)

In an apparent attempt to reinforce the argument, the possibility
is raised that the population of the metropolitan area might grow to
10,000,000.   This is rejected for reasons that 'have nothing to do with
the case' save to give good reason for forcibly limiting growth.   The
plan states that

>'Such a population would result in very high densities, so high
>that it would be impossible to provide those facilities necessary
>to urban life and this, in turn, would result in a decrease in
>population in future until a balance was achieved;
>
>government would have to spend a huge sum of money to provide
>the public utilities necessary for such a population and this
>would affect the efficiency of the administration;
>
>the imbalance in the allocation of monies between the city and
>other centres would lead to political problems;   and
>
>administrative and other kinds of services would be inadequate
>and would result in turmoil that, in turn, would stop the
>growth of the city.'   (Department of Town and Country Planning,
>1971.)

Both the First revised metropolitan plan and its lineal ancestor
appeared immediately before the results of a national census became available.   Both plans bemoan the lack of accurate, readily usable data and
the gathering of such information is urged on agencies of government as
being indispensable to planning.   But the kinds and worth of data which
are gathered by agencies of government were, it appears, not assessed.
The Department of Town and Country Planning should have amassed all data
collected in the decade since publication of the Greater Bangkok plan
2533.   In view of the acknowledged errors introduced into that plan by
the difference between the actual population in the metropolitan area
reported in the 1960 Census and the estimate of the consultants, revision
should have been delayed until the results of the 1970 Census were
available.

The First revised metropolitan plan, as the Greater Bangkok plan
2533, contains a good deal of pedantry and much space is devoted to
definitions, procedures and a simple iteration of the worth of city planning.   There is certainly need for such propaganda, but not in place of
planning.   Similarly, although the Department stresses the need to fulfil
certain other fundamental tasks in planning, such as determining measures

by which slums might be defined and classed, or standards for public
housing and land subdivisions fixed, there is no indication that these
needs have received serious consideration.   The First revised metropolitan plan is overly appealing to the eye and unnecessarily generous in
providing costly multi-coloured plates.   The concern with the 'finish'
of the publication is misplaced in what is properly a working paper.

The author of the Greater Bangkok plan 2533 believed a comprehensive plan to be concerned with the physical environment of a city or
region and consequently it is essentially a land use plan.   The First
revised metropolitan plan is also aimed mainly at defining plans for land
use and communications and is essentially a land use plan (Fig. 15.2).
Both plans represent the type of planning eschewed in the so-called 'new'
planning philosophy that considers strategic measures and provision of
the necessary fiscal, legal and administrative infrastructure, but does
not prepare a 'plan' as such.   This approach seeks to provide the necessary planning milieu by gradually turning the ad hoc project-by-project
approach into an integrated programme.   The merit of the 'new' philosophy is evident, but the land use plan has value.   Each agency involved
in developing the city follows the ad hoc approach, but each wants a guide
to overall growth.   'A land-use plan rooted in actual use, duly cognizant
of all projects contemplated by the many and various agencies responsible,
and merely filled out through a clear and simple extrapolation, is a
satisfying tactical device in working towards integrated, comprehensive
planning' (Sternstein, 1972:250).

The two land use plans appear to include approximately equal areas
but differ in their general configuration (Figs 15.2 and 15.4).   The
Greater Bangkok plan 2533 includes 780 square kilometers and the First
revised metropolitan plan only 732 square kilometers, but none of the
area covered in the Revised plan is slated for agricultural use, whereas
more than two-fifths of the area is so designated in the Greater Bangkok
plan 2533.   The area in urban uses in the First revised metropolitan plan
is more than half as much again as in the Greater Bangkok plan 2533.
This difference is in a similar proportion to the difference between the
populations projected for 1990.   The exclusion of fringing cultivated
lands from a plan of metropolitan land uses suggests an 'empty' countryside over which the city may sprawl if necessary or convenient.   In fact,

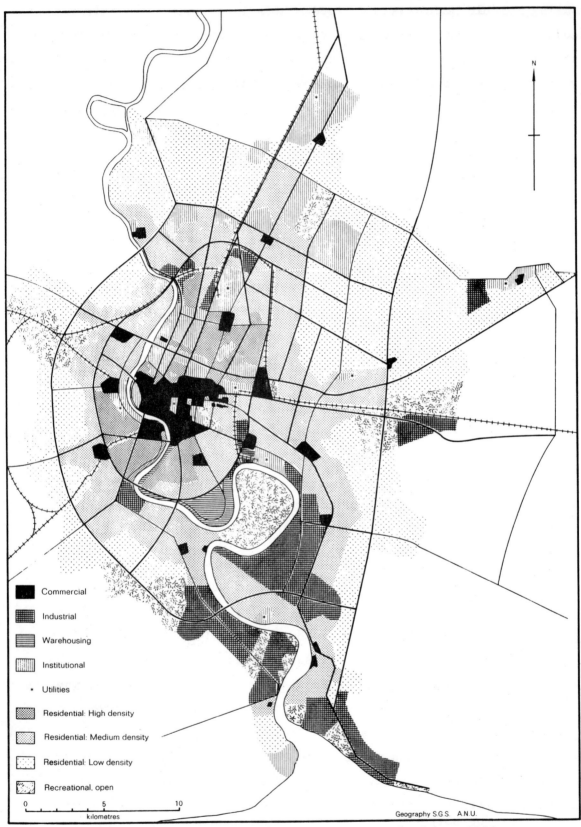

Commercial

Industrial

Warehousing

Institutional

• Utilities

Residential: High density

Residential: Medium density

Residential: Low density

Recreational, open

0   5   10
      kilometres

Geography S.G.S. A.N.U.

Fig. 15.2 First revised metropolitan plan: land use 1990.

the countryside is well populated and, in truth, a first aim of city
planning should be to contain this sprawl.   The identity of the metropolitan area comprises the city and the surrounding country yet the plans
give only cursory consideration to the countryside.   The inter-dependence
of city and countryside should be clear on the plan.   Removing the sheath
of agricultural land from the area in the Greater Bangkok plan 2533 reveals that the two plans are strikingly similar in configuration - the
fingers extending from the hand are simply fuller and less bold
in the Revised plan.

     The First revised metropolitan plan embraces the haphazard growth
of the past decade and the ungoverned developments which are scheduled.
The disposition of land use is more coherent than in the Greater Bangkok
plan 2533 although the general disposition of the various land uses is
similar in both plans.   Reducing the intricacy of the Greater Bangkok
plan 2533 increases the credibility of the First revised metropolitan
plan which emerges more as a guide than a goal.   This is not to imply
that the First revised metropolitan plan proffers no specific suggestions.
Several novel ideas are brought into the plan.   An example of a happier
thought is the national park proposed immediately south of the Port of
Bangkok on a piece of land almost completely surrounded by the Chao Phraya
River.   Here the river is not bridged and the island-like area remains
rural.   The Plan warns that the next five years will see the area built-
up and government is urged to seize the opportunity of keeping it as open
space.[2]   The uniqueness of the site was not noticed in the Greater
Bangkok plan 2533 and most of the area was scheduled for residential use.

---

2 It would surprise and delight me if the area were not already in the
hands of speculators. (Similarly, the proposed recreational use of
vacated Crown properties in the heart of the city seems a forlorn hope.)
A decade ago I wondered aloud in knowledgeable company as to why the
narrow neck of this bulbous peninsula-like area had not been cut through
and the river rechanneled.   I was told that a canal had been cut, but
not wide and deep for fear of greater intrusion of salt water into orchards
and fields.   These were already threatened by brackish tides made more
threatening by the withdrawal of underground water for use by the rapidly
increasing population and proliferating industry in the metropolitan area.
The location of the port along the loop in the river bounding the area was
a further obstacle.   Still, I fancy a cut through this scrawny neck, the
resiting of the port at the cut, and the blocking of the flow of salt
water upstream by a submerged dam and fresh water wall. It would be an
elegant solution. Given the port, another possibility would be to score
channels through the area to allow for much needed expansion. Naturally,

After an assessment of present conditions it is proposed in the
Revised plan that a large block of 'empty' land in the northeastern part
of the city be purchased by government and used for new offices and extensions to existing offices.   In the Greater Bangkok plan 2533 a new
government area was proposed just on the Thon Buri side of the Krung
Thon Bridge and extension of the existing government area was urged.
The authors of the First revised metropolitan plan argue that to extend
the area now used by government is virtually impossible since this is in
the heart of the city where land values are very high and surrounding
properties are in private hands.   The argument is true only in part,
for the existing national administrative centre could be expanded if the
military moved from a number of spacious encampments in the heart of the
city.   But the military will not move just now and so the possibility is
not mooted in the plan.   Accepting this as politic, the existing government area might be expanded in other ways, most obviously, upwards.
Another possibility is along the processional Ratchadamnoen Klang Boulevard which is now faced on both sides by squat, dismal, woefully inadequate and decrepit structures housing a mixed bag of activities.   These
buildings back onto an even more dismal, more decrepit lot of motley
structures housing an even more mixed assembly.   Ratchadamnoen Klang
Boulevard could be faced by efficient and attractive high-rise office
buildings, interconnected and with ample off-street parking.   These might
be backed by efficient and attractive high-rise apartment blocks, nicely
spaced and housing many of those employed in the adjacent offices.
Shopping and recreational facilities are already to hand and could be
readily extended (Sternstein, 1969).   Finance for this proposal would
be no more difficult to find than for any other scheme, and might perhaps
be less so since similar developments are under way in a number of large
cities.   Even New York and London, renowned for the efficiency of their
mass transit systems, acknowledge the need to turn the 'single purpose,
eight hours a day, five days a week, commercial center to a full-time,
well-balanced commercial, residential and sightseeing area where people
live, work and play....'.   In New York, the Battery Park City Corporation Authority, created in 1968, is to develop Battery Park City on 104

---

2 (cont'd) others have speculated about this unique area, but the idea
of a national park is new to me and I think it praiseworthy.

acres in lower Manhattan as a waterfront residential and commercial
community (State University of New York, 1968:6).

   The reason the First revised metropolitan plan rejected the Thon
Buri site which the Greater Bangkok plan 2533 proposed for government is
not stated, but it is obvious that the area designated has passed into
different use, mostly residential, during the intervening decade.   The
Revised metropolitan plan sees Thon Buri as a residential area more than
did the first plan.   This is consistent with present use, but does
encourage a dormitory-like Thon Buri in the face of increasing congestion
on the river crossings.

   Rationalisation of the Greater Bangkok plan 2533 is made possible
by the much more elaborate system of communications (particularly land
transport) proposed in the First revised metropolitan plan.   It is claimed
that the road system described will solve present traffic problems and
prevent these recurring in future or at least for the next 40 years or
more.[3]   The system comprises three ring roads, a number of radial and
cross-town roads, many lesser major roads and several new bridges across
the Chao Phraya River as well as a riverside drive which would overhang
the eastern bank and thus minimise costs of expropriating land and demo-
lishing buildings.[4]   The uncertainty of such a grandiose scheme being
implemented even in part is acknowledged and an alternate way to 'solve'
the traffic problem 'immediately' is proffered.   This would entail two
elevated roads with limited access - one above main canals for much of
its length, the other above a major avenue.   A monorail system has been
mooted and seems a better 'immediate' solution, but no mention is made of
it.   The Revised metropolitan plan warns that a huge financial outlay would
be required for the elevated roads but this may be no higher (and conceivably
lower) than the cost of providing a comparable portion of the proposed
ground-level system.   The elevated roadways scheme may quite possibly
find favour.   But this is unlikely to solve the traffic problem.   Proliferation of roadway, in itself, has not answered the traffic problem anywhere,

---

3   The system is necessary to 'solve' the traffic problem and would take
more than a few years to create.   At the present pace of roadway construction, a half century would be a foolhardy schedule.

4   The need for this riverside drive may be questioned as the plan includes
a number of proposals that would thin traffic in the area.

and as Fig. 15.3 shows, the number of private cars in Bangkok has increased more than three-fold in the last decade.   The pressure will undoubtedly continue to build up rapidly.

Traffic in the metropolitan area has been affected adversely by the railroad as 17 level crossings 'contribute to traffic congestion and when more roads are cut...this problem will make difficult the development of the communications system...' (Sternstein, 1971).   Several proposals to

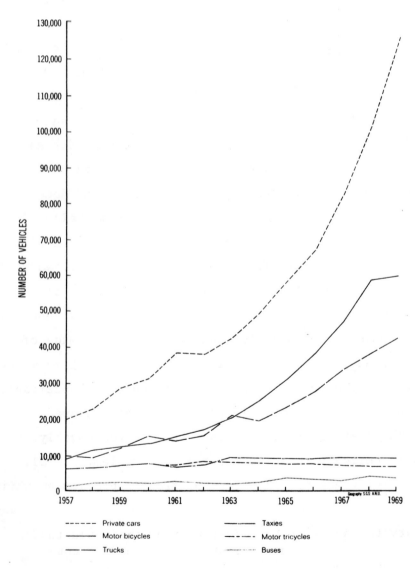

Fig. 15.3 Motor vehicle registrations, Bangkok-Thon Buri 1857-1969.

ameliorate the situation are made in the First revised metropolitan plan.
The more important are to elevate the track at each level crossing within the area included in the plan and to transfer petroleum from the Port
of Bangkok in the southern part of the city by pipeline to the Paholyothin Yard in the northern part of the city from where tank cars would be
dispatched to the provinces.   The Department of Town and Country Planning thinks the elevation of track at each road crossing possible and
notes that the Royal State Railway has considered this.   Until this can
be done it is suggested that the number of trains using Hua Lampong
Station, in the heart of the city, should be reduced to a minimum and
there should be no such trains during rush hours.

When built at the turn of the century, the Hua Lampong Station of
the State Railway was peripheral to the built-up area.   The Station is
now at the heart of the city and the question of moving it to a peripheral
site at the Paholyothin Yard could be raised.   But the Railway has
embarked on a grand redevelopment of the Hua Lampong Station, which houses
the main offices of the Railway and other facilities as well, and so this
seemingly sensible resolution of the problem is not considered in the
First revised metropolitan plan.   If the station were moved the traffic
problem would be alleviated and the area now occupied by railway instal-
lations and rights-of-way could be turned to other uses.   For example,
the central station could become a warehousing-wholesaling centre, a
central bus depot or the site of a residential complex housing those
employed in the surrounding commercial and institutional area.   The
rights-of-way could be used for roads, car parks, recreational grounds
or residential blocks - the possibilities are many and the opportunity
great.

Other proposals need closer examination of alternatives. Given the
difficulties of maintaining rail grades over elevated crossings it might
be easier to lower the roads or relocate and realign them.   Road layouts
should not be regarded as planned once and set forever.   To suggest that
rail services be suspended during rush hours and very much diminished at
other times overlooks the considerable and ever-growing number of commuters
travelling by train.   The suggestion overlooks the fact that the railway
is a service and must offer some convenience to users.   A petroleum

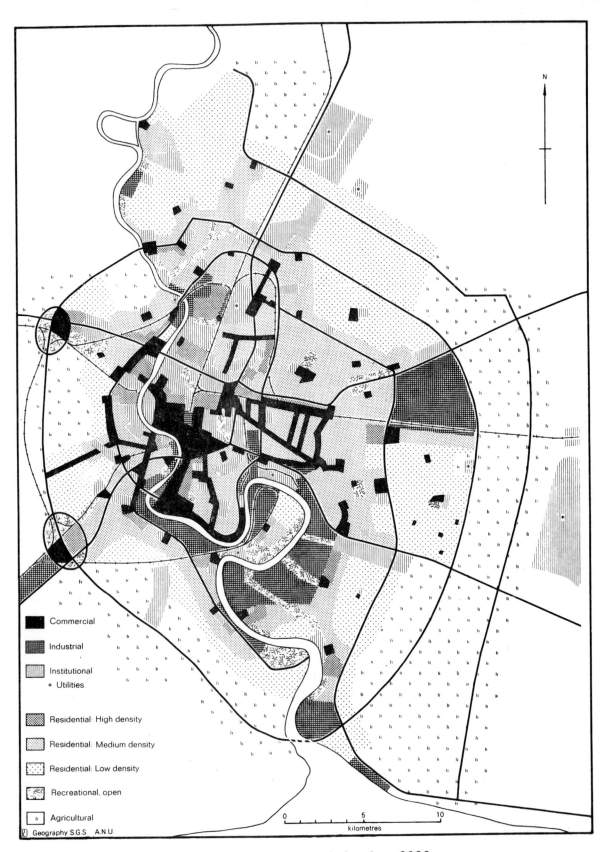

Fig. 15.4 Greater Bangkok plan 2000.

N.B.   Slightly generalised after a many coloured map on which it was sometimes
        difficult to determine differences of colour.

pipeline from the Port to the Paholyothin Yard appears at first sight to
be an eminently reasonable suggestion, but it may be entirely unnecessary
as it is already planned to carry petroleum directly up-country from the
new Laem Chabang deep-sea port without entering the metropolitan area.
The First revised metropolitan plan heartily endorses the proposed port
but appears to ignore its consequences.

4. GREATER BANGKOK PLAN 2543 (2000)

In concept and in execution the Memorandum describing activities under
the responsibility for planning and proffering advice concerning the
future of Bangkok, that is, the Greater Bangkok plan 2543, is not different from the Greater Bangkok plan 2533 or from the First revised metropolitan plan.   Like the latter it attempts revision of the first plan in
order to incorporate present and scheduled uses of land different from
those set out a decade before and to allow for a population of 6,500,000
anticipated in 2000 as against the 4,500,000 expected in 1990 (Fig. 15.4).
As in the Greater Bangkok plan 2533 the population of the metropolitan
area is fixed for the author foresees an insupportable 13,620,000 in the
year 2000 if growth is uncontrolled.   To accommodate 6,500,000 the
Greater Bangkok plan 2543 includes 975 square kilometers – 25 per cent
more land than in the Greater Bangkok plan 2533.   The former plan
schedules more land for industry, government and other institutions,
commerce and public utilities and less for residential use.   The areas
allocated for recreation and agriculture are similar in both plans
(Table 15.1).   Broadly the Greater Bangkok plan 2543 lies somewhere
between the Greater Bangkok plan 2533 and the First revised metropolitan
plan in land use allocations (Table 15.2) and in the 'fingers-from-the-
hand' configuration.   Non-agricultural uses cover 555 square kilometers
as against 460 square kilometers in the Greater Bangkok plan 2533 and 732
square kilometers in the First revised metropolitan plan, and the use of
land is set out more particularly than in the former and the system of
roads and railways is more elaborate than in the latter.   The three plans
do not form a sequence as the later two are contrary kin to the Greater
Bangkok plan 2533.   Essentially, the difference between them is in
emphasis.   The duplication of effort meant a waste of severely limited

Table 15.1: Land use allocations - Greater Bangkok plan 2533 (1990) and
Greater Bangkok plan 2543 (2000)

Land use	Greater Bangkok plan 2533		Greater Bangkok plan 2543	
	km^2	per cent	km^2	per cent
Agricultural	320	41.0	420	43.1
Residential	305	39.1	293	30.1
Industrial	39	5.1	71.5	7.3
Institutional	45	5.7	68.2	7.0
Utilities and services	26	3.3	46.7	4.8
Recreational	27	3.5	38.6	3.9
Commercial	18	2.3	37.5	3.8
Total	780	100.0	975.5	100.0

Sources: Chancharoensook, 1969; Litchfield, 1960.

time, money and manpower, and should have been avoided by the establishment of the Department of Town and Country Planning.

The different biases of the plans reflect the affiliations of the
authors.   The Department of Town and Country Planning particularises
developments in the nation's other centres as an integral part of the
plan for the metropolitan area; the Division of City Planning acknowledges
the vital importance of such development but offers no specific details.
The Division of City Planning is concerned with all forms of environmental
pollution in the urban area; the Department of Town and Country Planning,
though aware of the threat, does not study it.   The plans show many differences in detail in distribution of land use categories but, basically,
these stem from the greater decentralisation of the Greater Bangkok plan
2543 as against the greater deconcentration of the First revised metropolitan plan.   A fundamental difference between the two lies in the make
up and responsibility of the single metropolitan area planning authority
urged by both authors.   The Department sees this authority controlling
the administration concerned with implementing the comprehensive plan -
the Department's comprehensive plan.   The Division sees the metropolitan
planning authority (made up of the planning units of the 'four municipalities' - Bangkok, Thon Buri, Nonthaburi and Samut Prakan - and 'other
agencies of government concerned') formulating planning policy and preparing

Table 15.2: Non-agricultural land use allocations – Greater Bangkok plan
             2533 (1990), Greater Bangkok plan 2543 (2000) and First
             revised metropolitan plan

Land use	Greater Bangkok plan 2533 per cent	Greater Bangkok plan 2543 per cent	First revised metropolitan plan per cent
Residential	66.3	52.8	54.5
Industrial	8.6	12.9	11.0
Institutional	9.7	12.3	8.3
Utilities and services	5.6	8.4	*
Recreational	5.9	7.0	20.5
Commercial	3.9	6.7	5.8
Total	100.0	100.0	100.0

* The use 'Utilities and services' is not specified but such areas are
   probably included in 'Institutional'.

Sources: Chancharoensook, 1969; Department of Town and Country Planning,
          1971; Litchfield, 1960.

the comprehensive plan.   Obviously, the City Planning Division wants to
be free of the veto of the Department of Town and Country Planning and
since two of the 'four municipalities' have no planning unit and a lone man
is the unit in Thon Buri, the City Planning Division in the Bangkok Municipality would in fact be the new single metropolitan planning authority
under their proposed plan.   At present the Department of Town and Country
Planning is responsible for comprehensive planning of the metropolitan
area.

5.   PLAN TO ESTABLISH A NEW NATIONAL ADMINISTRATIVE CENTRE

Professor An Nimmanhaemindr's lecture and associated article, Solution to
the traffic problem and establishment of a new national administrative
centre, differs from the First revised metropolitan plan and the Greater
Bangkok plan 2543 in not being comprehensive (though the new national
administrative centre proposed would involve total planning of the metropolitan area) and in not noticing the Greater Bangkok plan 2533.   It is
also rather impassioned, as befits a lecture.   But Professor An argues
many views very similar to those expressed in the other plans.   For

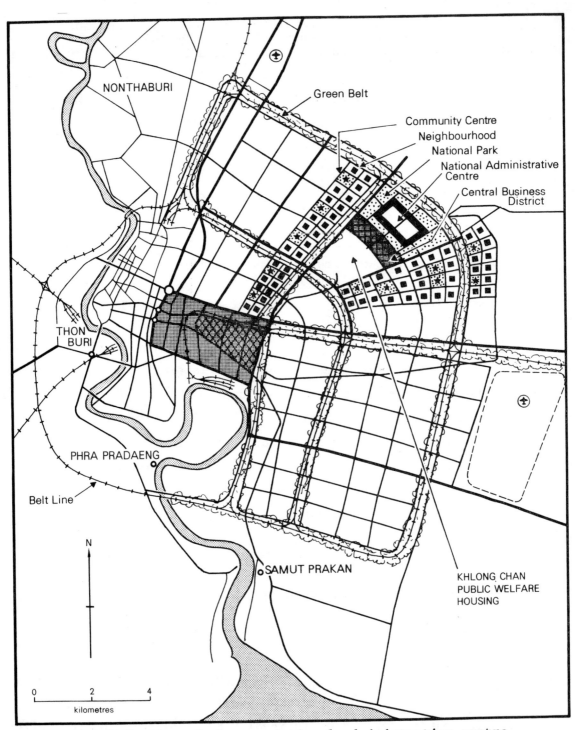

Fig. 15.5 Plan of the new national administrative centre.
The Plan is economical and multi-purpose. The centre of the new town (shaded
area) is away from the old built-up area and a belt line railway provides local
transport. The 'wheel' or 'spider-web' roadway system will be constructed in
the suburbs for the most part and on moderately or low priced land - empty
land mostly. This will reduce construction cost by five to ten times that in
the old crowded built-up area. Should the built-up area be extended in this
direction, it would be most opportune to establish a new national administrative centre and gain a new and proper residential area. This is not only an
economical project but will help solve the traffic problem.

Source: Nimmanhaemindr, 1970.

example, he notes the need to reorganise and extend the system of roads
and railways in the form of rings and radii; the need to develop mass
transportation; the need to control the use of land and the construction of buildings; the need to practice decentralisation and encourage
birth control.   All these amount to the need for a comprehensive plan.
His proposals to limit the population of Bangkok-Thon Buri to 3,500,000,
to remove the Port of Bangkok and to stop dredging the bar at the mouth
of the Chao Phraya River immediately, and to relocate all offices of the
central government at a new national administrative centre at Khlong Chan
in the suburbs of Bangkok (Fig. 15.5) are, however, strikingly different.
Such proposals have been greeted with more than dismay by responsible Thai
authorities.   Authority would probably like the population of Bangkok-
Thon Buri to be around 3,500,000 as the present population give problems
enough, but the population is already almost 3,500,000.   It appears
hopeless even to get administrative machinery going that could act to
encourage a slowing of growth in the foreseeable future - to reduce the
population absolutely seems impossible.   Again, there must be some among
the leadership who are aware of the blunder in siting the Port of Bangkok,
but to remove the Port now is unthinkable[5] and therefore to stop dredging
is irrational.

The crux of Professor An Nimmanhaemindr's thesis is the establishment of a new national administrative centre in the Bangkok suburbs. This
is not only to provide the Thai people with 'a new capital, beautiful,
properly planned and modern, like Washington, D.C.' or Canberra - an
'Administrative Suburb' if I may follow the term 'Industrial Suburb'
(Osborn, 1960:27) - but to solve the traffic problem most economically.
To cut or widen roads in the heart of the city is many times more costly
than in the suburbs.   Additionally, the new national capital would open
up new areas for residential use, relieve crowding in the city and allow
the conserving of places of historic and artistic worth.   The proposal is
thought impracticable and, although Professor An believes a good part of
the necessary outlay could be defrayed by the sale of present government
buildings and that the cost of the new centre would be less than the cost

_____
5 In fact, additions to the Port of Bangkok are underway and more are
planned, for even with a new deep-sea port (or two) shipping facilities
will be taxed, as trade will certainly grow rapidly in future.

of necessary improvements to present sites and structures, the present
economic and political situation, reflected in conservative budgeting,
supports this view.   Under a policy of decentralisation, too, the proposed wholesale relocation of offices of the central government may be
questioned.   What is proposed is a *recentralisation* and it is unlikely
that the benefits described would be realised.   What should be urged,
I feel, is a rational reconstruction of the administrative heart of the
city so that the single purpose, eight hours a day, five days a week,
administrative centre is once more a full-time, well-balanced administrative, commercial, residential and recreational area where people live,
work and play.

6.   CONCLUSION

The First revised metropolitan plan and, more so, the Greater Bangkok plan
2543 inherit a too conservative approach from the Greater Bangkok plan
2533.   Each posits a schedule that will allow in future only a city in
the wake of Western fashion.   Professor An Nimmanhaemindr's proposals
appear extreme but, in fact, are simple borrowings from the West and cannot lead to any real deviation from Western ways - despite the fact that
these ways are obviously wanting.   I think it fair to insist that the
great lesson to be learned from the city of the 'developed' world is what
not to do in the city of the 'developing' world.   To go this brutal way,
at speed, would be foolish.   To plan remedially is to forfeit the opportunity yet waiting.   But to grasp the chance needs resolute, knowledgeable
leaders: people in authority who are aware of what is going on in the
many and varied fields pertinent to urban development, and who know Bangkok.
At present there are no such people and so all the many and varied ills
of a remarkable and chaotic development appear equally urgent and hope-
lessly entangled.   Forced to do something, authority turns blindly to
the experts, but the experts are little more than technicians - even if
able technicians.   In consequence the planning of the metropolitan area
is too much a mimicry of happenings elsewhere: inevitably lagging behind
thinking elsewhere and not dedicated to discovering what is happening in
Bangkok.   No question, a real and a commendable effort went into the
making of these plans and proposals, but I cannot help believing that the

effort would have been better directed toward enquiry into those factors
fundamental to guiding the development of Bangkok.

Unique Bangkok, the most primate of cities, and embodiment of the
distinct and splendid Thai ethos, is rapidly becoming any mean 'modern'
city of recent generations and the planners seem intent on endorsing
this pattern.

REFERENCES

Chancharoensook, A., 1969.   Memorandum describing activities under the
        responsibility for planning and proffering advice concerning
        the future of Bangkok, Bangkok (in Thai). An edited translation
        appears in Sternstein, 1971:93-182.

Department of Town and Country Planning, 1971.   Report on the first revision
        of the plan for the metropolitan area, Bangkok (in Thai).   An
        edited translation appears in Sternstein, 1971:17-91.

Litchfield, Whiting, Bowne & Associates, 1960.   Greater Bangkok plan 2533,
        New York.

Nimmanhaemindr, A., 1970.   Solution to the traffic problem in Bangkok-Thon
        Buri and establishment of a new national administrative centre,
        Bangkok (in Thai).   An edited translation appears in Sternstein,
        1971:183-218.

Nims, C.R., 1963.   City planning in Thailand, Ministry of Interior, Bangkok.

Osborn, F.J., 1960.   'Preface' in Howard, E., Garden cities of tomorrow,
        Faber and Faber, London, pp. 9-28.

State University of New York, 1968.   'Battery Park City to cost $1.1
        billion', Metropolitan Area Digest 11 no. 5, p. 6.

Sternstein, L., 1969.   'Greater Bangkok metropolitan area: population
        growth and movement 1956-1960 and research for planning, the
        traffic problem', Greater Bangkok Metropolitan Area Population
        Studies, no. 2, Office of the Municipal Advisor, Bangkok
        Municipality.

Sternstein, L., 1971.   Planning the developing primate city: Bangkok 2000,
        Occasional Paper 9, Department of Geography, Australian National
        University.

Sternstein, L., 1972.   'Planning the future of Bangkok', in Dwyer, D. (ed.),
        The City as a centre of change in Asia, Centre of Asian Studies,
        University Press, Hong Kong, pp. 243-54.

CHAPTER 16

A NOTE ON FOREIGN ASSISTANCE TO THAILAND

Piew Phusavat*

1. INTRODUCTION

Foreign assistance is of great importance in world politics today.   It
is a concept with two very different facets: the first is an idealistic
principle that the world as a whole has a responsibility to extend the
benefits of modern technology to developing countries, to share the burden
of supporting populations with very low living standards, and to help the
less developed countries not to fall too far behind the advanced countries.
This is a valuable principle even though it can lead to naive ideas about
the kind of foreign assistance given by developed countries.   The other
aspect of foreign aid is more realistic.   It may be given and accepted
for political and strategic motives, to gain allies and influence public
opinion, or to strengthen friendly countries against various threats.
It may also be given for commercial motives, to expand markets and secure
preferences in the receiving countries.

The aim of this paper is to give a brief description of foreign
assistance as it affects Thailand.   It examines the sources and types of
technical assistance which Thailand has received over the past two decades,
and provides data on the distribution of aid expenditure over various
sectors of the economy (Tables 16.1 - 11, see pages 378-91).   In the
second half of the paper an assessment of key problems in the administration
of aid, from a recipient's viewpoint, leads to a summary conclusion indicating how these problems may best be avoided.

From Thailand's point of view foreign assistance should fall as far as
possible within the framework of its own development and strategic policies.

---

* Khun Piew Phusavat is Director-General of the Department of Technical and
Economic Co-operation, Bangkok.   The views expressed in this paper are those
of the author; they do not necessarily represent the views of the Royal
Thai Government.

The nation has to view the motives of the donors of aid realistically; it must also be conscious that the policies of foreign aid agencies, however well-intentioned, may result in aid of quite unsuitable, or even destructive, forms.

2.   FOREIGN LOANS

During the last decade Thailand has built up an outstanding external debt of about US$300,000,000 through official loan agreements.   This sum is equivalent to the value of about one-quarter of imports in a single year and about one-third of total foreign exchange reserves.   The government could have made use of its reserves to finance projects now aided by loans. But the loans have bolstered the country's economy considerably.   Further, some loan sources, particularly the World Bank, have given the government experience in the preparation and control of projects and have acted as friendly critics of the government's policies.   This help has been very valuable.

On the other hand, most foreign loans bear interest charges rather in excess of the interest earned on the increased exchange reserves. Furthermore conditions attached to loans almost always increase the cost of projects financed by loans to some extent.   The interest burden and the conditions attached to loans have to be weighed against the advantages to Thailand of greater exchange reserves and the benefits obtained from the projects which have been implemented.

3.   GRANT AID (TECHNICAL ASSISTANCE)

Thailand does not receive any grant aid in the form of transfers of foreign exchange.   In practice grant aid finances the provision of foreign experts, scholarships for Thai officials to study abroad, and imports of specific materials and equipment for use in agreed projects.   This sort of aid is usually called technical assistance because, according to the idealistic principle, it is intended to improve the technical and administrative resources of the country.   Measured in terms of costs, about 80 per cent of the US$50,000,000 of grant aid received by Thailand each year is

contributed by the United States of America.   Further important sources
are the various United Nations funds and specialised agencies, certain
Colombo Plan countries (particularly Australia, Canada, New Zealand and
the United Kingdom), other countries of which Germany is the most important,
and various private foundations.   Data relating to the period 1951-71 are
shown in Table 16.1.

Matching these differences in the magnitude of aid from the various
donor countries there are marked differences in the allocation of aid
within the Thai economy.   The United States, for example, has consistently
channelled a relatively small proportion of its aid to agricultural development in Thailand (7.5 per cent in 1970;   8.0 per cent in the period 1967-71),
while the United Nations agencies and other countries have variously emphasised health, agriculture, education and communications.   Data set out in
Tables 16.2 - 11 provide a detailed statement of the assistance which
Thailand has received and is now receiving from so many countries;   at the
same time the tables may be seen, in sum, as a record of substantial aid
experience on which the following observations have been based.

Grant aid is not entirely free, because the Thai government always
has to undertake various 'counterpart' expenditures as a condition for
receiving such aid.   Direct counterpart expenditures include the provision
of accommodation and travel allowances for experts, payment or part payment
of the air fares for Thai officials who are given scholarships abroad, and
payment for the transport in Thailand of imported materials and equipment.
The total cost of these 'direct counterpart' expenditures usually comes to
about 15 per cent of the total cost to the donors of grant aid.

Very often there are also 'indirect counterpart' expenditures which
pay for the manpower, buildings and other facilities provided by the Thai
government as its contribution to joint technical assistance projects.   The
funds which are separately budgeted for this purpose come to nearly 50 per
cent of the total cost to the donors of grant aid.   In a more general sense
the entire government development budget, which is now about 10 times the
total of all grant aid, may be considered as counterpart investment for
receiving foreign technical assistance.

Theoretically at least, there are two distinct kinds of technical assistance. What we may call direct assistance is intended to aid the government in carrying out specific tasks which have to be done. Secondly, indirect assistance is designed to improve the government's 'capability', or technical and administrative ability.

Direct assistance is required because the government lacks resources to carry out its present programmes effectively. It needs specialists in various fields and imported materials and equipment. Often these are most effectively supplied through grant aid programmes. The government could recruit and employ foreign specialists by using its own budget funds. This was a common practice 60 years ago and it still continues to some extent. But it is not easy to recruit foreign specialists on short-term contracts; problems over scales of remuneration, pension rights and professional qualifications make the direct employment of foreign specialists in substantial numbers quite impractical. Thus it is necessary to rely on grant aid programmes for the provision of foreign specialists and, some-times, for obtaining highly specialised technical equipment.

Indirect assistance is intended to build up the government's capacity to carry out future programmes. The most important form of this kind of aid is scholarships to enable Thai officials to study or train abroad. Again the Thai government could finance these scholarships itself, but the selection of courses and institutions and all the other necessary arrange-ments for a programme of study or training abroad are most easily made by a technical assistance donor country. A more suitable form of indirect assistance is on-the-job training and administrative development provided by foreign specialists working in Thailand. Still another form of in-direct assistance is the pressure exerted by technical assistance programmes for the creation of new institutions and for changes in government policy.

Most grant aid programmes combine elements of direct and indirect technical assistance. They are intended both to carry out specific admini-strative or development activities and to strengthen the government's long-run ability to carry out its programmes without further assistance.

(i)   Direct assistance

In Thailand the provision of direct technical assistance encounters

a number of difficulties which paradoxically result from the very sophistication of the apparatus of administration.   Any project requires both
technical and organisational services.   In principle foreign specialists
should supply technical skills while the Thai counterpart agency should
provide the necessary management and organisation.   Inevitably government
departments have all kinds of administrative deficiencies.   If foreign
specialists are restricted to a technical role they will experience frequent
frustrations because of organisational shortcomings.   But if the foreign
specialists themselves attempt to undertake an administrative role they
find themselves seriously hampered by their ignorance of the Thai administrative system.   There are three approaches to the resolution of this
dilemma: to restrict foreign specialists to a technical role and to
tolerate any organisational weaknesses which may arise;   to give foreign
staff a substantial administrative role within the framework of some
government agency;   or to set up an independent organisation largely
managed by the foreign staff.   Each of these alternative approaches
warrants further comment.

First, the approach which restricts foreign experts to a technical
role is commonly preferred by donor countries as there is a strong preference,
among aid donors, to give aid in the form of specific projects.   This
enables them to concentrate experts, scholarships and equipment into integrated programmes where the role of foreign assistance can be clearly
defined and performance can be more clearly assessed.   It also enables
the Thai government to provide more effective counterpart services by
concentrating suitable staff and facilities.   The difficulty is that
concentration of aid into projects usually means grouping foreign staff
into teams.   When foreign specialists find themselves operating as a group
they tend to develop an administrative role, and the consequences of any
organisation failures are magnified because they affect the whole group
rather than one or two individuals.   Consequently, the execution of
particular administrative or development tasks has been found to be most
effective if the foreign specialists are confined to a technical role.
In the case of joint projects, it should be understood that management is
entirely the responsibility of the government agencies and not of the
foreign staff who have to be prepared to tolerate organisational failures

and weaknesses.   At the same time, prior experience of the Thai administrative system and of the language will tremendously enhance the contribution that the foreign specialist can make towards the Thai organisation
concerned.

The second appraoch, to give foreign staff a substantial administrative role within some government agency, is the least satisfactory
solution of all.   Because of their relative lack of knowledge of the
Thai administrative system and of the Thai language, foreign staff are
likely to be led into repeated conflicts and misunderstandings.   In
principle the project manager and administrative staff should always be
Thai civil servants, with foreign staff confined to a technical role.

The last solution is only suitable for some short-run and well-
defined technical task.   In practice technical assistance is provided
by an independent self-contained organisation only on contracts, e.g. for
various technical design and feasibility studies, or very occasionally
for civil engineering construction work.   In most cases an independent
organisation is not satisfactory because of the need for administrative
coordination and because it does not lead to indirect improvement of the
government's administrative capabilities.

(ii)   Indirect assistance

The most controversial aspect of indirect assistance is the pressure
exerted by a programme to create new institutions, and to change government
policy or administrative methods.   This kind of change is potentially of
immense importance and thus often represents the principal objective of
the donors of technical assistance.   But it is here that the most direct
clashes of interest and opinion arise and in this field one must take a
realistic, rather than idealistic, view of aid programmes.

The amount of pressure for administrative reform exerted by different
foreign donors varies enormously.   The United States programme is by far
the most important in this respect both because of the amount of aid given
and because of the very large supporting staff based in Bangkok and in the
United States.   The United States programme is designed to achieve reform
and changes in government programmes with the primary purpose of thwarting

subversion and insurgency.   Many United Nations organisations also have
specific 'institution building' objectives designed to further the cause
of economic and social development.   Other bilateral aid programmes have
a host of explicit and implicit objectives to achieve administrative
reform, but they are of less consequence because the programmes are not
large enough to justify a substantial support organisation which could
develop this kind of pressure effectively.

Ideally, the formulation of projects should be undertaken by the
government's own executive agencies.   The Budget Bureau, the National
Economic Development Board and the Department of Technical and Economic
Co-operation (an agency whose principal role is to negotiate for, and
process, technical and economic assistance) are jointly responsible for
the selection and financing of government projects.   Even if the aid
donors have the same objectives as the government, they do not have a
sufficient knowledge of the Thai administrative system to formulate
effective measures for administrative change and reform.   The foreign
donor should contribute whatever technical assistance is available to
projects and programmes organised by the government.

(iii) Forms of assistance

Donors of aid often find it hard to decide the form in which technical assistance should be given, having to allocate funds between the
provision of experts or technicians under contract, overseas scholarships
for Thai officials, and the supply of materials and equipment.

Technical services should only be provided under contract for projects
which are suitable for execution by an independently organised group, i.e.
the design and feasibility studies discussed above.   It is not satisfactory
to use contractual services for other kinds of projects because a contract
team inevitably requires the administrative and managerial independence
which is so harmful to the successful implementation of a project within
the framework of a government agency.   Experts and technicians who are
hired on an individual basis must be given a clear technical role.   They
have to work under the direction and within the organisation provided by
the counterpart agency.   Thus in selecting experts and technicians

attention must be paid not only to their technical qualifications but
also to their ability to put up with the frustrations of working with an
unfamiliar and often imperfect administrative system.

A very large number of scholarships are offered to the government
each year through grant aid programmes.   It is often hard to find suitable candidates, partly for lack of officials with suitable prior qualifications and partly because too many personnel cannot be released from
their posts at any one time.   The need at present is to improve the quality
of the scholarship programme, firstly by shifting from fairly short, rather
general programmes of study to long-term high-level academic courses; and
secondly, by providing more intensive technical training.   Donor countries
should consider how to set up scholarship programmes which are specifically
suited to the needs of developing countries for high-level academic manpower,
and for specialist technical staff.

Materials and equipment may be incorporated into a grant aid programme
for two broad reasons.   Firstly the donor may wish to ensure that certain
essential supplies and equipment are available to the foreign experts and
technicians.   While the counterpart agency will always endeavour to provide these facilities, budgetary stringencies and delays may mean that they
cannot be provided immediately.   In this event the foreign donor has sometimes to provide supplies and equipment to the counterpart agency.   The use
of equipment given to a government agency must obviously be at the discre-
tion of the responsible officials.   Sometimes they will inevitably want to
use equipment for other top priority purposes;   it would be invidious not
to give them this freedom of action.

The second reason for using grant aid to supply materials and equipment is to encourage the government to carry out the particular programme
for which the aid is given.   To be realistic, this is usually one form of
the pressure discussed above which foreign aid often generates.   Thailand
does in fact need aid for imported materials and equipment because there
is a very large trade deficit only partly made up by a surplus on services.
Inflows of debt capital have maintained reserves but created a growing
external dependence.   The provision of imported equipment under grant aid
has been very useful in strengthening the foreign exchange position in the
past few years and will be increasingly required as the process of domestic

industrialisation continues to gather momentum.   This kind of aid is economically most significant because it makes a continued high rate of capital investment possible.

If donors of aid first consider what forms of assistance they are able to provide, the selection of suitable projects or fields for assistance is then much easier.   However, if specific projects or fields for assistance are chosen first, it often happens that unsuitable foreign experts and inappropriate scholarships are provided in an attempt to meet the requirements of a project for which the donor was not really in a position to offer technical assistance.

(iv) Fields of assistance

Ideally, after a donor has determined what forms of assistance can best be provided, the Thai Government can then suggest the projects or fields where the assistance can best be used.   However, donors of grant aid often like to select the projects and fields for assistance themselves; but these may conflict with the views and objectives of the recipient. While the Thai Government recognises the variety of motives that prompt aid giving, it feels that donors should follow the recommendations of NEDB, DTEC and the Budget Bureau.   This is because these agencies have the best information about development problems and policies, and are therefore best placed to judge where assistance can be best deployed.   The same agencies also perform a coordinating function which should not be by-passed. Nearly all Thai government offices feel that they are short of resources and would like to benefit from technical assistance programmes.   But they should not be encouraged to compete for the grant aid available, as this can easily result in the selection of unsound projects.   Nor are such departments necessarily in the best position to assess the priorities for the expenditure of counterpart funds and capital investment.

4. SUMMARY OF REQUIREMENTS FOR TECHNICAL ASSISTANCE

In conclusion, it may be useful to express, in summary form, the guidelines which my personal experience suggests are important for foreign assistance to Thailand.

(i)   Selection of projects and fields for assistance

Projects and fields for assistance should be chosen after consultation between the donor, DTEC, NEDB and the Budget Bureau, in the light of the specific objectives of the government's development programme and the donor's assistance programme.

(ii)   Formulation of projects

The donor and the counterpart agency should formulate projects with advice from DTEC, NEDB and the Budget Bureau.   They should take account of the remarks concerning execution of projects and use of different forms of assistance in the following paragraphs.

(iii) Execution of projects

With the exception of survey, feasibility and design contracts, responsibility for the administration and execution of a project should rest entirely with the counterpart government agency.   Foreign staff should be assigned to technical and not administrative roles, although they may have some reporting and administrative functions vis-à-vis the donor agency.   Foreign staff, returned trainees, equipment and supplies provided by a foreign donor for a project, should not be used for other purposes unless:-

    a) the project has terminated
    b) the donor agrees to the alternative uses, or
    c) in the judgement of the counterpart agency some sufficiently
        important emergency or new priority arises.

(iv)   Experts and technicians

Foreign staff should be assigned technical roles, taking nto consideration the ability of the donor to find specialists who will

    a) have adequate technical qualifications, and
    b) be able to operate under the administrative control of the
        counterpart government agency.

(v)   Contractual services

Technical services should only be hired under contract for the purpose of carrying out survey, feasibility and design studies.

(vi) Scholarships

Priority should be given to

a) specific technical training, and
b) long-term (two years or more) academic study.

(vii) Equipment and supplies

Donors should give serious attention to the provision of equipment
and supplies even if they have to be restricted to imports from the donor
country on a 'tied' basis.   Grant-financed equipment is valuable because

a) it can usually be readily procured in time to meet project
    requirements, and
b) it makes a contribution to the balance of payments which directly
    affects future prospects for the growth of the whole economy.

It is hoped that equipment and supplies could account for at least
60 per cent of the total cost of grant aid programmes.

Table 16.1: Total grant assistance to Thailand, 1951-1971
('000 US$)

Year	AID[a]	UN	Colombo Plan[b]	Other countries[c]	Volunteers	Total
1951 - 60	131,809	n.a.	4,142	718	n.a.	136,667
1961	7,168	1,871	2,265	460	4	11,768
1962	13,033	3,102	3,503	607	254	20,499
1963	16,255	1,925	3,734	684	947	23,545
1964	12,223	3,163	3,251	713	1,385	20,735
1965	18,711	3,114	2,968	1,425	1,374	27,592
1966	43,631	3,190	4,423	2,234	1,926	55,404
1967	54,964	3,885	5,676	3,923	1,814	70,262
1968	47,319	3,968	4,474	3,348	1,438	60,547
1969	37,871	3,118	3,932	3,279	1,876	50,076
1970	30,725	3,798	6,720	4,660	2,284	48,187
1971	23,000	3,504	6,000	3,381	2,424	38,309
Total	436,707	34,638	51,088	25,432	15,726	563,591

a Net obligations by fiscal year of AID (U.S. Agency of International Development) Project Assistance except 1969 and 1970. Figures quoted from Annual Financial Report Cumulative Data as of June 30, 1969. USCM/Thailand, November 1, 1969.

b 1954 - 60.

c 1959 - 60.

Table 16.2: Grant assistance by sector, source and type. Jan-Dec 1970
(US $)

Sector	AID[a]	United Nations	Colombo Plan	Other countries	Volunteers	Total	% Distribution
Agriculture & cooperatives	2,299,564	1,028,463	1,209,373	1,053,339	27,198	5,617,937	11.7
Industry & mining	569,100	549,517	92,230	231,170	-	1,442,017	3.0
Power	-	14,935	28,601	299,597	6,000	349,133	0.7
Communications	1,026,022	235,754	3,186,726	56,419	-	4,504,921	9.3
Health	3,496,390	641,445	345,464	167,088	532,541	5,182,928	10.8
Education	3,611,109	710,629	1,141,135	2,306,653	1,440,749	9,210,275	19.1
Community & social development	7,840,078	435,999	96,011	221,563	216,969	8,810,620	18.3
Administration	298,540	181,687	189,527	283,347	-	953,101	2.0
Public Safety	6,647,927	-	-	-	-	6,647,927	13.8
Unclassified	4,936,672	-	431,469	40,936	60,444	5,469,521	11.3
Total	30,725,402	3,798,429	6,720,536	4,660,112	2,283,901	48,188,380	100.0
%	63.8	7.9	13.9	9.7	4.7	100.0	

Type	%	%	%	%	%	%	
Experts	35	53	26	57	100	40	
Scholarships	11	16	23	32	-	15	
Equipment	54	31	51	11	-	45	
Total	100	100	100	100	100	100	

a U.S. obligation fiscal year 1970. The Thai fiscal year extends from 1 October to 30 September.

Table 16.3: U.S. programme assistance by sector and type, financial year 1970

(US $)

	Experts		Scholarships		Contract services		Equipment	Total	% Distri-bution
	No.	Value	No.	Value	No.	Value	Value	Value	
Agriculture	11	305,835	165	439,170	14	333,000	1,221,559	2,299,564	7.5
Industry	5	82,000	38	349,500	5	137,600	-	569,100	1.9
Power	-	-	-	-	-	-	-	-	-
Communications	12	489,000	18	78,000	-	-	459,022	1,026,022	3.3
Health	17	534,000	120	369,150	20	20,000	2,573,240	3,496,390	11.4
Education	9	205,000	134	1,154,000	11	650,000	1,602,109	3,611,109	11.7
Community & social development	50	1,360,000	197	492,550	11	421,000	5,566,528	7,840,078	25.5
Administration	5	93,800	44	134,430	5	-	70,310	298,540	1.0
Public Safety	89	1,377,000	192	185,308	26	457,360	4,628,259	6,647,927	21.6
Unclassified	132	4,164,886	24	280,000	5	52,400	439,386	4,936,672	16.1
Total	330	8,611,521	932	3,482,108	97	2,071,360	16,560,413	30,725,402	100.0

Table 16.4: U.N. assistance by sector, type and programme. Jan-Dec 1970
(US $)

| Sector | Experts | | | Scholarships | | | Equipment | Total | % Distri- |
	No.	M-mths[a]	Value	No.	M-mths[a]	Value	Value	Value	bution
Agriculture	41	445	847,725	18	186	96,930	83,808	1,028,463	27.1
Industry	23	178	339,090	16	55	38,827	171,600	549,517	14.4
Power	1	7	13,335	-	-	-	1,600	14,935	0.4
Communications	7	76	144,780	13	62	38,974	52,000	235,754	6.2
Health	7	63	120,015	33	166	102,630	418,800	641,445	16.9
Education	17	134	255,270	46	323	182,359	273,000	710,629	18.7
Community & social development	12	123	234,315	9	54	31,734	169,950	435,999	11.5
Administration	5	41	78,105	34	166	103,582	-	181,687	4.8
Unclassified	-	-	-	-	-	-	-	-	-
Total	113	1,067	2,032,635	169	1,012	595,036	1,170,758	3,798,429	100.0
Programme									
UNDP special fund	54	594	1,131,570	17	195	99,839	333,408	1,564,817	
UNDP/TA	31	257	489,585	21	163	89,919	15,350	594,854	
Regular programme	18	122	232,410	38	332	178,604	-	411,014	
Regional & inter-regional programme	10	94	179,070	93	322	226,674	-	405,744	
UNICEF	-	-	-	-	-	-	822,000	822,000	
Total	113	1,067	2,032,635	169	1,012	595,036	1,170,758	3,798,429	

a   Man-months.

Table 16.5: Special fund assistance by project, 1963-1975
(Plan figures, US $)

Name of project	Total value of assistance	1964	1965	1966	1967	1968	1969	1970	1971	1972	1973	1974	1975
							Value of assistance by year						
1. Civil Aviation Training Center	1,663,530	325,161	362,303	60,227	5,522	72,303	66,417	-	-	-	-	-	-
2. Bangkok Port siltation and Sriracha Port feasibility studies	1,014,404	-	220,987	-	-	-	-	-	-	-	-	-	-
3. Productivity center	708,126	158,199	144,074	114,874	59,786	923	-	-	-	-	-	-	-
4. Thon Buri Technical Institute	1,157,785	260,167	251,927	192,817	200,856	84,255	-	-	-	-	-	-	-
5. Research and Training Center for rice protection	733,967	54,950	98,137	161,330	136,325	117,400	90,700	35,384	-	-	-	-	-
6. Expansion of meteorological services	389,871	130,004	127,547	78,367	28,212	-	-	-	-	-	-	-	-
7. Paper and pulp material survey	557,300	175,400	214,300	145,330	12,900	-	-	-	-	-	-	-	-
8. Telecommunication training, test and development center	1,143,100	55,900	157,592	302,221	313,203	207,656	104,528	2,000	-	-	-	-	-
9. Technological Research Institute	924,900	26,800	126,600	226,200	163,400	129,300	192,600	60,000	-	-	-	-	-
10. Rubber development	936,000	12,920	92,243	146,548	183,314	226,200	218,950	55,825	-	-	-	-	-
11. Experimental and demonstration farm for irrigated agriculture	375,600	3,175	38,826	50,453	69,129	63,013	111,600	39,404	-	-	-	-	-
12. Mineral survey and mineral processing industries in the northeast	311,700	-	67,600	228,100	16,000	-	-	-	-	-	-	-	-
13. Small Industries Service Institute	949,700	-	-	46,615	139,008	252,546	239,231	204,100	68,200	-	-	-	-
14. Soil fertility research	941,352	-	-	76,282	130,200	204,700	204,900	202,484	122,786	-	-	-	-
15. Thon Buri technical teacher training	935,100	-	-	103,925	233,900	257,975	209,050	130,250	-	-	-	-	-
16. Soil survey and land classification	1,055,800	-	-	-	131,500	263,600	230,100	203,300	148,400	78,900	-	-	-
17. Management consultancy training	407,700	-	-	-	2,400	87,100	147,100	152,100	19,000	-	-	-	-
18. Strengthening plant protection services	974,800	-	-	-	-	-	32,400	249,500	347,000	199,500	75,300	60,700	10,400
19. National service for technical skill promotion and job-entry training for industry	1,034,800	-	-	-	-	4,500	137,600	420,300	290,400	131,900	50,100	-	-
Total	16,215,535	1,202,676	1,902,136	1,933,289	1,825,655	1,971,471	1,985,176	1,754,647	995,786	410,300	125,400	60,700	10,400

Note: The data in this table cover only projects begun in 1969 or earlier years: they do not show planned expenditure for new projects beginning in 1970 or later years.

Table 16.6: Colombo Plan assistance by country and type, 1967-1971
(US $)

Country	Experts			Fellowships			Equipment	Total
	No.	M-mths[a]	Value	No.	M-mths[a]	Value	Value	Value
Australia	124	1,533	1,696,120	409	9,677	2,529,701	6,691,585	11,190,406
Japan	449	2,472	3,200,652	594	3,532	945,081	3,754,886	7,900,619
New Zealand	196	1,478	1,950,467	156	2,949	820,445	1,104,617	3,875,529
United Kingdom	240	1,503	1,978,277	311	4,564	1,366,236	388,565	3,733,078
Canada	50	355	432,013	258	4,587	1,505,178	16,363	1,953,554
India	-	-	-	159	1,784	289,398	400	289,798
Malaysia	-	-	-	88	120	31,564	-	31,564
Philippines	-	-	-	3	72	11,150	-	11,150
Korea	-	-	-	1	24	5,143	-	5,143
Singapore	-	-	-	4	12	2,202	-	2,202
Total	1,149	7,341	9,530,529	1,983	27,321	7,506,098	11,956,416	28,993,043

a   Man-months.

Table 16.7: Colombo Plan assistance by project and type, Jan-Dec 1970
(US $)

Project	Government agency	Experts			Scholarships			Equipment	Total
		No.	M-mths	Value	No.	M-mths	Value	Value	Value
Australia									
1. Tak – Mae Sot highway	Highways D.	7	76	108,604	-	-	-	41,552	150,156
2. The Agricultural Research Centre of the Chao Phraya Basin at Chainat	Ministry of Communication	-	-	-	-	-	-	5,708	5,708
3. Thai-Australian land development	Land Development D.	5	34	48,586	-	-	-	240,784	289,370
4. Lom Sak-Chum Phae highway	Highways D.	18	54	77,166	-	-	-	1,776,003	1,853,169
Non-project	-	4	42	60,018	92	1,642	460,900	6,612	527,530
Total		34	206	294,374	92	1,642	460,900	2,070,659	2,825,933
Canada									
1. Comprehensive schools	Secondary Education D.	3	36	51,444	-	-	-	-	51,444
2. Khon Kaen University	Khon Kaen University	2	18	25,722	-	-	-	-	25,722
Non-project	-	1	5	7,145	63	1,151	375,935	3,146	386,226
Total		6	59	84,311	63	1,151	375,935	3,146	463,392
New Zealand									
1. Thai-New Zealand road project at Maha Sarakham	Highways D.	32	278	397,262	-	-	-	598,149	995,411
2. Pasture Demonstration Farm at Borabu	Land Development D.	2	19	27,151	-	-	-	5,521	32,672
3. Forest and Forest Industrial Training School	Royal Forestry D.	1	12	17,148	-	-	-	-	17,148
4. Civil aviation and agricultural aviation	Aviation D.	-	-	-	-	-	-	50,615	50,615
Non-project	-	4	33	47,157	31	638	178,411	6,029	231,597
Total		39	342	488,718	31	638	178,411	660,314	1,327,443
Malaysia – Non-project	-	-	-	-	32	36	10,492	-	10,492
India – Non-project	-	-	-	-	22	157	32,923	-	32,923
Philippines – Non-project	-	-	-	-	2	48	7,436	-	7,436
Total					56	241	50,851	-	50,851

Table 16.7 (cont'd)

Project	Government agency	Experts No.	Experts M-mths	Experts Value	Scholarships No.	Scholarships M-mths	Scholarships Value	Equipment Value	Total Value
United Kingdom									
1. Yom Basin study	Royal Irrigation D.	18	70	100,030	-	-	-	612	100,642
2. Deep sea port at Phuket	Ministry of Communication	2	2	2,858	-	-	-	-	2,858
3. Takfa cotton farm development	Agriculture D.	7	61	87,169	-	-	-	18,626	105,795
4. Permanent Language Centre	National Education Council	1	1	1,429	-	-	-	-	1,429
5. Chiang Mai University	Chiang Mai University	1	5	7,145	-	-	-	6,098	13,243
Non-project	-	20	117	167,193	74	1,232	363,664	28,507	559,364
Total		49	256	365,824	74	1,232	363,664	53,843	783,331
Japan									
1. Development of primary products for export	Agriculture D.	5	30	42,870	-	-	-	133,736	176,606
2. Sericultural Development Center	Agriculture D.	5	9	12,861	-	-	-	216,979	229,840
3. Rice development	Rice D.	1	10	14,290	-	-	-	5,395	19,685
4. National Cancer Institute	Medical Services D.	18	40	57,160	-	-	-	119,843	177,003
5. Virus disease control	Medical Science D.	2	3	4,287	-	-	-	35,118	39,405
6. Opnthalmology	Mahidol University	1	6	8,574	-	-	-	-	8,574
7. Experimental pathology	Mahidol University	1	2	2,858	-	-	-	-	2,858
8. Road construction and training center at Surat Thani	Highways D.	7	7	10,003	-	-	-	685	10,688
9. Nonthaburi Telecommunication Institute	Vocational Education D.	8	59	84,311	-	-	-	40,120	124,431
10. Provincial water supply	Public & Municipal Works D.	8	48	68,592	-	-	-	-	68,592
11. Ports of southern part of Thailand	Harbour D.	2	16	-	-	-	-	652	652
12. Marine shrimp culture development	Fisheries D.	-	-	-	-	-	-	257	257
Non-project	-	24	125	201,489	127	512	154,176	55,330	410,995
Total		81	355	507,295	127	512	154,176	608,115	1,269,586
Grand Total		209	1,218	1,740,522	443	5,416	1,583,937	3,396,077	6,720,536

Table 16.8: Other government and non-government assistance by source, 1959-1970
(US $000)

	1959-60	1961	1962	1963	1964	1965	1966	1967	1968	1969	1970	Total
France	50.3	50.8	74.9	95.6	87.1	118.1	176.0	472.4	363.3	358.5	568.2	2,415.2
Germany	626.8	267.8	295.1	314.2	314.3	814.2	904.7	1,313.6	1,011.9	1,094.2	1,669.9	8,626.7
Netherlands	13.1	9.7	18.6	25.5	20.6	31.9	79.5	136.5	164.8	251.2	240.0	991.4
Italy	14.4	-	16.4	4.9	-	-	-	2.6	16.3	2.5	10.2	67.3
Belgium	8.1	17.9	8.1	5.4	1.8	18.1	5.8	2.4	5.6	4.0	2.9	80.1
Austria	-	-	36.0	1.0	-	15.4	65.5	25.0	42.7	55.5	83.8	324.9
Denmark	3.7	97.8	106.1	102.6	113.5	167.1	133.9	198.1	85.8	194.8	326.0	1,529.4
Sweden	0.2	2.5	5.6	35.0	44.4	105.3	14.7	33.4	7.8	26.5	5.2	280.6
Israel	1.0	11.0	33.4	18.3	29.7	12.4	49.5	84.8	62.1	100.9	86.0	489.1
Swiss	-	2.6	13.1	57.5	57.9	102.6	8.8	16.8	32.2	-	3.8	295.3
United Arab Republic	-	-	-	23.7	36.8	36.5	2.3	-	-	-	-	99.3
Norway	-	-	-	-	7.4	3.2	14.6	37.5	26.3	21.3	51.9	162.2
The Republic of China	-	-	-	-	-	-	22.0	8.7	5.8	207.1	200.5	444.1
Finland	-	-	-	-	-	-	10.3	-	-	-	-	10.3
Korea	-	-	-	-	-	-	-	2.8	-	-	-	2.8
Greece	-	-	-	-	-	-	-	-	-	4.0	6.7	10.7
Foundations, Universities, etc.	n.a.	n.a.	n.a.	n.a.	n.a.	n.a.	746.5	1,588.0	1,523.2	958.9	1,405.0	6,221.6
Total	717.6	460.1	607.3	683.7	713.5	1,424.8	2,234.1	3,922.6	3,347.8	3,279.4	4,660.1	22,051.0

Table 16.9: Other countries and non-government assistance by project and type, Jan-Dec 1970
(US $)

Project	Government agency	Experts			Scholarships			Equipment	Total
		No.	M-mths	Value	No.	M-mths	Value	Value	Value
Germany									
1. Marine Fisheries Laboratory	Fisheries D.	2	24	34,296	4	12	6,664	11,977	52,937
2. Animal husbandry	Livestock D.	7	62	88,598	2	32	9,520	25,184	123,302
3. Geological and mineral survey	Mineral Resources D.	11	110	157,190	1	18	5,236	6,603	169,029
4. Yanhee area, 2nd stage	Provincial Electricity Authority	6	36	51,444	6	126	35,700	-	87,144
5. Public health research	Medical Science D.	5	46	65,734	11	159	47,362	9,635	122,731
6. Thai-German Technical Institute at Khon Khen	Vocational Education D.	7	58	82,882	9	220	58,072	5,411	146,365
7. Thai-German Technical Institute at Bang Saen	Vocational Education D.	3	36	51,444	4	96	26,656	53,193	131,293
8. Protein food from algae	Kasetsart University	1	3	4,287	2	8	3,808	-	8,095
9. Sara Buri self-help land settlement	Public Welfare D.	5	52	74,308	2	32	9,520	35,865	119,693
10. Cadastral survey	Land D.	2	24	34,296	1	18	5,236	4,040	43,572
11. Vehicle testing	Police D.	1	9	12,861	-	-	-	18,287	31,148
12. Wood Research Institute	Forestry D.	2	11	15,719	-	-	-	4,632	20,351
13. Training centre for agricultural training	Vocational Education D.	4	47	67,163	-	-	-	137,141	204,304
14. Thai-German Teachers Training College	Vocational Education D.	2	48	68,592	-	-	-	-	68,592
15. Mae-Kok hydro-power	National Energy Authority	7	35	50,015	-	-	-	80,602	130,617
16. The erection of dolphins at the Port of Bangkok	Port Authority	2	11	15,719	-	-	-	-	15,719
Non-project		10	86	122,894	25	211	72,114	-	195,008
Total		77	698	997,442	67	932	279,888	392,570	1,669,900
France									
1. Electricians training center	National Energy Authority	-	-	-	1	7	2,618	170	2,788
Non-project		26	202	288,658	76	1,003	276,794	-	565,452
Total		26	202	288,658	77	1,010	279,412	170	568,240
Netherlands									
1. Land Consolidation	Irrigation D.	7	28	40,012	4	14	7,140	-	47,152
2. Laem Krabang port	Port Authority	2	2	2,858	3	9	4,998	-	7,856
Non-project		3	17	24,293	56	471	160,650	-	184,943
Total		12	47	67,163	63	494	172,788	-	239,951

Table 16.9 (cont'd)

Project	Government agency	Experts			Scholarships			Equipment	Total
		No.	M-mths	Value	No.	M-mths	Value	Value	Value
Austria									
1. The establishment of Cholburi Technical Institute	Vocational Education D.	7	43	61,447	-	-	-	-	61,447
Non-project		-	-	-	7	66	22,372	-	22,372
Total		7	43	61,447	7	66	22,372	-	83,819
Israel									
1. Thai-Israel rural area development	Office of the Under Secretary of State Ministry of National Development	5	25	35,725	-	-	-	-	35,725
Non-project		11	19	27,151	13	45	23,086	-	50,237
Total		16	44	62,876	13	45	23,086	-	85,962
Denmark									
1. Dairy farm	Livestock D.	3	36	51,444	3	29	8,806	40,158	100,408
2. Teak improvement	Forestry D.	2	24	34,296	1	24	6,664	4,980	45,940
3. Marine Biological Centre	Fisheries D.	3	32	45,728	2	24	7,616	59,370	112,714
3. Technical cooperation silviculture and genetics of conifers	Forestry D.	2	24	34,296	-	-	-	4,577	38,873
Non-project		-	-	-	9	86	28,084	-	28,084
Total		10	116	165,764	15	163	51,170	109,085	326,019
The Republic of China									
1. Multi-purpose cooperation	Office of the Under Secretary of State Ministry of National Development	20	102	145,758	-	-	-	1,458	147,216
Non-project		3	10	14,290	22	76	39,032	-	53,322
Total		23	112	160,048	22	76	39,032	1,458	200,538

Table 16.9 (cont'd)

Project		Experts		Scholarships		Equipment	Total
	No.	M-mths	Value	No.	M-mths	Value	Value	Value
Sweden	Non-project	–	–	–	2	18	5,236	–	5,236
Norway	Non-project	–	–	–	15	158	51,884	–	51,884
Swiss	Non-project	–	–	–	6	8	3,808	–	3,808
Italy	Non-project	–	–	–	4	27	10,234	–	10,234
Greece	Non-project	–	–	–	1	24	6,664	–	6,664
Belgium	Non-pooject	–	–	–	1	12	2,856	–	2,856
Foundations & Universities etc. Non – project	69	615	878,835	125	1,310	526,166	–	1,405,001
Grand Total	240	1,877	2,682,233	418	4,343	1,474,596	503,283	4,660,112

Table 16.10: Volunteer service by sector and source, 1967-1971
(Value in US $)

Sector	PCV			GVS			CUSO			VSO			VSA			Total		
	No.	M-mths	Value	No.	M-mths	Value	No.	M-mths	Value	No.	M-mths	Value	No.	M-mths	Value	No.	M-mths	Value
Agriculture	20	68	34,296	3	15	10,622	2	8	1,700	1	25	2,450	2	50	7,382	29	177	56,450
Industry	1	3	1,313	-	-	-	-	-	-	-	-	-	-	-	-	1	3	1,313
Power	1	12	5,000	1	6	2,000	9	58	13,310	1	3	308	-	-	-	12	79	20,618
Health	460	4,890	2,196,988	38	403	210,311	20	102	17,975	21	202	25,548	1	6	720	490	5,603	2,451,542
Education	954	8,371	3,873,066	140	1,526	757,036	163	1,477	295,450	136	913	99,889	21	229	27,594	1,414	12,516	5,053,035
Community & Social Development	134	1,163	539,039	16	187	94,206	-	-	-	13	49	4,919	41	464	54,795	204	1,863	692,959
Administration	7	87	36,560	-	-	-	-	-	-	-	-	-	-	-	-	7	87	36,560
Unclassified	56	477	215,543	6	55	26,997	11	100	21,153	1	8	824	8	93	11,627	82	706	276,144
Total	1,633	15,071	6,901,805	204	2,192	1,101,172	205	1,745	349,588	173	1,200	133,938	73	842	102,118	2,239	21,034	8,588,621

PCV : Peace Corps Volunteer
GVS : German Volunteer Service
CUSO : Canadian University Service Overseas
VSO : Volunteer Service Overseas (U.K.)
VSA : Volunteer Service Agency (New Zealand)

Table 16.11: Foreign development loans to Thailand, 1970
(US $)

Activity	Source	Amount	Duration	Grace period	Interest rate
1. Industrial finance loan to Industrial Finance Corporation of Thailand (IFCT)	ADB	10,000,000	12 years	2 years	a
2. Sirikit power project	IBRD	46,500,000	20 "	5 "	7.0 per cent
3. Port project	IBRD	12,500,000	20 "	4 "	7.0 "
4. GAS turbine	Germany	1,404,371	10 "	2 "	6.0 "
5. Nam-Phrom-Hydroelectric	Japan	8,709,422	20 "	5 "	4.5 "
6. Lam Dom Nai distribution	Japan	2,284,153	20 "	5 "	4.5 "

a   Each part of the loan will bear interest rate at the ADB rate current at the time funds are committed for an approved project.

CHAPTER 17

AUSTRALIAN AID TO THAILAND

External Aid Branch
Department of Foreign Affairs*

1.   INTRODUCTION

Australian aid to Thailand began under the Colombo Plan in 1955 following
the acceptance in Ottawa in 1954 of Thailand as a full member of the Plan.
Australia has been accepting Thai trainees since 1952, but it was in 1955
that the sustained capital and technical assistance programme began.
Also in that year, the Australian Mission in Bangkok, then 10 years old,
was raised to the status of an Embassy.   In the 1955-6 financial year
Australia provided Thailand with medical equipment worth $A23,400, lignite
mining machinery worth $A120,000 and two experts to advise in the fields
of health and transportation.   The following year, Australia gave aid to
Thailand for the first time under the new SEATO Economic Aid Programme.

Australia has continued to give aid under these two programmes.
About 75 per cent has been financed under the Colombo Plan item of the
Department of Foreign Affairs vote, and 25 per cent under the SEATO economic aid item.   Although the Thai government continues to differentiate
between the two types of aid for political and administrative reasons, the
distinction for Australia between the two programmes has over the course
of time become somewhat blurred, and many types of projects may be financed
out of both items.

Since the inception of its aid programmes Australia has followed
policies of giving priority to bilateral over multilateral aid, and of
geographical concentration of aid in the Pacific and Southeast Asia.   Two-
thirds of Australia's aid goes to Papua New Guinea, but within the remainder of the bilateral programme Thailand receives high priority.   For the
past six years Australian aid to Thailand has averaged about $A3,000,000

* This paper was presented at the seminar by Mr R.G. Spratt, Assistant
Secretary, External Aid Branch, Department of Foreign Affairs, Canberra.

annually.   This is between seven and nine per cent of Australia's
bilateral aid to Asia.   In 1971/2 Thailand (7.0 per cent) was the third
largest recipient of Australian aid, after Indonesia (40 per cent) and
Bangladesh (13.3 per cent).   Table 17.1 shows the trend in Australia's
aid to Thailand;   Table 17.2 gives the size of Australia's aid to Thailand relative to other major recipients in Asia.   Up to 30 June 1972,
Australian bilateral aid to Thailand has amounted to over $A31,000,000.

Table 17.1:   Australian bilateral aid to Thailand
to 30 June 1972

Year	$A'000
Total to 30 June 1961	3,239.9
1961–62	1,356.6
1962–63	1,784.1
1963–64	1,884.5
1964–65	1,848.5
1965–66	3,195.8
1966–67	2,363.7
1967–68	2,912.6
1968–69	2,506.4
1969–70	3,322.1
1970–71	3,736.0
1971–72	3,129.1
Total to 30 June 1972	31,279.3

Table 17.2:   Australian bilateral aid to Asia

Country	Cumulative Total to 30/6/72	Aid in 1971/2	% of aid to Asia in 1971/2
Indonesia	81,242.7	17,824.0	39.9
Bangladesh	5,948.8	5,948.8	13.3
Thailand	31,279.3	3,129.1	7.0
Vietnam	24,427.4	3,016.7	6.8
Malaysia	29,242.2	2,913.8	6.5
India	82,578.9	2,901.2	6.5
Khmer Republic	8,064.9	1,759.6	3.9
Pakistan	40,811.0	1,404.2	3.1
Laos	9,787.3	1,227.5	2.8
Sri Lanka (Ceylon)	16,790.1	1,153.8	2.6
Burma	11,362.2	905.6	2.0
Other	26,525.5	2,518.6	5.6
Total	368,060.3	44,702.9	100.0

Thailand's relative importance as a recipient of Australian aid stems partly from the fact that it is one of the larger (population: 35,000,000) and less economically developed (GNP per capita: $A149) of Australia's Southeast Asian neighbours; partly from the close political association of the two governments in SEATO; and largely from the energy and efficiency with which Thai officials have sought and utilised aid from Australia.

2. COMPOSITION OF AUSTRALIA'S AID PROGRAMME

The main aims of assistance given by Australia fall into three categories: to increase Thailand's supply of skilled manpower; to develop the country's communications facilities; and to help raise economic, social and health standards in rural areas.   The bulk of aid under the Colombo Plan has been directed towards improving transport, communications, agriculture and irrigation, the mining industry, health and education.   Unlike SEATO aid, Colombo Plan aid has been of substantially the same type since its inception.   There has been no marked shift in emphasis of the projects, although the successful completion of our first joint roads project in 1966 led to further similar requests and ultimately to two more road and highway projects in succeeding years.   In brief, aid under the Plan has included several major projects in road construction, land development and irrigated agriculture; the provision of experts and the supply of a wide variety of equipment for mining, health, irrigation, agriculture, engineering, communications and education; and the training of several hundred Thai students in Australia.

The SEATO Economic Aid Programme has undergone considerable change in the 15 years of its operation.   It was begun originally as an earnest of Australia's wish to give fuller effect to Article III of the Manila Treaty regarding the promotion of economic progress and social well-being among member countries.   The first appropriations were $A4,000,000 in February 1956 and a further $A2,000,000 in February 1958, to support the defence efforts of the Asian SEATO countries - Pakistan, the Philippines, Thailand and South Vietnam.   In 1962 a further $A3,000,000 was appropriated for a three-year programme, and in 1967 Australia's aid under SEATO became a continuing annual commitment.

In the beginning about 39 per cent of this aid went to Pakistan
with the rest divided evenly between Thailand and the Philippines.
Vietnam received minor amounts before 1962, but since then the emphasis
has shifted strongly to Vietnam, also to Thailand and more recently the
Philippines.   SEATO economic aid up to 1965 continued to be related to
counter-insurgency activities and some of the projects in Thailand reflect this emphasis;   an example is the Armed Forces Vehicle Rebuild Workshop near Bangkok.

Since 1965, SEATO aid has not been confined to projects of this
character, although some of the civil aid projects undertaken could nevertheless be said to have some strategic importance.   These have included
the installation of two radio transmitters in the northeast and the Motor
Mechanics Training Centre in Bangkok (an adjunct to the Military Technical
Training School).   Jointly with other members of SEATO, Australia has
contributed staff and equipment to the Asian Institute of Technology in
Bangkok (formerly the Graduate School of Engineering) and to the Hill
Tribes Research Centre at Chiang Mai.   Thai students have been sponsored
to Australia under the SEATO programme.

(i)   Projects, experts and equipment

Between 1962 and 1966 Australia completed, in cooperation with Thai
staff, a project for the creation of a road construction centre at Khon
Kaen in northeast Thailand.   It involved the construction in the area of
169 kilometres of all-weather roads, 53 kilometres of access roads and
the design and surveying of a further 130 kilometres.   The major aim of
the project was to train Thai personnel in all aspects of road design,
construction and maintenance, and in the proper use, maintenance and
repair of equipment.   The construction of the roads was a sizable contribution to the region's feeder road system.

The total Australian contribution amounted to $A3,600,000, while
the Thai government financed local costs totalling $A2,600,000.   Australia
supplied equipment including tractors, scrapers, rollers and other
machinery.   Thirty-nine Australian staff including engineers, supervisors, instructors, geologists and accountants participated in the project over the course of four years.   The Thai Highways Department

provided buildings, local materials, fuel, staff (including the Project
Manager) and labour.   The agent from the Australian side was the Snowy
Mountains Hydro-Electric Authority, which since the virtual completion
of the Snowy Mountains Scheme has provided the expertise and organisation
for a number of overseas aid projects.[1]

In the course of implementing the project 40 Thai engineers, 160
operators, 80 mechanics and 30 supervisors received on-site training.
In addition a number of engineers, mechanics and operators received additional training in Australia;   the engineers for up to a year, and the
mechanics and operators for up to six months.   Courses at the Khon Kaen
Centre were provided during the wet season when construction work was
hampered.   The average cost per kilometre of road construction was about
$A15,000, excluding bridges and sealing.   Including bridges and sealing,
it was about $A23,000 per kilometre.

One particular achievement of the training programme was the success
of a deliberate policy of employing unskilled men, often with only rudi-
mentary education, and turning them into trained operators and mechanics.
On the other hand, the success of the project in opening up agricultural
land is considered by some to have been only moderate because of the lack
of a thorough pre-investment investigation.   The area was primarily a
subsistence area and thus not in immediate need of market outlets.   The

---

1   The Snowy Mountains Hydro Electric Authority has made a significant
contribution to Australia's aid programmes.   In Australia the Authority
used its own resources to develop the road network necessary for its
programme, in contrast to the use of contracts for the major construction
works of dams, tunnels, pipelines and power stations.   When the road
system in the Snowy Mountains was approaching completion arrangements
were made with the Authority to use its expertise and personnel on road
projects, commencing in Thailand.   Later the Authority contributed to
Australia's aid programme in other ways, such as the feasibility study,
design and supervision of construction of the Prek Thnot dam in the Khmer
Republic.

Because of the high international reputation of the Authority, together
with the continuing demand for its specialised services in Australia and
overseas, legislation was passed by the Australian Parliament establishing the Snowy Mountains Engineering Corporation when the hydro-electric
scheme was completed.   This enables the continued use of the expertise
developed by the Authority.

effectiveness of the feeder roads in bringing the rural people into contact with the rest of the community, and perhaps as a counter-insurgency measure, may in this case have been greater than its economic impact. The trained Thai staff are now continuing with the construction of further roads.

Against the background of results and close cooperation experienced in the Khon Kaen project, the Australian government was asked to assist in establishing another centre at Tak in northern Thailand for the construction of the Tak-Mae Sot Highway.   Construction commenced in 1966 and the road was opened by the Prime Minister of Thailand in December 1970 - nine months ahead of schedule.   The cost of the 87.5 kilometres of road which crosses the main part of the north-south mountain range was approximately $A16,000,000;   Thailand contributed approximately two-thirds and Australia one-third.

Specifically, the Thai contribution covered the equipment and head-quarters centre at Tak (on the main north-south highway between Chiang Mai and Bangkok) including office, workshop, laboratory and housing for both Thais and Australians;   sub-depots along the route as required, including the hills camp 30 kilometres up the road from Tak;   staff and personnel; plant and vehicles;   bridges and culverts;   construction and general materials including fuels and lubricants;   and some of the spare parts for plant and vehicles.   The Australian contribution embraced engineers and technical advisers;   equipment for road construction;   workshop tools for repair and servicing work;   laboratory equipment for quality control of roadworks;   supplies of spare parts for plant and vehicles;   training aids;   and sedan cars.

The Thai authority was again the Highways Department, an efficient and reliable organisation.   The Australians were again from the Snowy Mountains Authority, with long experience of road construction in difficult mountainous terrain such as that between Tak and Mae Sot on the Burmese border.   The project centre at Tak became, on completion of the project, the headquarters of a new field division of the Highways Department, and the equipment supplied by Australia remained at the centre or was transferred to other works of the Department.

This stretch of highway replaced the existing low standard track, which was in effect single-lane and, during the wet season, virtually impassable even to four-wheel drive vehicles.   It helped to reduce the isolation of the people of the Mae Muey valley (Mae Sot) and will provide access to better education and medical care, as well as increasing markets for the area's produce.

Evidence of the continued use of staff and equipment is seen in the commencement of the Lom Sak-Chum Phae Highway in 1970, as the Tak-Mae Sot road was nearing completion.   The road from Lom Sak to Chum Phae is intended to close the last gap in the east-west trans-Thailand highway from Mae Sot to Ubon, and like the Tak-Mae Sot road, it will be part of the planned Asian Highway.   Construction of this 105 kilometres of highway is expected to be completed by 1974.   Total cost is estimated to be approximately $A20,000,000, of which Australia will contribute one-third.   At July 1972, Australia had spent $A3,500,000.   This project was the first road construction to be based upon thorough pre-investment studies; a technical feasibility report was made by the Snowy Mountains Authority and an economic analysis by the Australian Department of National Development.   The same team of Snowy Mountains Authority engineers has moved to this project and is expected to number about 30 men at the peak construction period.

As with the other two roads, the Thai authority involved is the Highways Department and many of the contributions and responsibilities of the two governments will be the same.   For the first time, the responsibilities have been expressed in a formal agreement.

A further road project was commenced in 1971 in Prachuap Khiri Khan in south Thailand.   As part of a multi-purpose venture by the Thai Office of Accelerated Rural Development, Australia is to assist in the construction of a number of feeder and access roads to link villages with main outlet roads.   Australia's commitment is four expert staff - project manager, a civil supervisor, mechanical supervisor and a technician - and essential heavy construction equipment and spares, to the value of about $A1,300,000 over four years.   The newly formed Snowy Mountains Engineering Corporation is acting as the Australian government's agent for the project, which is based on a feasibility study published by the Snowy Mountains Hydro Electric Authority in February 1970.

Other major recent and current projects are in two fields which could be broadly described as agriculture and technical education.   In agriculture, work is being undertaken firstly on land development in Nan province of northern Thailand, and secondly on crops and cultivation techniques at Chai Nat in the Central Plain.   The Nan project, with which Australia has been associated since 1965, is financed under the Colombo Plan, and is being undertaken in conjunction with the Thai Department of Land Development.   It will involve a $A700,000 contribution by Australia.   An innovation in this case has been the arrangement for the University of New England to carry out the Australian side of the project (which involves on the one hand land survey, classification, clearing, redistribution and tenure, and on the other, the examination of possible crops and cultivation techniques to displace or supplement shifting cultivation on unirrigated river terraces).

At Chai Nat, Australian soil scientists and agronomists are helping to train Thai research and extension staff in determining the suitability of various crops for growing under irrigation in the Central Plain. Attention is being concentrated on training Thai staff both in Thailand and in Australia; 10 Thai scientists are presently (1972) doing postgraduate studies at various Australian universities.

In all, up to 30 June 1972, over 200 Australian experts had served in Thailand under the Colombo Plan; of these 44 were then in the country, serving in a variety of fields.

(ii) Training

The training courses undertaken reflect the priorities of the recipient government.   Australia each year offers Thailand a 'quota' of scholarships.   The Thai authorities decide how to allocate these as between graduate, undergraduate and non-university training.   A competitive examination is held for the Australian awards but students are told by the Thai government in which fields of training they can be obtained.   (In addition to the quota, there are a fairly large number of 'over-quota' awards offered annually for particular ad hoc courses of various types.   Additionally, if one country does not use up all its quota awards, they may be transferred to another country later in the year.   Eighty new awards were made to Thailand in the financial year 1971/2 (Table 17.3).)

Table 17.3: Aid to Thailand - training

Field of training	Cumulative no. of students up to 30/6/72	Students in Australia at 30/6/72	New awards made in financial year 1971/2
Engineering (acad.)	126	60	4
Education (ad hoc)	139	26	24
Science (acad.)	88	33	6
Medicine and health	80	10	3
Education (acad.)	75	14	3
Economics	68	14	2
Nursing	55	2	Nil
Agriculture	72	12	15
Engineering (ad hoc)	46	Nil	3
Public administration gen.	43	2	5
Police and legal	27	2	2
Science (ad hoc)	30	2	Nil
Social studies	24	9	1
Industry	7	Nil	Nil
Public administration spec.	23	4	4
Arts	17	10	Nil
Transport	19	Nil	Nil
Mining	22	1	2
Journalism	14	Nil	Nil
Trade	19	2	3
Dentistry	9	Nil	Nil
Livestock	8	2	1
Surveying	7	Nil	Nil
Aviation	5	Nil	Nil
Food technology	5	Nil	Nil
Communications	4	Nil	Nil
Libraries	6	2	2
Veterinary science	3	Nil	Nil
Architecture	3	2	Nil
Accountancy	3	Nil	Nil
Forestry	2	Nil	Nil
Banking and insurance	1	Nil	Nil
Meteorology	2	1	Nil
Textiles	1	Nil	Nil
34 fields of training	1,053	210	80

The primary emphasis in Thai training in Australia has been on undergraduate education. This partly reflects belief of the Thai authorities
that Thai universities do not yet produce sufficient numbers of graduates
for the country's needs, and partly the fact that most other aid donors
do not provide awards for undergraduates.   Thailand is currently planning

a system of regional universities and it is hoped that graduates of Australian universities will be part of a pool of graduates from which staff
can be recruited.   Other countries, such as Korea, which for some time
concentrated on undergraduate education, eventually moved to post-graduate
courses and it is expected that Thailand will follow this trend as their
regional university system is established.

Recently, Thailand has been sending a higher proportion of its
students on courses other than formal academic ones.   This has not been
due to any change in Thai priorities but rather to a change in the Australian training programme.   Over the past four to five years a series of
International Training Courses has been specially developed for overseas
students by the International Training Section of the Department of Foreign
Affairs, in collaboration with other public and private institutions.
These courses usually last about three months and are normally for government officials or private businessmen from the particular field, whether
it is export development or bridge engineering.   The courses are usually
fairly practical in nature and permit students to see Australian methods
in use; not so that they can be introduced elsewhere, but to see how they
can be adapted to the conditions of the countries from which the students
come.   Twenty-four such courses were held in 1971-72.   Awards for such
courses are often not counted against a country's 'quota' and are thus
additional to normal awards.   An increasing number of Thai students have
participated in such courses as road and bridge design, trade promotion,
agricultural marketing, photogrammetry and prison administration.   However, Thailand has not always been able to take up as many of these awards
as it wished, due to some nominees being found to require a larger amount
of preliminary English tuition than time allowed.

Language is of course a problem in all the training assistance given
to Thailand, but measures have been taken to overcome it.   Thai undergraduate scholars usually come to Australia several months before their
university courses begin, for English language training and familiarisa-
tion in Australian study practices and methods.   To assist in the development of English language programmes in Thailand, special over-quota awards
are offered annually for intensive English courses at the English Teaching
Centre, North Sydney (ETC), for Special English Language Fellowship (SELF)

Courses at a number of private institutions, and for the Diploma course
in the Teaching of English as a Foreign Language (TEFL) at the University
of Sydney.   In 1971-72 six ETC, 16 SELF and five TEFL awards were granted.
As far as private students are concerned they had, until recently, to
pass an English language test before they were permitted entry into
Australia as students, but a new policy has been adopted permitting the
entry of Thai (and also Indonesian and Japanese) students to undertake
nine months English-language training.

        Another relatively new field of training is termed 'project train-
ing'.   Under this award scheme, Thai counterpart personnel on Australian
aid projects in Thailand are selected by Australian experts and the Thai
government for study in their particular field in Australia.   This is in
line with the general aim of Thai-Australian cooperation on projects,
which is that on completion of a project there should be sufficient trained
Thai personnel available to maintain projects and to undertake new ones.

        Officially sponsored Thai students also come to Australia for train-
ing under the SEATO Civilian Aid Programme, various United Nations agency
fellowships (such as WHO, FAO, ILO, Unesco etc.), and World Intellectual
Property Organisation fellowships.   They would also be eligible to come
to Australia under the ASPAC Fellowship Exchange Programme, if they so
desired.

        In addition to students being brought here under the Aid programmes,
a large number of Thai private students have been trained in Australia.
In so far as their fees do not cover the full cost of their training in
Australian institutions, there is a considerable government subsidy to
assist training.   It is notable that the large majority of these students
return to Thailand and remain there to use their skills in their home
country.   In June 1971 there were 270 private Thai students in Australia
of whom 80 were at primary or secondary school, 46 at universities, and
43 at technical or advanced colleges of education.   The remainder were
undergoing other forms of training, mainly at tertiary institutions.

(iii) Practical administration of aid

        The basic premise of Australia's aid programme is that bilateral
aid is given in response to specific requests from the governments of

recipient countries.   In the early years of Australian aid to Thailand,
ideas for aid projects were submitted by the Thai Technical and Economic
Committee.   The responsibility for making formal requests to the Australian government through its Embassy now rests with two Thai government
agencies.   The Department of Technical and Economic Cooperation is responsible for coordinating Colombo Plan aid, and the Ministry of Foreign
Affairs for SEATO aid.   The requests coming through these bodies must
be from the Thai government as a whole, not from an individual department.

While this is the formal position, in practice the Australian
Embassy may bring to the notice of Thai officials Australia's capacity
to assist in a particular field.   In recent years formal requests have
become part of a continuing dialogue between officials of the two governments, usually in Bangkok.   This constant bilateral exchange of information is reinforced by the opportunities for consultation presented by
the Colombo Plan Consultative Committee and the Development Assistance
Group in Bangkok.   Although in the course of discussions the Embassy
might make a suggestion of possible Australian aid, for Thai consideration, the value of that form of aid is critically examined by the two
governments separately or jointly before it is mutually agreed as being
satisfactory.   Australia does not provide goods simply because they are
surplus to Australia's requirements.   For example, Thailand, being a
rice exporter, has not received any Australian food aid.   Indeed in its
food aid programme to neighbouring Asian countries, Australia has been
conscious of Thailand's exporting position.

In practice, the governments receiving Australian aid tend to
request more aid of a type with which they are already familiar and
which they know Australia can provide.   Australian road projects in
Thailand and the series of Australian town water-supply projects in
South Vietnam are illustrations of this tendency.

After a formal request has been made, if it is not duplicating the
efforts of another donor and if funds are available, the first step usually
taken is a feasibility study by an expert or a team.   Not all projects
require formal feasibility studies, but with the increased professional-
ism of Australia's aid programme the value of such studies has become
recognised and they are being applied with increasing sophistication to
more and more Australian projects.

The series of roads projects is a good example of this trend.
Although it was the third road project undertaken, the Lom Sak-Chum Phae
Highway was the first to be subject to a benefit-cost analysis.   The
second project, the Tak-Mae Sot Highway, was undertaken after comparatively little investigation, and there was no signed agreement concerning
the responsibilities of the two governments.   The Lom Sak-Chum Phae
Highway is indicative of the present thoroughness with which projects
are considered.   After both technical and economic analyses, subsequent
discussions led to a formal signed agreement specifying Australian and
Thai responsibilities, including the vital maintenance responsibilities
and Australia's training obligations.   The importance now being assigned
by Thailand to thorough investigation is evident in the list of requirements for Thailand's third Five Year Plan.   This includes details of a
large number of pre-investment studies aimed at identifying potential
capital projects, and determining engineering and economic feasibilities
of projects within the framework of the Plan.

The administration of Australia's aid has also been strengthened
by the appointment of staff working full-time on aid to the Australian
Embassy.   The first aid administrator was appointed to an Australian
Embassy in 1965 and to the Embassy in Bangkok in 1968.   There are at
present three officials, headed by a First Secretary, dealing full-time
with Australian aid matters in Thailand.

To avoid duplication of investigations and ultimately of projects,
the coordination of aid requests is essential.   There is sometimes a
tendency on the part of recipient governments or individual departments,
anxious to proceed with a project, to request the same assistance from
several donors.   This problem has been largely overcome in Thailand by
coordination through the Development Assistance Group.   The Group, originally known as the Development Assistance Committee for Thailand, was set
up in 1962 to consider problems of aid coordination and opportunities for
extending assistance to Thailand.

The Group's role centres on the exchange of information among its
members.   Information is provided by the Thai government on the state of
the economy, economic planning and foreign assistance requirements, and
by the members, including Australia, on their current and proposed aid
programmes.   Such exchanges assist the Thai government to assess donor

interest in certain projects and to determine the best directions in which
to channel requests, and assist donors with the formulation of specific
programmes of assistance.   The primary responsibility for aid coordination
rests of course with the Thai government.

Recently, Australia agreed to participate in a series of working
groups set up under the Development Assistance Group for Thailand.   These
informal groups will consist of representatives of the donor country, of the
National Economic Development Board, of the Department of Technical and
Economic Cooperation and relevant departments.   The discussion is to be
informal and on a bilateral basis, to determine the scope of Australia's
foreign assistance programme for the third Five Year Plan.

3.   VALUE OF AUSTRALIAN AID

Australia provides only about two to three per cent of Thailand's total
foreign assistance and Australia's aid alone could not be expected to make
a dramatic contribution to Thailand's economy.   If the achievements have
been modest, so have the aims, and this has been recognised by both governments.

Nevertheless, both governments consider that Australian aid has had
an impact in the areas in which it has been directed - but unfortunately
for the time being, such a belief can only be based on the subjective
evaluation of the officials concerned.   The development of evaluation
methods has not kept pace with the rapid growth in Australia's aid.   There
can be little doubt that projects such as the road-building undertakings
have been technical successes and have also succeeded in training Thai
teams to take over the task of road building and road maintenance.   However, no systematic evaluation has as yet been undertaken of the economic,
social and political effects of these projects.

This situation is expected to change with the establishment in 1971
of a Review and Evaluation Section within the Aid Branch of the Department
of Foreign Affairs.   The section will undertake both prior evaluation of
projects and post hoc review of their success or failure in economic and
social terms.

Evaluation of training assistance has also begun only in recent years. It is of course a difficult exercise, involving a number of non-quantifiable factors. The International Training Section now sends to Colombo Plan students questionnaires seeking their own evaluation of their training and the use being made of it in their home countries. Unfortunately, until recently, the Thai authorities had not given permission for the questionnaires to be sent to Thai students. This misunderstanding has now been resolved, but it is too early to discuss the results of the few questionnaires so far returned.

Some preliminary work on the evaluation of training has been published (Keats, 1969). As Keats pointed out, the results of this study must be viewed with some caution as it was based on a small sample of mailed questionnaires, which were returned voluntarily by students, and on subsequent interviews.

These preliminary results do not all lead in the same direction. On the one hand, Thai students, in comparison with those from other Asian countries, rank very highly in the degree to which their skills are used on their return. They experienced least employment delay on their return; they were more likely than students from other Asian countries to be employed in their main field of study and remain in it; and most returning Thai students were employed by the government and thought government employment most desirable. Thai students rank very highly also, according to the criteria used, on their lack of community alienation. On the other hand, Australian qualifications were not highly regarded in comparison with equivalent qualifications gained in Thailand and elsewhere overseas. Thailand was generally, along with Ceylon, lowest on the list showing the degree to which Australian qualifications were an advantage in gaining membership of professional groups, appointment to jobs, better salaries and promotion. Furthermore, in reply to the question as to whether or not the former student felt he was helping to meet national needs, Thai students ranked equal lowest.

There are two further comments that may be made on the quality of Australian aid. First, all Australian aid is in the form of grants. It does not carry repayment obligations. Thailand, in requesting aid for its Third Development Plan has pointed to the increasing burden of debt repayment, and asked for an increased proportion of its aid as grants.

Secondly, although Australian aid is tied aid, the provisions are sensibly interpreted and Australian aid is not closely associated with export promotion or private profitability. The general rule is that goods and services must be purchased from Australia and be of two-thirds Australian content. However, this rule is waived if there are sound economic reasons for doing so, and Australian aid is not tied to commercial transactions. In certain cases - such as third country training awards and our contribution to the construction of the Asian Institute of Technology in Bangkok - our aid is completely untied. Being grant aid, Australian aid is in any case not open to the same objections as the tying of loans. The financing of local costs by the Thai government, in fact, serves useful purposes. It ensures that projects are genuinely exercises in development cooperation rather than an imposition by the donor country of the aid it wants to give; it also ensures that the recipient country will closely assess the value to it of any project requested and take a continuing interest in it after its completion.

On the whole, both the Thai and Australian governments seem well satisfied with their mutual cooperation for economic development. No major problems have arisen out of the aid relationship. The projects undertaken have been well carried out and technically at least, have achieved their aims. The training aspect of the roads projects discussed above may not have been conducive to the lowest cost operation, but it has maximised the long term effects of the particular projects. Australia is a small donor and its aid programme has had a modest economic impact in Thailand; aid has at the same time, through cooperation in development, increased the links between the two countries and improved their understanding of one another.

REFERENCE

Keats, D.M., 1969. Back in Asia : a follow-up study of Australian-
trained Asian students, Department of Economics, Research
School of Pacific Studies, Australian National University,
Canberra.

APPENDIX I

AUSTRALIAN BILATERAL AID TO THAILAND UNDER BOTH THE COLOMBO PLAN
AND THE SEATO AID PROGRAMMES, BY CATEGORY 1968/9 TO 1971/2

($A)

Category	1968/9	1969/70	1970/1	1971/2
Colombo Plan				
Projects and equipment	1,455,574	2,152,935	2,570,283	2,100,494
Experts	163,324	215,472	225,439	102,977
Training	416,383	612,166	622,355	644,637
Sub totals	2,035,281	2,980,573	3,418,077	2,848,108
SEATO				
Projects and equipment	393,813	314,056	199,514	252,287
Experts	50,145	6,949	86,912	5,419
Civil training	26,311	14,994	19,898	8,290
Defence training	825	5,519	11,596	15,021
Sub totals	471,094	341,518	317,920	281,017
Grand totals	2,506,375	3,322,091	3,735,997	3,129,125

APPENDIX II

AUSTRALIAN ECONOMIC AID TO THAILAND

Projects and technical assistance (excluding training) by field of activity

Field of activity	Project	Programme	Description
AGRICULTURE Land and water use, farm machinery and tools	Central Region Agri- cultural Centre, Chai Nat, Central Thailand	Colombo Plan	Part of the Greater Chao Phraya Development Pro- ject (financed by IBRD). Research into double cropping, and development of crops and farming techniques suitable to the Central Plain. Experts: agronomists; soil scientists. Equipment: agricultural research and laboratory equipment; chemicals; vehicles. Controlled through Chai Nat Research Advisory Committee (C.S.I.R.O. and Foreign Affairs) Current to end 1974.
	Tank Irrigation Construction, Northeast Thailand	Colombo Plan	Supply of equipment for construction of tank sites and access roads near Korat in N.E. Thai- land. Earth moving and other vehicles; water- ing trucks; concrete mixers; soil compactors; spare parts; mobile workshop. Followed inves- tigation and report, 1965. Complete (1970-1). Total cost about $A600,000.
	Thai-Australian Land Development, North Thailand	Colombo Plan	Land use survey, establishment of research stations, clearing and development of upland areas in Ping, Yang, Yom and Nan valleys for permanent cultivation. Experts: geographers; agricultural scientists; mechanic. Equipment: vehicles; tractors; cultivation equipment; earth moving machinery. Agents: University of New England and Thai Department of Land Development. Current to June 1973. Commenced 1965.

Field of activity	Project	Programme	Description
	Accelerated Rural Development Programme, South Thailand	Colombo Plan	Experts only, to assist and advise Thai Office of Accelerated Rural Development, in: (a) development of a cost accounting system to enable funds to be used with maximum effectiveness; (b) engineering planning and review. Current to June 1972.
	Pasture Improvement, Khon Kaen, Northeast Thailand	Colombo Plan	Research into pasture improvement and undersowing of upland crops with tropical pasture (Townsville stylo). Expert: research agronomist. Equipment: research and laboratory equipment; chemicals; seeds; vehicle. Agents: University of Queensland and Applied Scientific Research Corporation of Thailand. Current to 1974.
	Tha Bo Irrigation Pumps, North Thailand	SEATO	Provision and installation of five irrigation pumps - three at Tha Bo and two at Sri Chiang Mai in North Thailand, located on Mekong River, to provide water for rural cooperatives in nearby districts. Experts: engineer. Completed 1970-1. Approximately $A130,000.
EDUCATION			
Primary and secondary education	Bhumipol King's College	Colombo Plan	Senior Master/English teacher only. Salary subsidised by Thai government. Completed December 1970.
Technical education and training	Military Technical Training School, Bangkok	SEATO	Establishment of the school to provide comprehensive trade training to all three branches of Thai armed forces. Joint Thai/Australian project. Experts, building materials, lathes, workshop machinery, vehicles. Completed 1963. Approximately $A400,000.

Field of activity	Project	Programme	Description
	Motor Mechanics Training Centre, Bangkok	SEATO	Joint Thai/Australian project. Part of M.T.T.S. Purpose to train 120 vehicle mechanics a year and instruct selected mechanics in repairing trucks, jeeps and other light transport vehicles. Experts: technical advisory team. Equipment: workshop machinery, vehicle instructional aids. Agents: Department of the Army and Supreme Command Headquarters of Thailand. Current to December 1972. Commenced 1967. Cost: about $A900,000.
	Electronics Wing – M.T.T.S. Bangkok	SEATO	Establishment of an electronics wing at the M.T.T.S. to provide a continuing supply of electronics tradesmen for the Thai services. Joint Thai/Australian Project. Provision of experts and technical equipment. Period 1971-2 – 1976-7. Approximate cost $A900,000.
	North Bangkok Engineering School	Colombo Plan	Provision of experts to advise in methods of instruction of various trades, and assist in developing curricula. Experts: teaching instructors. Equipment: workshop training equipment and tools. Completed 1970. Commenced 1965.
	Asian Institute of Technology	SEATO	Appointment of Professor (1967-70) and member of Board of Trustees (current). Contribution to building of new administrative block, as part of new campus. Expert: architect for feasibility study. Current.
	D.T.E.C. Language Institute	Colombo Plan	Teaching of English language to Thai government officials to level sufficient to enable them to take up their Colombo Plan scholarships. Expert: Lecturer in English. Current 1968-73.

Field of activity	Project	Programme	Description
Higher education and research	Mobile Research Laboratory	Colombo Plan	Used by Faculty of Tropical Medicine, University of Medical Sciences, for training of doctors for Post-graduate Diploma in Tropical Medicine and Hygiene. Equipment: Land rover and equipped caravan. Complete. Shipped 1969. Approximately $A13,000.
Other educational and cultural activities	Transmitter for Ministry of Education, Bangkok Technical Institute	Colombo Plan	Provision of a 10KW radio transmitter and 300 metre mast, with auxiliary equipment followed by a survey of school broadcasting facilities by Australian expert in 1962. Installation by Thai contractor at Australian expense. Other equipment: 3000 transistor radios for school broadcasts. Completed 1969.
HEALTH AND SANITATION			
Health services	Horses for serum production, Bangkok	Colombo Plan	Supply to the Pasteur Research Institute of horses to provide the serum used in production of anti-venene. Equipment only: 150 horses sent in 1961, then 20 horses a year 1966-8. Jeep supplied in 1962 for horse farm.
	Other health services (including the above-mentioned Mobile Research Laboratory) and aid for medical education and training	Colombo Plan	Supply of variety of equipment of hospitals and health services: sterilizers, x-ray and cardiographic equipment etc.; a heart-lung machine for the New Medical School; equipment for vaccine production; 2 landrover ambulances for Princess Mother's Medical Volunteer Organisation; books for the Neurological Research Institute, Prasat Hospital; 94 ambulances. Mobile Research Laboratory used also as diagnostic clinic in remote areas.

Field of activity	Project	Programme	Description
INDUSTRY AND TECHNOLOGY			
Transport and communications	Civic Action Programme	SEATO	Supply of anaesthetic apparatus to Ubon Hospital by RAAF. Complete 1971.
	Radio Transmitters, Khon Kaen and Korat, North Thailand	SEATO	Installation of two 50KW radio transmitters for agricultural education and general broadcasting in the Northeast. Completed 1966, but subsequent repair of masts after lightning damage. Equipment maintenance expert, and transmitter components. Completed 1971
	Khon Kaen feeder roads, Northeast Thailand	Colombo Plan	Joint Thai/Australian project. Construction of 160 km of all-weather roads, 53 km of access roads and design and survey of 130 km. Main aim was training of Thai personnel. Equipment: tractors, scrapers, rollers and other heavy machinery, spare parts etc. Experts: 39 staff – engineers, supervisors, instructors, geologists, accountants. Training: on-site training of Thai personnel, and additional training in Australia for some of the Thai engineers, operators and mechanics. Agent: Snowy Mountains Hydro Electric Authority. Completed 1966. Australian contribution $3.6m. Total cost $A6,200,000.
	Tak-Mae Sot Highway, North Thailand	Colombo Plan	Joint Thai/Australian project. Construction of 89 kms of highway from Tak (NW Thailand) to Mae Sot (Burmese border). Part of Asian Highway. Equipment: earth moving, road construction, survey and design, maintenance and repair soil testing, vehicles, spare parts etc. Experts: engineers, administrative officers, foremen-mechanics, works supervisors, technical officers. Agent: S.M.H.E.A. Completed 1970. Total project cost about $A16,000,000. Australian contribution one-third.

Field of activity	Project	Programme	Description
	Lom Sak–Chum Phae Highway, North Thailand	Colombo Plan	Joint Thai/Australian project. Construction of 106 km of highway. Adopted on basis of feasibility study (S.M.H.E.A.) and economic analysis (Dept. of National Development). Part of Asian Highway. Equipment: earth moving, road construction, survey and design, soil testing, maintenance and repairs etc. Spare parts procurement a Thai responsibility. Experts: engineers, foremen-mechanics, works supervisors, technical officers, administrative officers. Agent: Snowy Mountains Engineering Corporation Current. Began 1970. Estimated total project cost $A20,000,000. Australian contribution one-third.
Transport and communications	Prachuap Khiri Khan, South Thailand	Colombo Plan	Part of multi-purpose venture by Thai Office of Accelerated Rural Development (ARD). Assistance with construction of feeder and access roads to link villages with outlet roads in Prachuap Khiri Khan province. Equipment: essential heavy construction equipment and spares. Experts: project manager, civil supervisor, technicians. Agent: S.M.E.C. Feasibility study by S.M.H.E.A. Current. Began 1971 for four years. Australia's contribution approximately $A1,300,000.
	Army Vehicle Rebuild Workshop, Bangkok	SEATO	Establishment of workshop for Thai armed forces. Joint Thai/Australian project. Equipment: vehicle repair machinery, building materials instructional equipment, tools. Experts: army personnel to assist in construction and train Thai instructors.

Field of activity	Project	Programme	Description
			Completed 1968. Cost about $A950,000. Tripartite Agreement (Thai, Australian and U.S. Forces) reactivated Australian assistance. Provision of additional machinery and a team of experts. Complete 1970-2.
Mining and manufacturing	Thai Lignite Industry Mae Moh (North Thailand) Krabi (South Thailand)	Colombo Plan	Provision of equipment and experts for lignite industry since Thai Lignite Authority set up in 1954. One of the longest running projects. Equipment: crushing and screening plant, two diesel locos and eight hopper wagons, 100 railway trucks, supply and installation of lignite conveyor belt for Mae Moh (North Tahiland). Experts: installation experts, advisers on exploitation of mining deposits. Complete. Cost about $A1,400,000.
PUBLIC ADMINISTRATION ECONOMICS, FINANCE AND SOCIAL WELFARE			
Community development	Hill Tribes Research Centre Chiang Mai, North Thailand	SEATO	Commenced 1964. Centre run by Thai government, with SEATO assistance, to promote socio-economic development of hill tribes. Experts: anthropologists, agricultural scientist, radio programme adviser for organisation and administration of the Centre. Trained and assisted research staff. Equipment: mainly agricultural research equipment, vehicles. Current. Experts: technical adviser, tropical agronomist.
MISCELLANEOUS	Provision of equipment and experts	Colombo Plan SEATO	Experts on short term assignments and individual items of equipment have been provided to a number of other projects.